Just A
Simple Wedding

Other *For Better or For Worse*® Collections

Home Sweat Home
Seniors' Discount
Teaching Is a Learning Experience!
She's Turning into One of Them!
Never Wink at a Worried Woman
Striking a Chord
Reality Check
With This Ring
Family Business
Graduation: A Time for Change
The Big 5-0
Sunshine and Shadow
Middle Age Spread
Growing Like a Weed
Love Just Screws Everything Up
Starting from Scratch
"There Goes My Baby!"
Things Are Looking Up . . .
What, Me Pregnant?
If This Is a Lecture, How Long Will It Be?
Pushing 40
It's All Downhill from Here
Keep the Home Fries Burning
The Last Straw
Just One More Hug
"It Must Be Nice to Be Little"
Is This "One of Those Days," Daddy?
I've Got the One-More-Washload Blues . . .

Retrospectives

Suddenly Silver: 25 Years of For Better or For Worse®
All About April
The Lives Behind the Lines: 20 Years of For Better or For Worse®
Remembering Farley: A Tribute to the Life of Our Favorite Cartoon Dog
It's the Thought That Counts . . . Fifteenth Anniversary Collection
A Look Inside . . . For Better or For Worse®: The 10th Anniversary Collection

With Andie Parton

I Love My Grandpa!
So You're Going to Be a Grandma!
Graduation: Just the Beginning!
Leaving Home
Wags and Kisses

Just A Simple Wedding

A *For Better or For Worse*® Collection by Lynn Johnston

**Andrews McMeel
Publishing, LLC**

Kansas City

For Better or For Worse® is distributed by Universal Press Syndicate.

09 10 11 12 13 RR2 10 9 8 7 6 5 4 3 2 1

ISBN-13: 978-0-7407-8097-4
ISBN-10: 0-7407-8097-2

Library of Congress Control Number: 2008939975

www.andrewsmcmeel.com

www.FBorFW.com

For Jim Andrews, who saw
potential in a new comic strip
artist, and for John McMeel,
who made it happen.
For Lee Salem, all my editors,
and for everyone who has
guided, supported, and contributed
in so many ways . . . a grateful
thanks.

I have always enjoyed working
with a team. You have been
more than co-workers; you've
been part of my extended family.

Thank you all for this past twenty-nine years.

Sincerely,

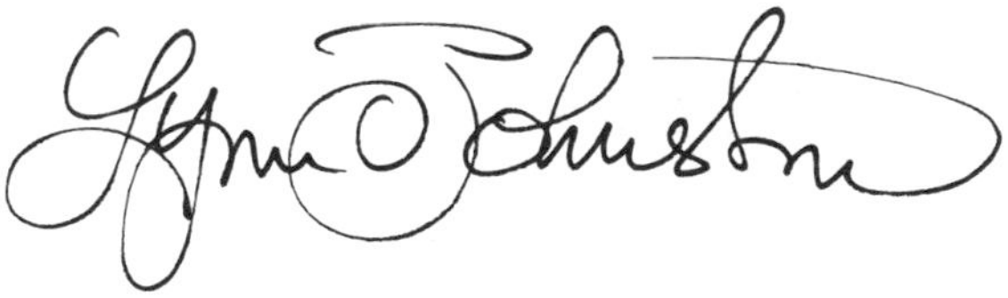

Introduction

This is the last of the *For Better or For Worse* collection books. With this, the saga goes on in everyone's imagination—not just mine! Michael and Deanna now live in the Patterson house on Sharon Park Drive. Their children are the ages that Michael and his sister were when the story began and now, a new generation takes flight.

I wanted to chronicle the cycle of life that brings a family back to its roots; back to babies and puppies and new friends; back to the shelter of Mom, Dad, and favorite toys; back to the home.

Many people have grown up and grown old with the Patterson family. They have written to me over the years to tell me that their children have graduated with Elizabeth, their son is getting married, or a new baby is on the way.

Your letters are all part of the privilege I have enjoyed; part of the fun and the challenge it's been in producing a small, daily glimpse into a personal perspective on family life.

So much entertainment focuses on the negative, the hostile, the selfish, the cruel. I firmly believe that our society is good; that most people are giving and forgiving; that most parents are nurturing and responsible; that children of all ages are loving, conscientious, and respectful. Teenagers are competent and caring. The next generation can be trusted to take on the world they're about to inherit and the future will be prosperous in their hands.

For me, this has been and will continue to be the most wonderful job on earth. I sat with Bill Hoest, shortly before he died, on the seawall beneath his lovely stone "castle." (Bill did *The Lockhorns, Laugh Parade, Agatha Crumm, Howard Huge, Bumper Snickers,* and more!) It was a cool autumn morning. We talked about comic strips; about being comic strip artists. The water between Connecticut and his home on Long Island was an old photograph gray. The sound of the waves took our attention away from his frailty. "I've had the best job anyone could ask for," he said, warming his hands on his coffee mug. "I've been a writer, an artist, a comic, a philosopher—and, I married the love of my life, who's supported me all the way. I did the best I could do. I'm happy with what I've done—and, if I'm allowed to come back here . . . I'm going to do it all over again!"

Well, that's how I feel. I agree with Bill. If there's something on the other side, and I firmly believe there is . . . if there's a chance I can ask a favor of the powers that be, I'd say, "Can I have a ticket for another ride? Can I please have the gift again? Because I'd like to go back and do it all over. For Better or For Worse."

See you in the funny papers!

Lynn Johnston

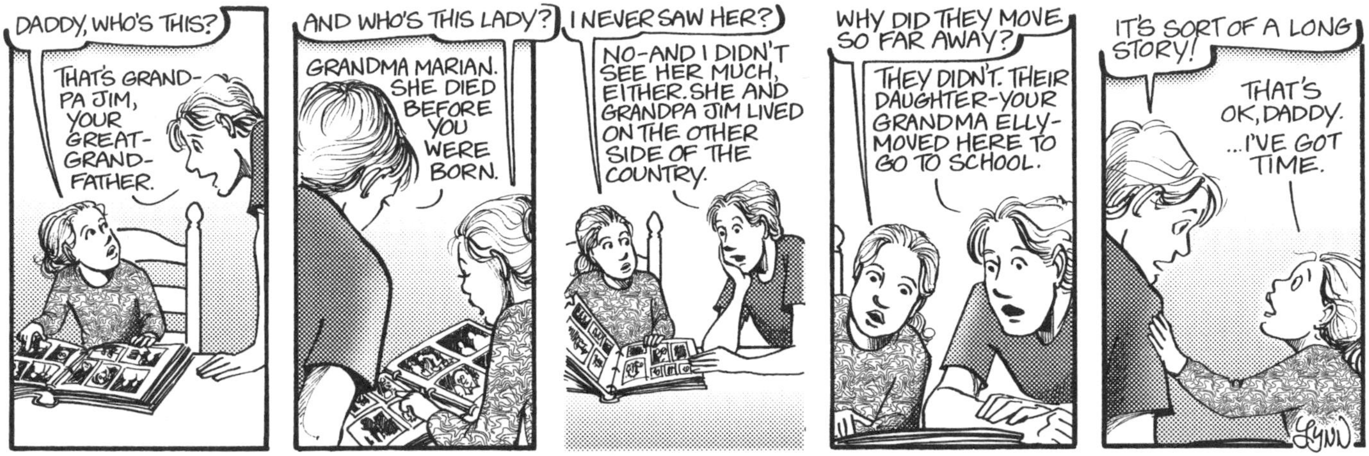
DADDY, WHO'S THIS?
THAT'S GRANDPA JIM, YOUR GREAT-GRANDFATHER.
AND WHO'S THIS LADY?
GRANDMA MARIAN. SHE DIED BEFORE YOU WERE BORN.
I NEVER SAW HER?
NO-AND I DIDN'T SEE HER MUCH, EITHER. SHE AND GRANDPA JIM LIVED ON THE OTHER SIDE OF THE COUNTRY.
WHY DID THEY MOVE SO FAR AWAY?
THEY DIDN'T. THEIR DAUGHTER-YOUR GRANDMA ELLY-MOVED HERE TO GO TO SCHOOL.
IT'S SORT OF A LONG STORY!
THAT'S OK, DADDY. ...I'VE GOT TIME.
LYNN

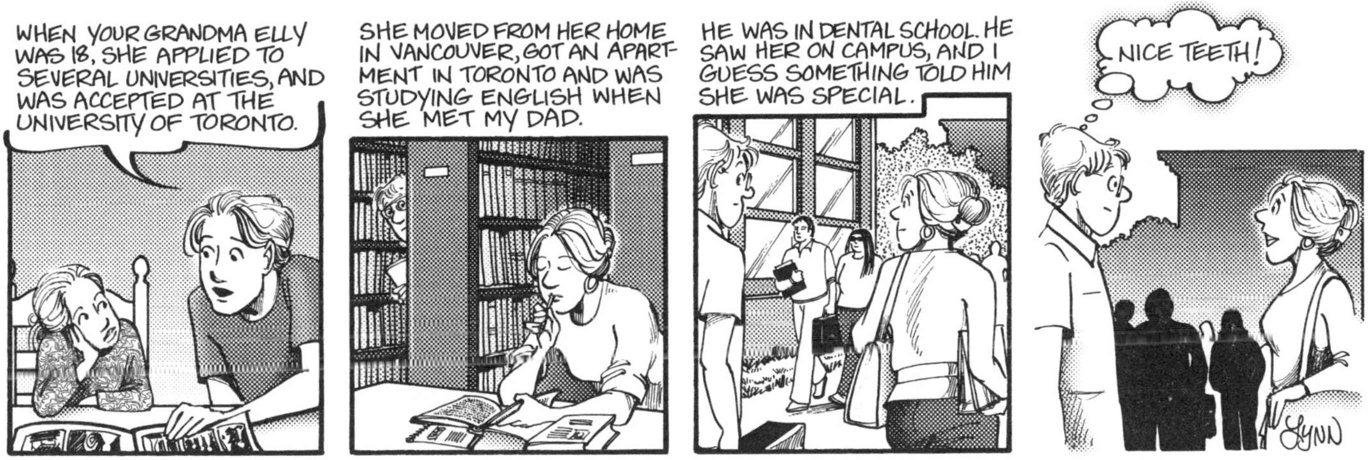
WHEN YOUR GRANDMA ELLY WAS 18, SHE APPLIED TO SEVERAL UNIVERSITIES, AND WAS ACCEPTED AT THE UNIVERSITY OF TORONTO.
SHE MOVED FROM HER HOME IN VANCOUVER, GOT AN APARTMENT IN TORONTO AND WAS STUDYING ENGLISH WHEN SHE MET MY DAD.
HE WAS IN DENTAL SCHOOL. HE SAW HER ON CAMPUS, AND I GUESS SOMETHING TOLD HIM SHE WAS SPECIAL.
NICE TEETH!
LYNN

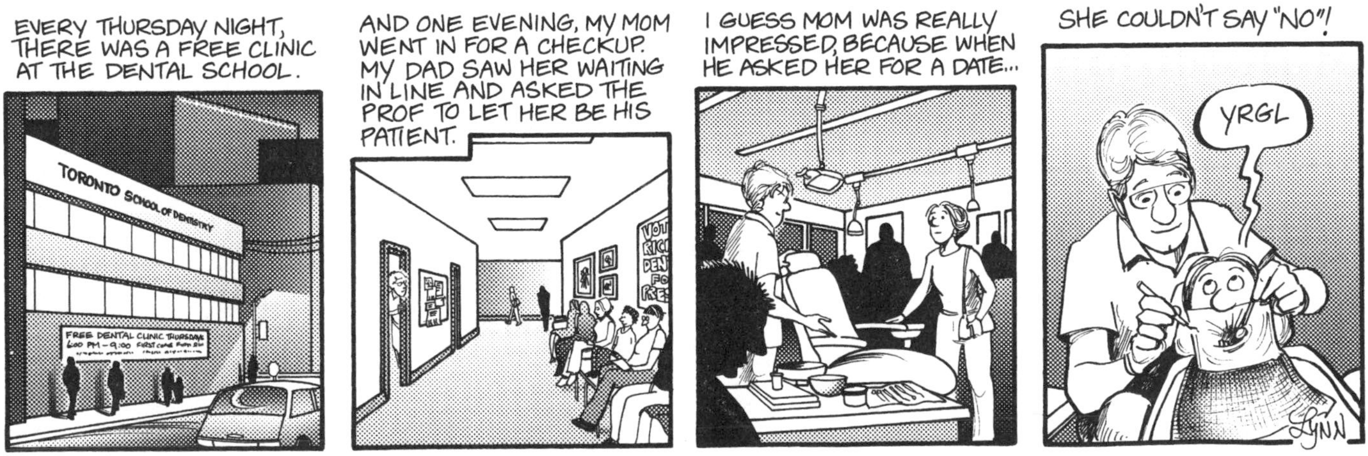
EVERY THURSDAY NIGHT, THERE WAS A FREE CLINIC AT THE DENTAL SCHOOL.
TORONTO SCHOOL OF DENTISTRY
FREE DENTAL CLINIC THURSDAYS
AND ONE EVENING, MY MOM WENT IN FOR A CHECKUP. MY DAD SAW HER WAITING IN LINE AND ASKED THE PROF TO LET HER BE HIS PATIENT.
I GUESS MOM WAS REALLY IMPRESSED, BECAUSE WHEN HE ASKED HER FOR A DATE...
SHE COULDN'T SAY "NO"!
YRGL
LYNN

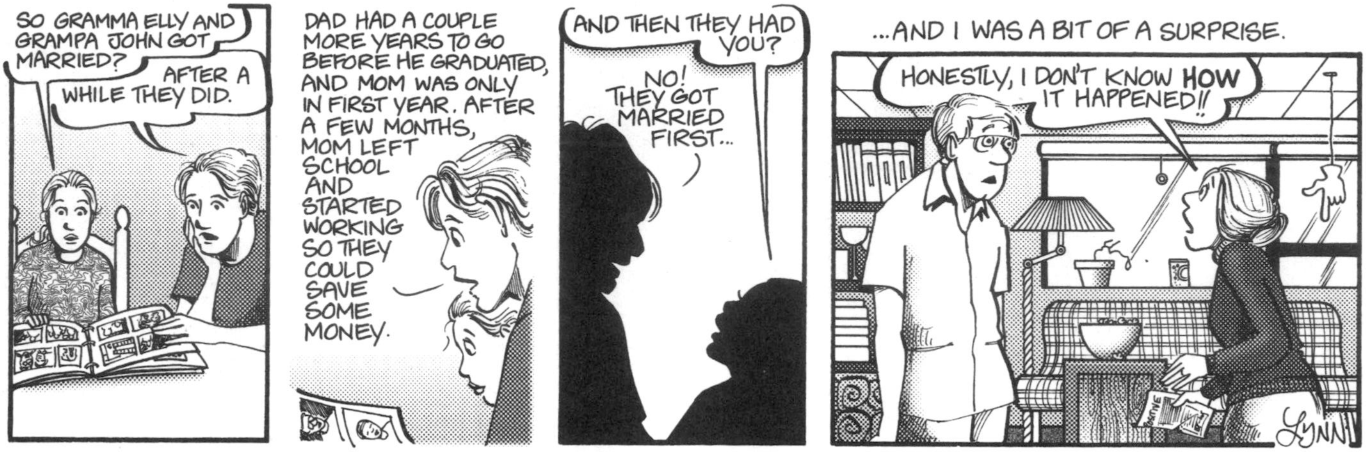
SO GRAMMA ELLY AND GRAMPA JOHN GOT MARRIED?
AFTER A WHILE THEY DID.
DAD HAD A COUPLE MORE YEARS TO GO BEFORE HE GRADUATED, AND MOM WAS ONLY IN FIRST YEAR. AFTER A FEW MONTHS, MOM LEFT SCHOOL AND STARTED WORKING SO THEY COULD SAVE SOME MONEY.
AND THEN THEY HAD YOU?
NO! THEY GOT MARRIED FIRST...
...AND I WAS A BIT OF A SURPRISE.
HONESTLY, I DON'T KNOW **HOW** IT HAPPENED!!
LYNN

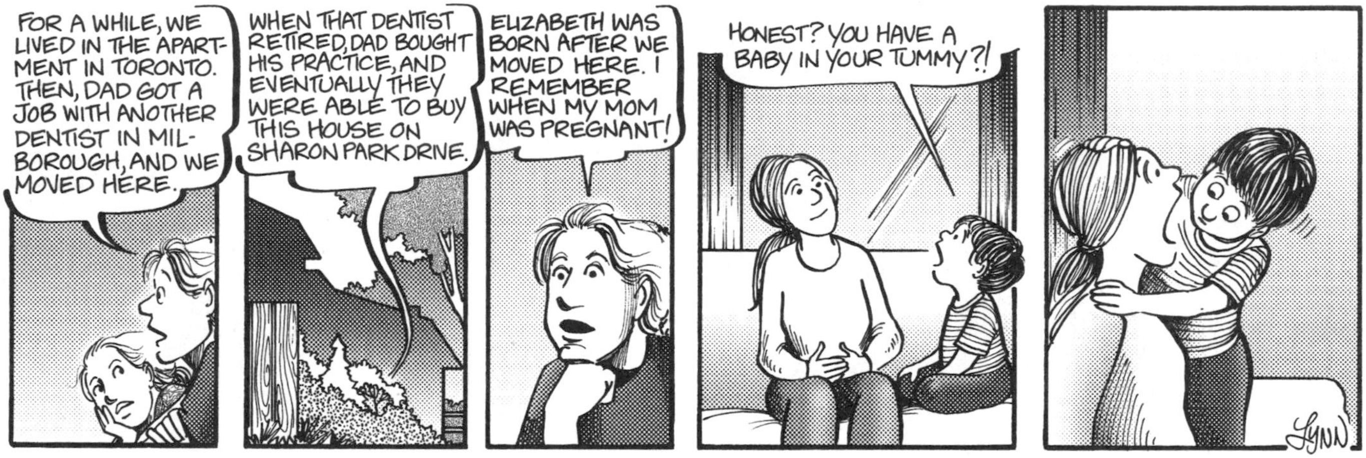
FOR A WHILE, WE LIVED IN THE APARTMENT IN TORONTO. THEN, DAD GOT A JOB WITH ANOTHER DENTIST IN MILBOROUGH, AND WE MOVED HERE.
WHEN THAT DENTIST RETIRED, DAD BOUGHT HIS PRACTICE, AND EVENTUALLY THEY WERE ABLE TO BUY THIS HOUSE ON SHARON PARK DRIVE.
ELIZABETH WAS BORN AFTER WE MOVED HERE. I REMEMBER WHEN MY MOM WAS PREGNANT!
HONEST? YOU HAVE A BABY IN YOUR TUMMY?!
LYNN

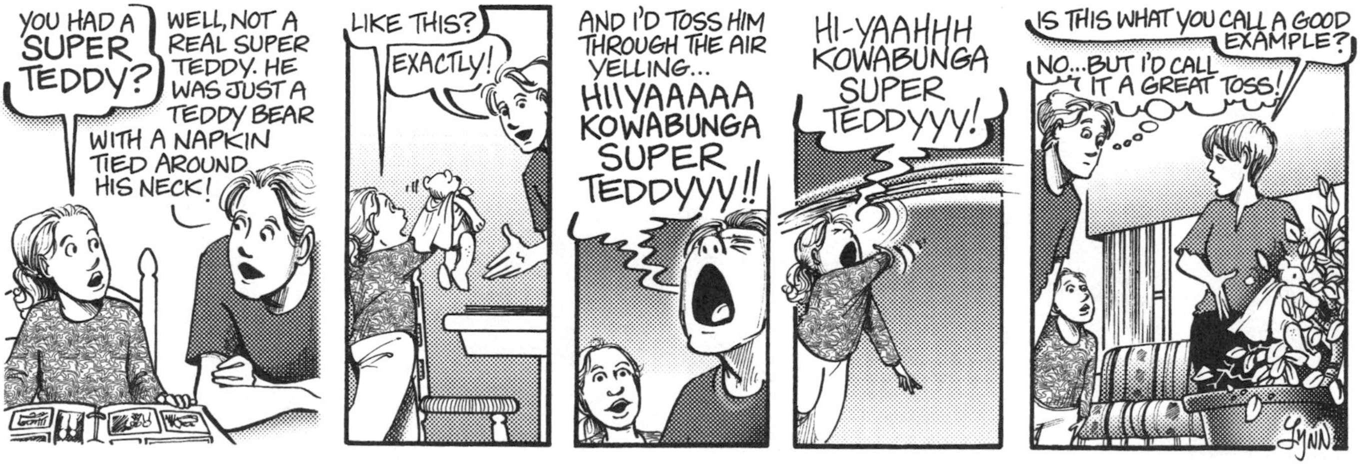
YOU HAD A SUPER TEDDY?
WELL, NOT A REAL SUPER TEDDY. HE WAS JUST A TEDDY BEAR WITH A NAPKIN TIED AROUND HIS NECK!
LIKE THIS?
EXACTLY!
AND I'D TOSS HIM THROUGH THE AIR YELLING... HIIYAAAAA KOWABUNGA SUPER TEDDYYY!!
HI-YAAHHH KOWABUNGA SUPER TEDDYYY!
IS THIS WHAT YOU CALL A GOOD EXAMPLE?
NO...BUT I'D CALL IT A GREAT TOSS!
LYNN

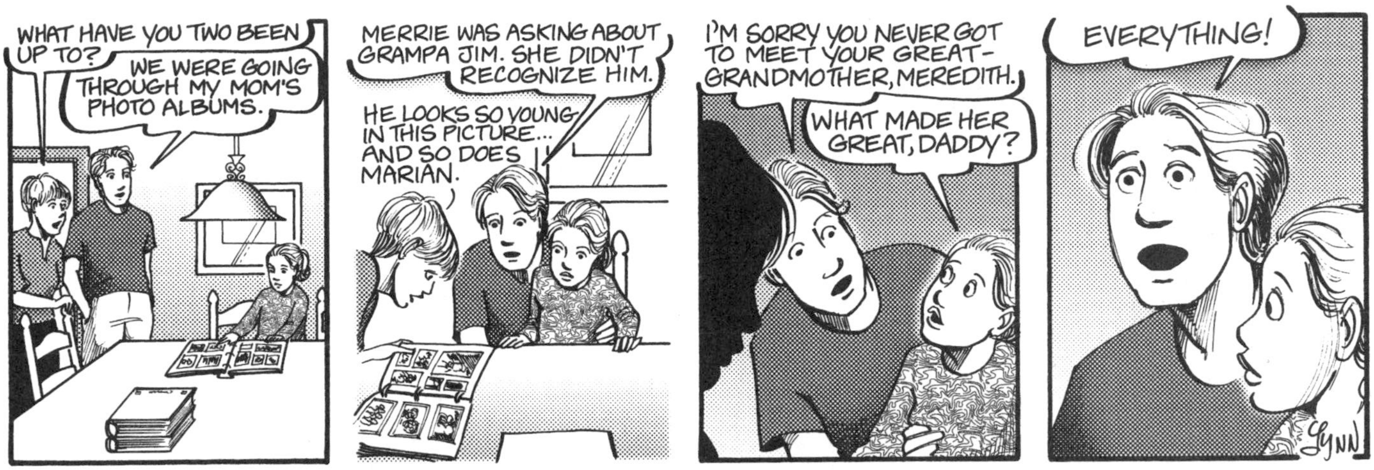
WHAT HAVE YOU TWO BEEN UP TO?
WE WERE GOING THROUGH MY MOM'S PHOTO ALBUMS.
MERRIE WAS ASKING ABOUT GRAMPA JIM. SHE DIDN'T RECOGNIZE HIM.
HE LOOKS SO YOUNG IN THIS PICTURE... AND SO DOES MARIAN.
I'M SORRY YOU NEVER GOT TO MEET YOUR GREAT-GRANDMOTHER, MEREDITH.
WHAT MADE HER GREAT, DADDY?
EVERYTHING!
LYNN

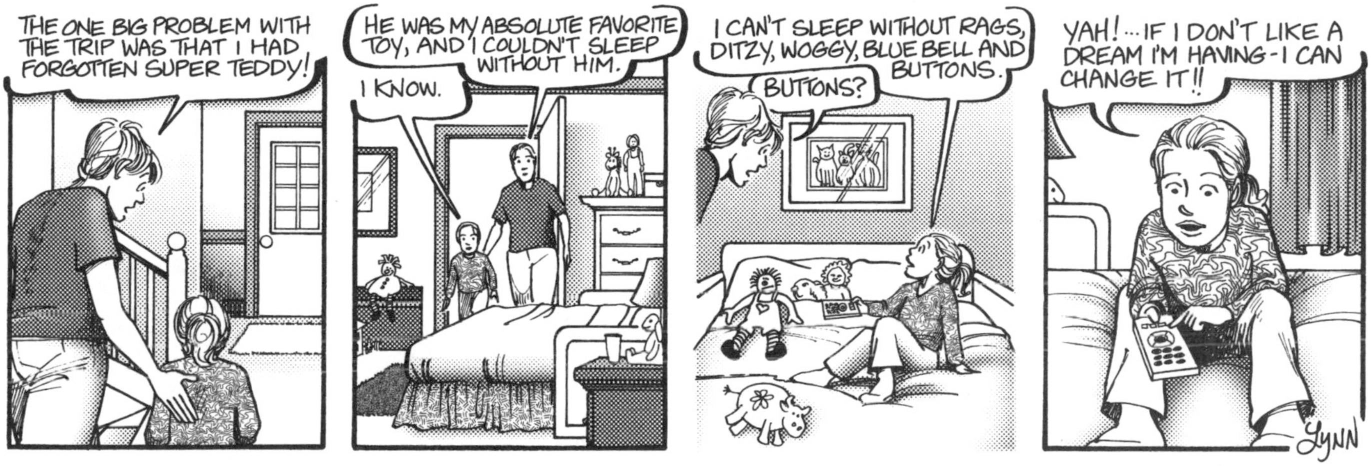
THE ONE BIG PROBLEM WITH THE TRIP WAS THAT I HAD FORGOTTEN SUPER TEDDY!
HE WAS MY ABSOLUTE FAVORITE TOY, AND I COULDN'T SLEEP WITHOUT HIM.
I KNOW.
I CAN'T SLEEP WITHOUT RAGS, DITZY, WOGGY, BLUE BELL AND BUTTONS.
BUTTONS?
YAH! ...IF I DON'T LIKE A DREAM I'M HAVING - I CAN CHANGE IT!!
LYNN

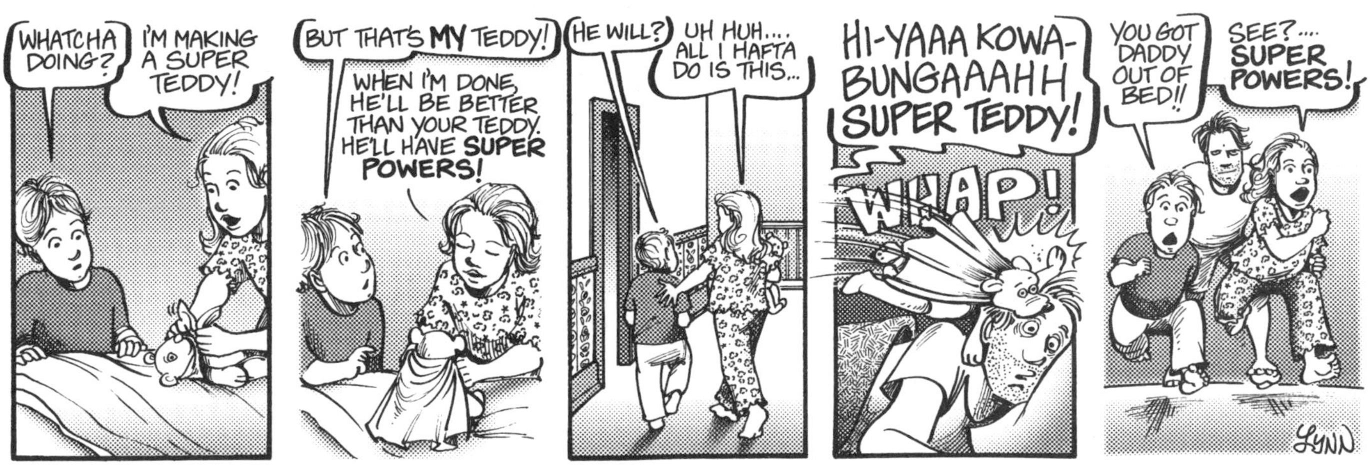
WHATCHA DOING?
I'M MAKING A SUPER TEDDY!
BUT THAT'S MY TEDDY!
WHEN I'M DONE, HE'LL BE BETTER THAN YOUR TEDDY. HE'LL HAVE SUPER POWERS!
HE WILL?
UH HUH.... ALL I HAFTA DO IS THIS...
HI-YAAA KOWA-BUNGAAAHH SUPER TEDDY!
WHAP!
YOU GOT DADDY OUT OF BED!!
SEE?.... SUPER POWERS!
LYNN

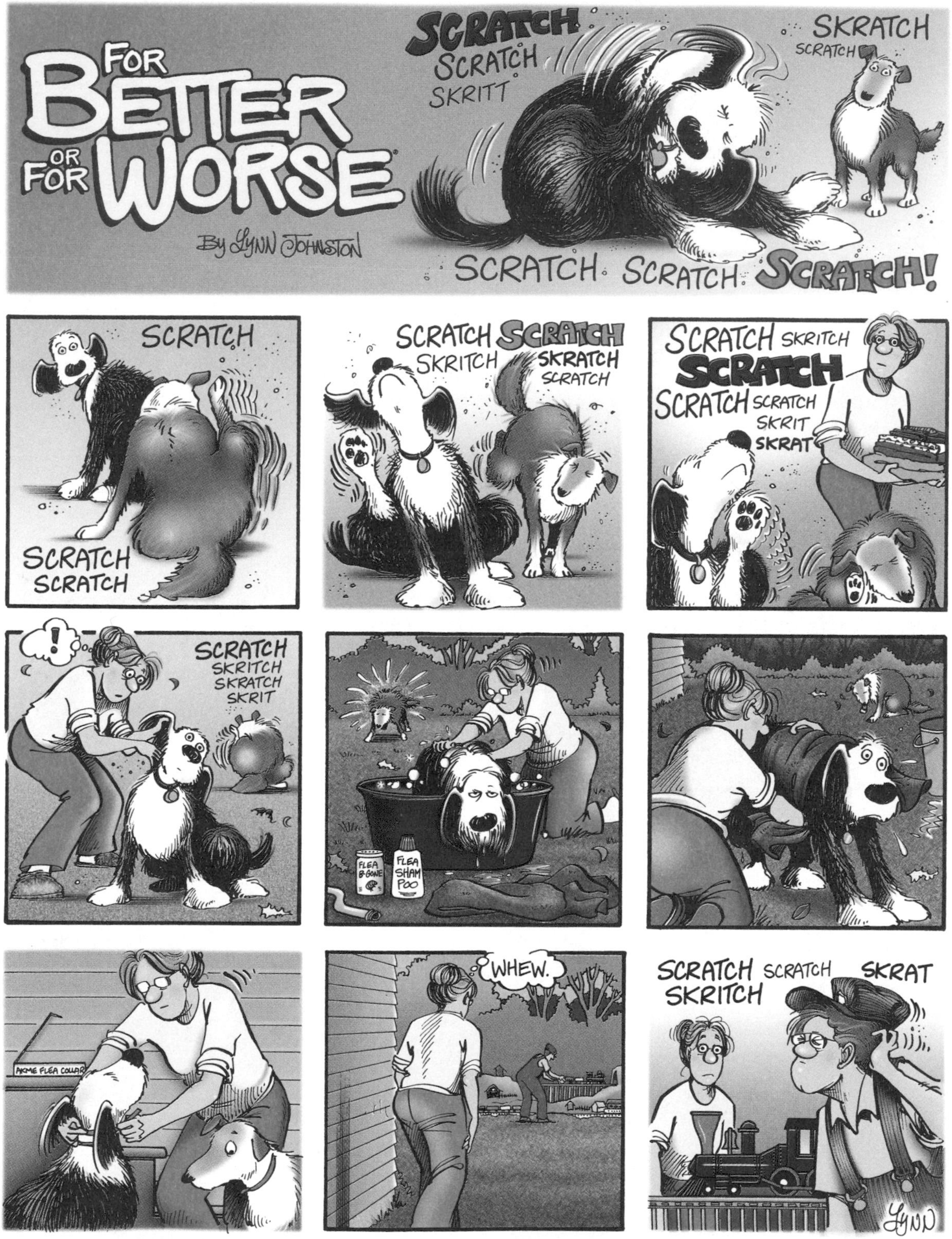
FOR BETTER OR FOR WORSE
By Lynn Johnston
SCRATCH SCRATCH SKRITT
SKRATCH SCRATCH
SCRATCH SCRATCH SCRATCH!
SCRATCH
SCRATCH SCRATCH
SCRATCH SCRATCH SKRITCH
SKRATCH SCRATCH
SCRATCH SKRITCH
SCRATCH
SCRATCH SCRATCH SKRIT SKRAT
!
SCRATCH SKRITCH SKRATCH SKRIT
FLEA B-GONE
FLEA SHAM POO
AKME FLEA COLLAR
WHEW.
SCRATCH SCRATCH SKRAT
SKRITCH
LYNN

FOR BETTER OR FOR WORSE
BY LYNN JOHNSTON
YAWNNN
SCRATCH
WOW. YOU'RE GETTING QUITE A PAUNCH THERE, HONEY!
WHAT PAUNCH? I DON'T HAVE A PAUNCH!!
WHAT I HAVE IS RELAXED AB-DOMINALS.
ALL I HAVE TO DO IS TIGHTEN THE ABS A BIT!
IT DOESN'T TAKE MUCH TO FLATTEN THIS OUT.
...JUST A FEW SPECIFIC EXERCISES.
WHEN I'M READY, I'LL GO DOWN TO THE GYM AND TAKE CARE OF IT.
THERE'S NOTHING WRONG WITH RELAXED ABDOMINALS.
PTooi
...IF IT WAS AN ACTUAL PAUNCH, I'D BE WORRIED ABOUT IT.
LYNN

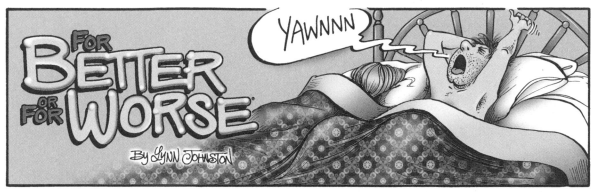

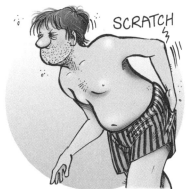

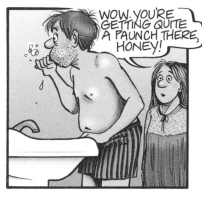

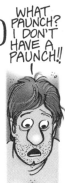

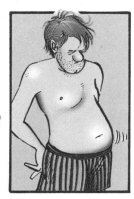

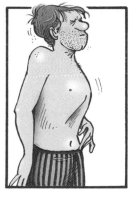

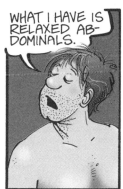

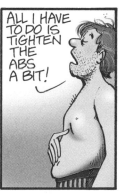

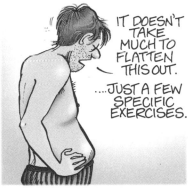

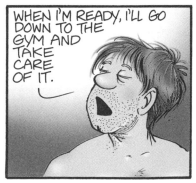

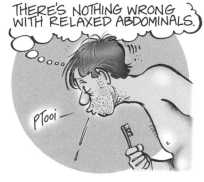

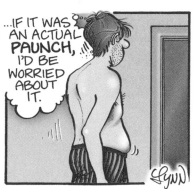

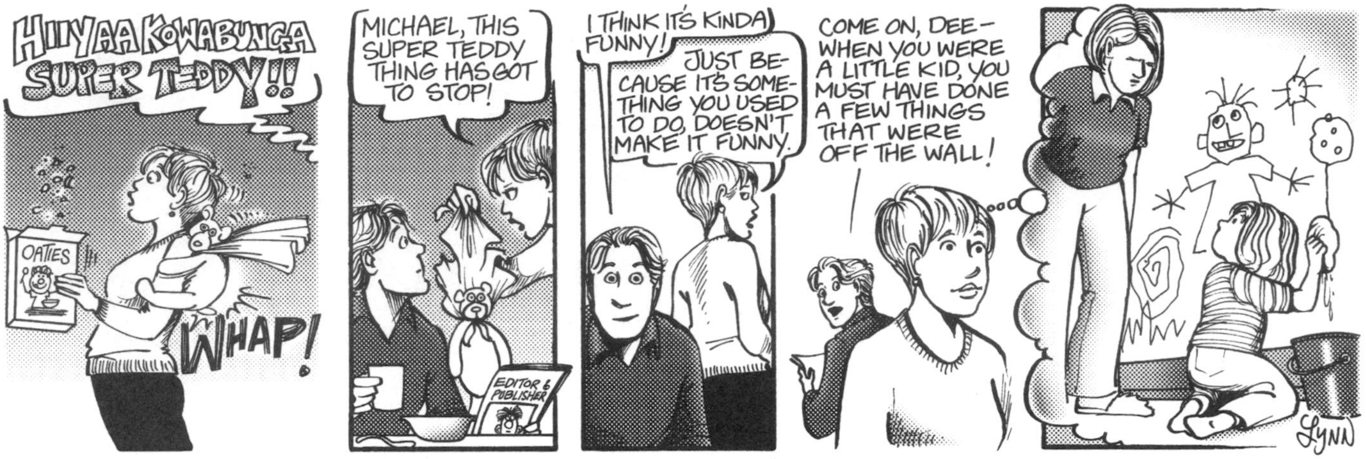
HIIYAA KOWABUNGA SUPER TEDDY!!
OATIES
WHAP!
MICHAEL, THIS SUPER TEDDY THING HAS GOT TO STOP!
EDITOR & PUBLISHER
I THINK IT'S KINDA FUNNY!
JUST BECAUSE IT'S SOMETHING YOU USED TO DO, DOESN'T MAKE IT FUNNY.
COME ON, DEE— WHEN YOU WERE A LITTLE KID, YOU MUST HAVE DONE A FEW THINGS THAT WERE OFF THE WALL!
LYNN

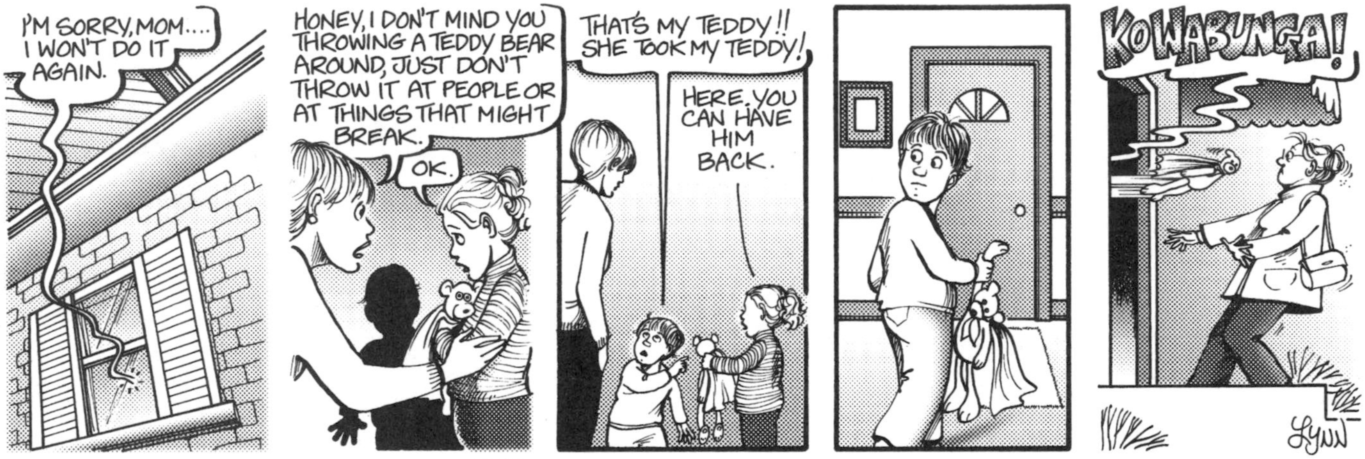
I'M SORRY, MOM.... I WON'T DO IT AGAIN.
HONEY, I DON'T MIND YOU THROWING A TEDDY BEAR AROUND, JUST DON'T THROW IT AT PEOPLE OR AT THINGS THAT MIGHT BREAK.
OK.
THAT'S MY TEDDY!! SHE TOOK MY TEDDY!
HERE, YOU CAN HAVE HIM BACK.
KOWABUNGA!
LYNN

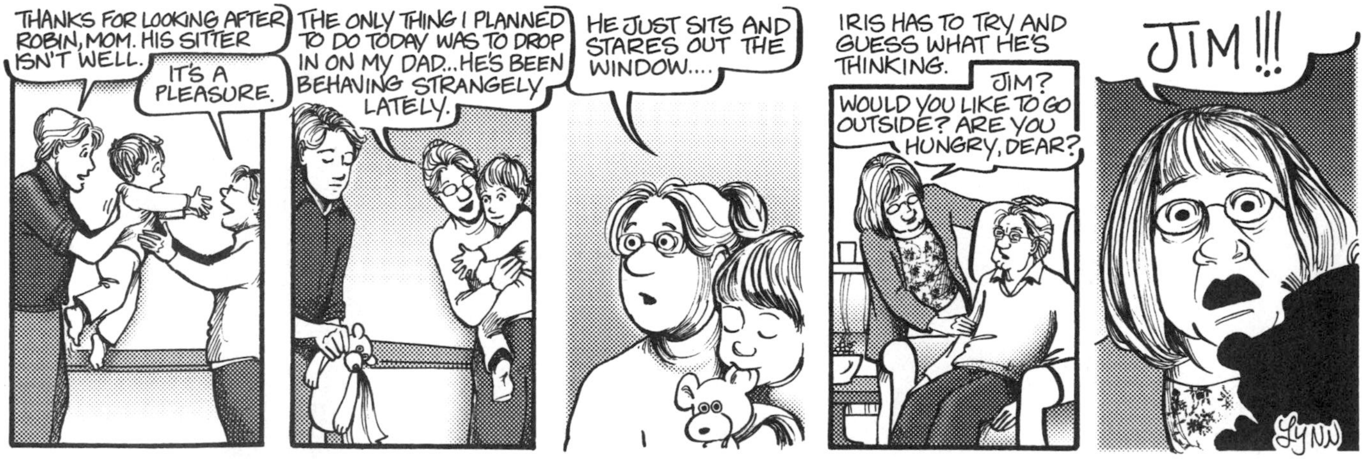
THANKS FOR LOOKING AFTER ROBIN, MOM. HIS SITTER ISN'T WELL.
IT'S A PLEASURE.
THE ONLY THING I PLANNED TO DO TODAY WAS TO DROP IN ON MY DAD...HE'S BEEN BEHAVING STRANGELY LATELY.
HE JUST SITS AND STARES OUT THE WINDOW....
IRIS HAS TO TRY AND GUESS WHAT HE'S THINKING.
JIM? WOULD YOU LIKE TO GO OUTSIDE? ARE YOU HUNGRY, DEAR?
JIM!!!
LYNN

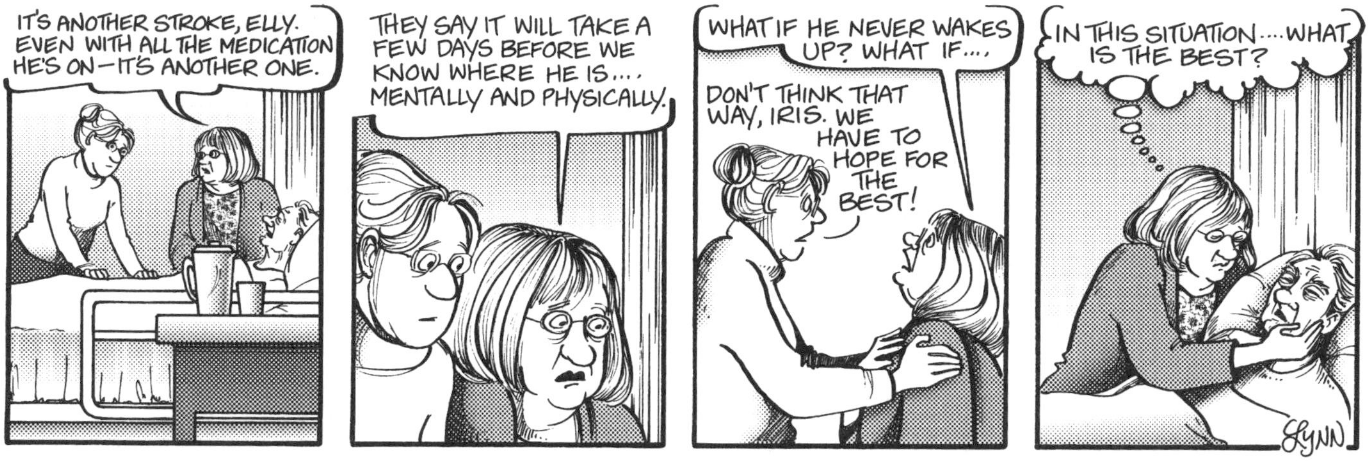
IT'S ANOTHER STROKE, ELLY. EVEN WITH ALL THE MEDICATION HE'S ON—IT'S ANOTHER ONE.
THEY SAY IT WILL TAKE A FEW DAYS BEFORE WE KNOW WHERE HE IS.... MENTALLY AND PHYSICALLY.
WHAT IF HE NEVER WAKES UP? WHAT IF....
DON'T THINK THAT WAY, IRIS. WE HAVE TO HOPE FOR THE BEST!
IN THIS SITUATION....WHAT IS THE BEST?
LYNN

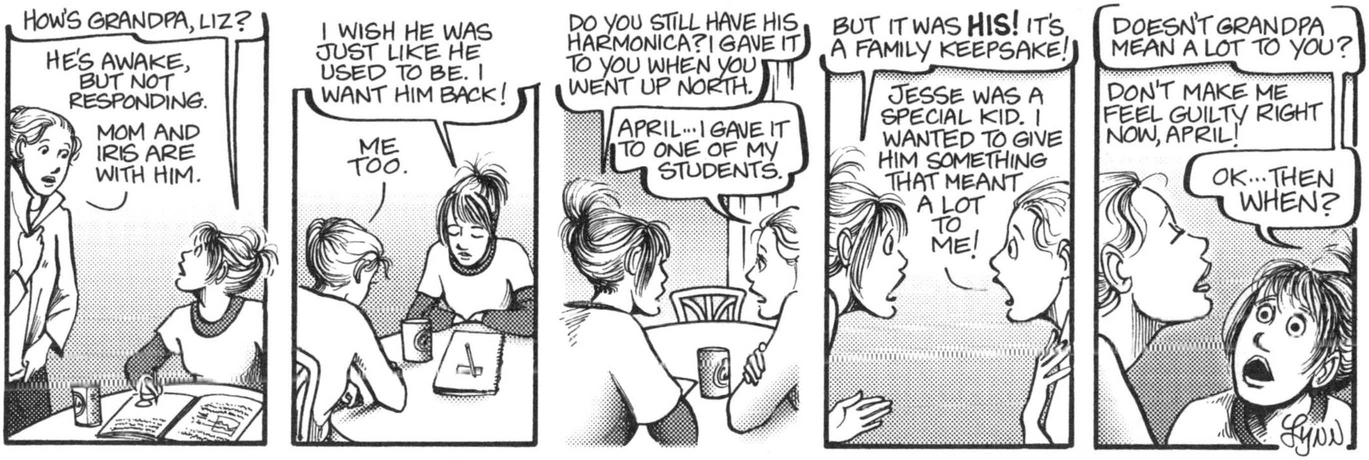
HOW'S GRANDPA, LIZ?
HE'S AWAKE, BUT NOT RESPONDING.
MOM AND IRIS ARE WITH HIM.
I WISH HE WAS JUST LIKE HE USED TO BE. I WANT HIM BACK!
ME TOO.
DO YOU STILL HAVE HIS HARMONICA? I GAVE IT TO YOU WHEN YOU WENT UP NORTH.
APRIL...I GAVE IT TO ONE OF MY STUDENTS.
BUT IT WAS HIS! IT'S A FAMILY KEEPSAKE!
JESSE WAS A SPECIAL KID. I WANTED TO GIVE HIM SOMETHING THAT MEANT A LOT TO ME!
DOESN'T GRANDPA MEAN A LOT TO YOU?
DON'T MAKE ME FEEL GUILTY RIGHT NOW, APRIL!
OK...THEN WHEN?
LYNN

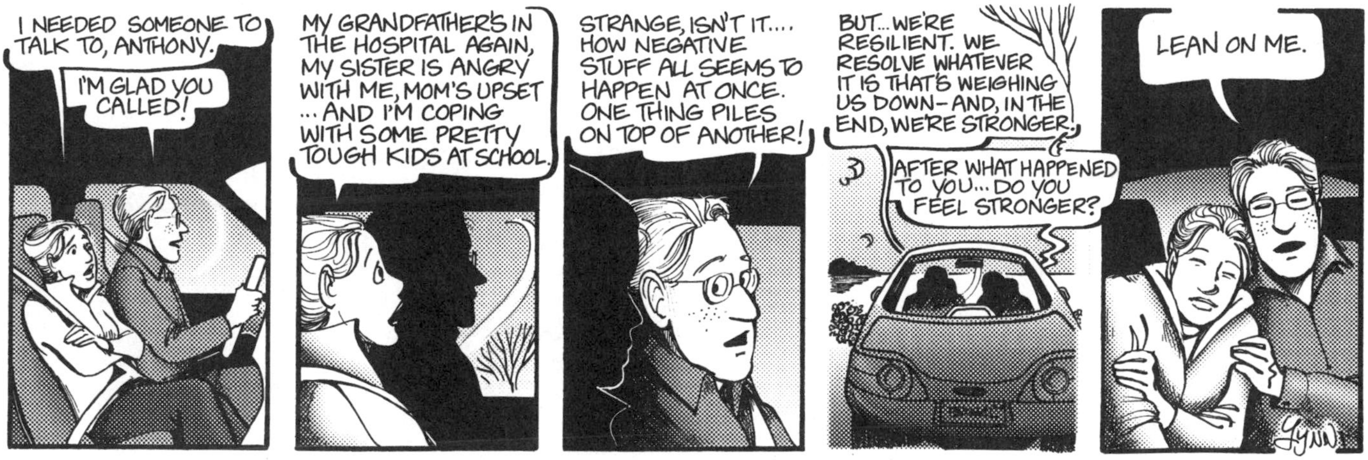
I NEEDED SOMEONE TO TALK TO, ANTHONY.
I'M GLAD YOU CALLED!
MY GRANDFATHER'S IN THE HOSPITAL AGAIN, MY SISTER IS ANGRY WITH ME, MOM'S UPSET ...AND I'M COPING WITH SOME PRETTY TOUGH KIDS AT SCHOOL.
STRANGE, ISN'T IT.... HOW NEGATIVE STUFF ALL SEEMS TO HAPPEN AT ONCE. ONE THING PILES ON TOP OF ANOTHER!
BUT...WE'RE RESILIENT. WE RESOLVE WHATEVER IT IS THAT'S WEIGHING US DOWN—AND, IN THE END, WE'RE STRONGER.
AFTER WHAT HAPPENED TO YOU...DO YOU FEEL STRONGER?
LEAN ON ME.
LYNN

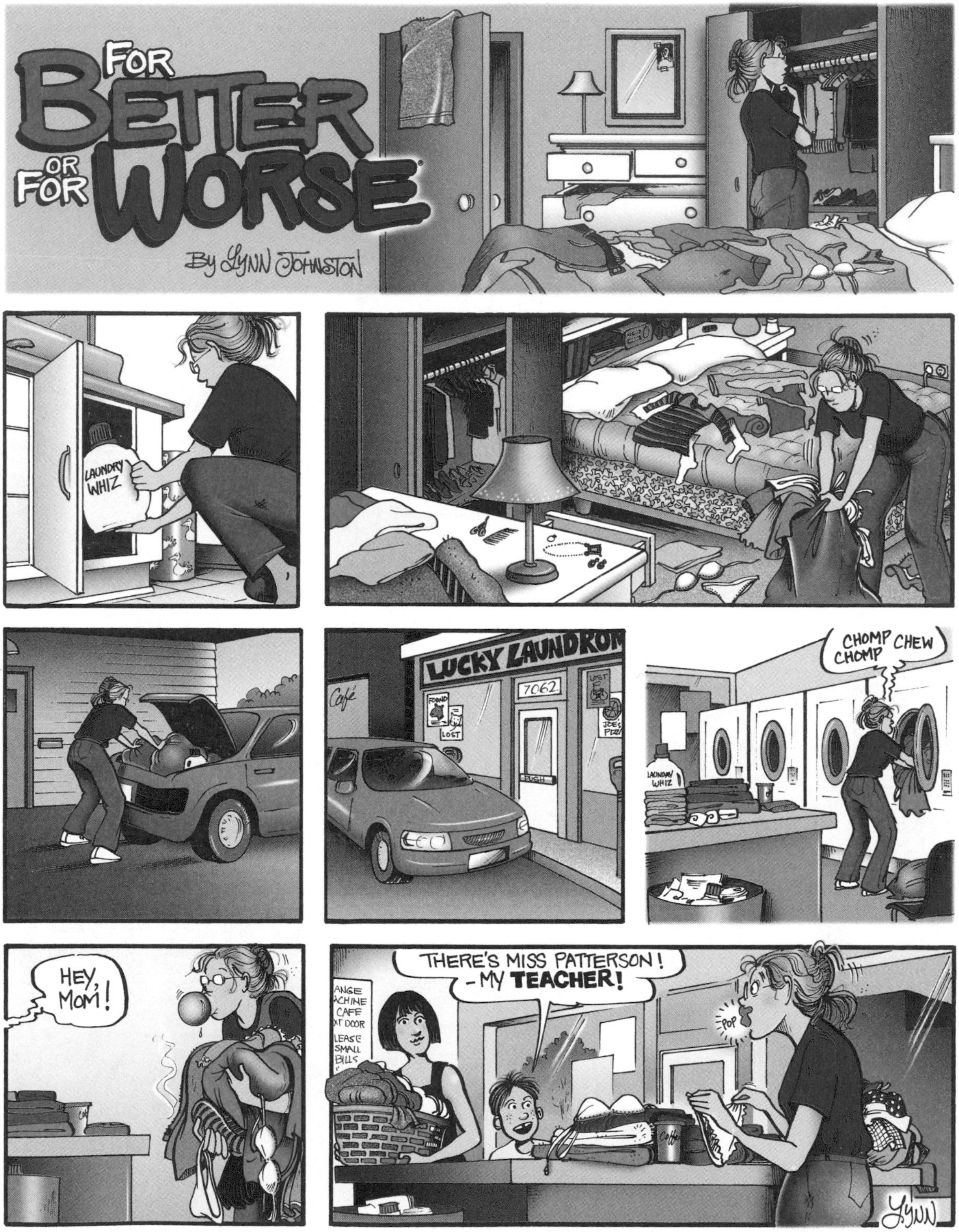
For Better or For Worse
By Lynn Johnston
LAUNDRY WHIZ
LUCKY LAUNDROM
7062
LOST
FOUND
LOST
CHOMP CHOMP CHEW
HEY, MOM!
THERE'S MISS PATTERSON! - MY **TEACHER!**
POP
LYNN

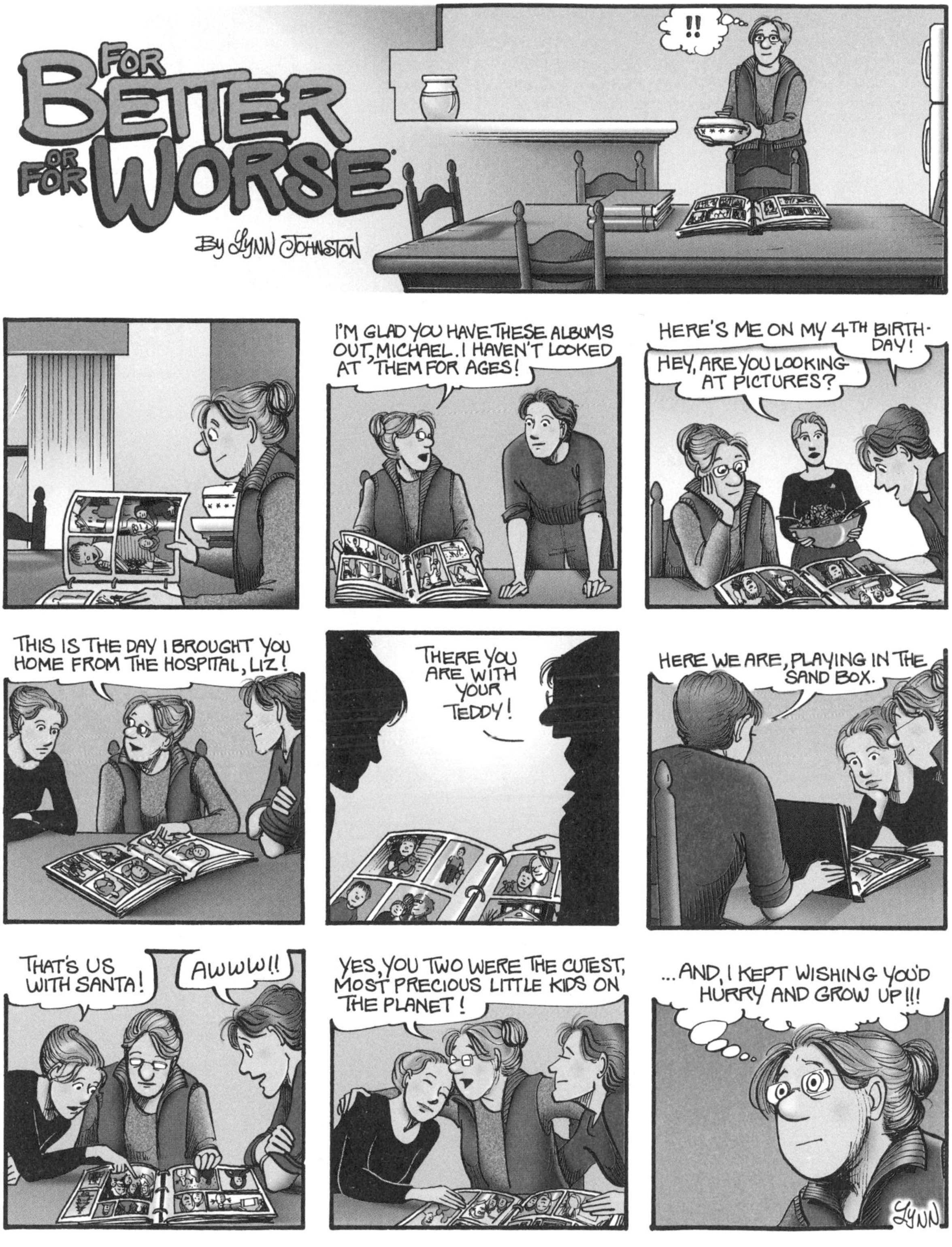
FOR BETTER OR FOR WORSE
By Lynn Johnston
!!
I'M GLAD YOU HAVE THESE ALBUMS OUT, MICHAEL. I HAVEN'T LOOKED AT THEM FOR AGES!
HERE'S ME ON MY 4TH BIRTH-DAY!
HEY, ARE YOU LOOKING AT PICTURES?
THIS IS THE DAY I BROUGHT YOU HOME FROM THE HOSPITAL, LIZ!
THERE YOU ARE WITH YOUR TEDDY!
HERE WE ARE, PLAYING IN THE SAND BOX.
THAT'S US WITH SANTA!
AWWW!!
YES, YOU TWO WERE THE CUTEST, MOST PRECIOUS LITTLE KIDS ON THE PLANET!
...AND, I KEPT WISHING YOU'D HURRY AND GROW UP!!!
LYNN

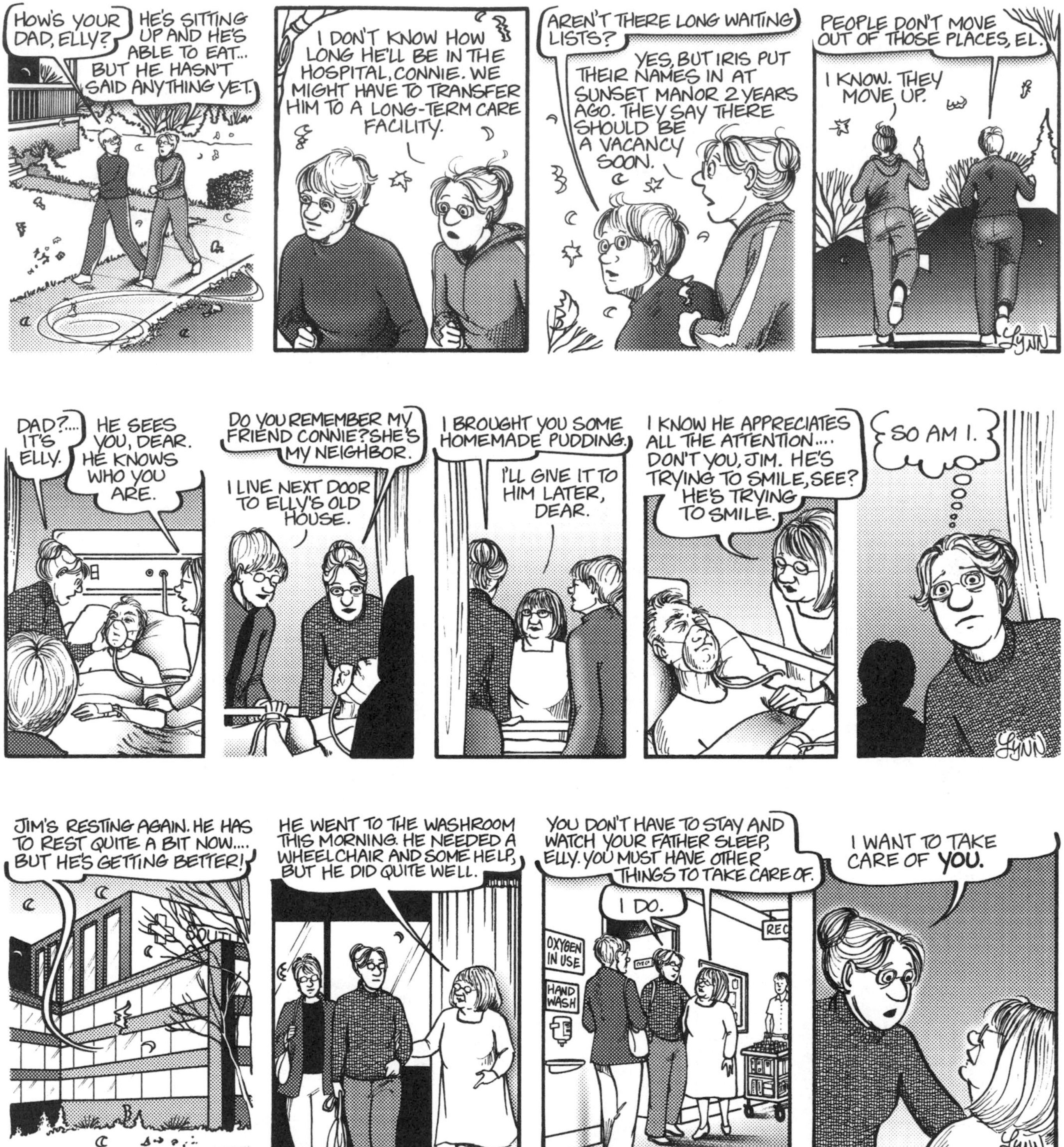
HOW'S YOUR DAD, ELLY?
HE'S SITTING UP AND HE'S ABLE TO EAT... BUT HE HASN'T SAID ANYTHING YET.
I DON'T KNOW HOW LONG HE'LL BE IN THE HOSPITAL, CONNIE. WE MIGHT HAVE TO TRANSFER HIM TO A LONG-TERM CARE FACILITY.
AREN'T THERE LONG WAITING LISTS?
YES, BUT IRIS PUT THEIR NAMES IN AT SUNSET MANOR 2 YEARS AGO. THEY SAY THERE SHOULD BE A VACANCY SOON.
PEOPLE DON'T MOVE OUT OF THOSE PLACES, EL.
I KNOW. THEY MOVE UP.
LYNN
DAD?.... IT'S ELLY.
HE SEES YOU, DEAR. HE KNOWS WHO YOU ARE.
DO YOU REMEMBER MY FRIEND CONNIE? SHE'S MY NEIGHBOR.
I LIVE NEXT DOOR TO ELLY'S OLD HOUSE.
I BROUGHT YOU SOME HOMEMADE PUDDING.
I'LL GIVE IT TO HIM LATER, DEAR.
I KNOW HE APPRECIATES ALL THE ATTENTION.... DON'T YOU, JIM. HE'S TRYING TO SMILE, SEE? HE'S TRYING TO SMILE.
SO AM I.
LYNN
JIM'S RESTING AGAIN. HE HAS TO REST QUITE A BIT NOW.... BUT HE'S GETTING BETTER!
HE WENT TO THE WASHROOM THIS MORNING. HE NEEDED A WHEELCHAIR AND SOME HELP, BUT HE DID QUITE WELL.
YOU DON'T HAVE TO STAY AND WATCH YOUR FATHER SLEEP, ELLY. YOU MUST HAVE OTHER THINGS TO TAKE CARE OF.
I DO.
OXYGEN IN USE
HAND WASH
I WANT TO TAKE CARE OF **YOU.**
LYNN

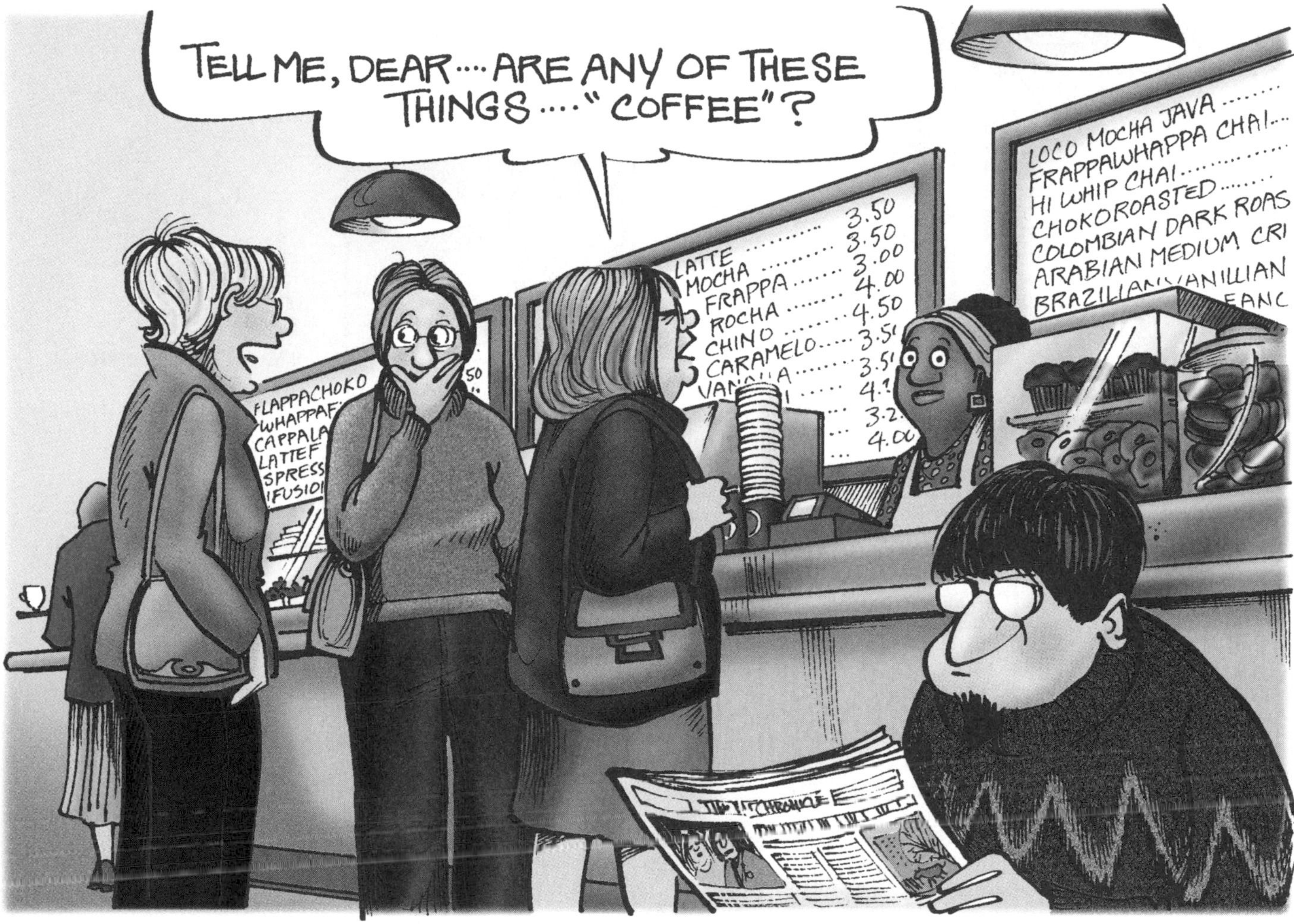
TELL ME, DEAR.... ARE ANY OF THESE THINGS...."COFFEE"?
LATTE 3.50
MOCHA 3.50
FRAPPA 3.00
ROCHA 4.00
CHINO 4.50
CARAMELO
LOCO MOCHA JAVA
FRAPPAWHAPPA CHAI
HI WHIP CHAI
CHOKOROASTED
COLOMBIAN DARK ROAS
ARABIAN MEDIUM CRI
FLAPPACHOKO
CAPPALA
LATTEF
SPRESS

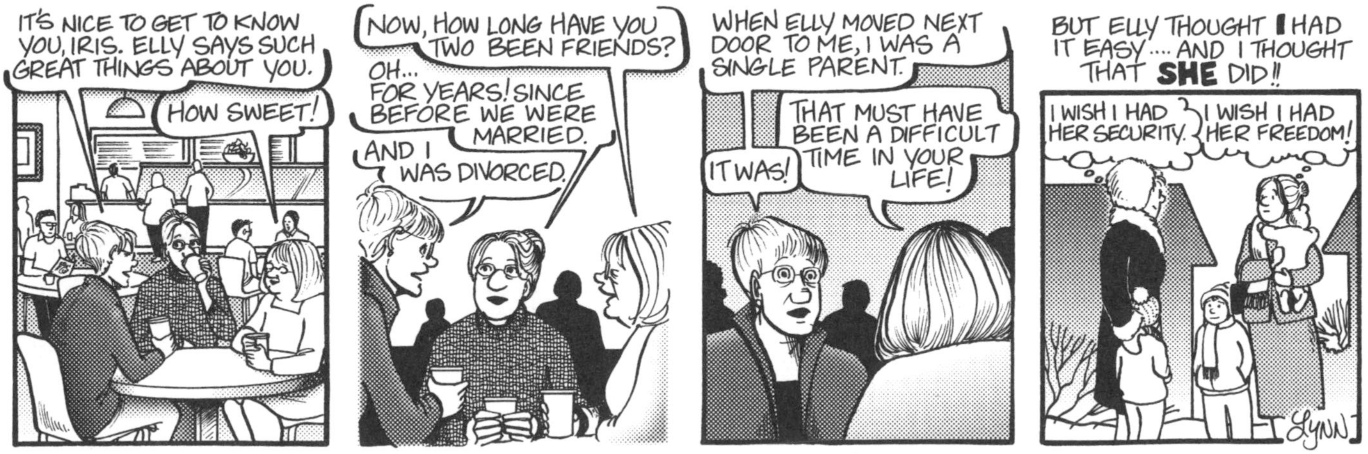
IT'S NICE TO GET TO KNOW YOU, IRIS. ELLY SAYS SUCH GREAT THINGS ABOUT YOU.
HOW SWEET!
NOW, HOW LONG HAVE YOU TWO BEEN FRIENDS?
OH... FOR YEARS! SINCE BEFORE WE WERE MARRIED.
AND I WAS DIVORCED.
WHEN ELLY MOVED NEXT DOOR TO ME, I WAS A SINGLE PARENT.
IT WAS!
THAT MUST HAVE BEEN A DIFFICULT TIME IN YOUR LIFE!
BUT ELLY THOUGHT I HAD IT EASY.... AND I THOUGHT THAT SHE DID!!
I WISH I HAD HER SECURITY.
I WISH I HAD HER FREEDOM!
LYNN

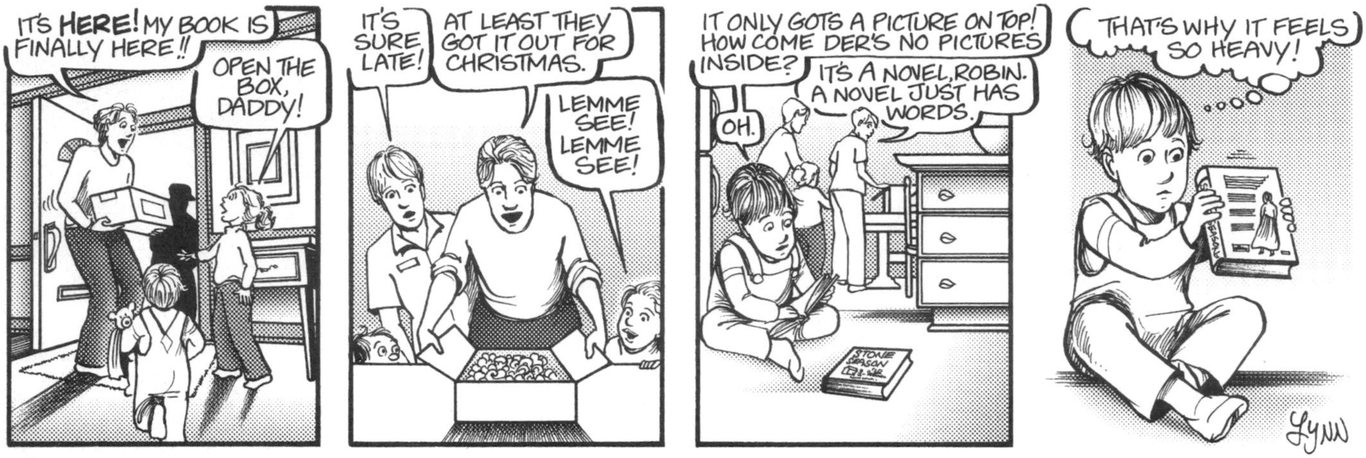
IT'S **HERE!** MY BOOK IS FINALLY HERE!!
OPEN THE BOX, DADDY!
IT'S SURE LATE!
AT LEAST THEY GOT IT OUT FOR CHRISTMAS.
LEMME SEE! LEMME SEE!
IT ONLY GOTS A PICTURE ON TOP! HOW COME DER'S NO PICTURES INSIDE?
IT'S A NOVEL, ROBIN. A NOVEL JUST HAS WORDS.
OH.
STONE SEASON
THAT'S WHY IT FEELS SO HEAVY!
LYNN

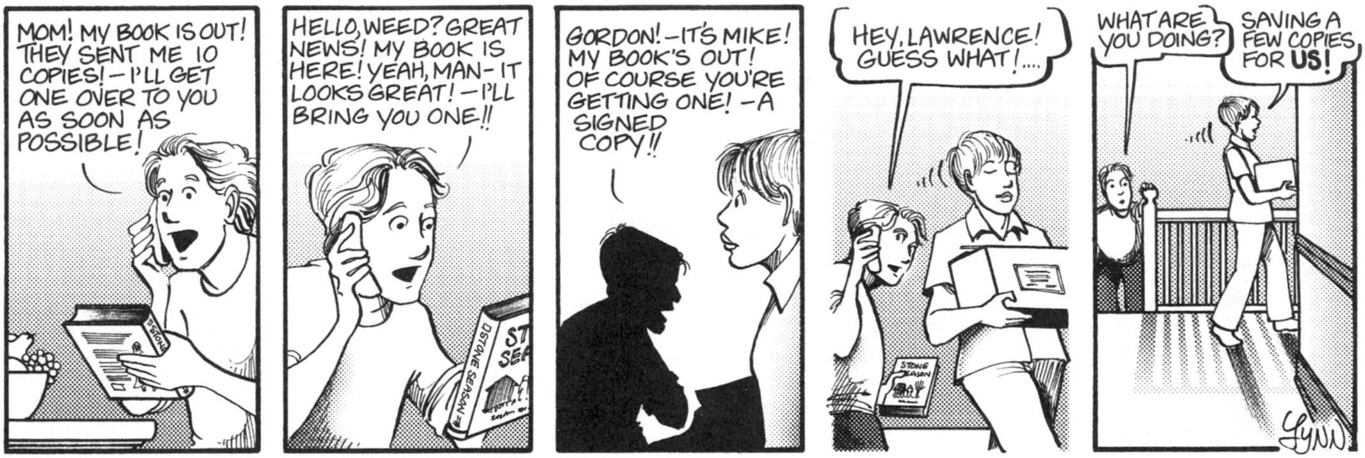
MOM! MY BOOK IS OUT! THEY SENT ME 10 COPIES! – I'LL GET ONE OVER TO YOU AS SOON AS POSSIBLE!
HELLO, WEED? GREAT NEWS! MY BOOK IS HERE! YEAH, MAN – IT LOOKS GREAT! – I'LL BRING YOU ONE!!
STONE SEASON
GORDON! – IT'S MIKE! MY BOOK'S OUT! OF COURSE YOU'RE GETTING ONE! – A SIGNED COPY!!
HEY, LAWRENCE! GUESS WHAT!....
STONE SEASON
WHAT ARE YOU DOING?
SAVING A FEW COPIES FOR **US!**
LYNN

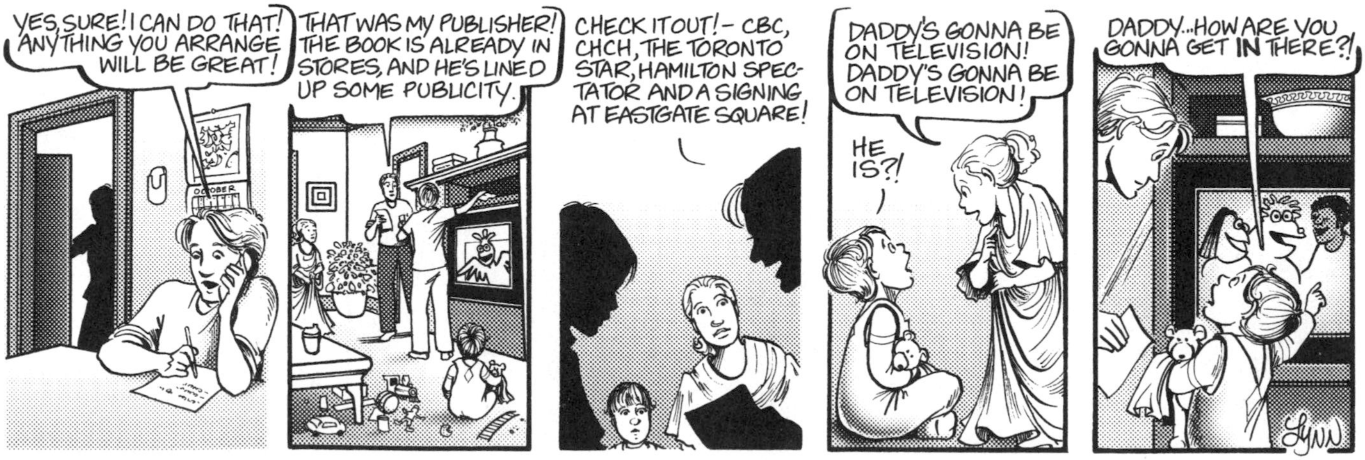
YES, SURE! I CAN DO THAT! ANYTHING YOU ARRANGE WILL BE GREAT!
OCTOBER
THAT WAS MY PUBLISHER! THE BOOK IS ALREADY IN STORES, AND HE'S LINED UP SOME PUBLICITY.
CHECK IT OUT! – CBC, CHCH, THE TORONTO STAR, HAMILTON SPECTATOR AND A SIGNING AT EASTGATE SQUARE!
DADDY'S GONNA BE ON TELEVISION! DADDY'S GONNA BE ON TELEVISION!
HE IS?!
DADDY...HOW ARE YOU GONNA GET **IN** THERE?!
LYNN

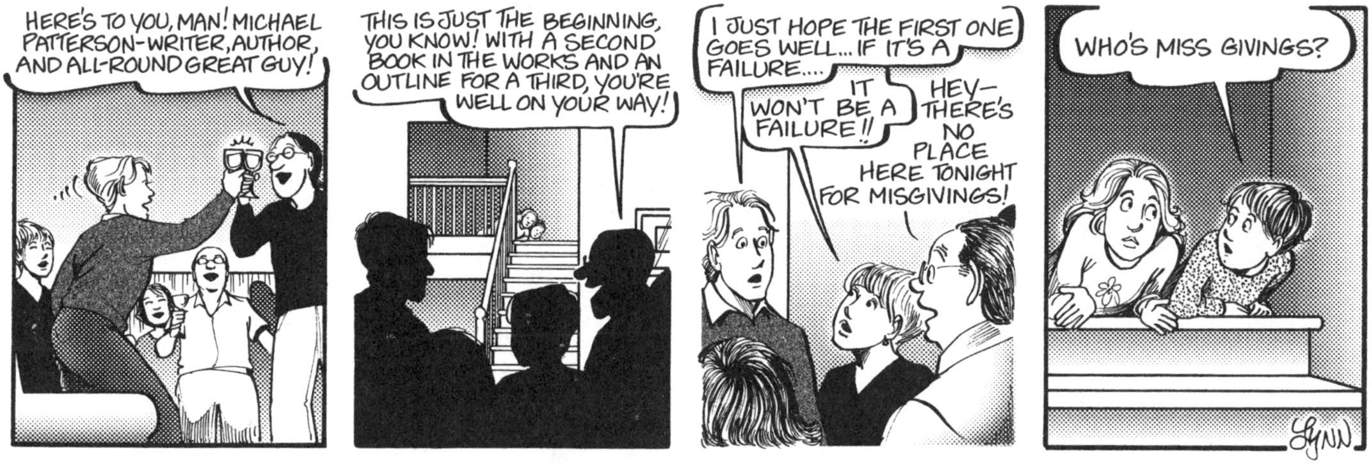
HERE'S TO YOU, MAN! MICHAEL PATTERSON-WRITER, AUTHOR, AND ALL-ROUND GREAT GUY!
THIS IS JUST THE BEGINNING, YOU KNOW! WITH A SECOND BOOK IN THE WORKS AND AN OUTLINE FOR A THIRD, YOU'RE WELL ON YOUR WAY!
I JUST HOPE THE FIRST ONE GOES WELL... IF IT'S A FAILURE....
IT WON'T BE A FAILURE!!
HEY– THERE'S NO PLACE HERE TONIGHT FOR MISGIVINGS!
WHO'S MISS GIVINGS?
LYNN

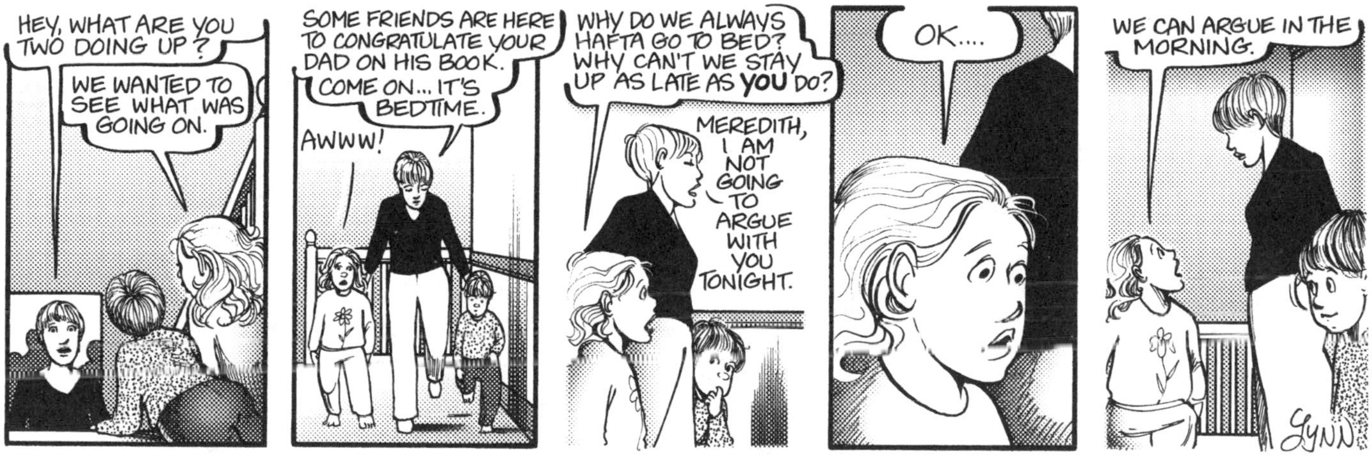
HEY, WHAT ARE YOU TWO DOING UP?
WE WANTED TO SEE WHAT WAS GOING ON.
SOME FRIENDS ARE HERE TO CONGRATULATE YOUR DAD ON HIS BOOK.
COME ON... IT'S BEDTIME.
AWWW!
WHY DO WE ALWAYS HAFTA GO TO BED? WHY CAN'T WE STAY UP AS LATE AS **YOU** DO?
MEREDITH, I AM NOT GOING TO ARGUE WITH YOU TONIGHT.
OK....
WE CAN ARGUE IN THE MORNING.
LYNN

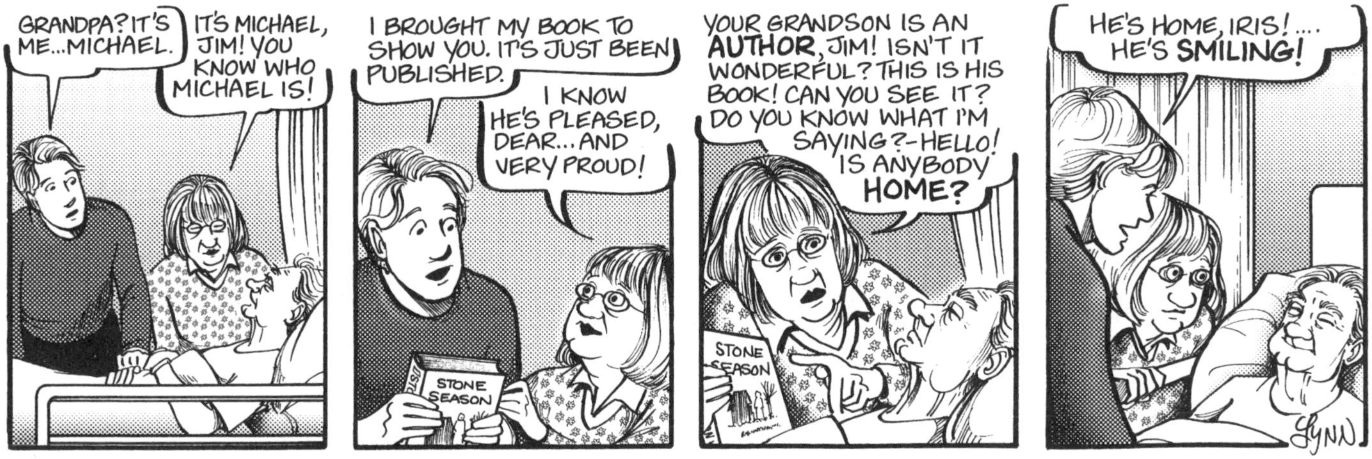
GRANDPA? IT'S ME...MICHAEL.
IT'S MICHAEL, JIM! YOU KNOW WHO MICHAEL IS!
I BROUGHT MY BOOK TO SHOW YOU. IT'S JUST BEEN PUBLISHED.
I KNOW HE'S PLEASED, DEAR... AND VERY PROUD!
STONE SEASON
YOUR GRANDSON IS AN **AUTHOR**, JIM! ISN'T IT WONDERFUL? THIS IS HIS BOOK! CAN YOU SEE IT? DO YOU KNOW WHAT I'M SAYING?-HELLO! IS ANYBODY **HOME?**
STONE SEASON
HE'S HOME, IRIS!.... HE'S **SMILING!**
LYNN

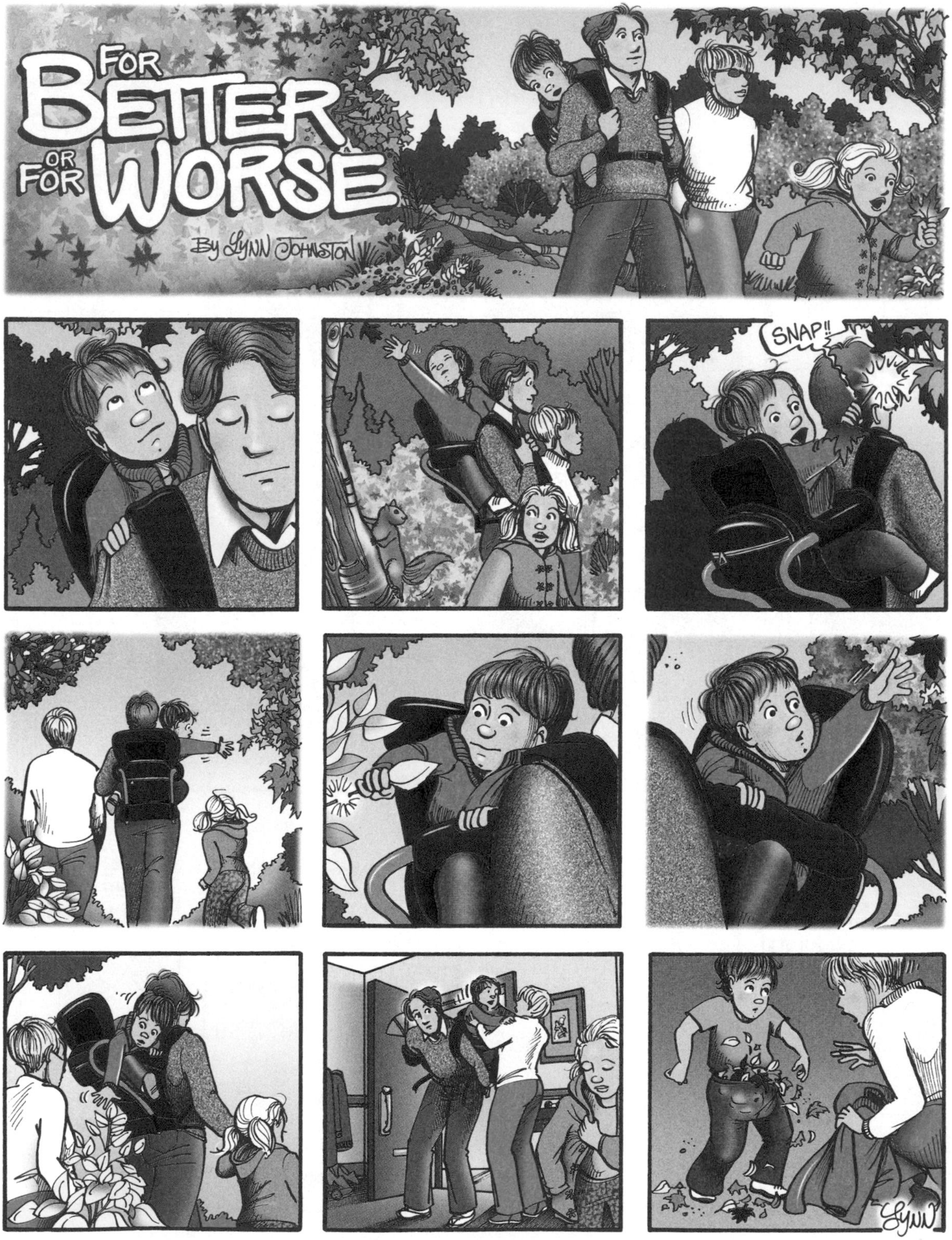
FOR BETTER OR FOR WORSE
By Lynn Johnston
SNAP!!
Lynn

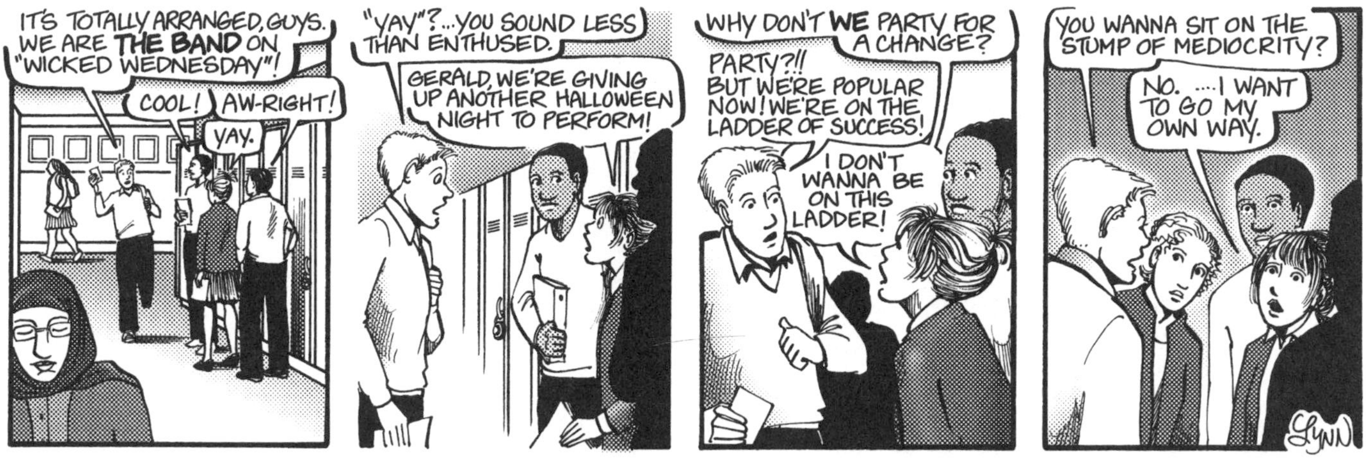
IT'S TOTALLY ARRANGED, GUYS. WE ARE **THE BAND** ON "WICKED WEDNESDAY"!
COOL!
AW-RIGHT!
YAY.
"YAY"?...YOU SOUND LESS THAN ENTHUSED.
GERALD, WE'RE GIVING UP ANOTHER HALLOWEEN NIGHT TO PERFORM!
WHY DON'T **WE** PARTY FOR A CHANGE?
PARTY?!! BUT WE'RE POPULAR NOW! WE'RE ON THE LADDER OF SUCCESS!
I DON'T WANNA BE ON THIS LADDER!
YOU WANNA SIT ON THE STUMP OF MEDIOCRITY?
NO. ....I WANT TO GO MY OWN WAY.
LYNN

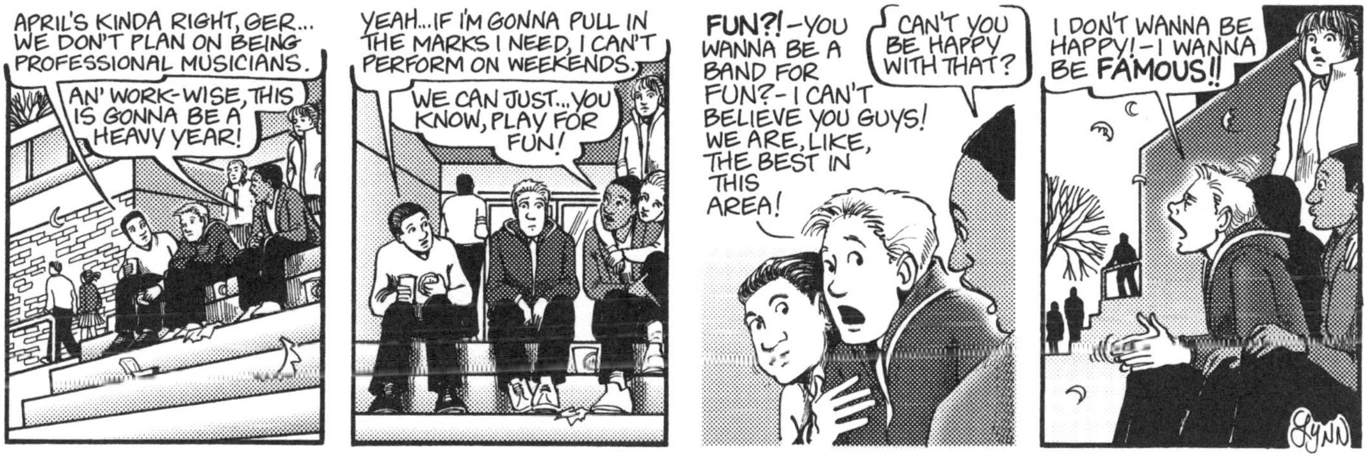
APRIL'S KINDA RIGHT, GER... WE DON'T PLAN ON BEING PROFESSIONAL MUSICIANS.
AN' WORK-WISE, THIS IS GONNA BE A HEAVY YEAR!
YEAH...IF I'M GONNA PULL IN THE MARKS I NEED, I CAN'T PERFORM ON WEEKENDS.
WE CAN JUST...YOU KNOW, PLAY FOR FUN!
FUN?! -YOU WANNA BE A BAND FOR FUN?- I CAN'T BELIEVE YOU GUYS! WE ARE, LIKE, THE BEST IN THIS AREA!
CAN'T YOU BE HAPPY WITH THAT?
I DON'T WANNA BE HAPPY! -I WANNA BE **FAMOUS!!**
LYNN

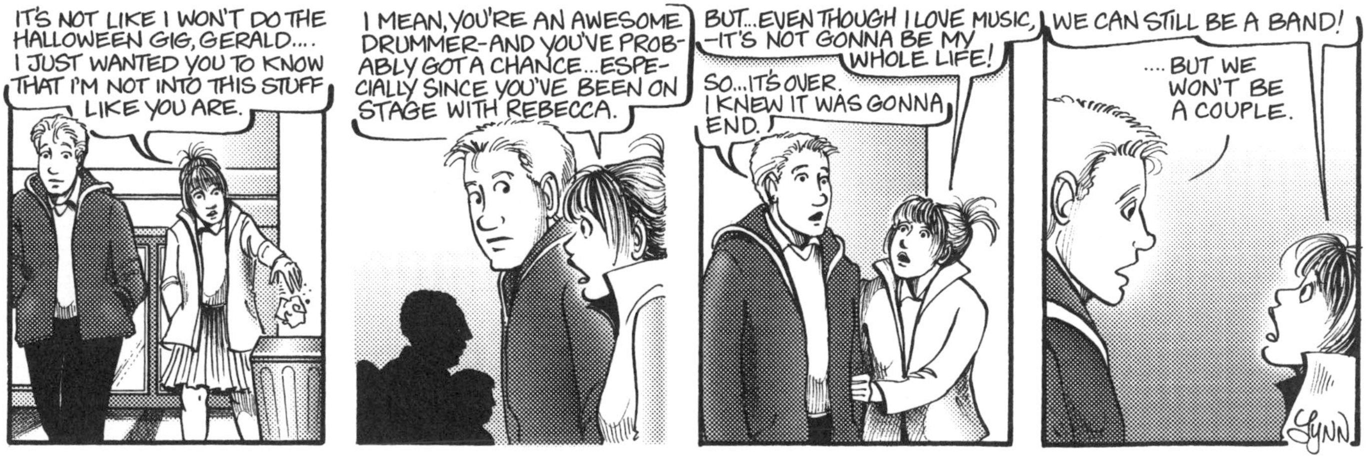
IT'S NOT LIKE I WON'T DO THE HALLOWEEN GIG, GERALD.... I JUST WANTED YOU TO KNOW THAT I'M NOT INTO THIS STUFF LIKE YOU ARE.
I MEAN, YOU'RE AN AWESOME DRUMMER-AND YOU'VE PROBABLY GOT A CHANCE...ESPECIALLY SINCE YOU'VE BEEN ON STAGE WITH REBECCA.
BUT...EVEN THOUGH I LOVE MUSIC, -IT'S NOT GONNA BE MY WHOLE LIFE!
SO...IT'S OVER. I KNEW IT WAS GONNA END.
WE CAN STILL BE A BAND!
....BUT WE WON'T BE A COUPLE.
LYNN

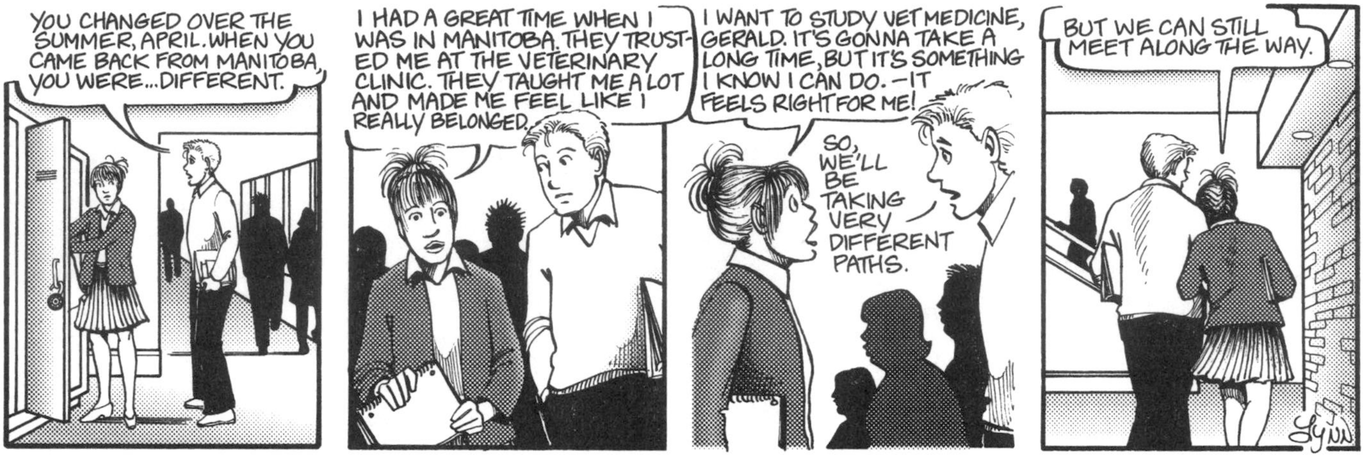
YOU CHANGED OVER THE SUMMER, APRIL. WHEN YOU CAME BACK FROM MANITOBA, YOU WERE...DIFFERENT.
I HAD A GREAT TIME WHEN I WAS IN MANITOBA. THEY TRUSTED ME AT THE VETERINARY CLINIC. THEY TAUGHT ME A LOT AND MADE ME FEEL LIKE I REALLY BELONGED.
I WANT TO STUDY VET MEDICINE, GERALD. IT'S GONNA TAKE A LONG TIME, BUT IT'S SOMETHING I KNOW I CAN DO. —IT FEELS RIGHT FOR ME!
SO, WE'LL BE TAKING VERY DIFFERENT PATHS.
BUT WE CAN STILL MEET ALONG THE WAY.
LYNN

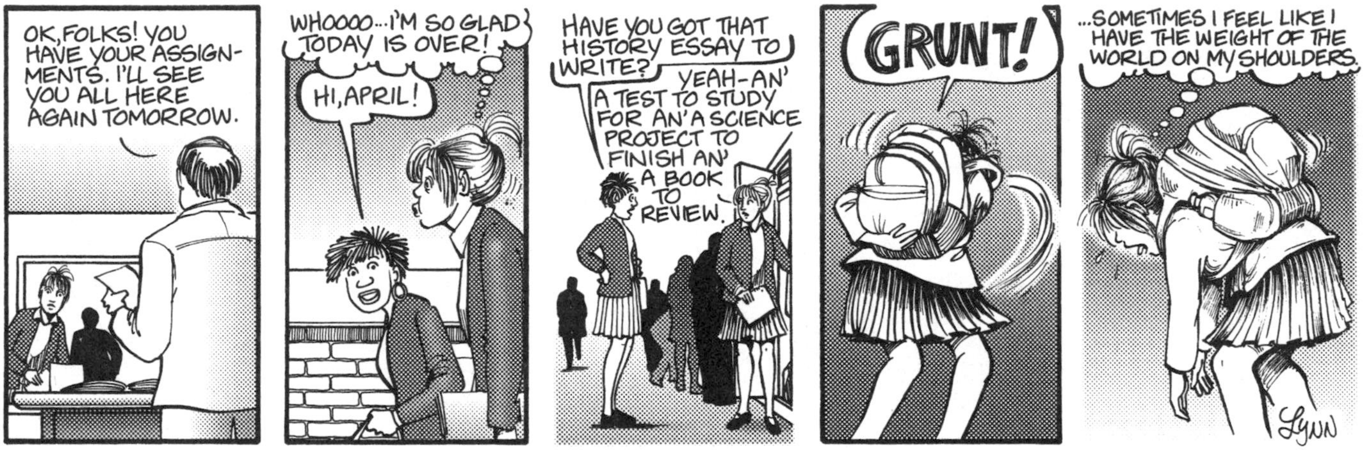
OK, FOLKS! YOU HAVE YOUR ASSIGNMENTS. I'LL SEE YOU ALL HERE AGAIN TOMORROW.
WHOOOO...I'M SO GLAD TODAY IS OVER!
HI, APRIL!
HAVE YOU GOT THAT HISTORY ESSAY TO WRITE?
YEAH-AN' A TEST TO STUDY FOR AN' A SCIENCE PROJECT TO FINISH AN' A BOOK TO REVIEW.
GRUNT!
...SOMETIMES I FEEL LIKE I HAVE THE WEIGHT OF THE WORLD ON MY SHOULDERS.
LYNN

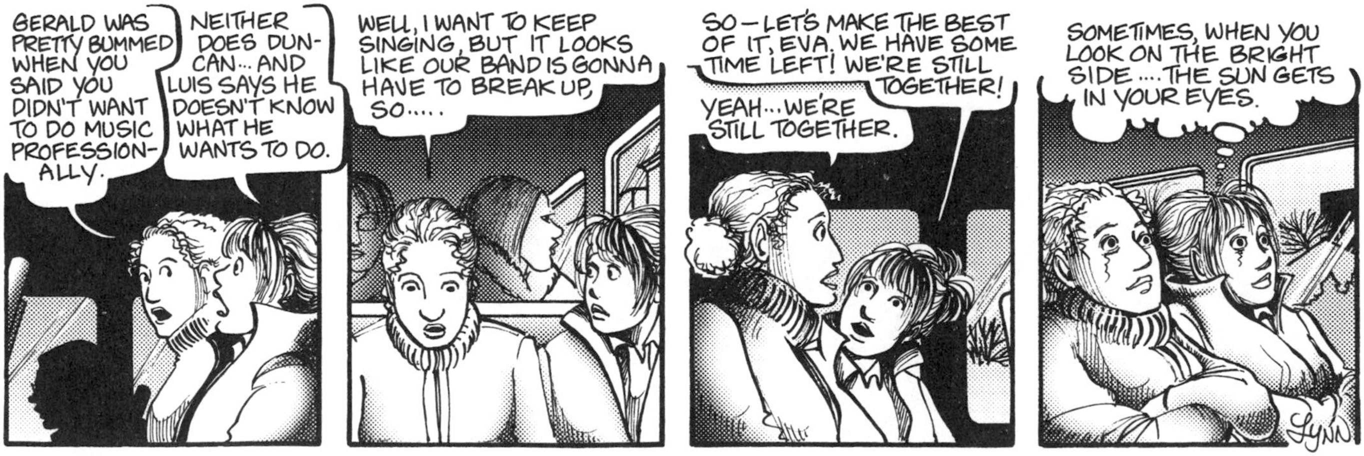
GERALD WAS PRETTY BUMMED WHEN YOU SAID YOU DIDN'T WANT TO DO MUSIC PROFESSIONALLY.
NEITHER DOES DUNCAN... AND LUIS SAYS HE DOESN'T KNOW WHAT HE WANTS TO DO.
WELL, I WANT TO KEEP SINGING, BUT IT LOOKS LIKE OUR BAND IS GONNA HAVE TO BREAK UP, SO.....
SO — LET'S MAKE THE BEST OF IT, EVA. WE HAVE SOME TIME LEFT! WE'RE STILL TOGETHER!
YEAH... WE'RE STILL TOGETHER.
SOMETIMES, WHEN YOU LOOK ON THE BRIGHT SIDE .... THE SUN GETS IN YOUR EYES.
LYNN

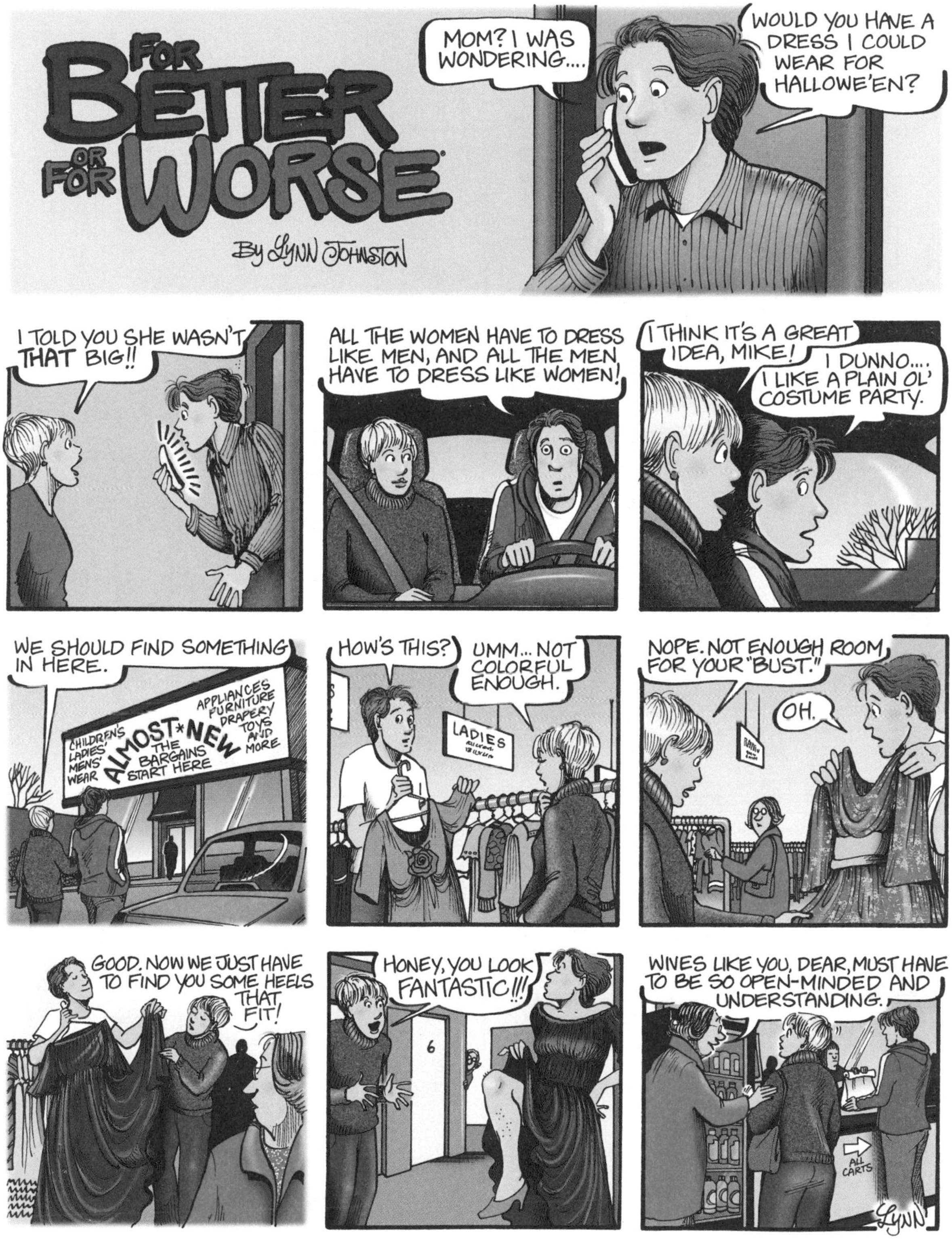
FOR BETTER OR FOR WORSE
By Lynn Johnston
MOM? I WAS WONDERING....
WOULD YOU HAVE A DRESS I COULD WEAR FOR HALLOWE'EN?
I TOLD YOU SHE WASN'T THAT BIG!!
ALL THE WOMEN HAVE TO DRESS LIKE MEN, AND ALL THE MEN HAVE TO DRESS LIKE WOMEN!
I THINK IT'S A GREAT IDEA, MIKE!
I DUNNO.... I LIKE A PLAIN OL' COSTUME PARTY.
WE SHOULD FIND SOMETHING IN HERE.
CHILDREN'S LADIES' MENS' WEAR
ALMOST*NEW
THE BARGAINS START HERE
APPLIANCES FURNITURE DRAPERY TOYS AND MORE
HOW'S THIS?
UMM... NOT COLORFUL ENOUGH.
LADIES
NOPE. NOT ENOUGH ROOM FOR YOUR "BUST."
OH.
GOOD. NOW WE JUST HAVE TO FIND YOU SOME HEELS THAT FIT!
HONEY, YOU LOOK FANTASTIC!!!
6
WIVES LIKE YOU, DEAR, MUST HAVE TO BE SO OPEN-MINDED AND UNDERSTANDING.
ALL CARTS
LYNN

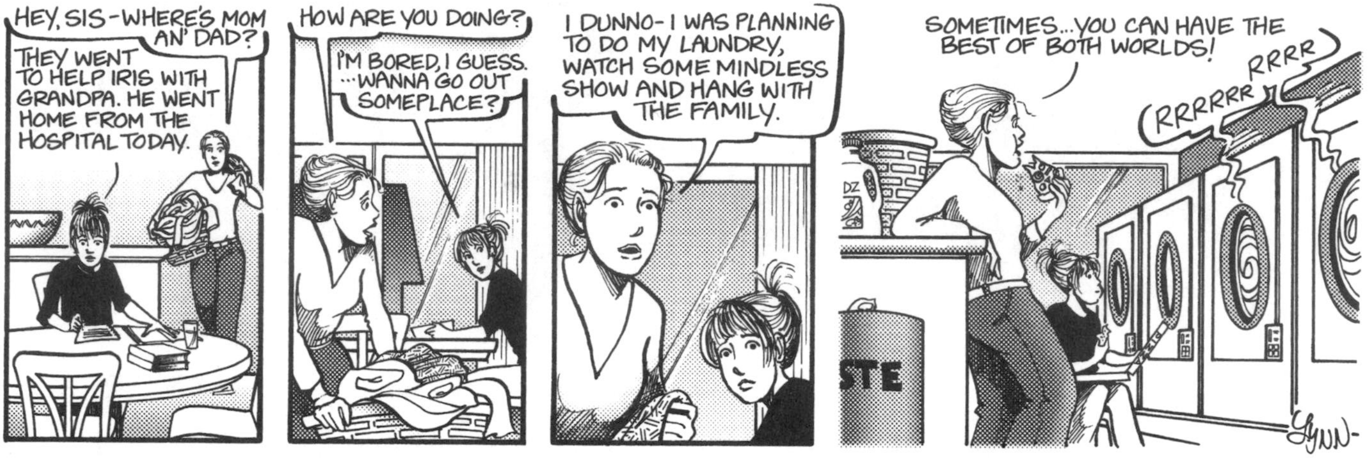
HEY, SIS-WHERE'S MOM AN' DAD?
THEY WENT TO HELP IRIS WITH GRANDPA. HE WENT HOME FROM THE HOSPITAL TODAY.
HOW ARE YOU DOING?
I'M BORED, I GUESS. ...WANNA GO OUT SOMEPLACE?
I DUNNO- I WAS PLANNING TO DO MY LAUNDRY, WATCH SOME MINDLESS SHOW AND HANG WITH THE FAMILY.
SOMETIMES...YOU CAN HAVE THE BEST OF BOTH WORLDS!
RRRRRR
RRRR
STE

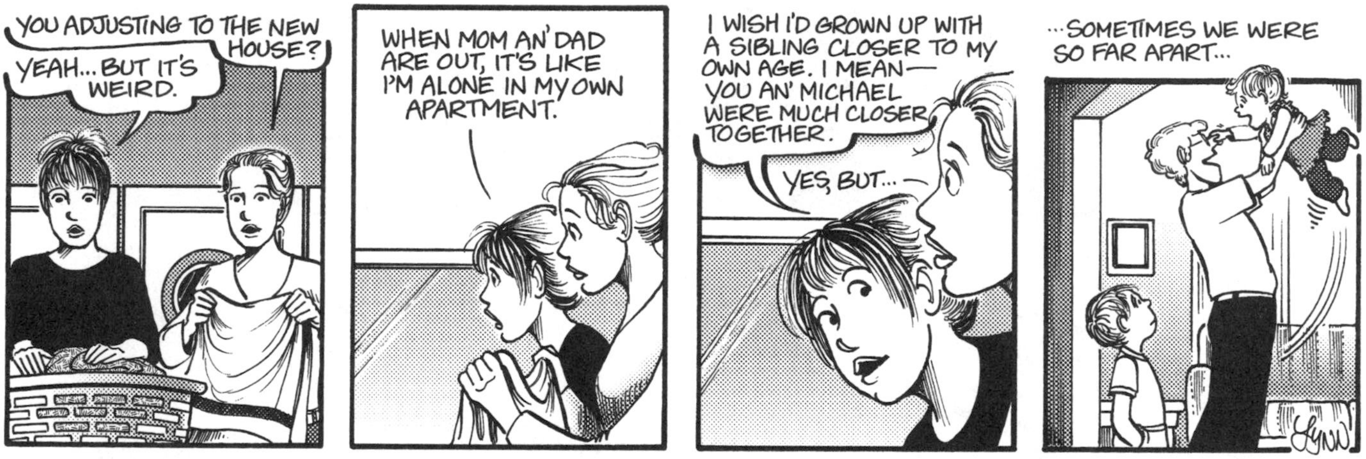
YOU ADJUSTING TO THE NEW HOUSE?
YEAH... BUT IT'S WEIRD.
WHEN MOM AN' DAD ARE OUT, IT'S LIKE I'M ALONE IN MY OWN APARTMENT.
I WISH I'D GROWN UP WITH A SIBLING CLOSER TO MY OWN AGE. I MEAN— YOU AN' MICHAEL WERE MUCH CLOSER TOGETHER.
YES, BUT...
...SOMETIMES WE WERE SO FAR APART...

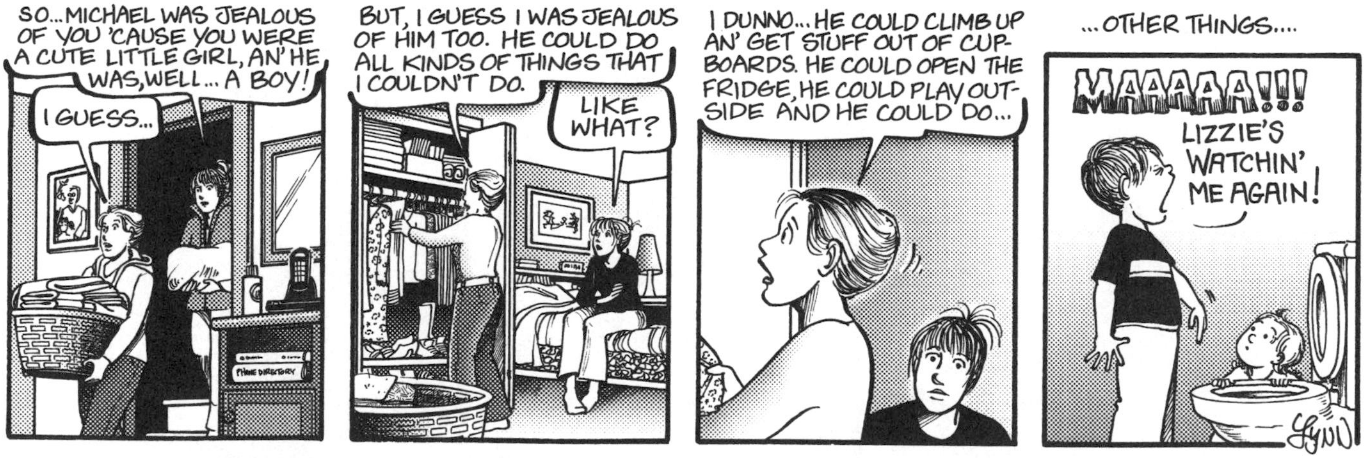
SO...MICHAEL WAS JEALOUS OF YOU 'CAUSE YOU WERE A CUTE LITTLE GIRL, AN' HE WAS, WELL... A BOY!
I GUESS...
BUT, I GUESS I WAS JEALOUS OF HIM TOO. HE COULD DO ALL KINDS OF THINGS THAT I COULDN'T DO.
LIKE WHAT?
I DUNNO... HE COULD CLIMB UP AN' GET STUFF OUT OF CUPBOARDS. HE COULD OPEN THE FRIDGE, HE COULD PLAY OUTSIDE AND HE COULD DO...
...OTHER THINGS....
MAAAAA!!!
LIZZIE'S WATCHIN' ME AGAIN!

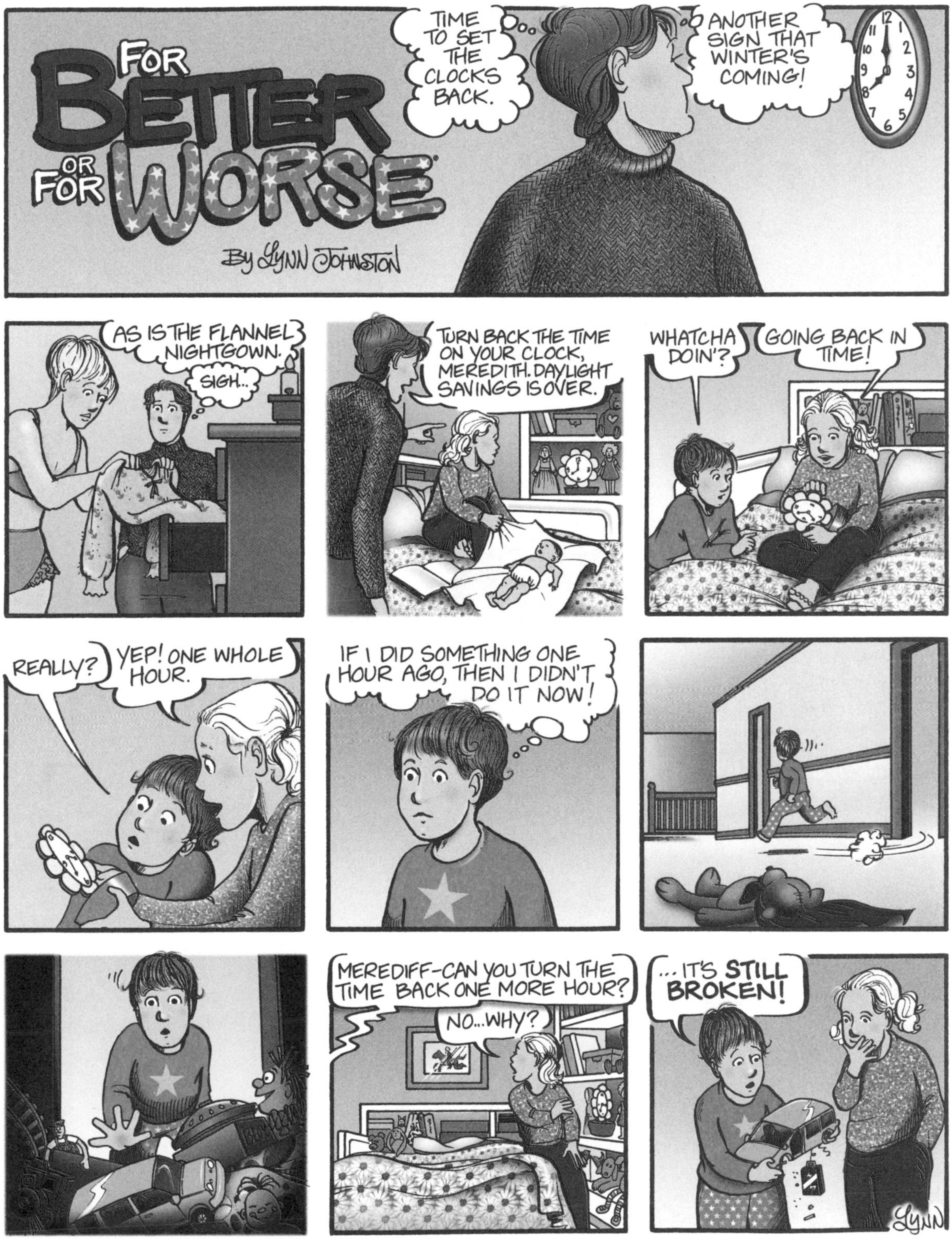
FOR BETTER OR FOR WORSE
BY LYNN JOHNSTON
TIME TO SET THE CLOCKS BACK.
ANOTHER SIGN THAT WINTER'S COMING!
AS IS THE FLANNEL NIGHTGOWN.
SIGH...
TURN BACK THE TIME ON YOUR CLOCK, MEREDITH. DAYLIGHT SAVINGS IS OVER.
WHATCHA DOIN'?
GOING BACK IN TIME!
REALLY?
YEP! ONE WHOLE HOUR.
IF I DID SOMETHING ONE HOUR AGO, THEN I DIDN'T DO IT NOW!
MEREDIFF–CAN YOU TURN THE TIME BACK ONE MORE HOUR?
NO...WHY?
...IT'S STILL BROKEN!
LYNN

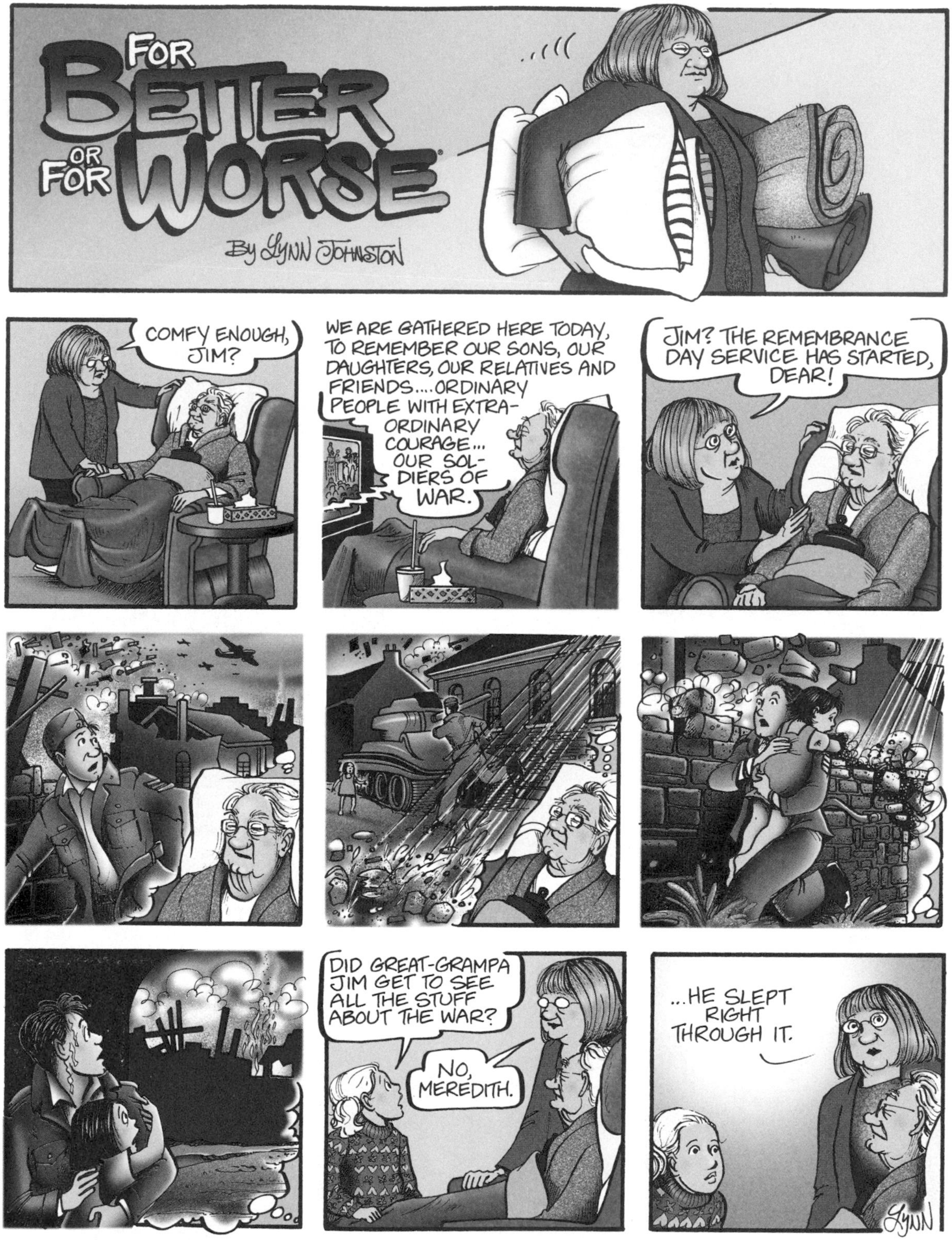
FOR BETTER OR FOR WORSE
BY LYNN JOHNSTON
COMFY ENOUGH, JIM?
WE ARE GATHERED HERE TODAY, TO REMEMBER OUR SONS, OUR DAUGHTERS, OUR RELATIVES AND FRIENDS....ORDINARY PEOPLE WITH EXTRA-ORDINARY COURAGE... OUR SOL-DIERS OF WAR.
JIM? THE REMEMBRANCE DAY SERVICE HAS STARTED, DEAR!
DID GREAT-GRAMPA JIM GET TO SEE ALL THE STUFF ABOUT THE WAR?
NO, MEREDITH.
...HE SLEPT RIGHT THROUGH IT.
LYNN

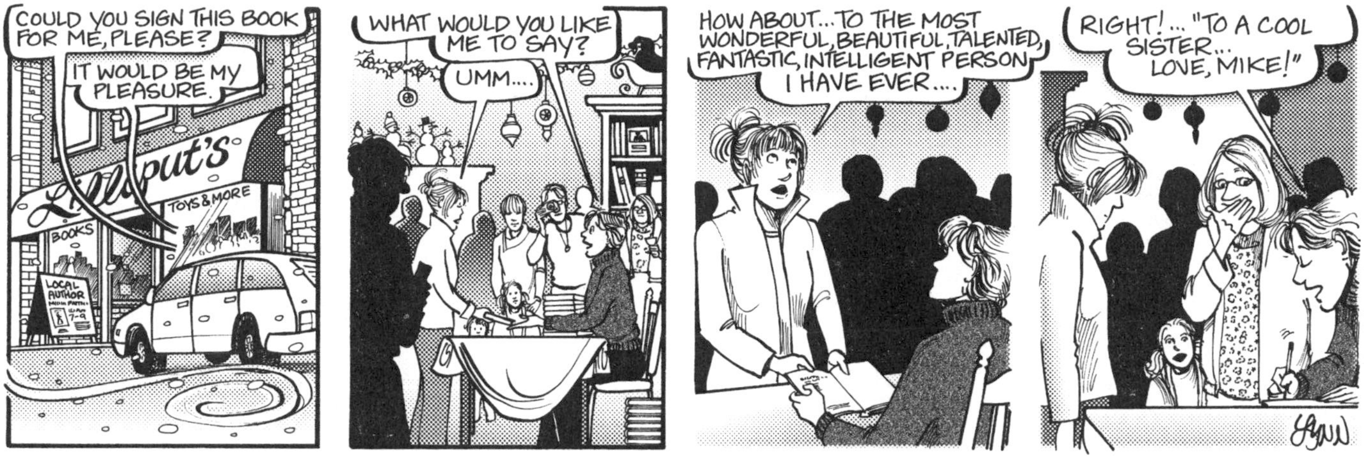
COULD YOU SIGN THIS BOOK FOR ME, PLEASE?
IT WOULD BE MY PLEASURE.
TOYS & MORE
BOOKS
LOCAL AUTHOR
WHAT WOULD YOU LIKE ME TO SAY?
UMM....
HOW ABOUT... TO THE MOST WONDERFUL, BEAUTIFUL, TALENTED, FANTASTIC, INTELLIGENT PERSON I HAVE EVER....
RIGHT! ... "TO A COOL SISTER... LOVE, MIKE!"
LYNN

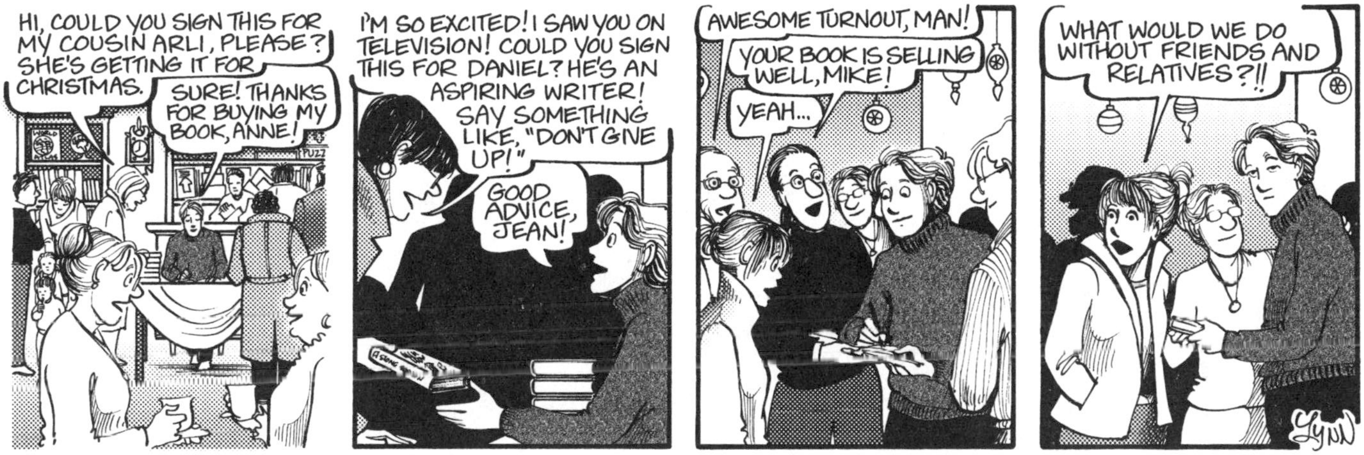
HI, COULD YOU SIGN THIS FOR MY COUSIN ARLI, PLEASE? SHE'S GETTING IT FOR CHRISTMAS.
SURE! THANKS FOR BUYING MY BOOK, ANNE!
I'M SO EXCITED! I SAW YOU ON TELEVISION! COULD YOU SIGN THIS FOR DANIEL? HE'S AN ASPIRING WRITER! SAY SOMETHING LIKE, "DON'T GIVE UP!"
GOOD ADVICE, JEAN!
AWESOME TURNOUT, MAN!
YOUR BOOK IS SELLING WELL, MIKE!
YEAH...
WHAT WOULD WE DO WITHOUT FRIENDS AND RELATIVES?!!
LYNN

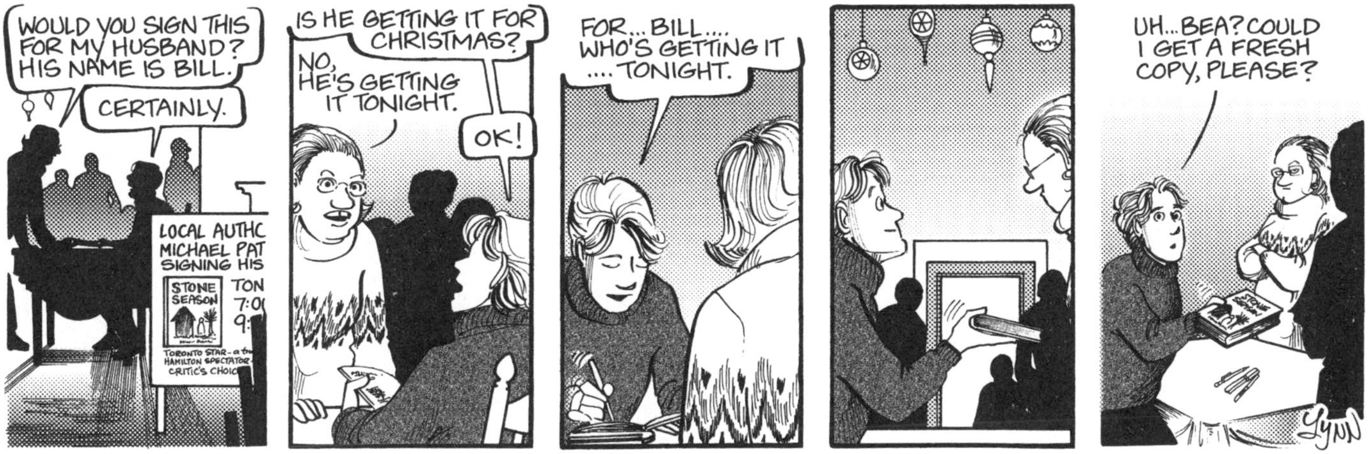
WOULD YOU SIGN THIS FOR MY HUSBAND? HIS NAME IS BILL.
CERTAINLY.
LOCAL AUTHC
MICHAEL PAT
SIGNING HIS
STONE SEASON
TON
7:0
9:
TORONTO STAR
HAMILTON SPECTATOR
CRITIC'S CHOICE
IS HE GETTING IT FOR CHRISTMAS?
NO, HE'S GETTING IT TONIGHT.
OK!
FOR... BILL.... WHO'S GETTING IT .... TONIGHT.
UH... BEA? COULD I GET A FRESH COPY, PLEASE?
LYNN

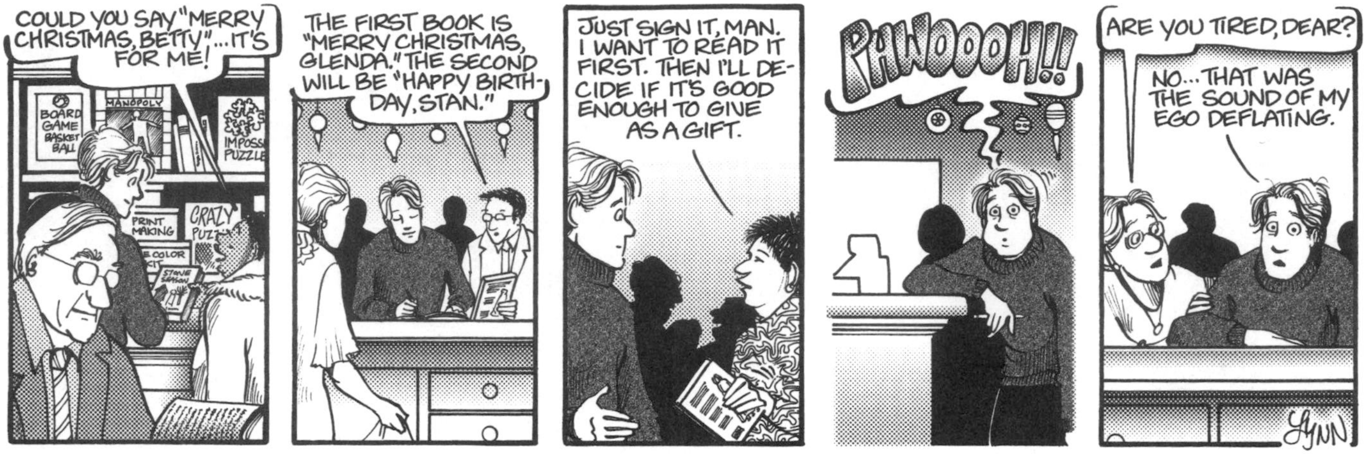
COULD YOU SAY "MERRY CHRISTMAS, BETTY"... IT'S FOR ME!
THE FIRST BOOK IS "MERRY CHRISTMAS, GLENDA." THE SECOND WILL BE "HAPPY BIRTH-DAY, STAN."
JUST SIGN IT, MAN. I WANT TO READ IT FIRST. THEN I'LL DE-CIDE IF IT'S GOOD ENOUGH TO GIVE AS A GIFT.
PHWOOOOH!!
ARE YOU TIRED, DEAR?
NO... THAT WAS THE SOUND OF MY EGO DEFLATING.
Lynn

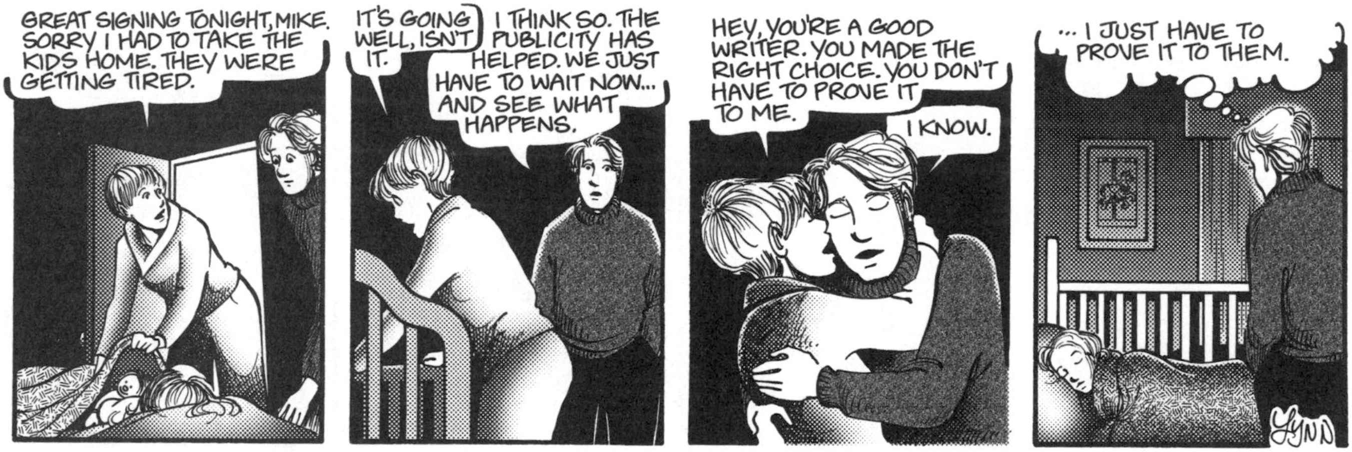
GREAT SIGNING TONIGHT, MIKE. SORRY I HAD TO TAKE THE KIDS HOME. THEY WERE GETTING TIRED.
IT'S GOING WELL, ISN'T IT.
I THINK SO. THE PUBLICITY HAS HELPED. WE JUST HAVE TO WAIT NOW... AND SEE WHAT HAPPENS.
HEY, YOU'RE A GOOD WRITER. YOU MADE THE RIGHT CHOICE. YOU DON'T HAVE TO PROVE IT TO ME.
I KNOW.
... I JUST HAVE TO PROVE IT TO THEM.
Lynn

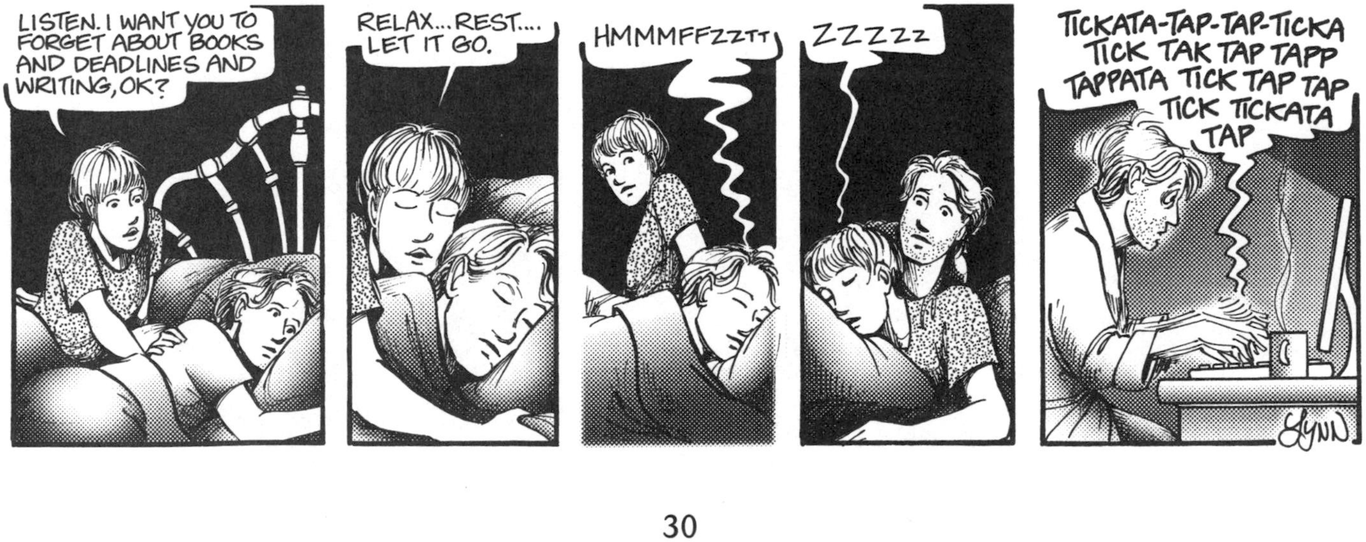
LISTEN. I WANT YOU TO FORGET ABOUT BOOKS AND DEADLINES AND WRITING, OK?
RELAX... REST.... LET IT GO.
HMMMFFzzTT
ZZZZz
TICKATA-TAP-TAP-TICKA TICK TAK TAP TAPP TAPPATA TICK TAP TAP TICK TICKATA TAP
Lynn

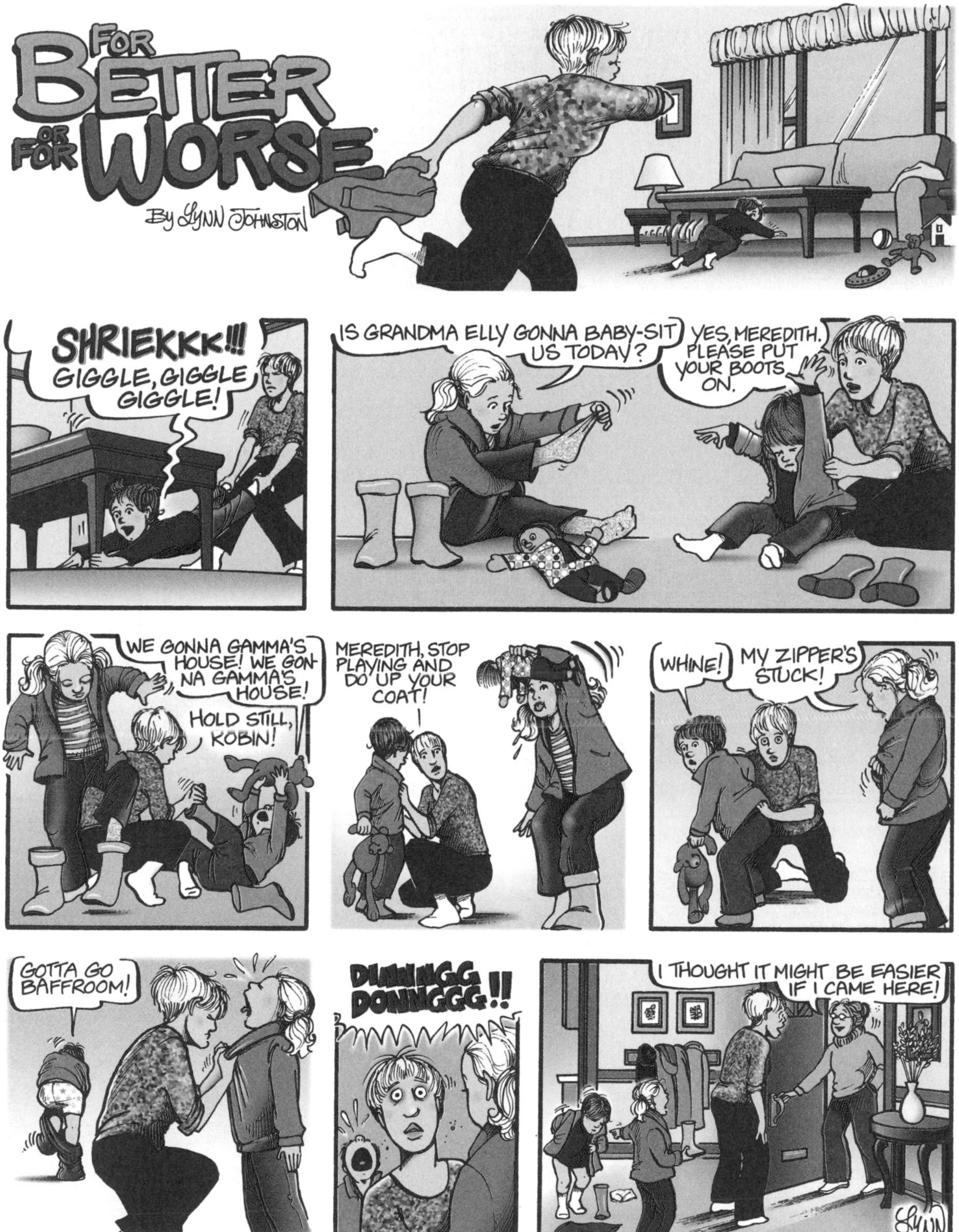
FOR BETTER OR FOR WORSE
BY LYNN JOHNSTON
SHRIEKKK!!!
GIGGLE, GIGGLE GIGGLE, GIGGLE!
IS GRANDMA ELLY GONNA BABY-SIT US TODAY?
YES, MEREDITH. PLEASE PUT YOUR BOOTS ON.
WE GONNA GAMMA'S HOUSE! WE GONNA GAMMA'S HOUSE!
HOLD STILL, ROBIN!
MEREDITH, STOP PLAYING AND DO UP YOUR COAT!
WHINE!
MY ZIPPER'S STUCK!
GOTTA GO BAFFROOM!
DINNNGG DONNGGG!!
I THOUGHT IT MIGHT BE EASIER IF I CAME HERE!
LYNN

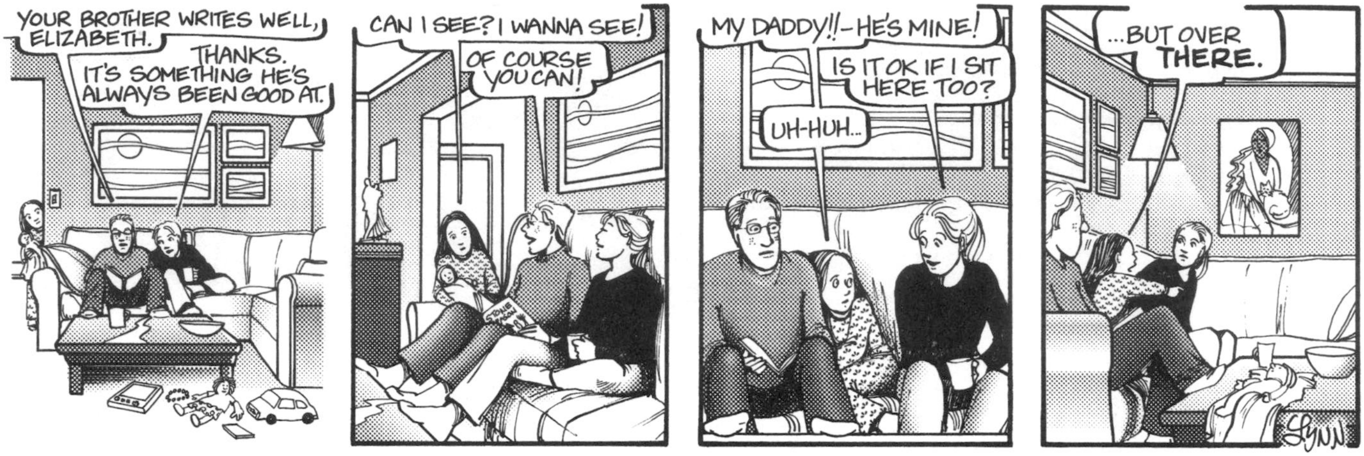
YOUR BROTHER WRITES WELL, ELIZABETH.
THANKS. IT'S SOMETHING HE'S ALWAYS BEEN GOOD AT.
CAN I SEE? I WANNA SEE!
OF COURSE YOU CAN!
MY DADDY!!- HE'S MINE!
IS IT OK IF I SIT HERE TOO?
UH-HUH...
...BUT OVER THERE.
LYNN

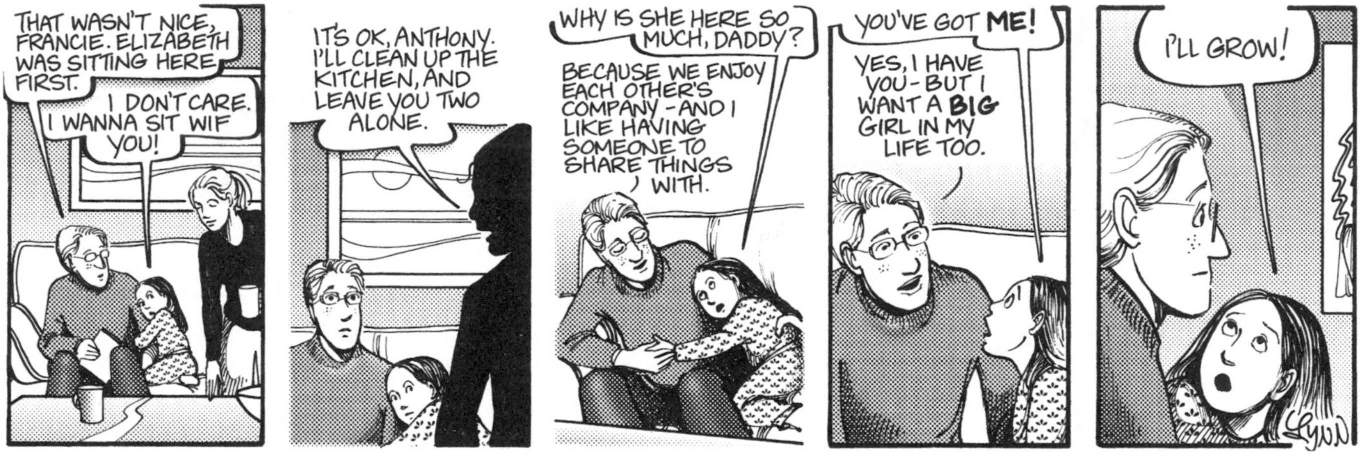
THAT WASN'T NICE, FRANCIE. ELIZABETH WAS SITTING HERE FIRST.
I DON'T CARE. I WANNA SIT WIF YOU!
IT'S OK, ANTHONY. I'LL CLEAN UP THE KITCHEN, AND LEAVE YOU TWO ALONE.
WHY IS SHE HERE SO MUCH, DADDY?
BECAUSE WE ENJOY EACH OTHER'S COMPANY - AND I LIKE HAVING SOMEONE TO SHARE THINGS WITH.
YOU'VE GOT ME!
YES, I HAVE YOU - BUT I WANT A BIG GIRL IN MY LIFE TOO.
I'LL GROW!
LYNN

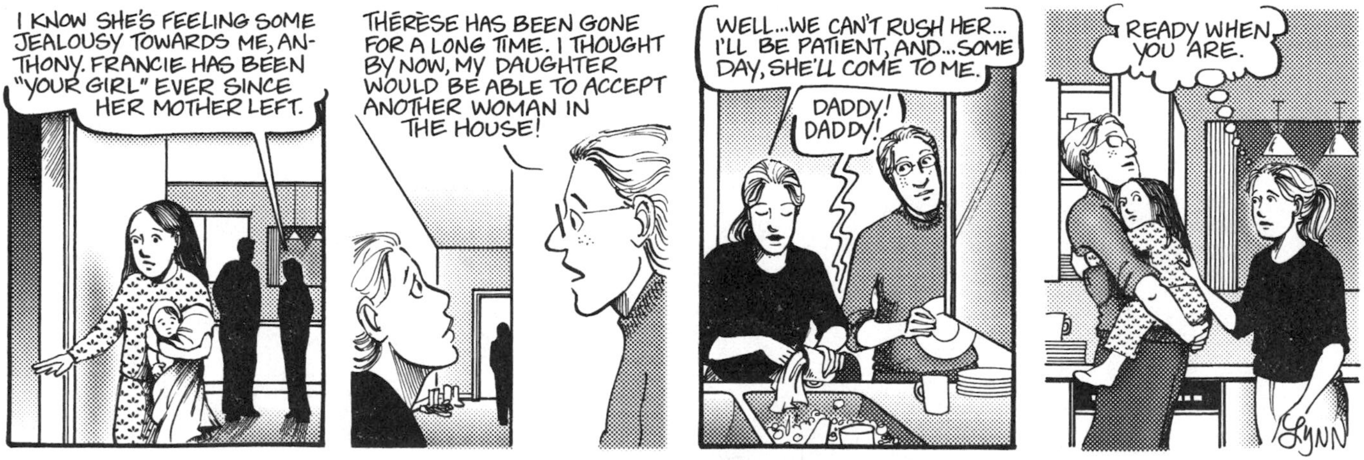
I KNOW SHE'S FEELING SOME JEALOUSY TOWARDS ME, ANTHONY. FRANCIE HAS BEEN "YOUR GIRL" EVER SINCE HER MOTHER LEFT.
THÉRÈSE HAS BEEN GONE FOR A LONG TIME. I THOUGHT BY NOW, MY DAUGHTER WOULD BE ABLE TO ACCEPT ANOTHER WOMAN IN THE HOUSE!
WELL... WE CAN'T RUSH HER... I'LL BE PATIENT, AND... SOME DAY, SHE'LL COME TO ME.
DADDY! DADDY!
READY WHEN YOU ARE.
LYNN

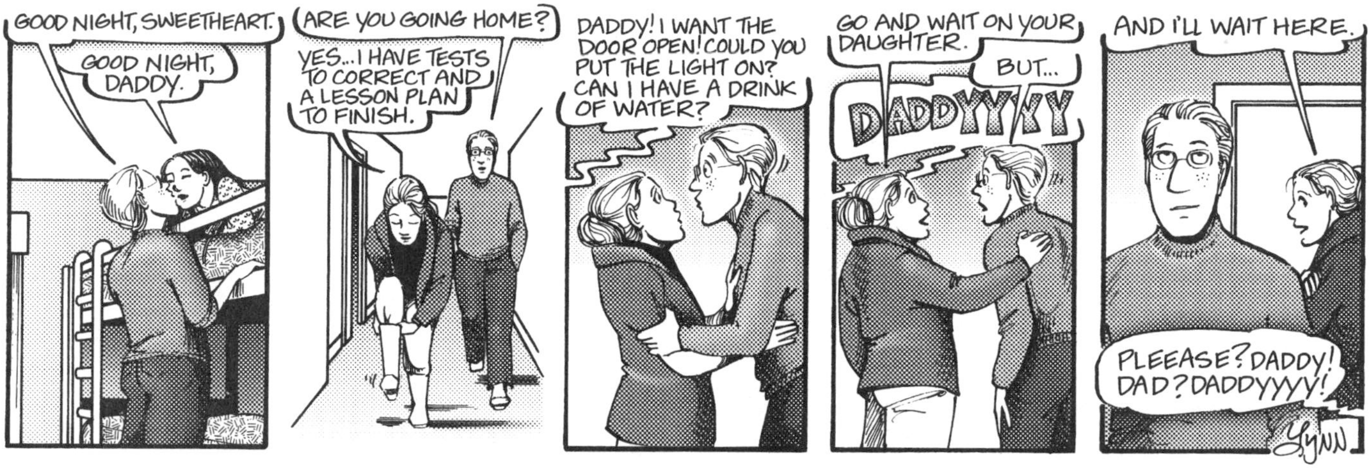
GOOD NIGHT, SWEETHEART.
GOOD NIGHT, DADDY.
ARE YOU GOING HOME?
YES...I HAVE TESTS TO CORRECT AND A LESSON PLAN TO FINISH.
DADDY! I WANT THE DOOR OPEN! COULD YOU PUT THE LIGHT ON? CAN I HAVE A DRINK OF WATER?
GO AND WAIT ON YOUR DAUGHTER.
BUT...
DADDYYYY
AND I'LL WAIT HERE.
PLEEASE? DADDY! DAD? DADDYYYY!
LYNN

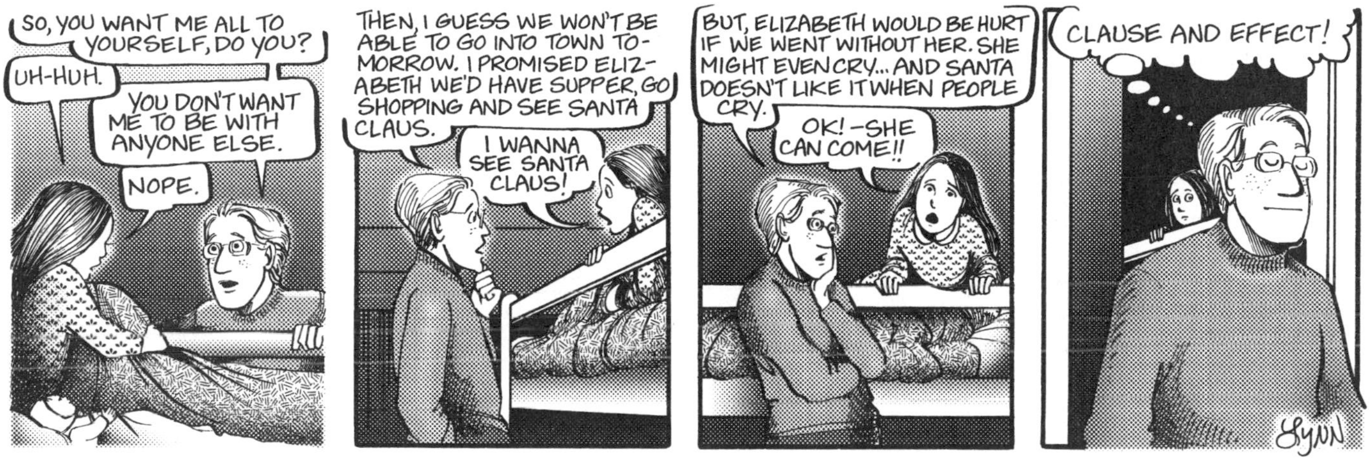
SO, YOU WANT ME ALL TO YOURSELF, DO YOU?
UH-HUH.
YOU DON'T WANT ME TO BE WITH ANYONE ELSE.
NOPE.
THEN, I GUESS WE WON'T BE ABLE TO GO INTO TOWN TO-MORROW. I PROMISED ELIZ-ABETH WE'D HAVE SUPPER, GO SHOPPING AND SEE SANTA CLAUS.
I WANNA SEE SANTA CLAUS!
BUT, ELIZABETH WOULD BE HURT IF WE WENT WITHOUT HER. SHE MIGHT EVEN CRY... AND SANTA DOESN'T LIKE IT WHEN PEOPLE CRY.
OK! –SHE CAN COME!!
CLAUSE AND EFFECT!
LYNN

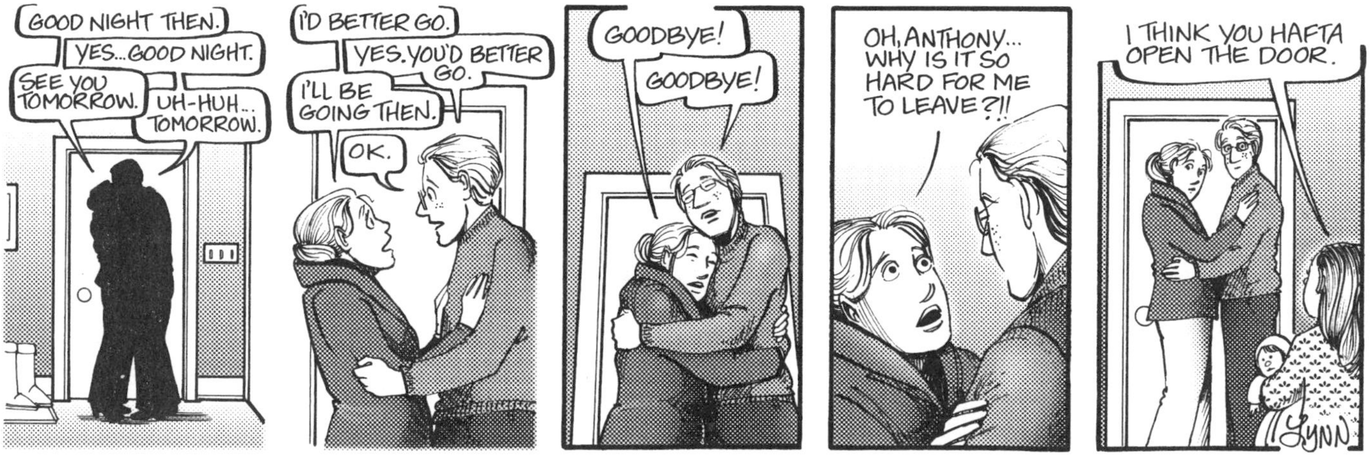
GOOD NIGHT THEN.
YES...GOOD NIGHT.
SEE YOU TOMORROW.
UH-HUH... TOMORROW.
I'D BETTER GO.
YES. YOU'D BETTER GO.
I'LL BE GOING THEN.
OK.
GOODBYE!
GOODBYE!
OH, ANTHONY... WHY IS IT SO HARD FOR ME TO LEAVE?!!
I THINK YOU HAFTA OPEN THE DOOR.
LYNN

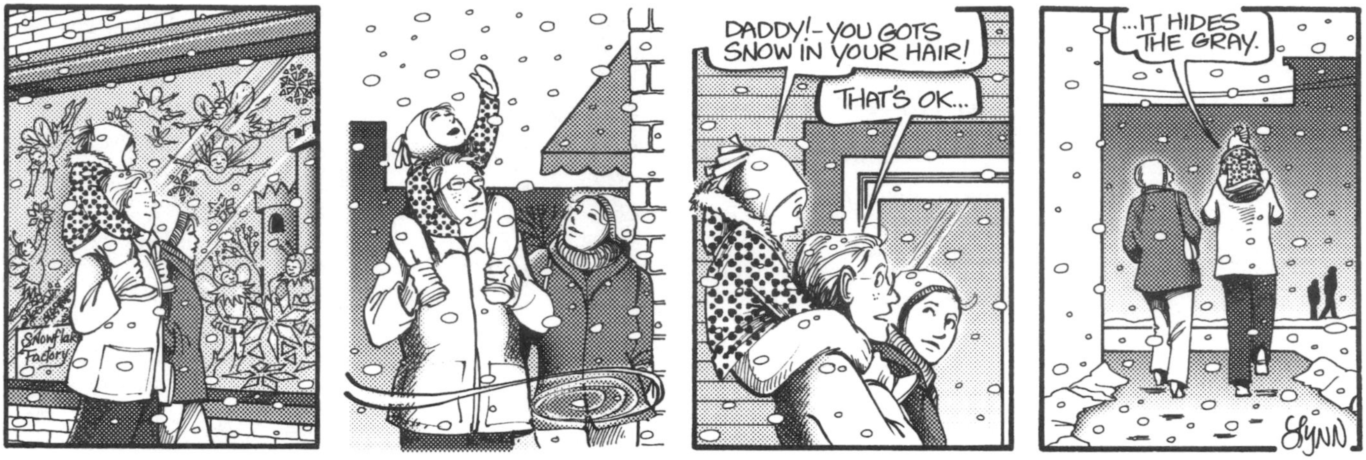
DADDY! - YOU GOTS SNOW IN YOUR HAIR!
THAT'S OK...
...IT HIDES THE GRAY.
LYNN

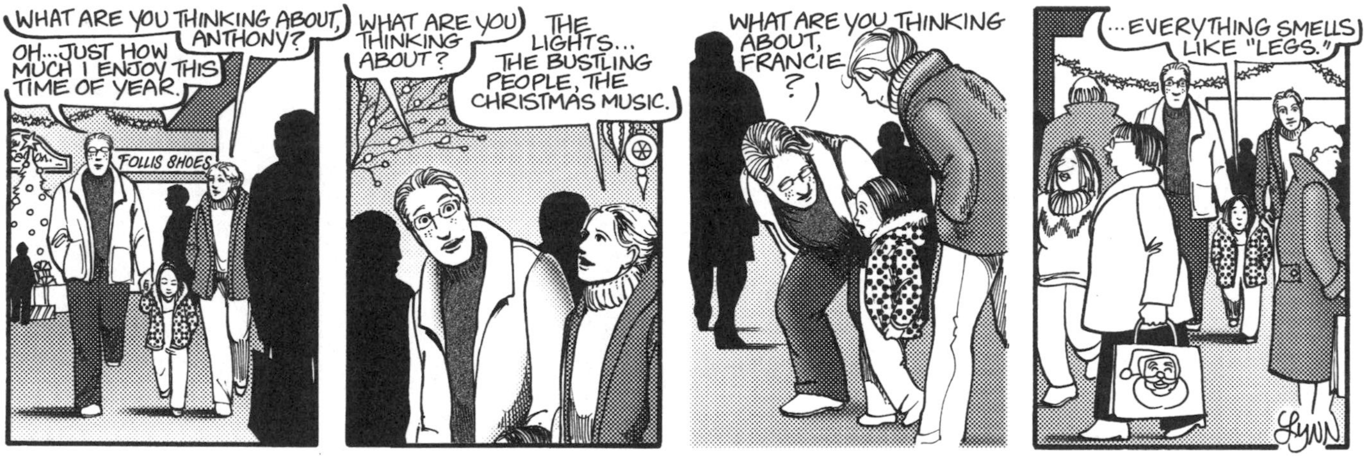
WHAT ARE YOU THINKING ABOUT, ANTHONY?
OH...JUST HOW MUCH I ENJOY THIS TIME OF YEAR.
FOLLIS SHOES
WHAT ARE YOU THINKING ABOUT?
THE LIGHTS... THE BUSTLING PEOPLE, THE CHRISTMAS MUSIC.
WHAT ARE YOU THINKING ABOUT, FRANCIE?
...EVERYTHING SMELLS LIKE "LEGS."
LYNN

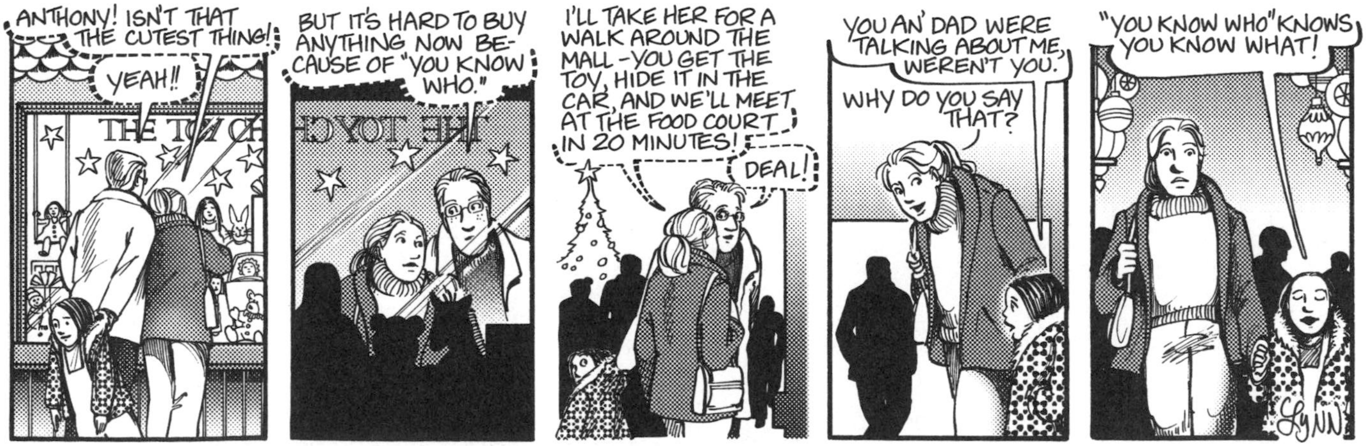
ANTHONY! ISN'T THAT THE CUTEST THING!
YEAH!!
BUT IT'S HARD TO BUY ANYTHING NOW BECAUSE OF "YOU KNOW WHO."
I'LL TAKE HER FOR A WALK AROUND THE MALL - YOU GET THE TOY, HIDE IT IN THE CAR, AND WE'LL MEET AT THE FOOD COURT IN 20 MINUTES!
DEAL!
YOU AN' DAD WERE TALKING ABOUT ME, WEREN'T YOU.
WHY DO YOU SAY THAT?
"YOU KNOW WHO" KNOWS YOU KNOW WHAT!
LYNN

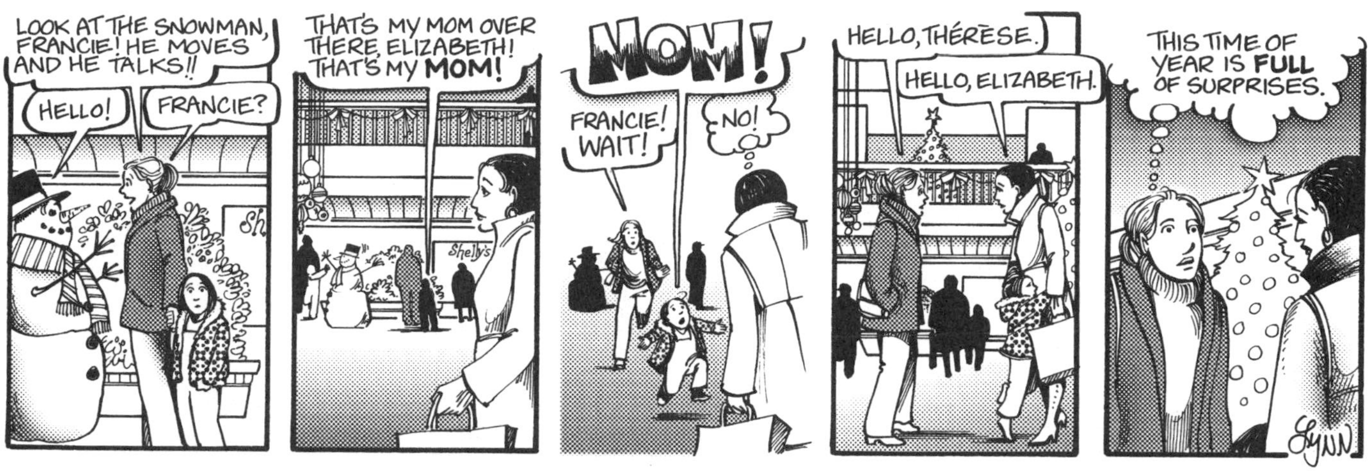
LOOK AT THE SNOWMAN, FRANCIE! HE MOVES AND HE TALKS!!
HELLO!
FRANCIE?
THAT'S MY MOM OVER THERE, ELIZABETH! THAT'S MY MOM!
Shelly's
MOM!
FRANCIE! WAIT!
NO!
HELLO, THÉRÈSE.
HELLO, ELIZABETH.
THIS TIME OF YEAR IS FULL OF SURPRISES.
LYNN

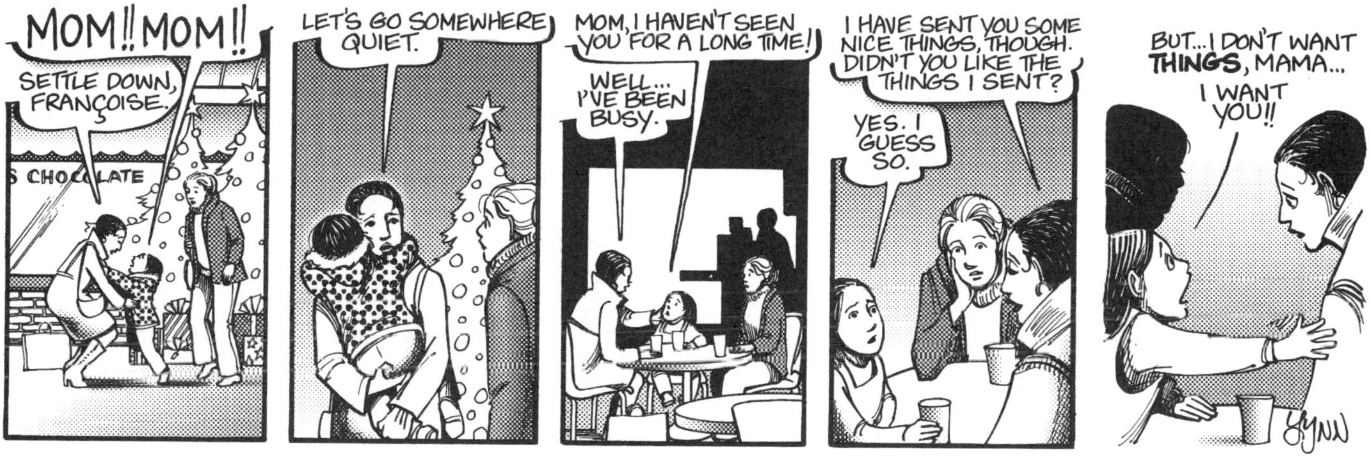
MOM!! MOM!!
SETTLE DOWN, FRANÇOISE.
S CHOCOLATE
LET'S GO SOMEWHERE QUIET.
MOM, I HAVEN'T SEEN YOU FOR A LONG TIME!
WELL... I'VE BEEN BUSY.
I HAVE SENT YOU SOME NICE THINGS, THOUGH. DIDN'T YOU LIKE THE THINGS I SENT?
YES. I GUESS SO.
BUT... I DON'T WANT THINGS, MAMA...
I WANT YOU!!
LYNN

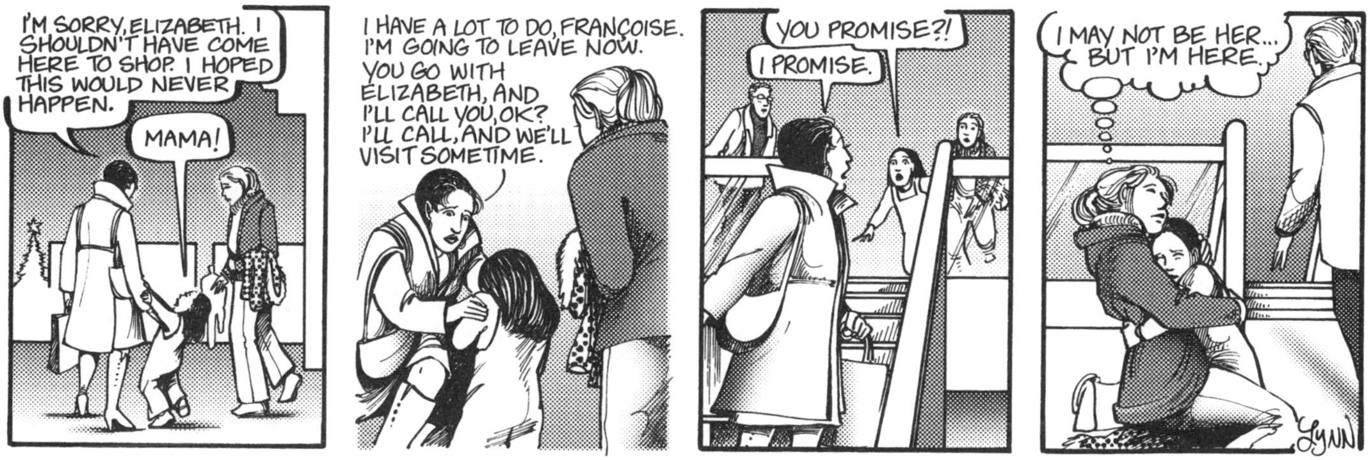
I'M SORRY, ELIZABETH. I SHOULDN'T HAVE COME HERE TO SHOP. I HOPED THIS WOULD NEVER HAPPEN.
MAMA!
I HAVE A LOT TO DO, FRANÇOISE. I'M GOING TO LEAVE NOW.
YOU GO WITH ELIZABETH, AND I'LL CALL YOU, OK? I'LL CALL, AND WE'LL VISIT SOMETIME.
YOU PROMISE?!
I PROMISE.
I MAY NOT BE HER... BUT I'M HERE.
LYNN

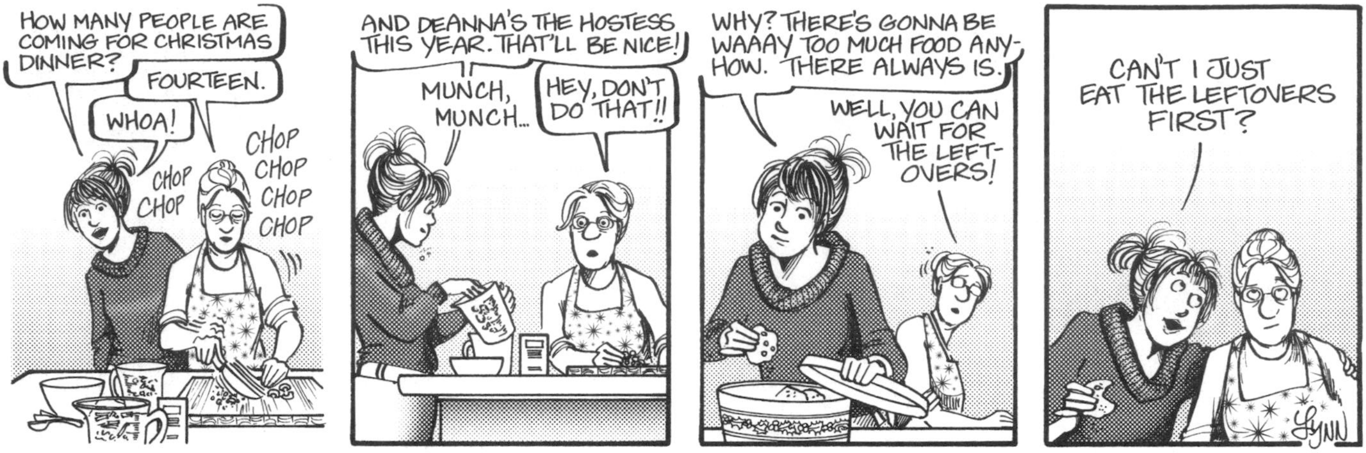
HOW MANY PEOPLE ARE COMING FOR CHRISTMAS DINNER?
FOURTEEN.
WHOA!
CHOP CHOP
CHOP CHOP CHOP CHOP
AND DEANNA'S THE HOSTESS THIS YEAR. THAT'LL BE NICE!
MUNCH, MUNCH...
HEY, DON'T DO THAT!!
WHY? THERE'S GONNA BE WAAAY TOO MUCH FOOD ANY-HOW. THERE ALWAYS IS.
WELL, YOU CAN WAIT FOR THE LEFT-OVERS!
CAN'T I JUST EAT THE LEFTOVERS FIRST?
LYNN

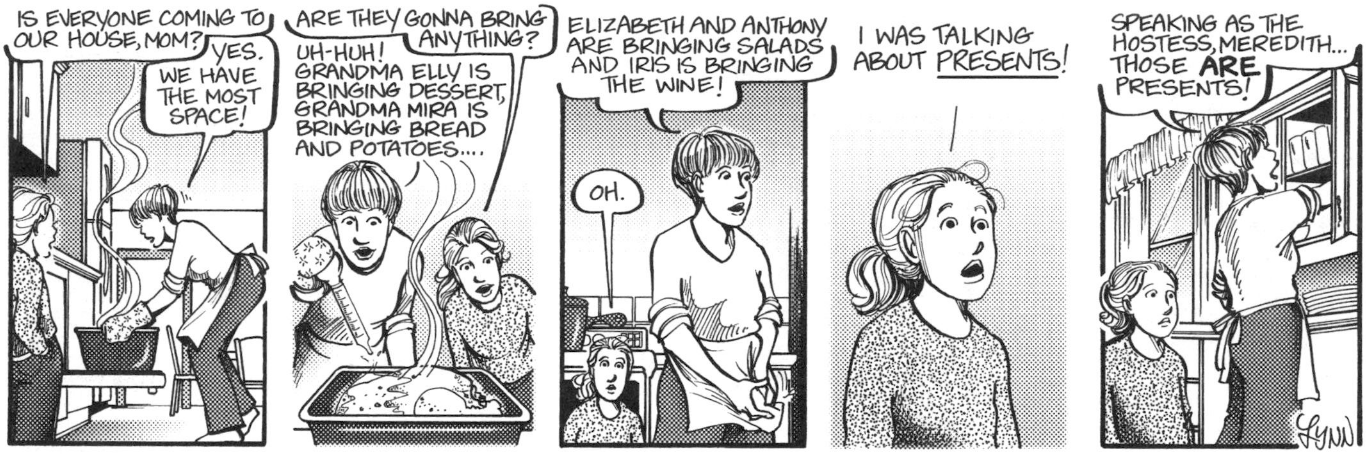
IS EVERYONE COMING TO OUR HOUSE, MOM?
YES. WE HAVE THE MOST SPACE!
ARE THEY GONNA BRING ANYTHING?
UH-HUH! GRANDMA ELLY IS BRINGING DESSERT, GRANDMA MIRA IS BRINGING BREAD AND POTATOES....
ELIZABETH AND ANTHONY ARE BRINGING SALADS AND IRIS IS BRINGING THE WINE!
OH.
I WAS TALKING ABOUT PRESENTS!
SPEAKING AS THE HOSTESS, MEREDITH... THOSE ARE PRESENTS!
LYNN

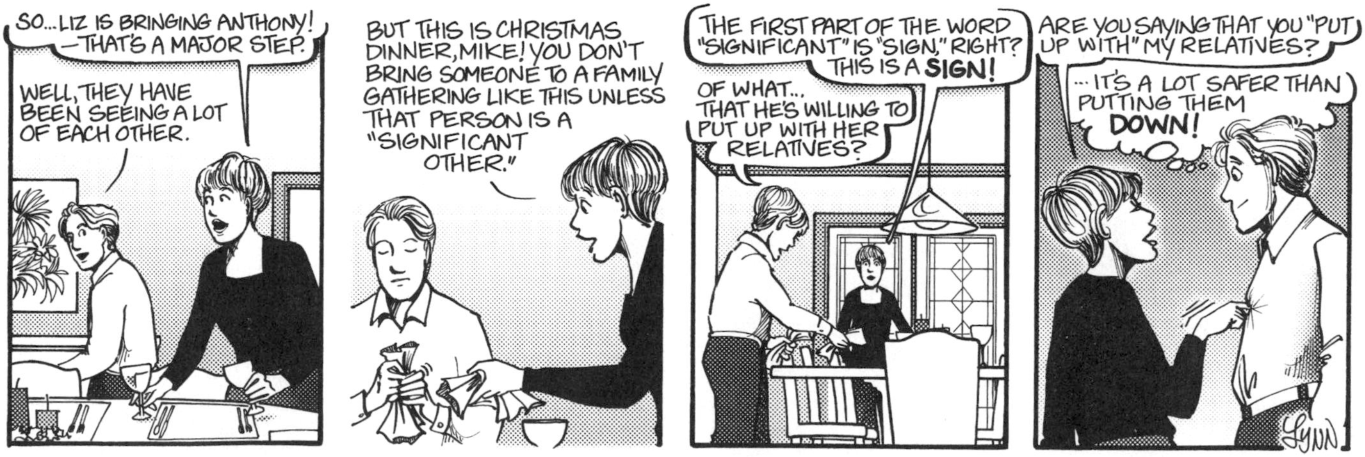
SO...LIZ IS BRINGING ANTHONY! —THAT'S A MAJOR STEP.
WELL, THEY HAVE BEEN SEEING A LOT OF EACH OTHER.
BUT THIS IS CHRISTMAS DINNER, MIKE! YOU DON'T BRING SOMEONE TO A FAMILY GATHERING LIKE THIS UNLESS THAT PERSON IS A "SIGNIFICANT OTHER."
THE FIRST PART OF THE WORD "SIGNIFICANT" IS "SIGN," RIGHT? THIS IS A SIGN!
OF WHAT... THAT HE'S WILLING TO PUT UP WITH HER RELATIVES?
ARE YOU SAYING THAT YOU "PUT UP WITH" MY RELATIVES?
...IT'S A LOT SAFER THAN PUTTING THEM DOWN!
LYNN

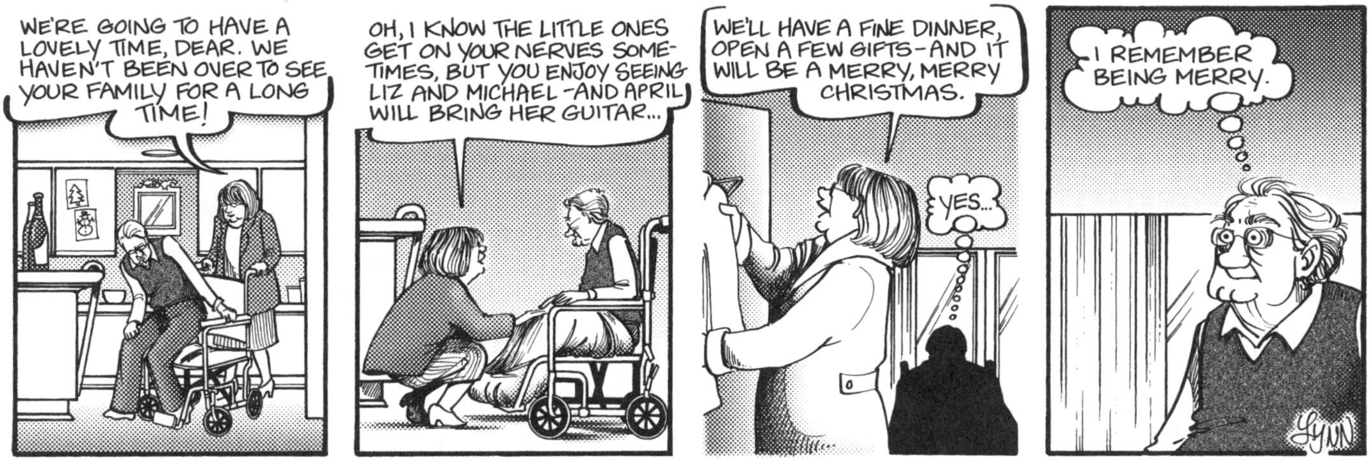
WE'RE GOING TO HAVE A LOVELY TIME, DEAR. WE HAVEN'T BEEN OVER TO SEE YOUR FAMILY FOR A LONG TIME!
OH, I KNOW THE LITTLE ONES GET ON YOUR NERVES SOMETIMES, BUT YOU ENJOY SEEING LIZ AND MICHAEL -AND APRIL WILL BRING HER GUITAR...
WE'LL HAVE A FINE DINNER, OPEN A FEW GIFTS-AND IT WILL BE A MERRY, MERRY CHRISTMAS.
YES...
I REMEMBER BEING MERRY.
LYNN

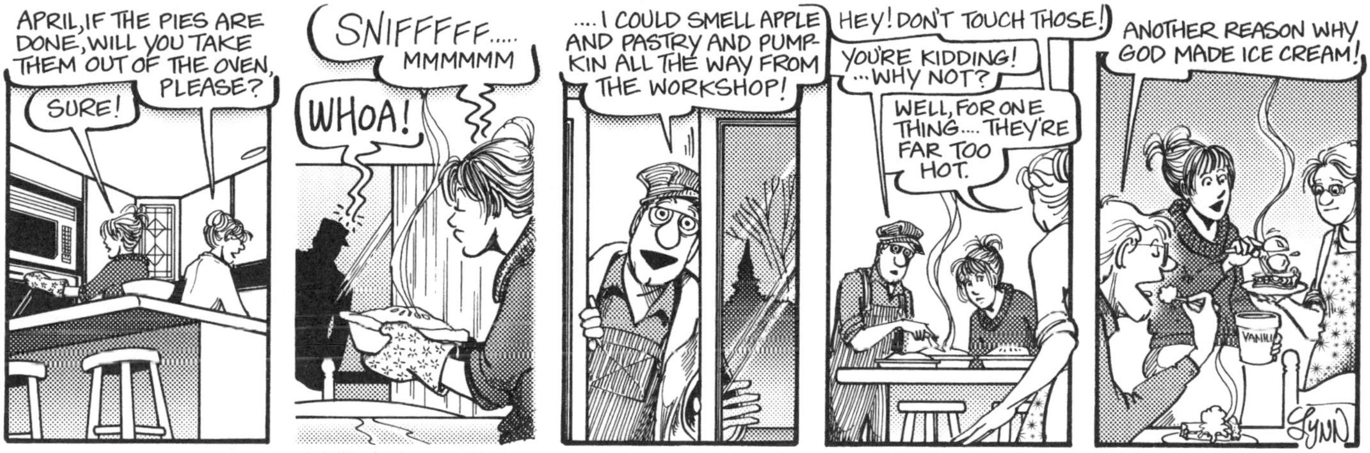
APRIL, IF THE PIES ARE DONE, WILL YOU TAKE THEM OUT OF THE OVEN, PLEASE?
SURE!
SNIFFFFF..... MMMMMM
WHOA!
....I COULD SMELL APPLE AND PASTRY AND PUMPKIN ALL THE WAY FROM THE WORKSHOP!
HEY! DON'T TOUCH THOSE!
YOU'RE KIDDING! ...WHY NOT?
WELL, FOR ONE THING.... THEY'RE FAR TOO HOT.
ANOTHER REASON WHY GOD MADE ICE CREAM!
LYNN

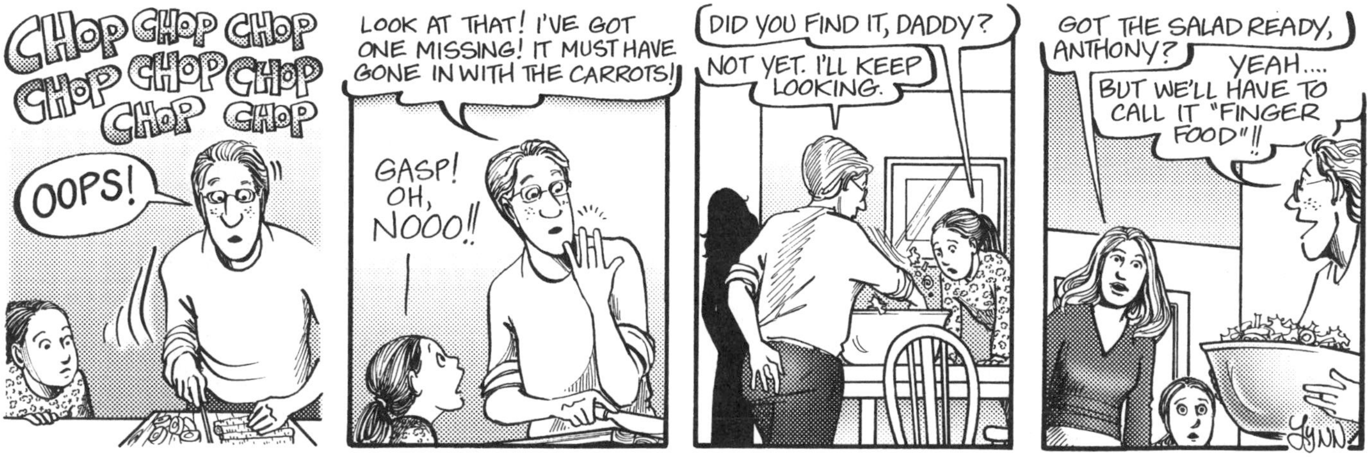
CHOP CHOP CHOP CHOP CHOP CHOP CHOP CHOP
OOPS!
LOOK AT THAT! I'VE GOT ONE MISSING! IT MUST HAVE GONE IN WITH THE CARROTS!
GASP! OH, NOOO!!
DID YOU FIND IT, DADDY?
NOT YET. I'LL KEEP LOOKING.
GOT THE SALAD READY, ANTHONY?
YEAH.... BUT WE'LL HAVE TO CALL IT "FINGER FOOD"!!
LYNN

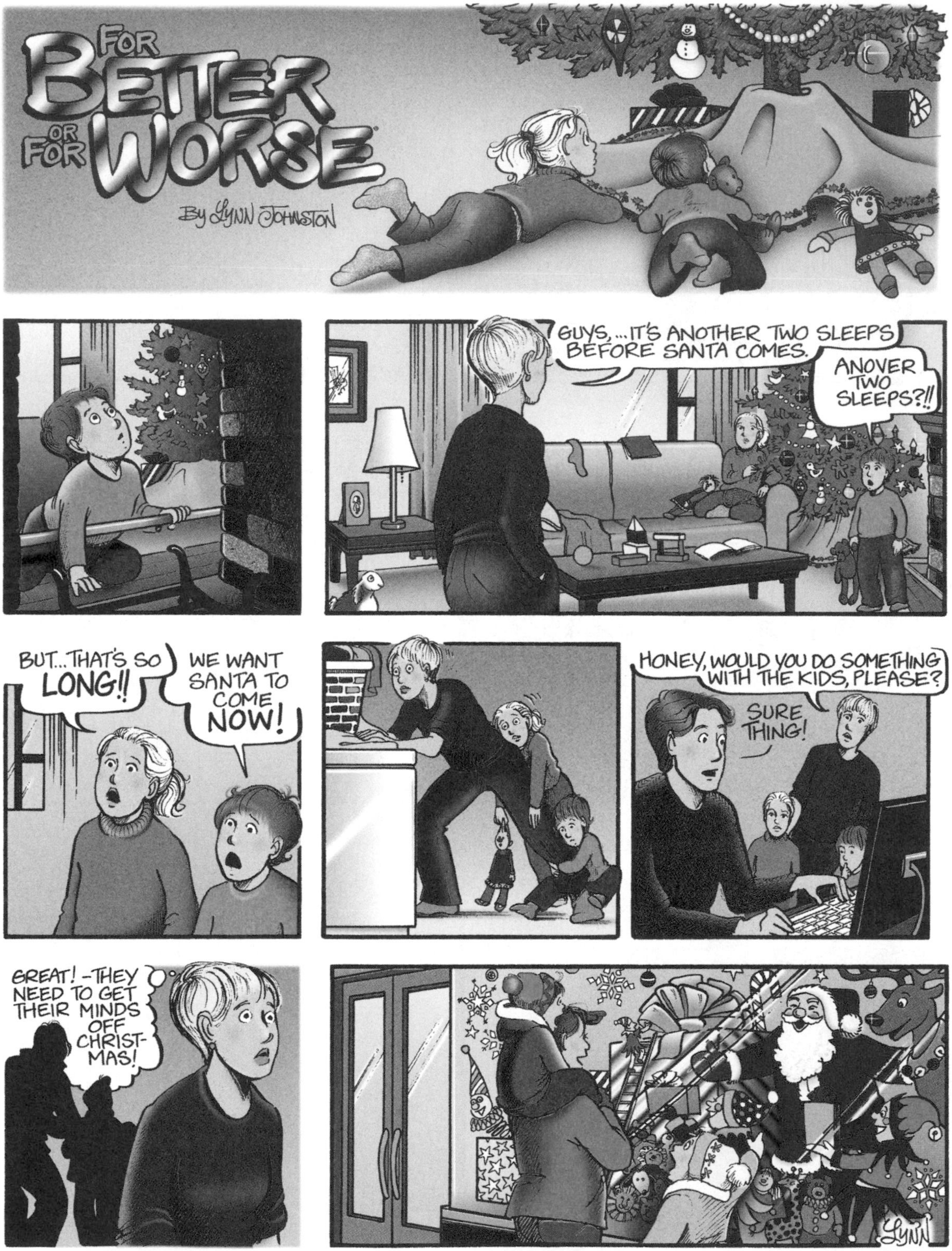

FOR BETTER OR FOR WORSE
BY LYNN JOHNSTON
GUYS, ...IT'S ANOTHER TWO SLEEPS BEFORE SANTA COMES.
ANOVER TWO SLEEPS?!!
BUT...THAT'S SO LONG!!
WE WANT SANTA TO COME NOW!
HONEY, WOULD YOU DO SOMETHING WITH THE KIDS, PLEASE?
SURE THING!
GREAT! -THEY NEED TO GET THEIR MINDS OFF CHRIST-MAS!
LYNN

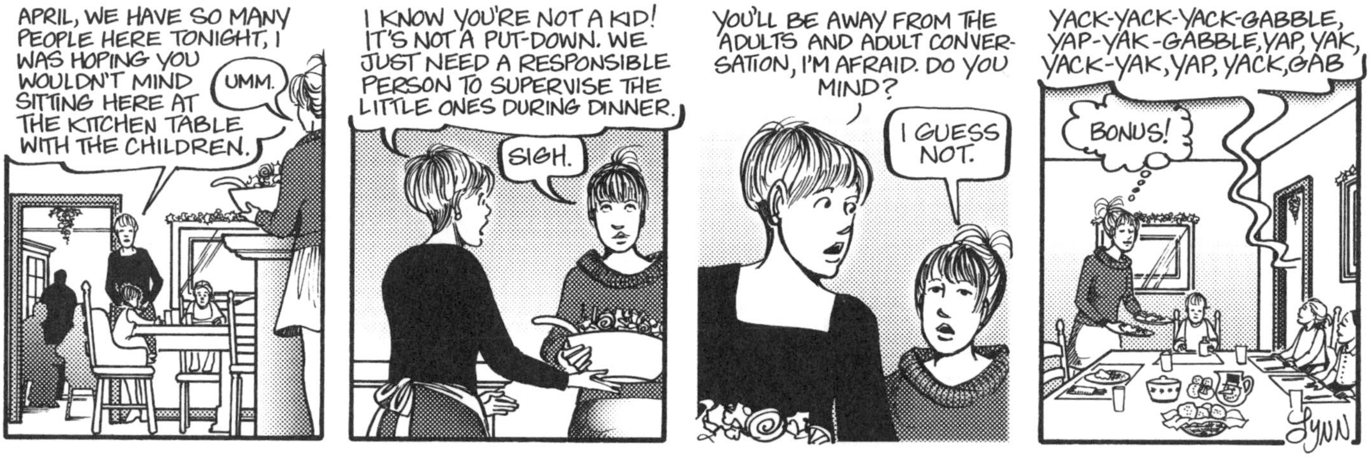
APRIL, WE HAVE SO MANY PEOPLE HERE TONIGHT, I WAS HOPING YOU WOULDN'T MIND SITTING HERE AT THE KITCHEN TABLE WITH THE CHILDREN.
UMM.
I KNOW YOU'RE NOT A KID! IT'S NOT A PUT-DOWN. WE JUST NEED A RESPONSIBLE PERSON TO SUPERVISE THE LITTLE ONES DURING DINNER.
SIGH.
YOU'LL BE AWAY FROM THE ADULTS AND ADULT CONVERSATION, I'M AFRAID. DO YOU MIND?
I GUESS NOT.
YACK-YACK-YACK-GABBLE, YAP-YAK-GABBLE, YAP, YAK, YACK-YAK, YAP, YACK, GAB
BONUS!
LYNN

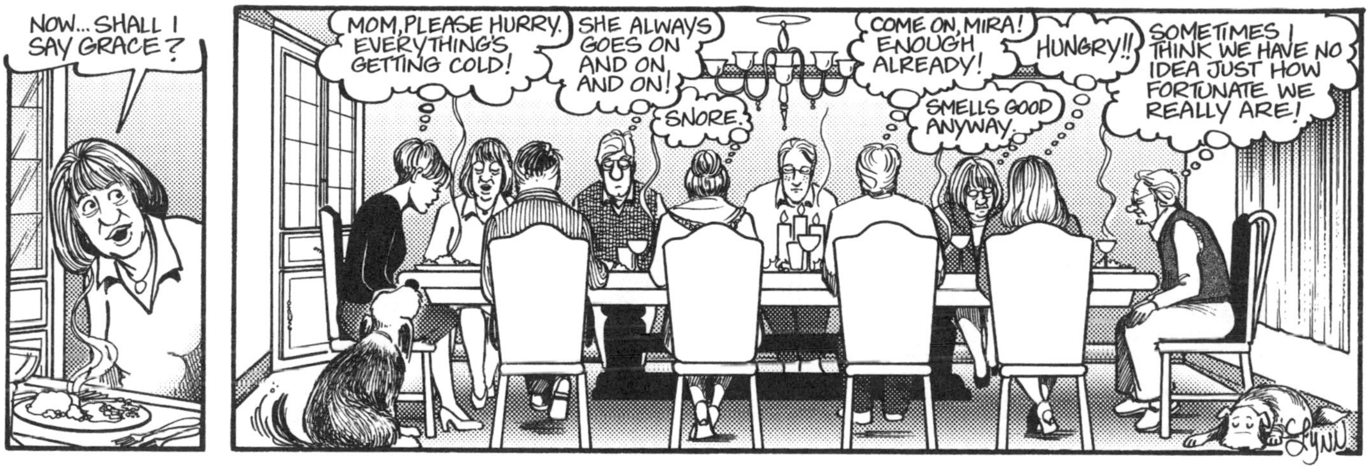
NOW... SHALL I SAY GRACE?
MOM, PLEASE HURRY. EVERYTHING'S GETTING COLD!
SHE ALWAYS GOES ON AND ON AND ON!
SNORE.
COME ON, MIRA! ENOUGH ALREADY!
HUNGRY!!
SMELLS GOOD ANYWAY.
SOMETIMES I THINK WE HAVE NO IDEA JUST HOW FORTUNATE WE REALLY ARE!
LYNN

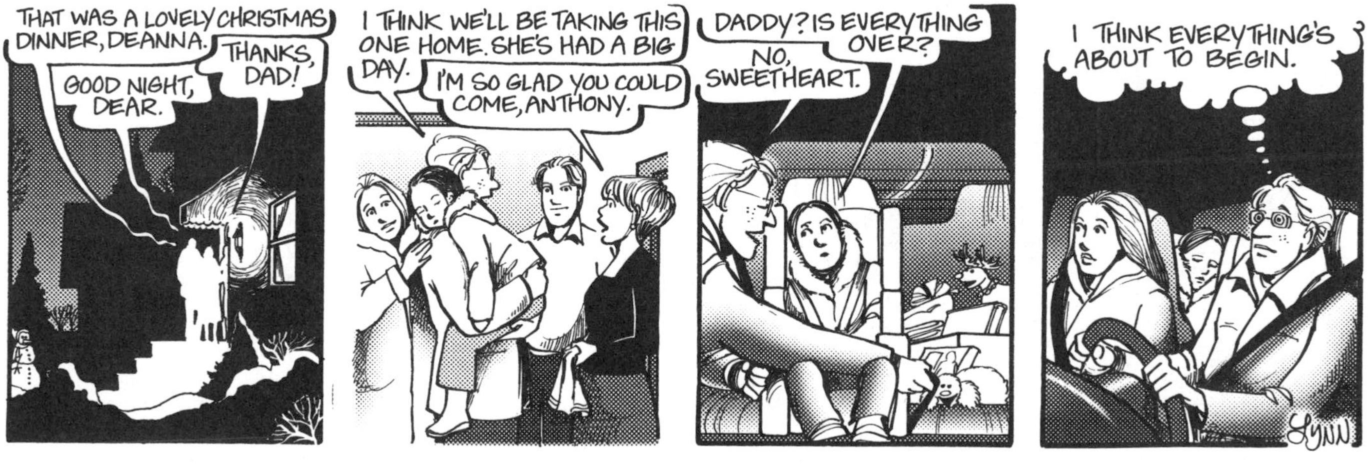
THAT WAS A LOVELY CHRISTMAS DINNER, DEANNA.
GOOD NIGHT, DEAR.
THANKS, DAD!
I THINK WE'LL BE TAKING THIS ONE HOME. SHE'S HAD A BIG DAY.
I'M SO GLAD YOU COULD COME, ANTHONY.
DADDY? IS EVERYTHING OVER?
NO, SWEETHEART.
I THINK EVERYTHING'S ABOUT TO BEGIN.
LYNN

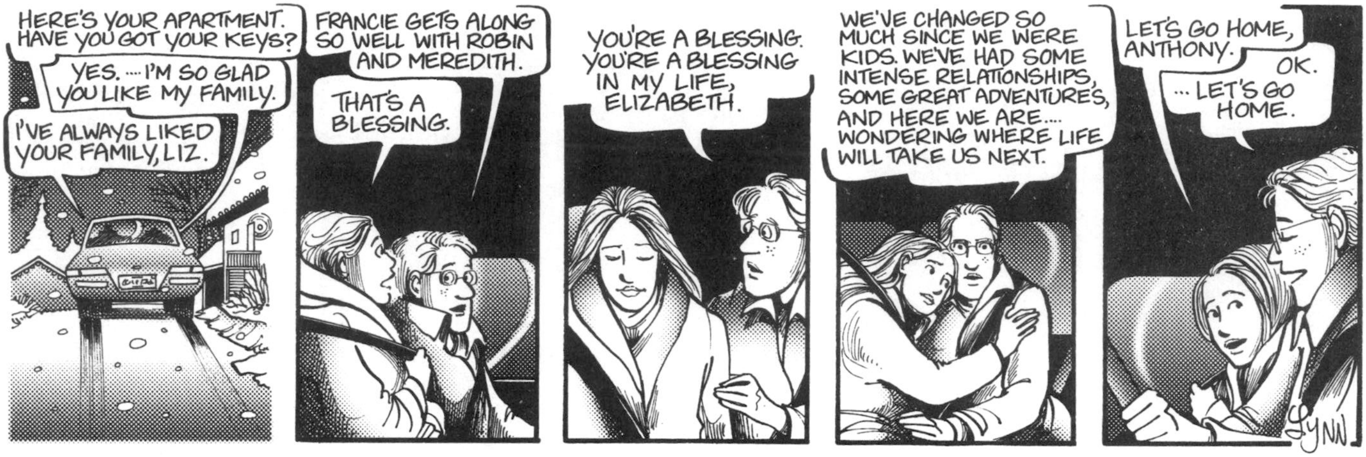
HERE'S YOUR APARTMENT. HAVE YOU GOT YOUR KEYS?
YES. .... I'M SO GLAD YOU LIKE MY FAMILY.
I'VE ALWAYS LIKED YOUR FAMILY, LIZ.
FRANCIE GETS ALONG SO WELL WITH ROBIN AND MEREDITH.
THAT'S A BLESSING.
YOU'RE A BLESSING. YOU'RE A BLESSING IN MY LIFE, ELIZABETH.
WE'VE CHANGED SO MUCH SINCE WE WERE KIDS. WE'VE HAD SOME INTENSE RELATIONSHIPS, SOME GREAT ADVENTURES, AND HERE WE ARE.... WONDERING WHERE LIFE WILL TAKE US NEXT.
LET'S GO HOME, ANTHONY.
OK.
... LET'S GO HOME.
LYNN

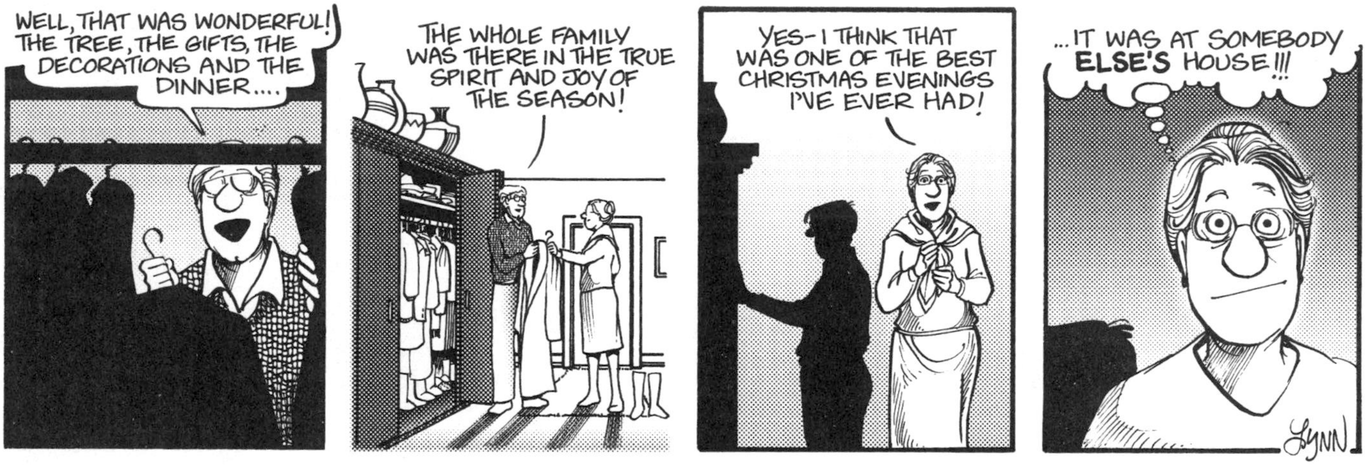
WELL, THAT WAS WONDERFUL! THE TREE, THE GIFTS, THE DECORATIONS AND THE DINNER....
THE WHOLE FAMILY WAS THERE IN THE TRUE SPIRIT AND JOY OF THE SEASON!
YES- I THINK THAT WAS ONE OF THE BEST CHRISTMAS EVENINGS I'VE EVER HAD!
... IT WAS AT SOMEBODY **ELSE'S** HOUSE!!!
LYNN

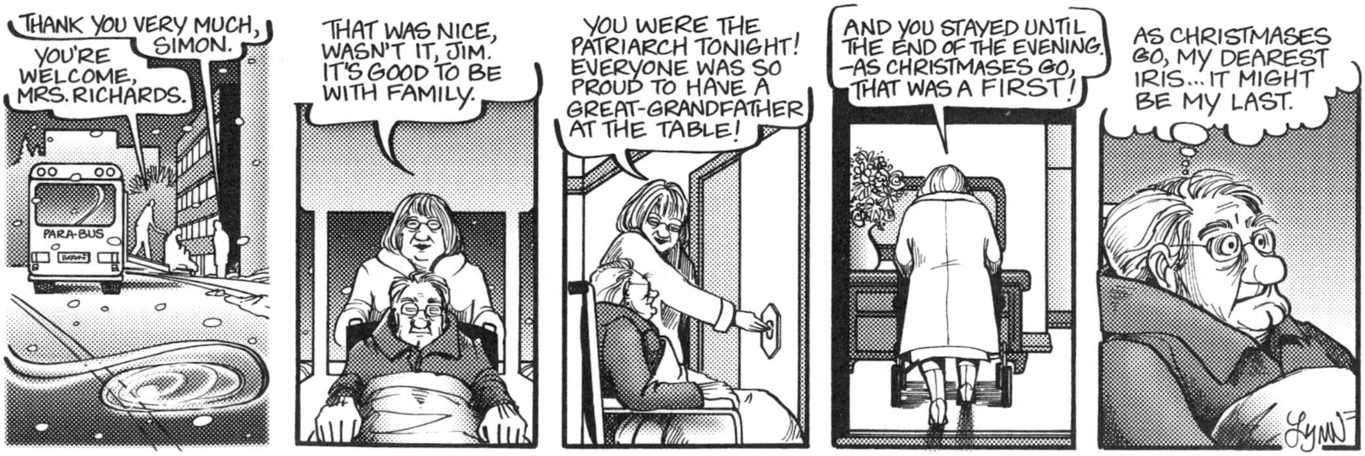
THANK YOU VERY MUCH, SIMON.
YOU'RE WELCOME, MRS. RICHARDS.
PARA-BUS
THAT WAS NICE, WASN'T IT, JIM. IT'S GOOD TO BE WITH FAMILY.
YOU WERE THE PATRIARCH TONIGHT! EVERYONE WAS SO PROUD TO HAVE A GREAT-GRANDFATHER AT THE TABLE!
AND YOU STAYED UNTIL THE END OF THE EVENING. -AS CHRISTMASES GO, THAT WAS A FIRST!
AS CHRISTMASES GO, MY DEAREST IRIS... IT MIGHT BE MY LAST.
LYNN

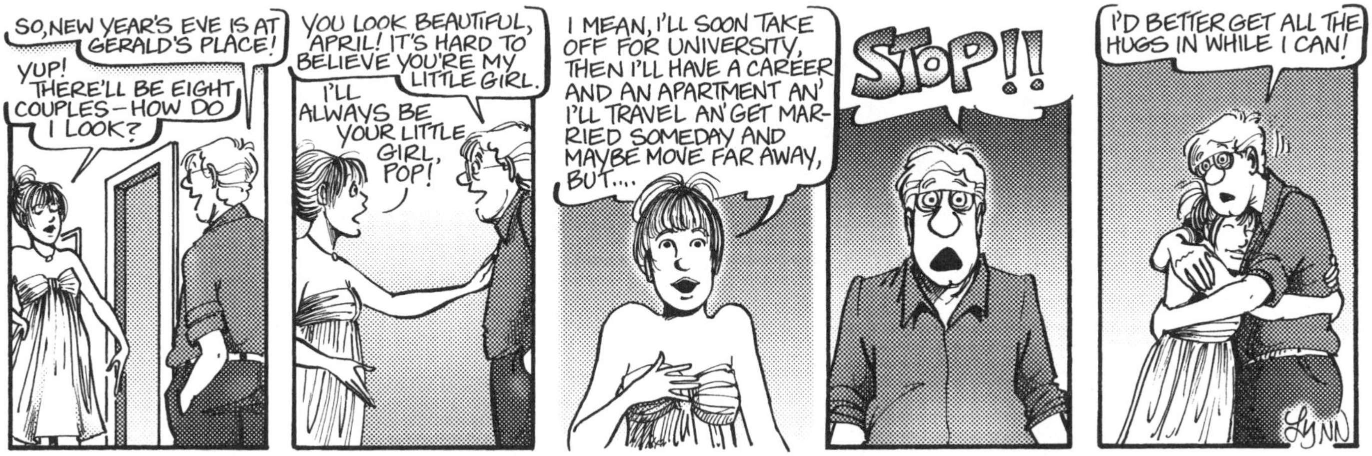
SO, NEW YEAR'S EVE IS AT GERALD'S PLACE!
YUP! THERE'LL BE EIGHT COUPLES – HOW DO I LOOK?
YOU LOOK BEAUTIFUL, APRIL! IT'S HARD TO BELIEVE YOU'RE MY LITTLE GIRL.
I'LL ALWAYS BE YOUR LITTLE GIRL, POP!
I MEAN, I'LL SOON TAKE OFF FOR UNIVERSITY, THEN I'LL HAVE A CAREER AND AN APARTMENT AN' I'LL TRAVEL AN' GET MARRIED SOMEDAY AND MAYBE MOVE FAR AWAY, BUT....
STOP!!
I'D BETTER GET ALL THE HUGS IN WHILE I CAN!
LYNN

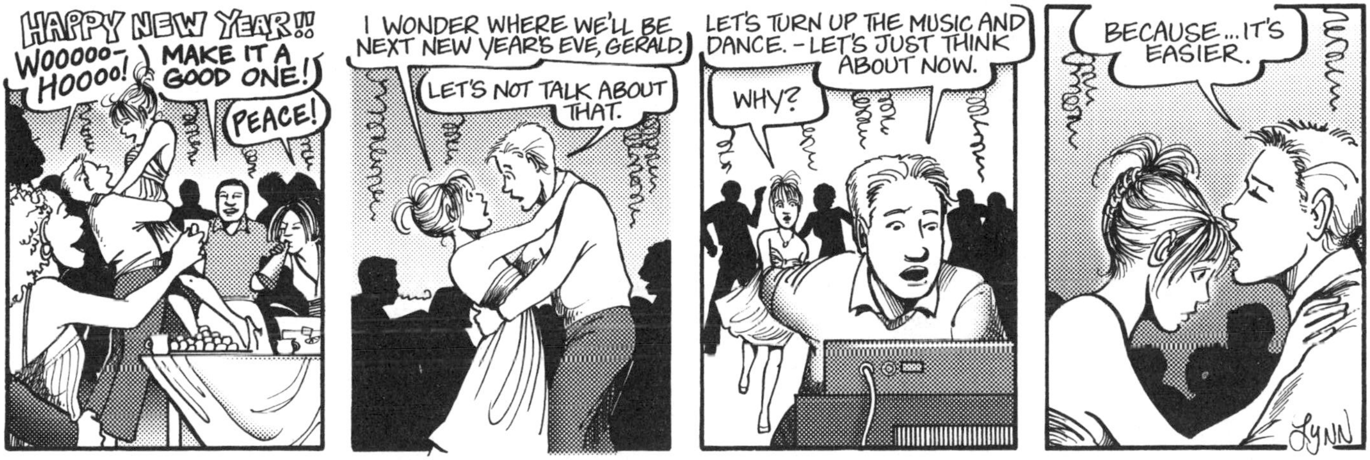
HAPPY NEW YEAR!!
WOOOOO-HOOOO!
MAKE IT A GOOD ONE!
PEACE!
I WONDER WHERE WE'LL BE NEXT NEW YEAR'S EVE, GERALD.
LET'S NOT TALK ABOUT THAT.
WHY?
LET'S TURN UP THE MUSIC AND DANCE. – LET'S JUST THINK ABOUT NOW.
BECAUSE ... IT'S EASIER.
LYNN

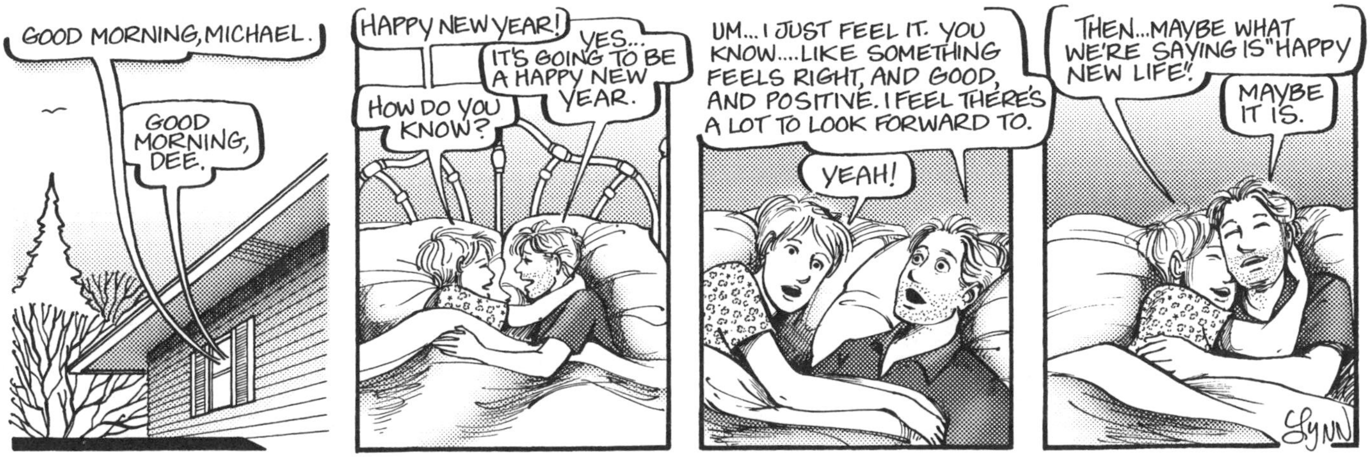
GOOD MORNING, MICHAEL.
GOOD MORNING, DEE.
HAPPY NEW YEAR!
YES... IT'S GOING TO BE A HAPPY NEW YEAR.
HOW DO YOU KNOW?
UM... I JUST FEEL IT. YOU KNOW.... LIKE SOMETHING FEELS RIGHT, AND GOOD, AND POSITIVE. I FEEL THERE'S A LOT TO LOOK FORWARD TO.
YEAH!
THEN... MAYBE WHAT WE'RE SAYING IS "HAPPY NEW LIFE!"
MAYBE IT IS.
LYNN

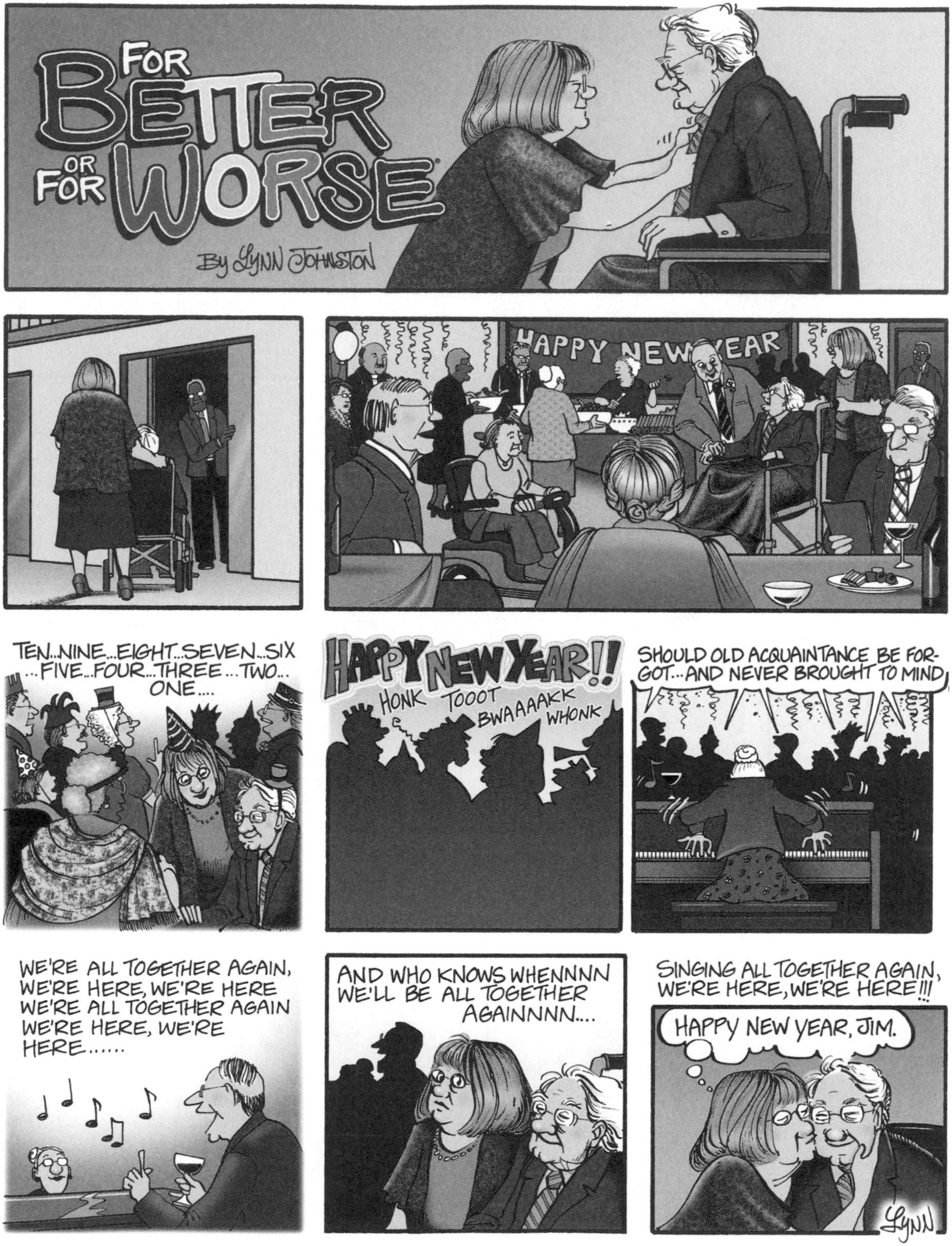

FOR BETTER OR FOR WORSE
BY LYNN JOHNSTON
HAPPY NEW YEAR
TEN...NINE...EIGHT...SEVEN...SIX ...FIVE...FOUR...THREE...TWO... ONE....
HAPPY NEW YEAR!!
HONK
TOOOT
BWAAAAKK
WHONK
SHOULD OLD ACQUAINTANCE BE FOR-GOT...AND NEVER BROUGHT TO MIND,
WE'RE ALL TOGETHER AGAIN, WE'RE HERE, WE'RE HERE WE'RE ALL TOGETHER AGAIN WE'RE HERE, WE'RE HERE......
AND WHO KNOWS WHENNNN WE'LL BE ALL TOGETHER AGAINNNN....
SINGING ALL TOGETHER AGAIN, WE'RE HERE, WE'RE HERE!!!
HAPPY NEW YEAR, JIM.
LYNN

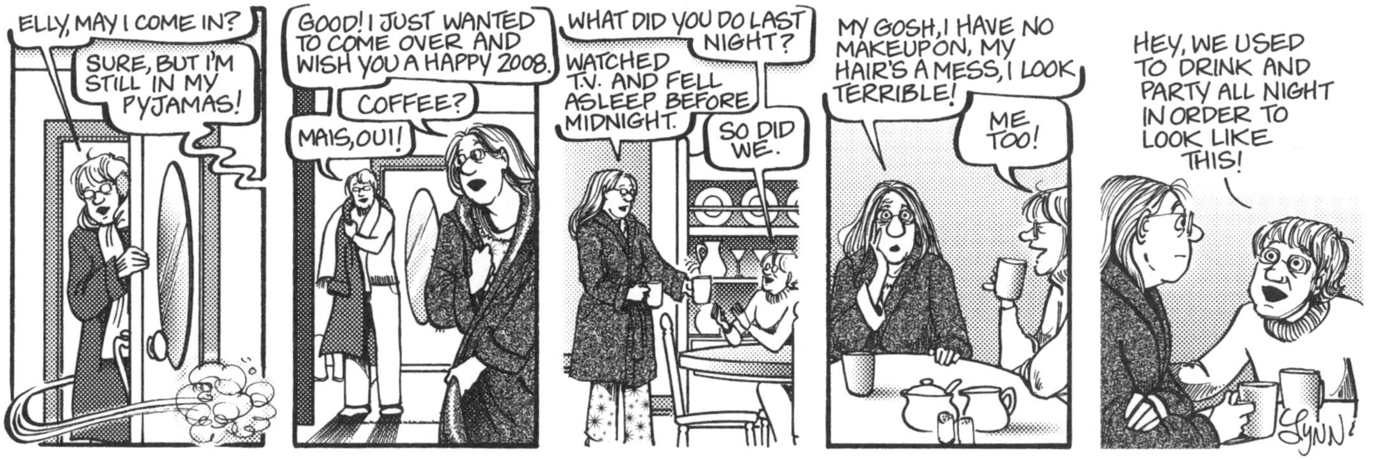
ELLY, MAY I COME IN?
SURE, BUT I'M STILL IN MY PYJAMAS!
GOOD! I JUST WANTED TO COME OVER AND WISH YOU A HAPPY 2008.
COFFEE?
MAIS, OUI!
WHAT DID YOU DO LAST NIGHT?
WATCHED T.V. AND FELL ASLEEP BEFORE MIDNIGHT.
SO DID WE.
MY GOSH, I HAVE NO MAKEUP ON, MY HAIR'S A MESS, I LOOK TERRIBLE!
ME TOO!
HEY, WE USED TO DRINK AND PARTY ALL NIGHT IN ORDER TO LOOK LIKE THIS!
LYNN

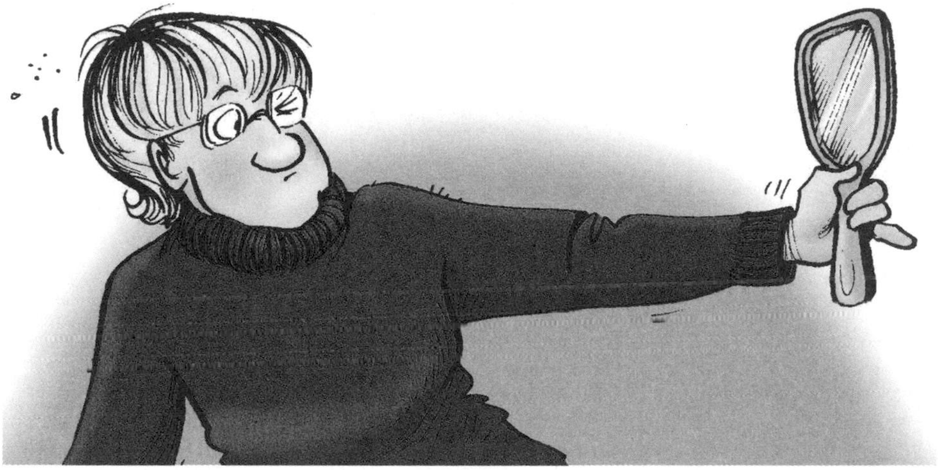

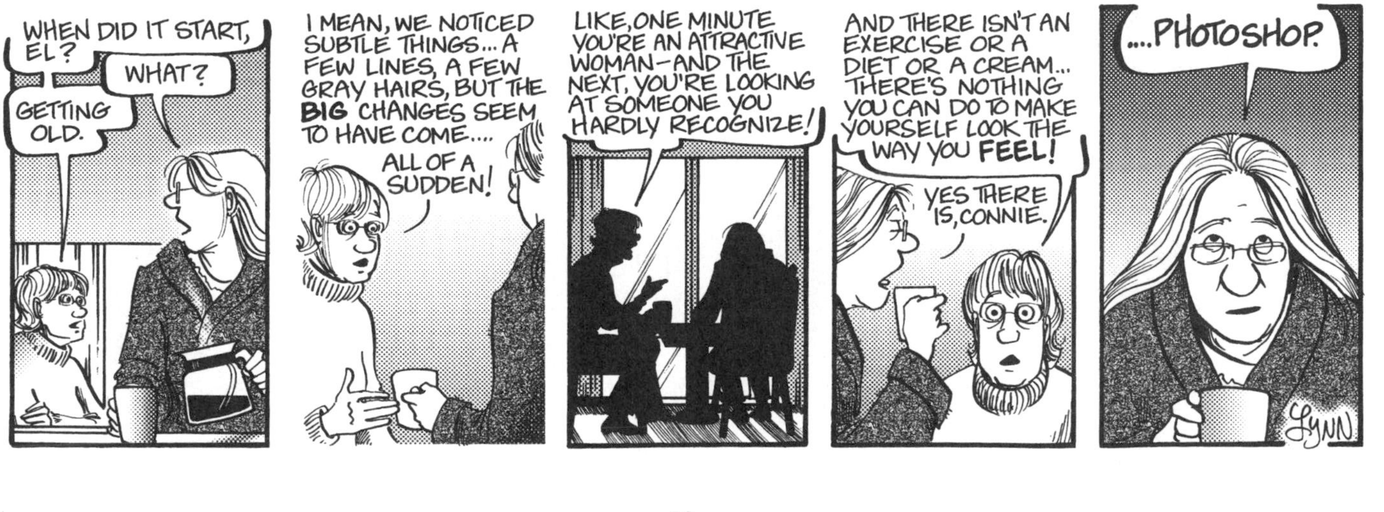
WHEN DID IT START, EL?
WHAT?
GETTING OLD.
I MEAN, WE NOTICED SUBTLE THINGS... A FEW LINES, A FEW GRAY HAIRS, BUT THE **BIG** CHANGES SEEM TO HAVE COME....
ALL OF A SUDDEN!
LIKE, ONE MINUTE YOU'RE AN ATTRACTIVE WOMAN—AND THE NEXT, YOU'RE LOOKING AT SOMEONE YOU HARDLY RECOGNIZE!
AND THERE ISN'T AN EXERCISE OR A DIET OR A CREAM... THERE'S NOTHING YOU CAN DO TO MAKE YOURSELF LOOK THE WAY YOU **FEEL**!
YES THERE IS, CONNIE.
....PHOTOSHOP.
LYNN

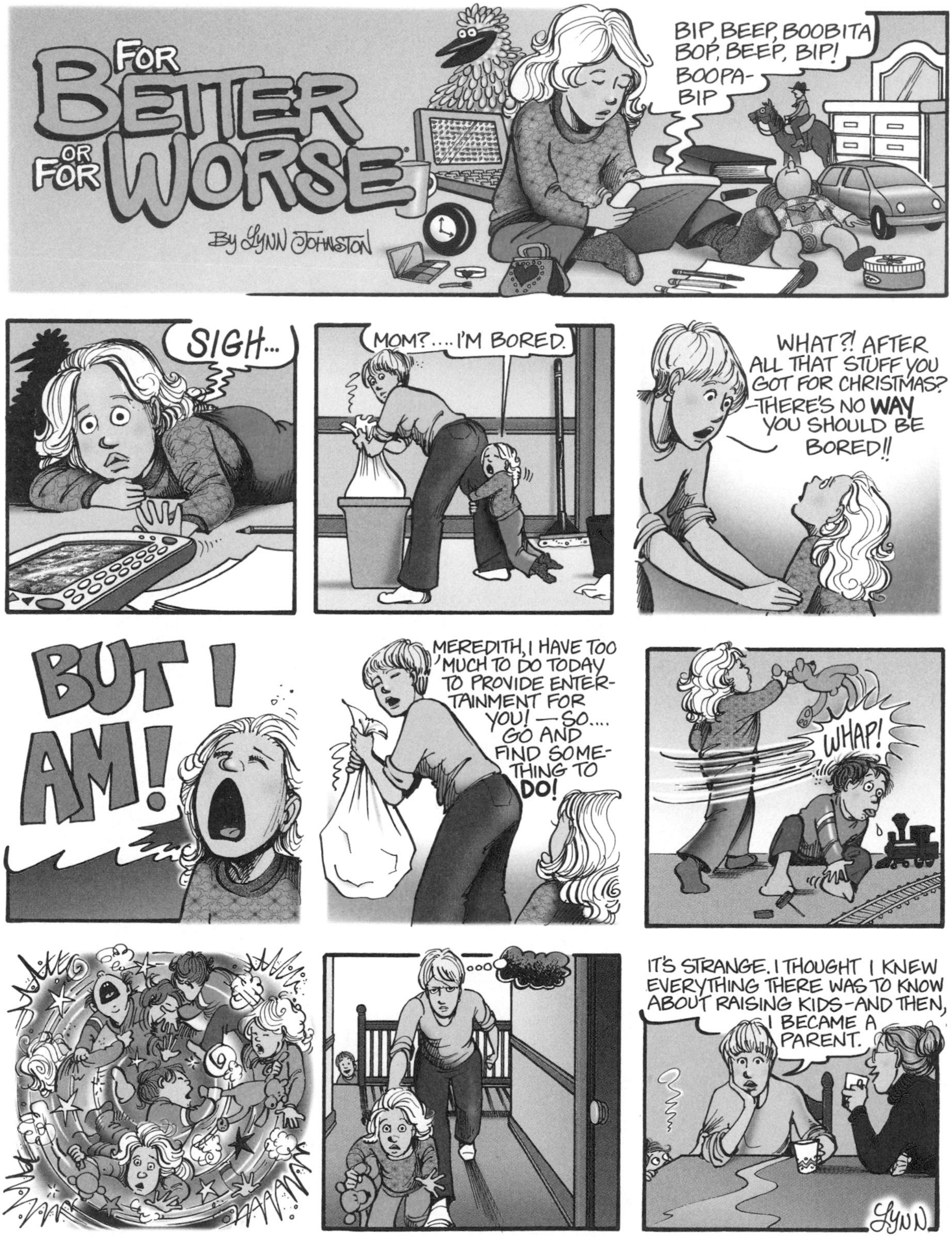
FOR BETTER OR FOR WORSE
By Lynn Johnston
BIP, BEEP, BOOBITA BOP, BEEP, BIP! BOOPA-BIP
SIGH...
MOM?.... I'M BORED.
WHAT?! AFTER ALL THAT STUFF YOU GOT FOR CHRISTMAS? -THERE'S NO WAY YOU SHOULD BE BORED!!
BUT I AM!
MEREDITH, I HAVE TOO MUCH TO DO TODAY TO PROVIDE ENTERTAINMENT FOR YOU! — SO.... GO AND FIND SOMETHING TO DO!
WHAP!
IT'S STRANGE. I THOUGHT I KNEW EVERYTHING THERE WAS TO KNOW ABOUT RAISING KIDS-AND THEN, I BECAME A PARENT.
LYNN

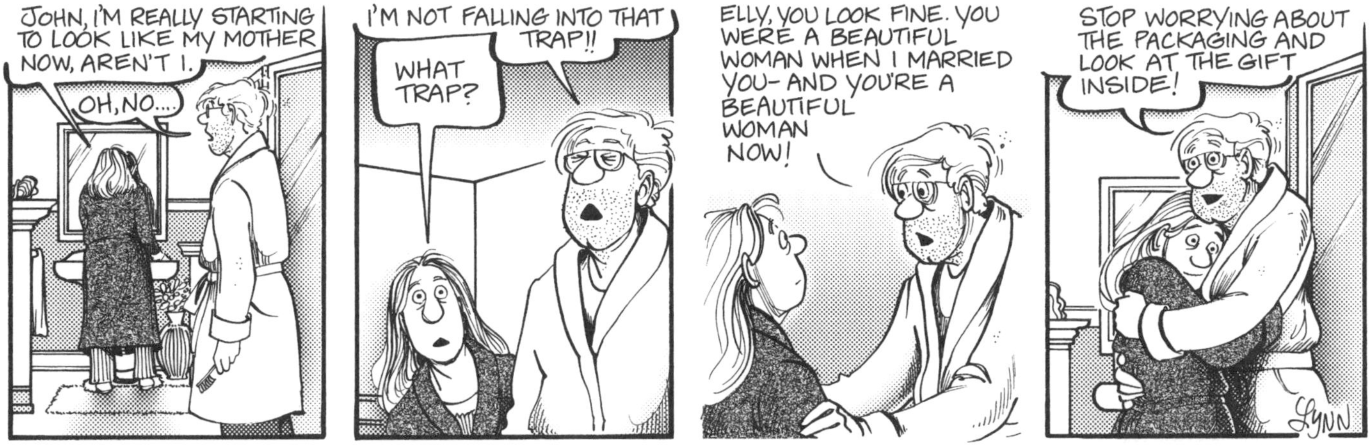
JOHN, I'M REALLY STARTING TO LOOK LIKE MY MOTHER NOW, AREN'T I.
OH, NO....
I'M NOT FALLING INTO THAT TRAP!!
WHAT TRAP?
ELLY, YOU LOOK FINE. YOU WERE A BEAUTIFUL WOMAN WHEN I MARRIED YOU- AND YOU'RE A BEAUTIFUL WOMAN NOW!
STOP WORRYING ABOUT THE PACKAGING AND LOOK AT THE GIFT INSIDE!
LYNN

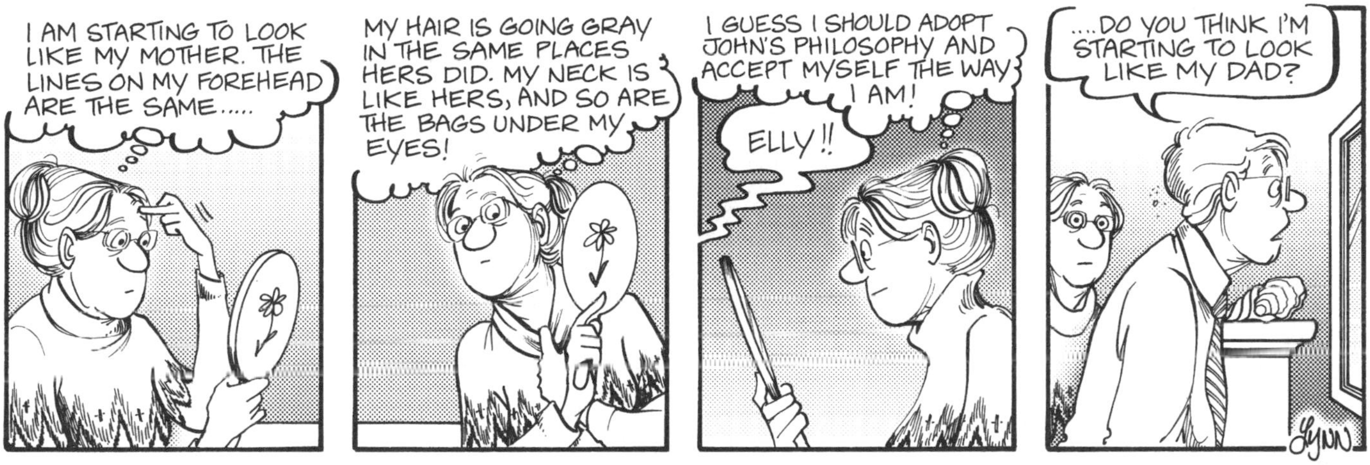
I AM STARTING TO LOOK LIKE MY MOTHER. THE LINES ON MY FOREHEAD ARE THE SAME.....
MY HAIR IS GOING GRAY IN THE SAME PLACES HERS DID. MY NECK IS LIKE HERS, AND SO ARE THE BAGS UNDER MY EYES!
I GUESS I SHOULD ADOPT JOHN'S PHILOSOPHY AND ACCEPT MYSELF THE WAY I AM!
ELLY!!
....DO YOU THINK I'M STARTING TO LOOK LIKE MY DAD?
LYNN

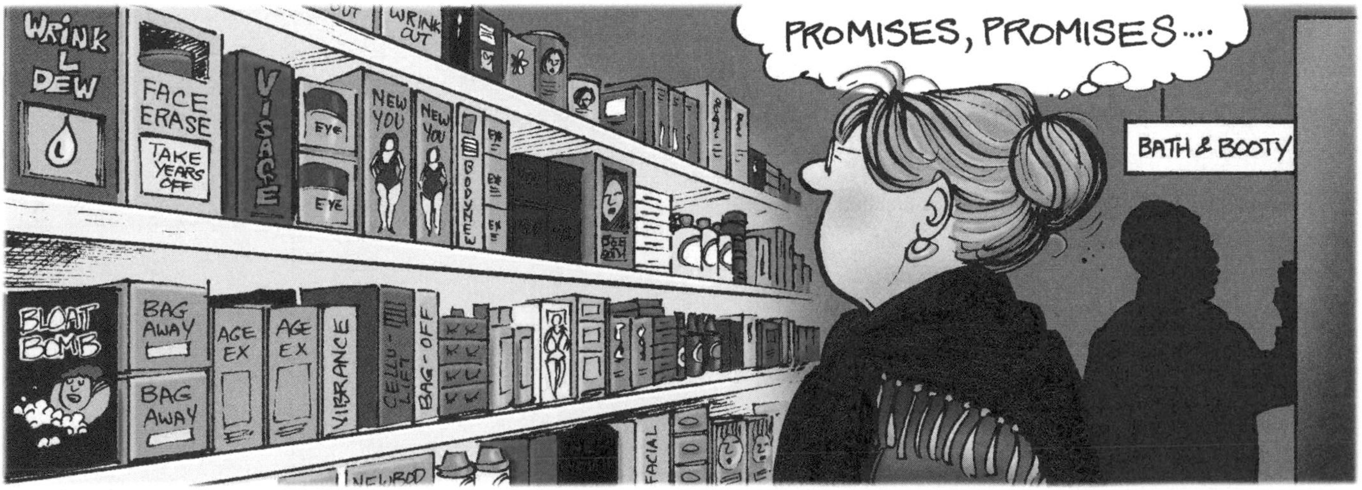
WRINK L DEW
FACE ERASE
TAKE YEARS OFF
VISAGE
NEW YOU
NEW YOU
BODYNEW
EYE
EYE
WRINK OUT
BLOAT BOMB
BAG AWAY
BAG AWAY
AGE EX
AGE EX
VIBRANCE
CELLU-LIFT
BAG-OFF
FACIAL
NEWBOD
PROMISES, PROMISES....
BATH & BOOTY

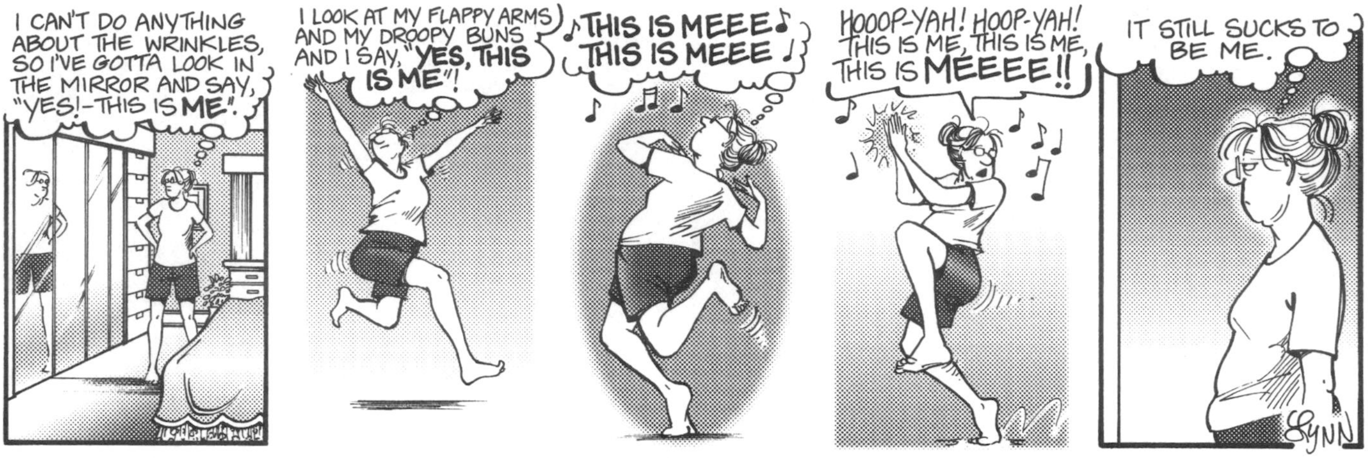
I CAN'T DO ANYTHING ABOUT THE WRINKLES, SO I'VE GOTTA LOOK IN THE MIRROR AND SAY, "YES!–THIS IS ME".
I LOOK AT MY FLAPPY ARMS AND MY DROOPY BUNS AND I SAY, "YES, THIS IS ME"!
THIS IS MEEE THIS IS MEEE
HOOOP-YAH! HOOP-YAH! THIS IS ME, THIS IS ME, THIS IS MEEEE!!
IT STILL SUCKS TO BE ME.
LYNN

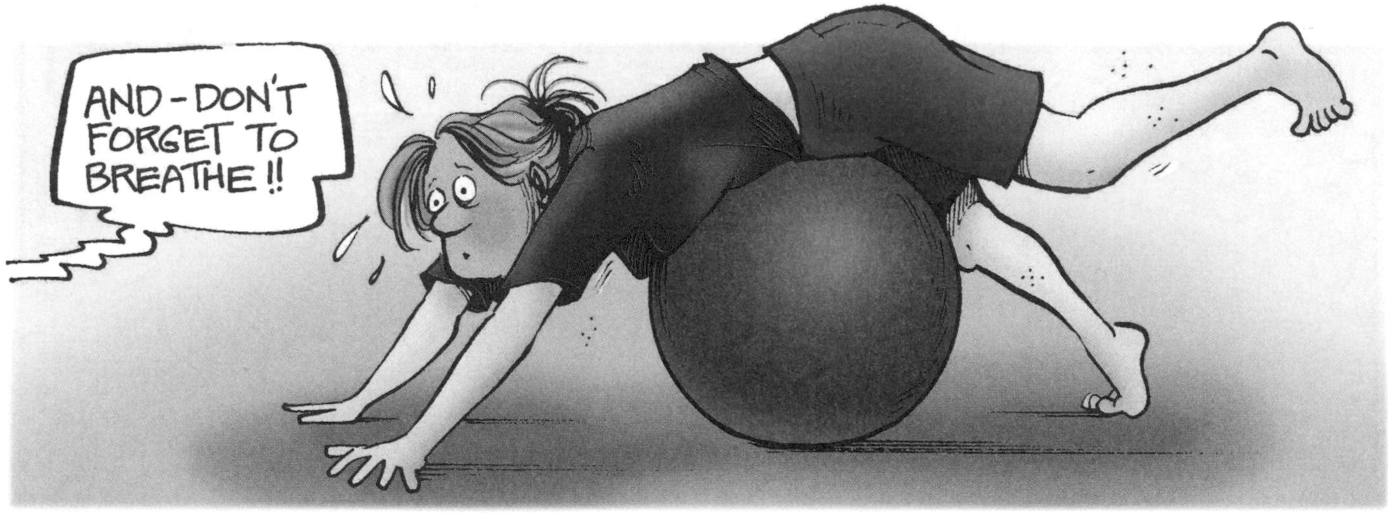
AND-DON'T FORGET TO BREATHE!!

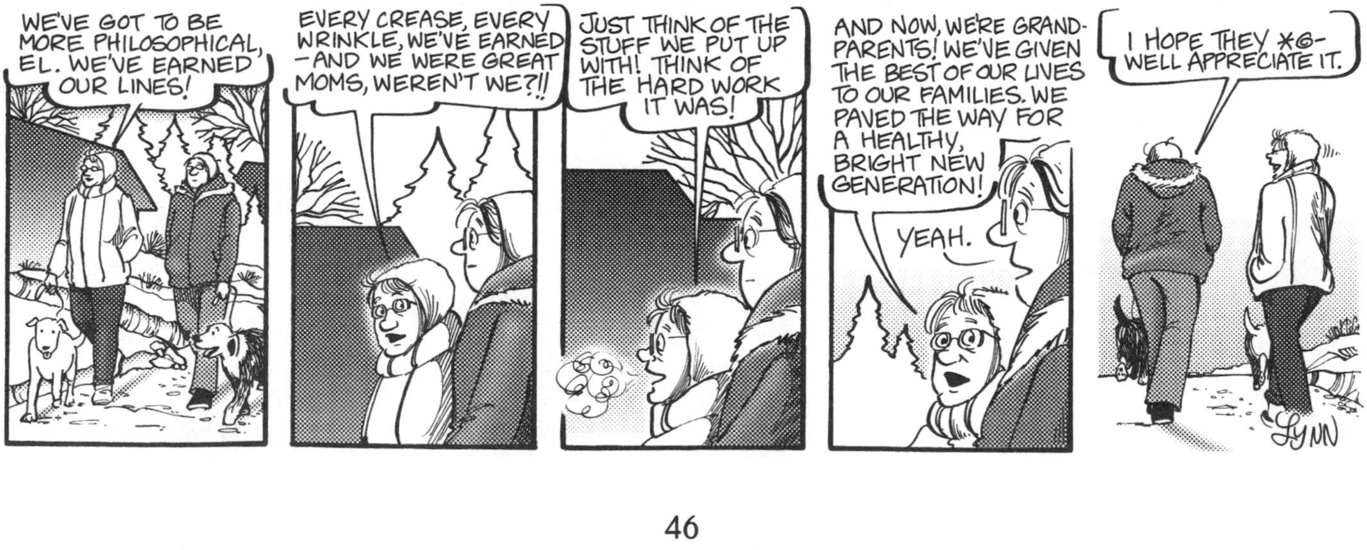
WE'VE GOT TO BE MORE PHILOSOPHICAL, EL. WE'VE EARNED OUR LINES!
EVERY CREASE, EVERY WRINKLE, WE'VE EARNED –AND WE WERE GREAT MOMS, WEREN'T WE?!!
JUST THINK OF THE STUFF WE PUT UP WITH! THINK OF THE HARD WORK IT WAS!
AND NOW, WE'RE GRAND-PARENTS! WE'VE GIVEN THE BEST OF OUR LIVES TO OUR FAMILIES. WE PAVED THE WAY FOR A HEALTHY, BRIGHT NEW GENERATION!
YEAH.
I HOPE THEY *@-WELL APPRECIATE IT.
LYNN

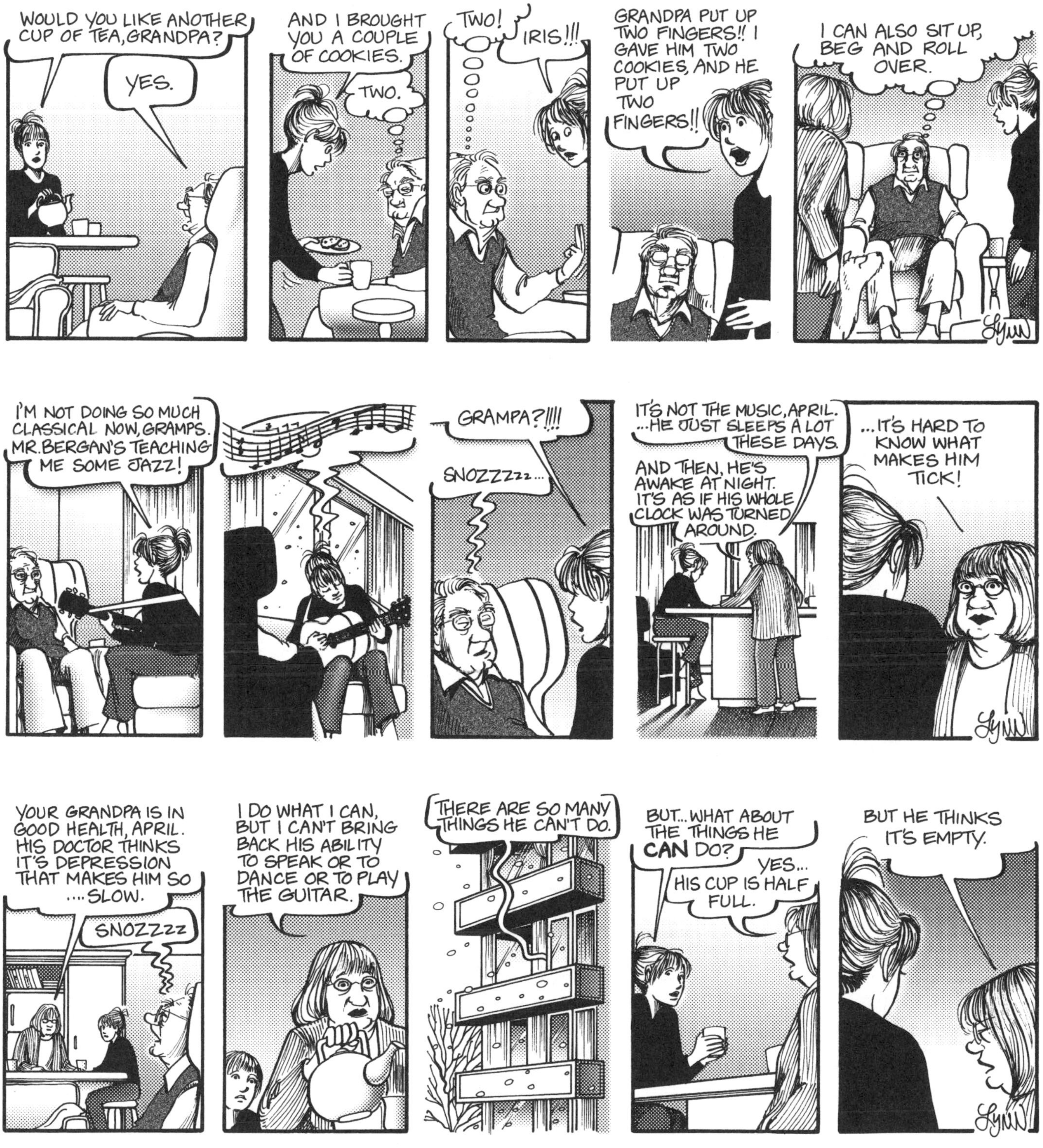
WOULD YOU LIKE ANOTHER CUP OF TEA, GRANDPA?
YES.
AND I BROUGHT YOU A COUPLE OF COOKIES.
TWO.
TWO!
IRIS!!!
GRANDPA PUT UP TWO FINGERS!! I GAVE HIM TWO COOKIES, AND HE PUT UP TWO FINGERS!!
I CAN ALSO SIT UP, BEG AND ROLL OVER.
LYNN
I'M NOT DOING SO MUCH CLASSICAL NOW, GRAMPS. MR. BERGAN'S TEACHING ME SOME JAZZ!
GRAMPA?!!!!
SNOZZZzz...
IT'S NOT THE MUSIC, APRIL. ...HE JUST SLEEPS A LOT THESE DAYS.
AND THEN, HE'S AWAKE AT NIGHT. IT'S AS IF HIS WHOLE CLOCK WAS TURNED AROUND.
...IT'S HARD TO KNOW WHAT MAKES HIM TICK!
LYNN
YOUR GRANDPA IS IN GOOD HEALTH, APRIL. HIS DOCTOR THINKS IT'S DEPRESSION THAT MAKES HIM SO ....SLOW.
SNOZZZzz
I DO WHAT I CAN, BUT I CAN'T BRING BACK HIS ABILITY TO SPEAK OR TO DANCE OR TO PLAY THE GUITAR.
THERE ARE SO MANY THINGS HE CAN'T DO.
BUT... WHAT ABOUT THE THINGS HE CAN DO?
YES... HIS CUP IS HALF FULL.
BUT HE THINKS IT'S EMPTY.
LYNN

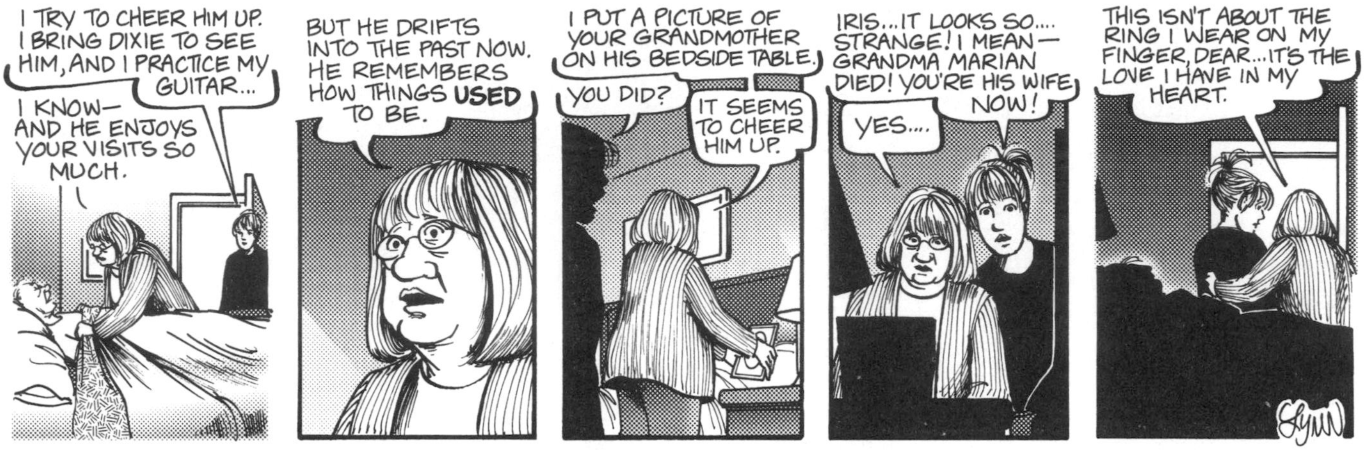
I TRY TO CHEER HIM UP. I BRING DIXIE TO SEE HIM, AND I PRACTICE MY GUITAR...
I KNOW— AND HE ENJOYS YOUR VISITS SO MUCH.
BUT HE DRIFTS INTO THE PAST NOW. HE REMEMBERS HOW THINGS **USED** TO BE.
I PUT A PICTURE OF YOUR GRANDMOTHER ON HIS BEDSIDE TABLE.
YOU DID?
IT SEEMS TO CHEER HIM UP.
IRIS...IT LOOKS SO.... STRANGE! I MEAN— GRANDMA MARIAN DIED! YOU'RE HIS WIFE NOW!
YES....
THIS ISN'T ABOUT THE RING I WEAR ON MY FINGER, DEAR...IT'S THE LOVE I HAVE IN MY HEART.
Lynn

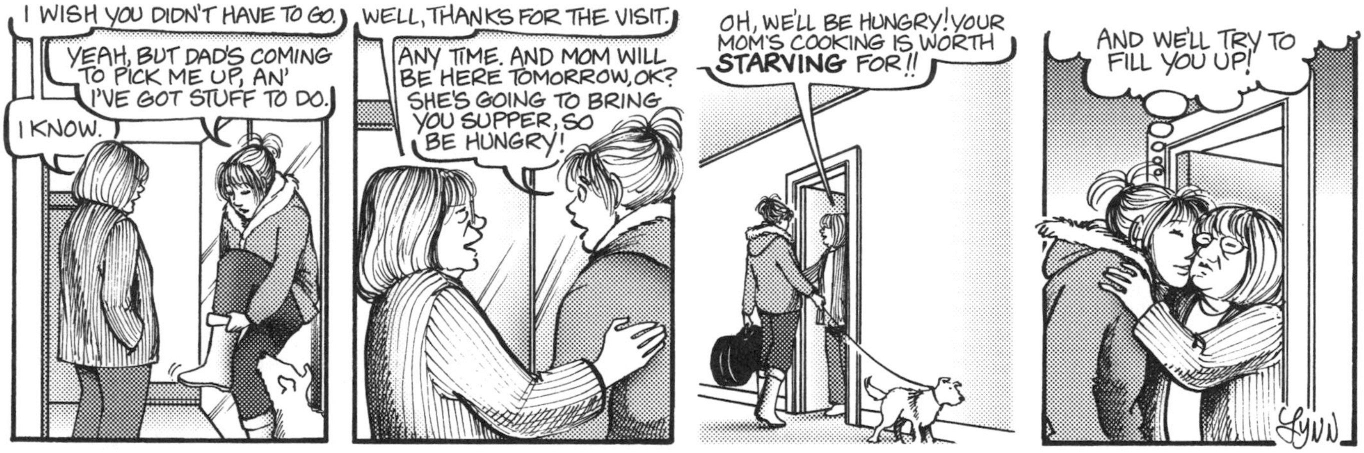
I WISH YOU DIDN'T HAVE TO GO.
YEAH, BUT DAD'S COMING TO PICK ME UP, AN' I'VE GOT STUFF TO DO.
I KNOW.
WELL, THANKS FOR THE VISIT.
ANY TIME. AND MOM WILL BE HERE TOMORROW, OK? SHE'S GOING TO BRING YOU SUPPER, SO BE HUNGRY!
OH, WE'LL BE HUNGRY! YOUR MOM'S COOKING IS WORTH **STARVING** FOR!!
AND WE'LL TRY TO FILL YOU UP!
Lynn

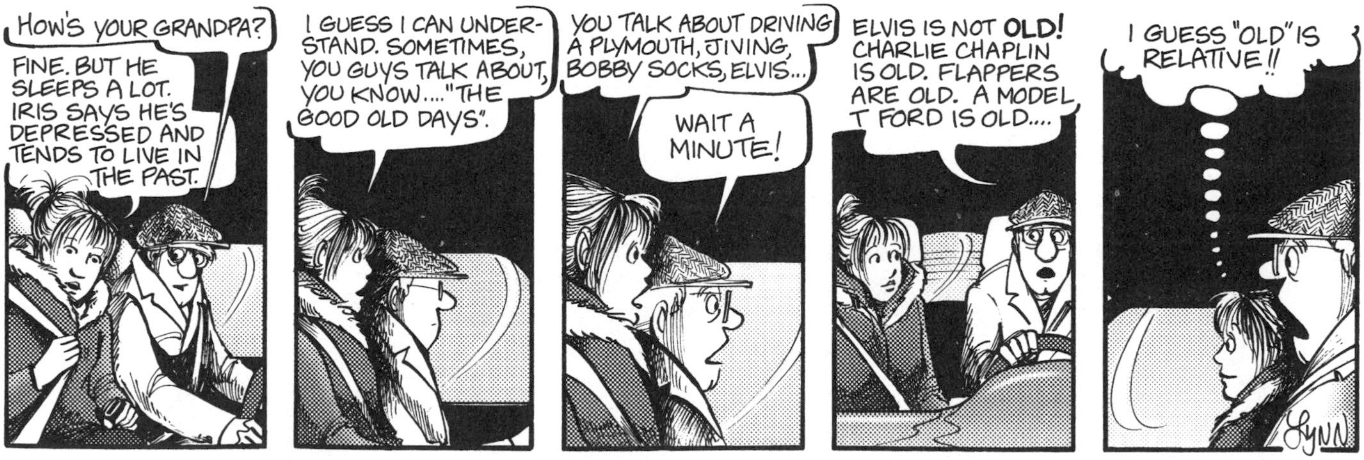
HOW'S YOUR GRANDPA?
FINE. BUT HE SLEEPS A LOT. IRIS SAYS HE'S DEPRESSED AND TENDS TO LIVE IN THE PAST.
I GUESS I CAN UNDERSTAND. SOMETIMES, YOU GUYS TALK ABOUT, YOU KNOW...."THE GOOD OLD DAYS".
YOU TALK ABOUT DRIVING A PLYMOUTH, JIVING, BOBBY SOCKS, ELVIS...
WAIT A MINUTE!
ELVIS IS NOT **OLD!** CHARLIE CHAPLIN IS OLD. FLAPPERS ARE OLD. A MODEL T FORD IS OLD....
I GUESS "OLD" IS RELATIVE!!
Lynn

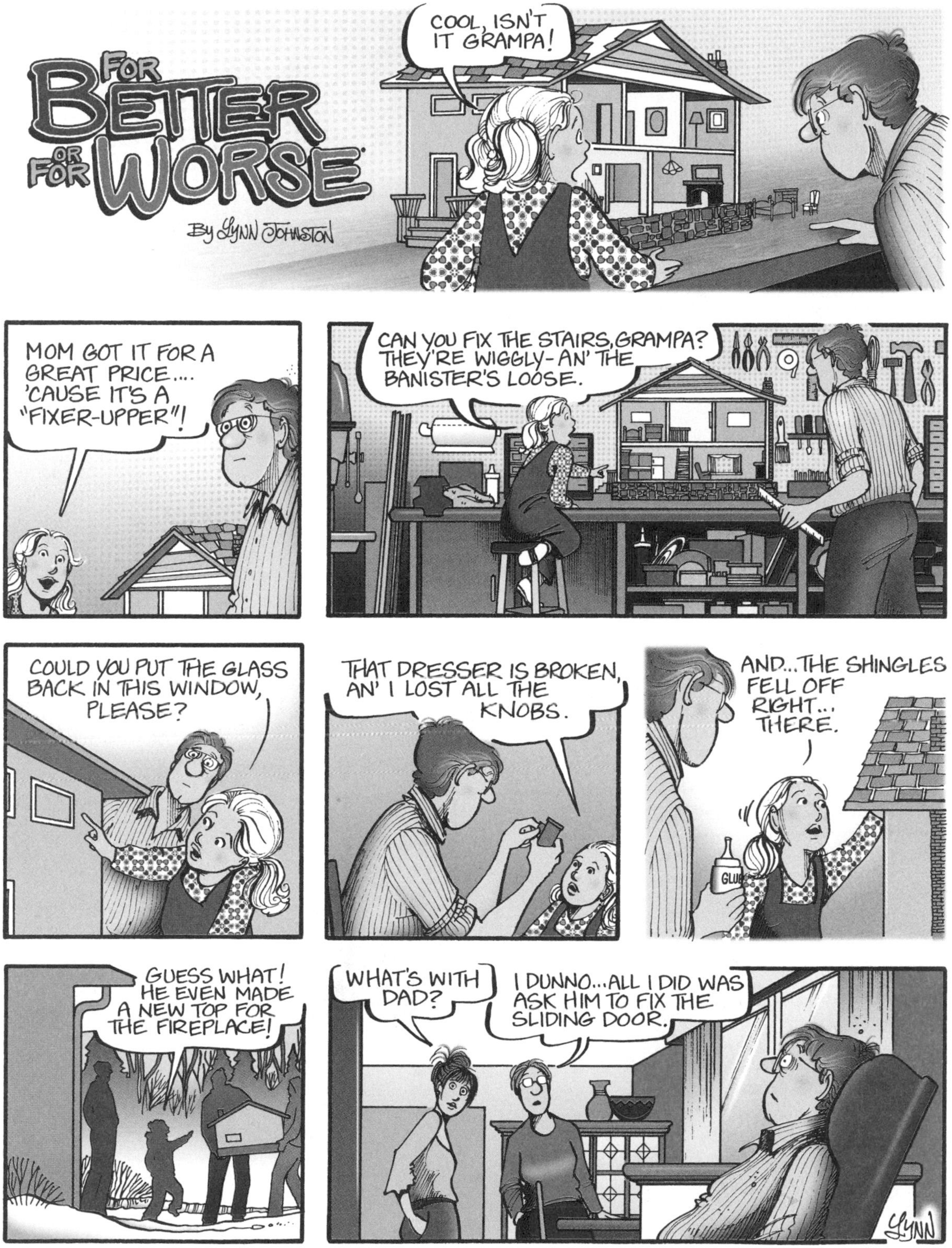
COOL, ISN'T IT GRAMPA!
FOR BETTER OR FOR WORSE
BY LYNN JOHNSTON
MOM GOT IT FOR A GREAT PRICE.... 'CAUSE IT'S A "FIXER-UPPER"!
CAN YOU FIX THE STAIRS, GRAMPA? THEY'RE WIGGLY- AN' THE BANISTER'S LOOSE.
COULD YOU PUT THE GLASS BACK IN THIS WINDOW, PLEASE?
THAT DRESSER IS BROKEN, AN' I LOST ALL THE KNOBS.
AND... THE SHINGLES FELL OFF RIGHT... THERE.
GLUE
GUESS WHAT! HE EVEN MADE A NEW TOP FOR THE FIREPLACE!
WHAT'S WITH DAD?
I DUNNO... ALL I DID WAS ASK HIM TO FIX THE SLIDING DOOR.
LYNN

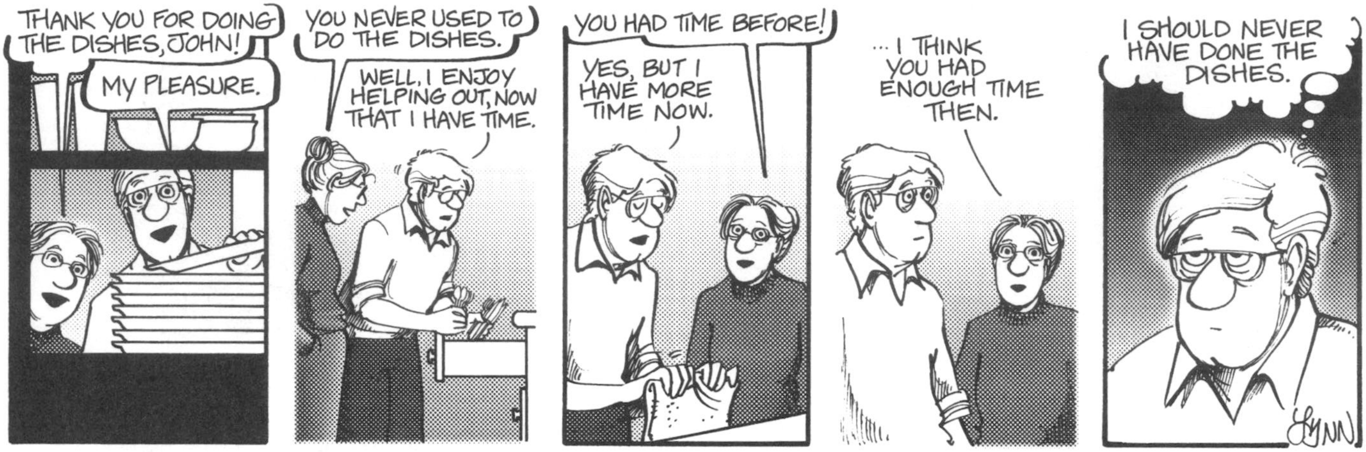
THANK YOU FOR DOING THE DISHES, JOHN!
MY PLEASURE.
YOU NEVER USED TO DO THE DISHES.
WELL, I ENJOY HELPING OUT, NOW THAT I HAVE TIME.
YOU HAD TIME BEFORE!
YES, BUT I HAVE MORE TIME NOW.
... I THINK YOU HAD ENOUGH TIME THEN.
I SHOULD NEVER HAVE DONE THE DISHES.
LYNN

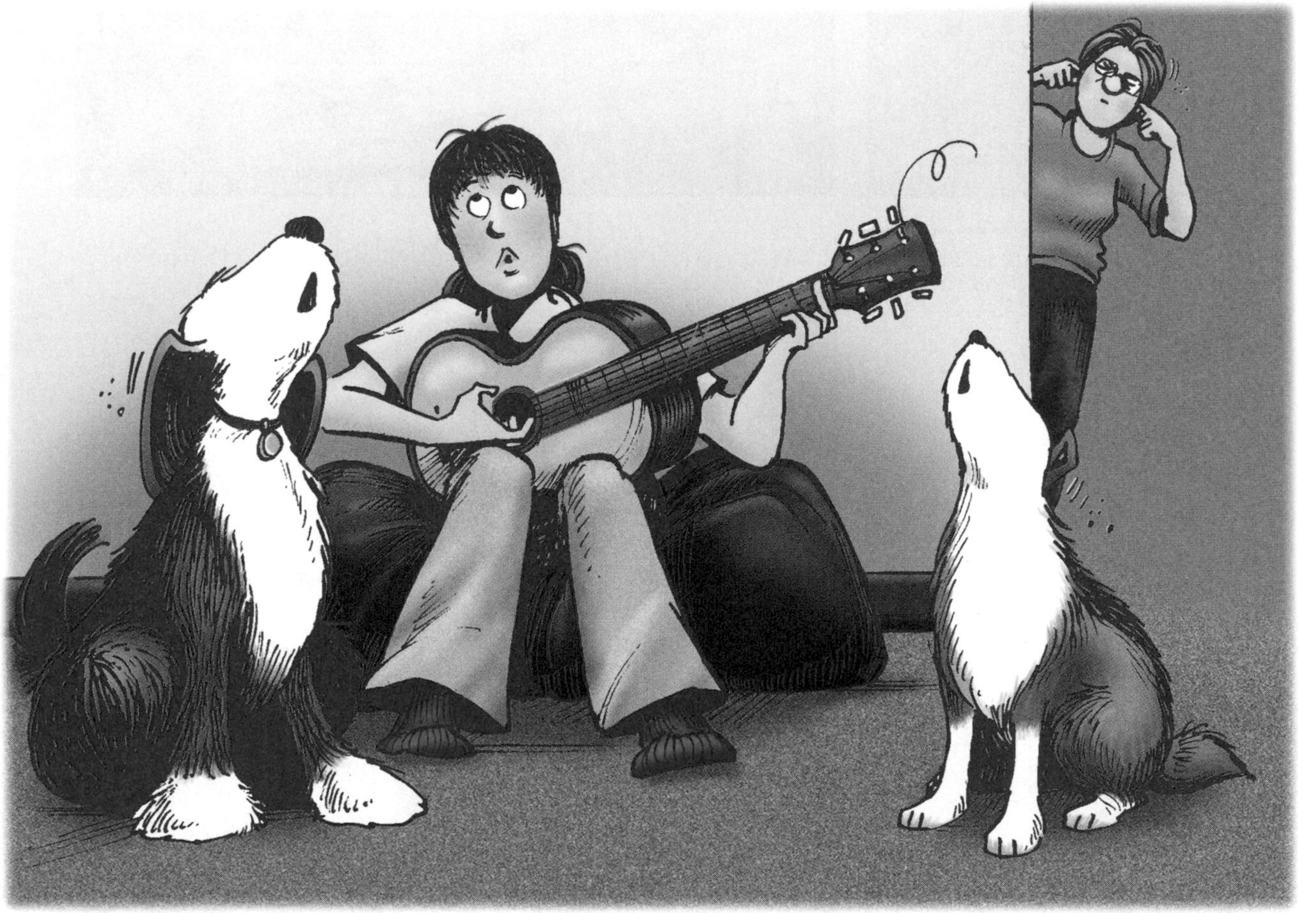

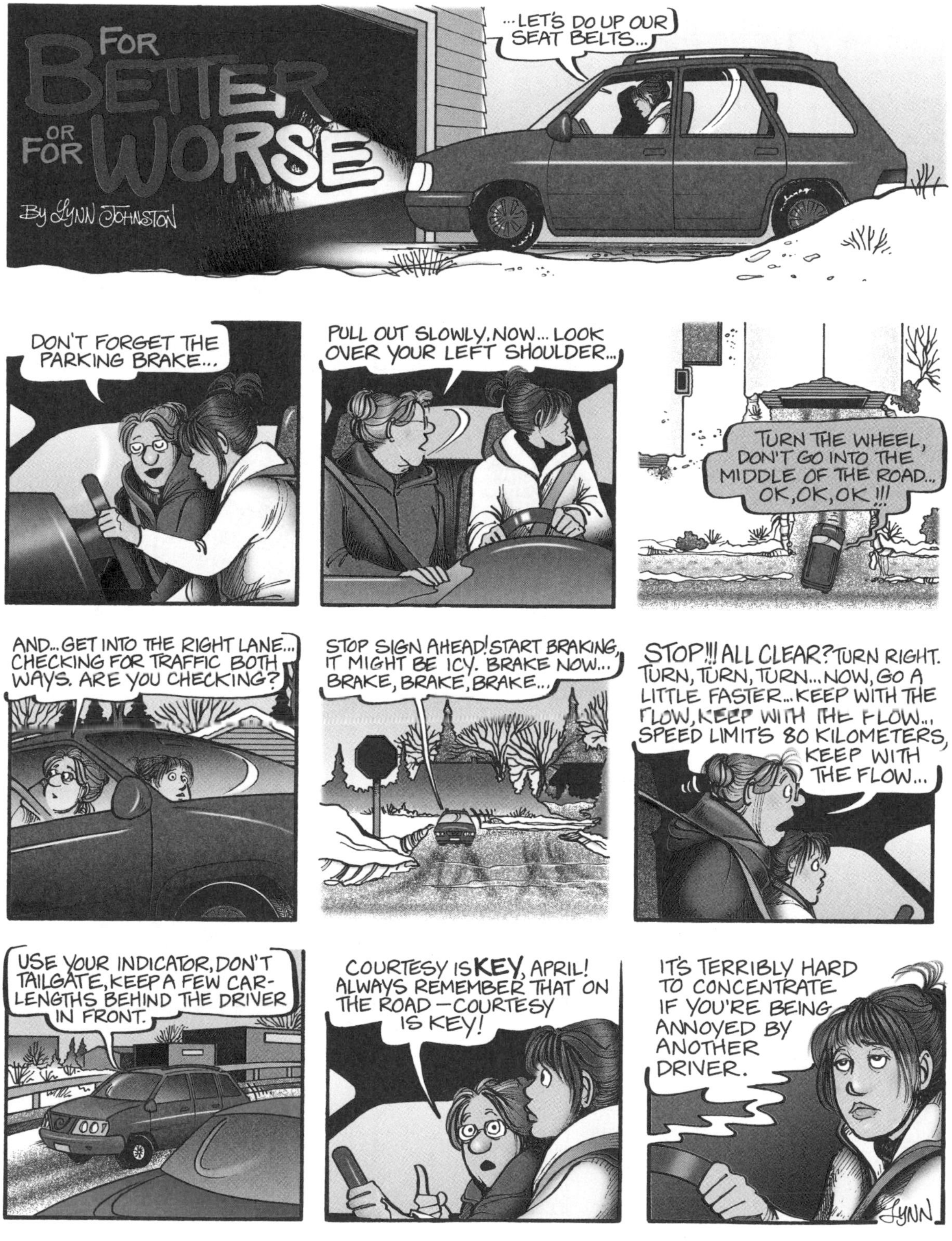
FOR BETTER OR FOR WORSE
By Lynn Johnston
...LET'S DO UP OUR SEAT BELTS...
DON'T FORGET THE PARKING BRAKE...
PULL OUT SLOWLY, NOW... LOOK OVER YOUR LEFT SHOULDER...
TURN THE WHEEL, DON'T GO INTO THE MIDDLE OF THE ROAD... OK, OK, OK !!!
AND...GET INTO THE RIGHT LANE... CHECKING FOR TRAFFIC BOTH WAYS. ARE YOU CHECKING?
STOP SIGN AHEAD! START BRAKING, IT MIGHT BE ICY. BRAKE NOW... BRAKE, BRAKE, BRAKE...
STOP!!! ALL CLEAR? TURN RIGHT. TURN, TURN, TURN... NOW, GO A LITTLE FASTER... KEEP WITH THE FLOW, KEEP WITH THE FLOW... SPEED LIMIT'S 80 KILOMETERS, KEEP WITH THE FLOW...
USE YOUR INDICATOR, DON'T TAILGATE, KEEP A FEW CAR-LENGTHS BEHIND THE DRIVER IN FRONT.
COURTESY IS KEY, APRIL! ALWAYS REMEMBER THAT ON THE ROAD — COURTESY IS KEY!
IT'S TERRIBLY HARD TO CONCENTRATE IF YOU'RE BEING ANNOYED BY ANOTHER DRIVER.
LYNN

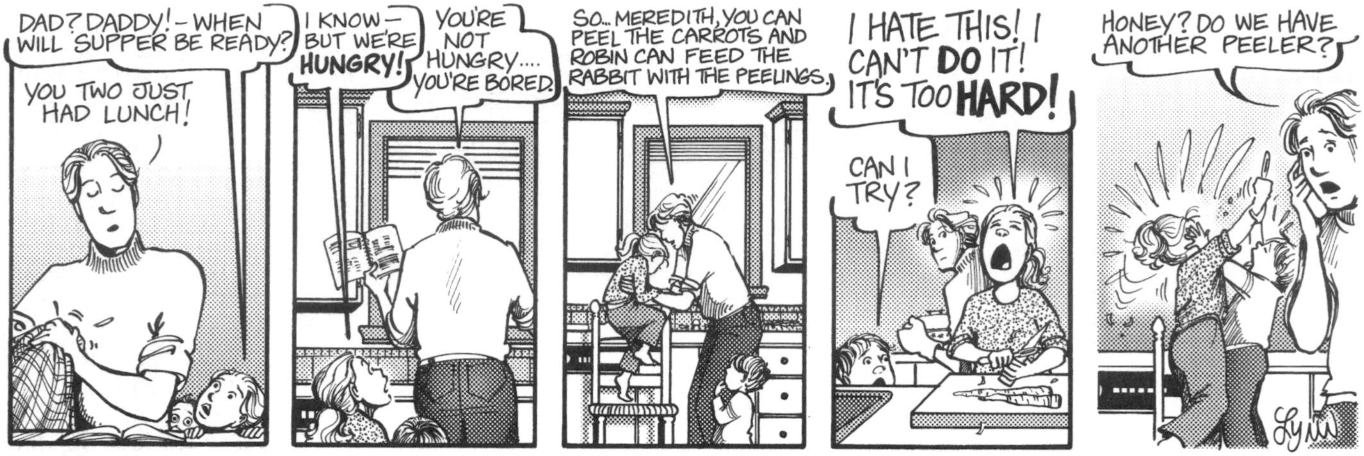
DAD? DADDY! – WHEN WILL SUPPER BE READY?
YOU TWO JUST HAD LUNCH!
I KNOW – BUT WE'RE **HUNGRY!**
YOU'RE NOT HUNGRY.... YOU'RE BORED.
SO... MEREDITH, YOU CAN PEEL THE CARROTS AND ROBIN CAN FEED THE RABBIT WITH THE PEELINGS.
I HATE THIS! I CAN'T **DO** IT! IT'S TOO **HARD!**
CAN I TRY?
HONEY? DO WE HAVE ANOTHER PEELER?

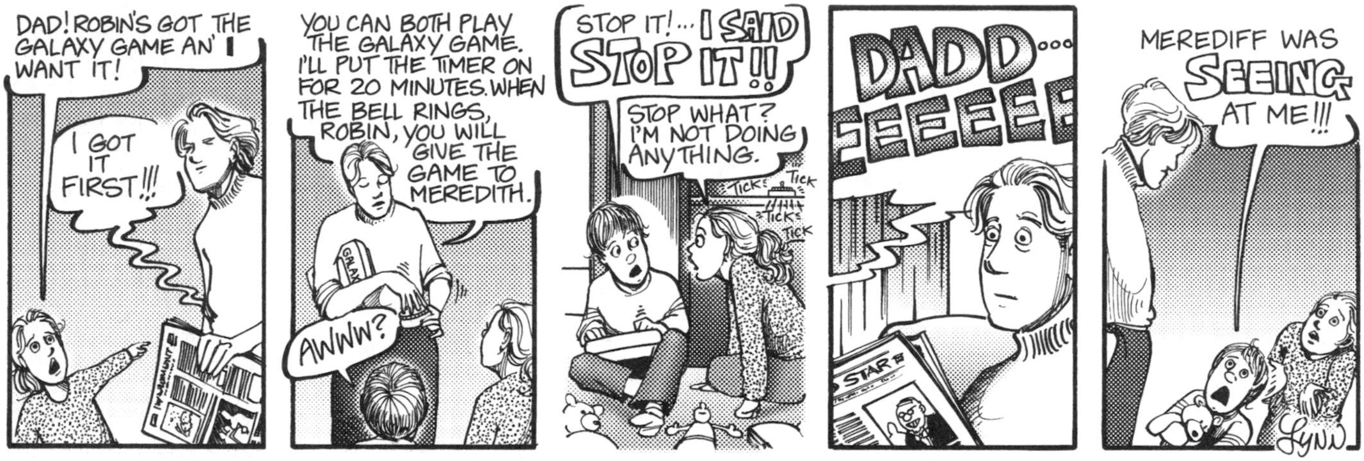
DAD! ROBIN'S GOT THE GALAXY GAME AN' **I** WANT IT!
I GOT IT FIRST!!!
YOU CAN BOTH PLAY THE GALAXY GAME. I'LL PUT THE TIMER ON FOR 20 MINUTES. WHEN THE BELL RINGS, ROBIN, YOU WILL GIVE THE GAME TO MEREDITH.
AWWW?
STOP IT!... **I SAID STOP IT!!**
STOP WHAT? I'M NOT DOING ANYTHING.
TICK TICK TICK TICK
DADD... EEEEEEE
MEREDIFF WAS **SEEING** AT ME!!!

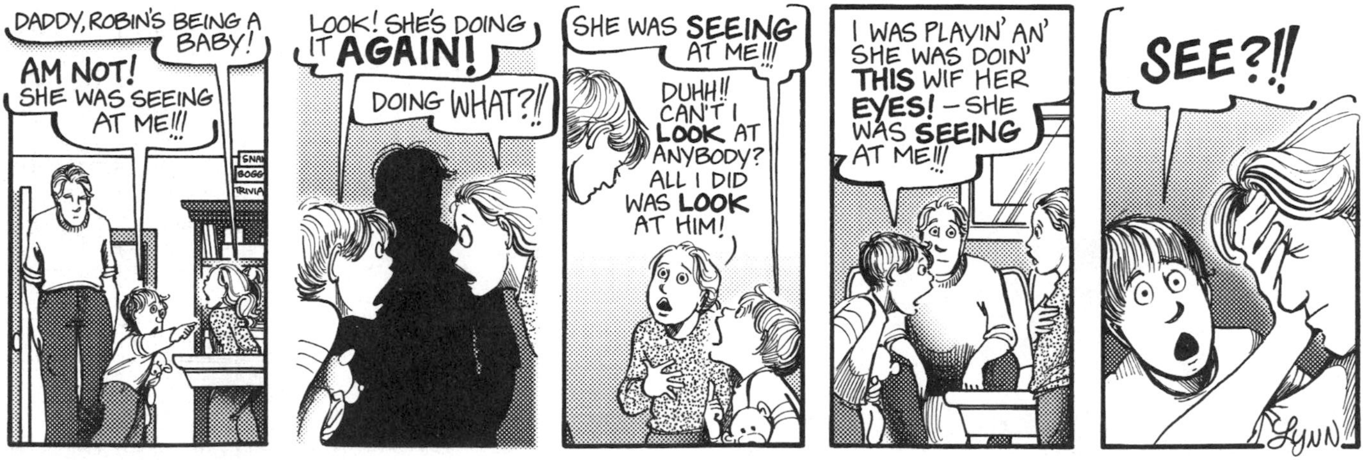
DADDY, ROBIN'S BEING A BABY!
AM NOT! SHE WAS SEEING AT ME!!!
LOOK! SHE'S DOING IT **AGAIN!**
DOING WHAT?!!
SHE WAS **SEEING** AT ME!!!
DUHH!! CAN'T I **LOOK** AT ANYBODY? ALL I DID WAS **LOOK** AT HIM!
I WAS PLAYIN' AN' SHE WAS DOIN' **THIS** WIF HER **EYES!** – SHE WAS **SEEING** AT ME!!!
SEE?!!

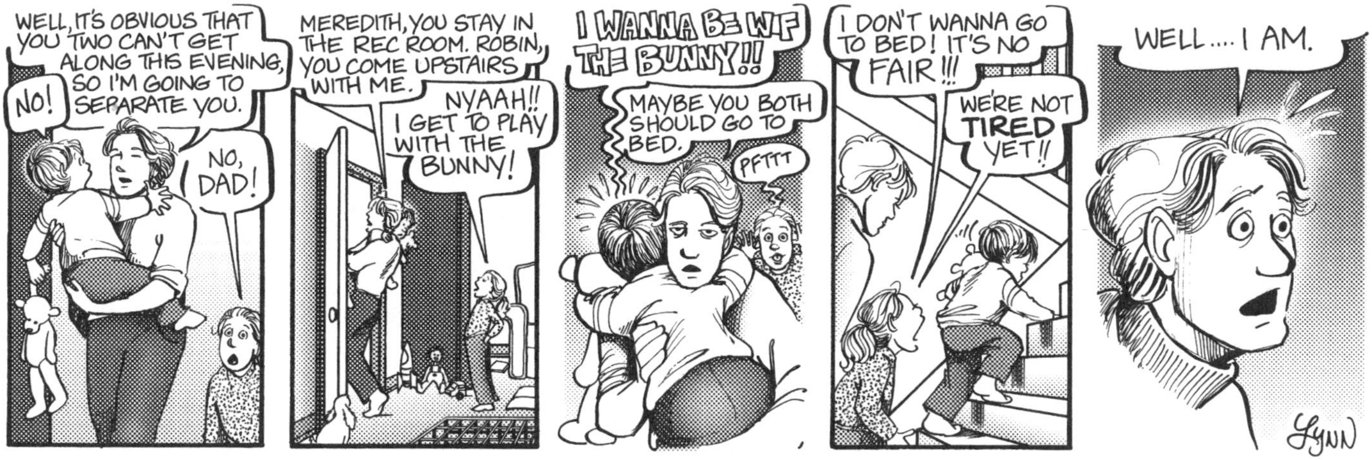
WELL, IT'S OBVIOUS THAT YOU TWO CAN'T GET ALONG THIS EVENING, SO I'M GOING TO SEPARATE YOU.
NO!
NO, DAD!
MEREDITH, YOU STAY IN THE REC ROOM. ROBIN, YOU COME UPSTAIRS WITH ME.
NYAAH!! I GET TO PLAY WITH THE BUNNY!
I WANNA BE WIF THE BUNNY!!
MAYBE YOU BOTH SHOULD GO TO BED.
PFTTT
I DON'T WANNA GO TO BED! IT'S NO FAIR!!!
WE'RE NOT TIRED YET!!
WELL.... I AM.
LYNN

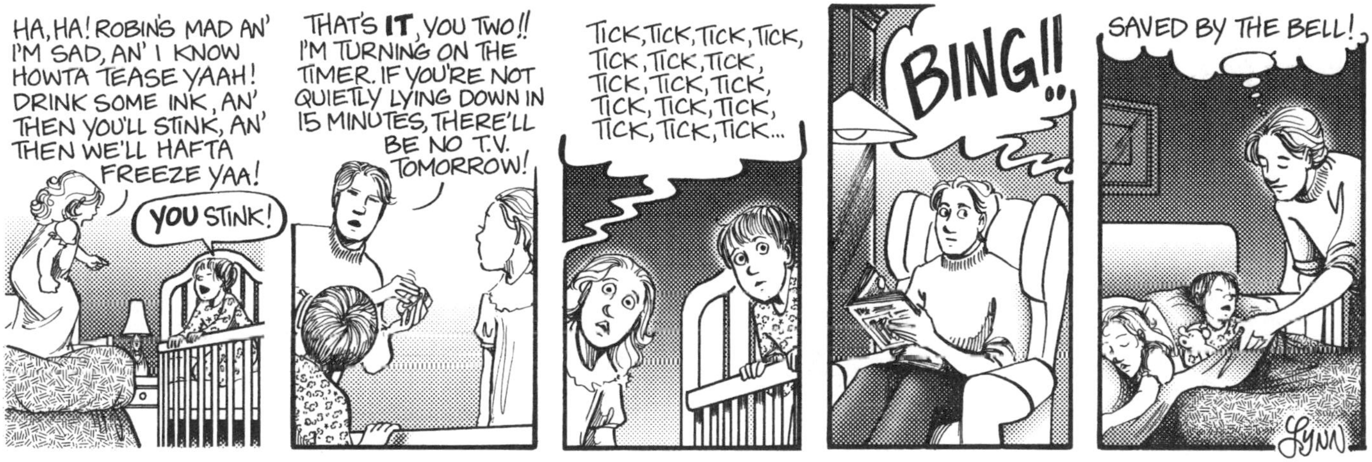
HA, HA! ROBIN'S MAD AN' I'M SAD, AN' I KNOW HOWTA TEASE YAAH! DRINK SOME INK, AN' THEN YOU'LL STINK, AN' THEN WE'LL HAFTA FREEZE YAA!
YOU STINK!
THAT'S IT, YOU TWO!! I'M TURNING ON THE TIMER. IF YOU'RE NOT QUIETLY LYING DOWN IN 15 MINUTES, THERE'LL BE NO T.V. TOMORROW!
TICK, TICK, TICK, TICK, TICK, TICK, TICK, TICK, TICK, TICK, TICK, TICK, TICK, TICK, TICK, TICK...
BING!!
SAVED BY THE BELL!
LYNN

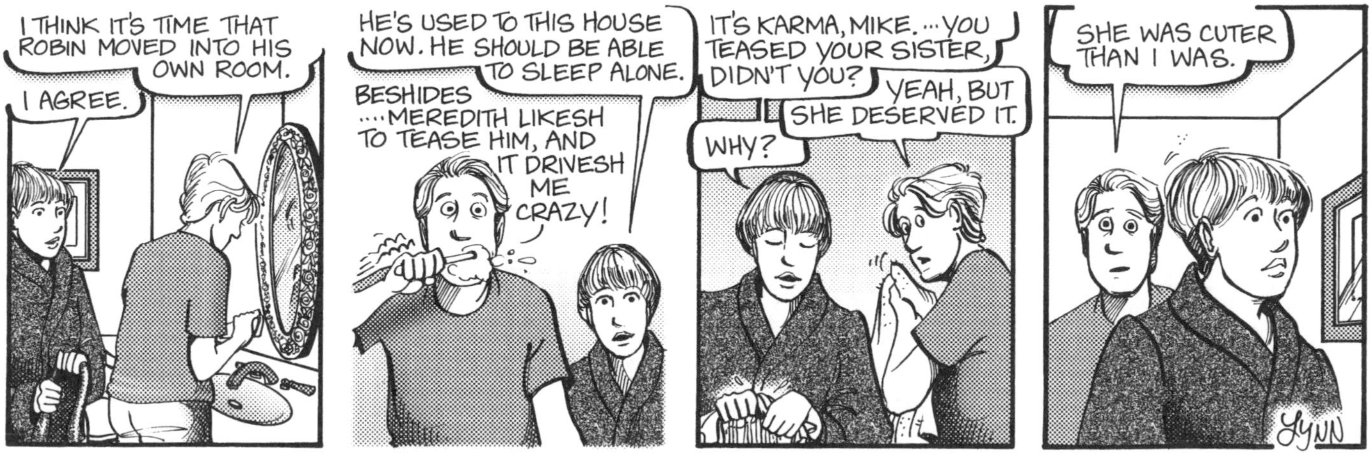
I THINK IT'S TIME THAT ROBIN MOVED INTO HIS OWN ROOM.
I AGREE.
HE'S USED TO THIS HOUSE NOW. HE SHOULD BE ABLE TO SLEEP ALONE.
BESHIDES ....MEREDITH LIKESH TO TEASE HIM, AND IT DRIVESH ME CRAZY!
IT'S KARMA, MIKE. ... YOU TEASED YOUR SISTER, DIDN'T YOU?
YEAH, BUT SHE DESERVED IT.
WHY?
SHE WAS CUTER THAN I WAS.
LYNN

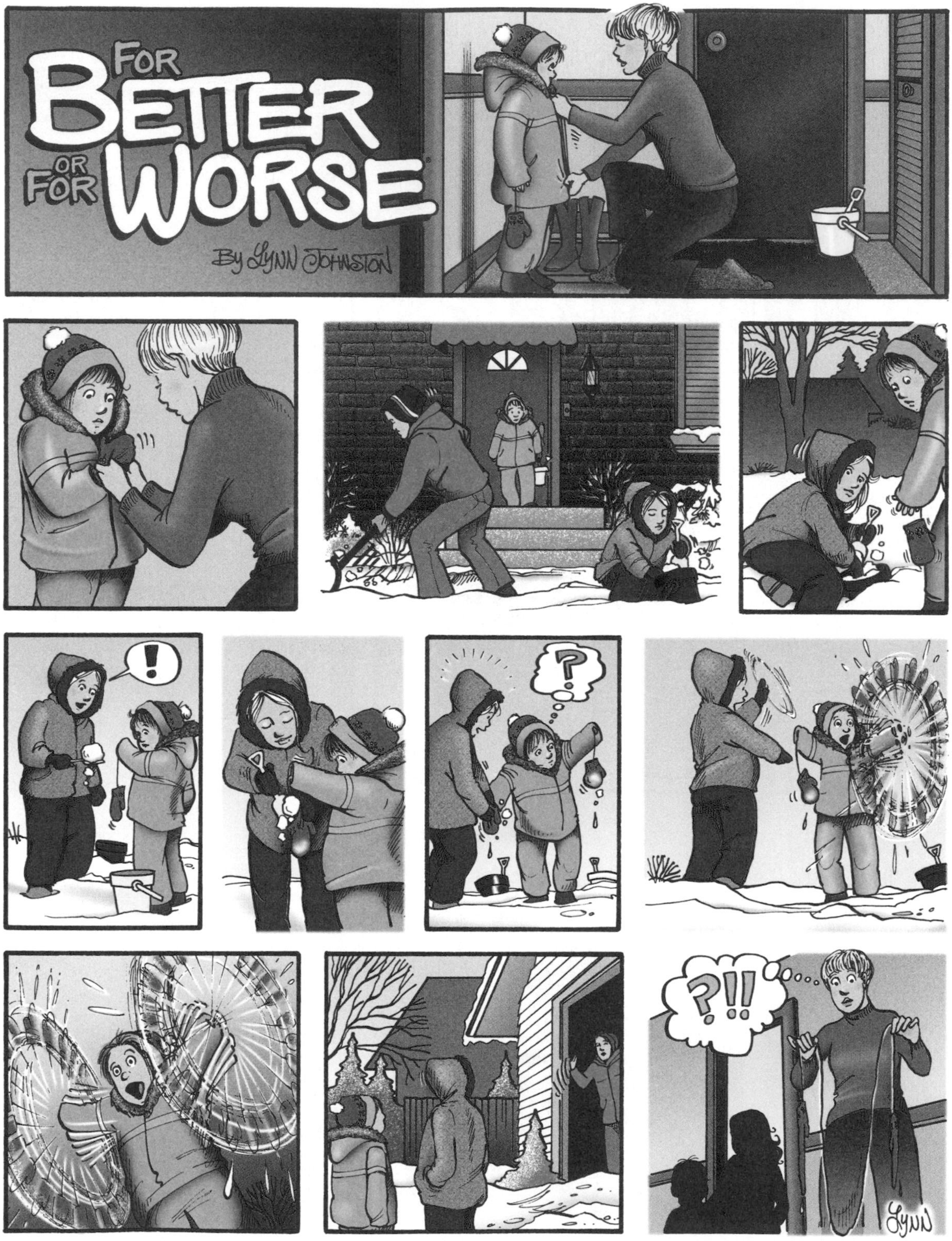
For Better or For Worse
By Lynn Johnston
!
?
?!!
Lynn

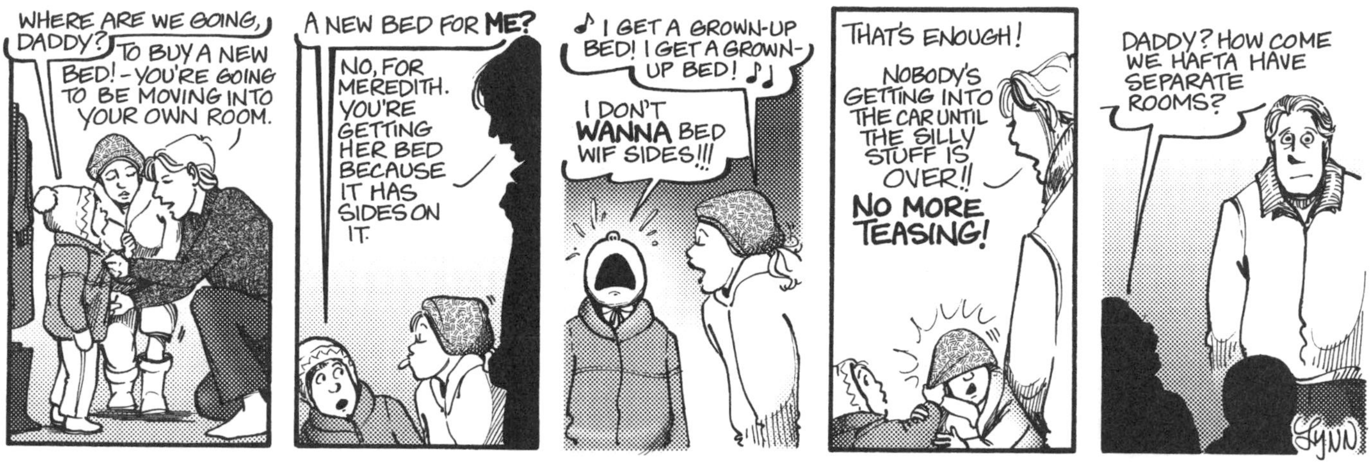
WHERE ARE WE GOING, DADDY?
TO BUY A NEW BED! - YOU'RE GOING TO BE MOVING INTO YOUR OWN ROOM.
A NEW BED FOR **ME?**
NO, FOR MEREDITH. YOU'RE GETTING HER BED BECAUSE IT HAS SIDES ON IT.
♪ I GET A GROWN-UP BED! I GET A GROWN-UP BED! ♪♩
I DON'T **WANNA** BED WIF SIDES!!!
THAT'S ENOUGH!
NOBODY'S GETTING INTO THE CAR UNTIL THE SILLY STUFF IS OVER!!
NO MORE TEASING!
DADDY? HOW COME WE HAFTA HAVE SEPARATE ROOMS?
LYNN

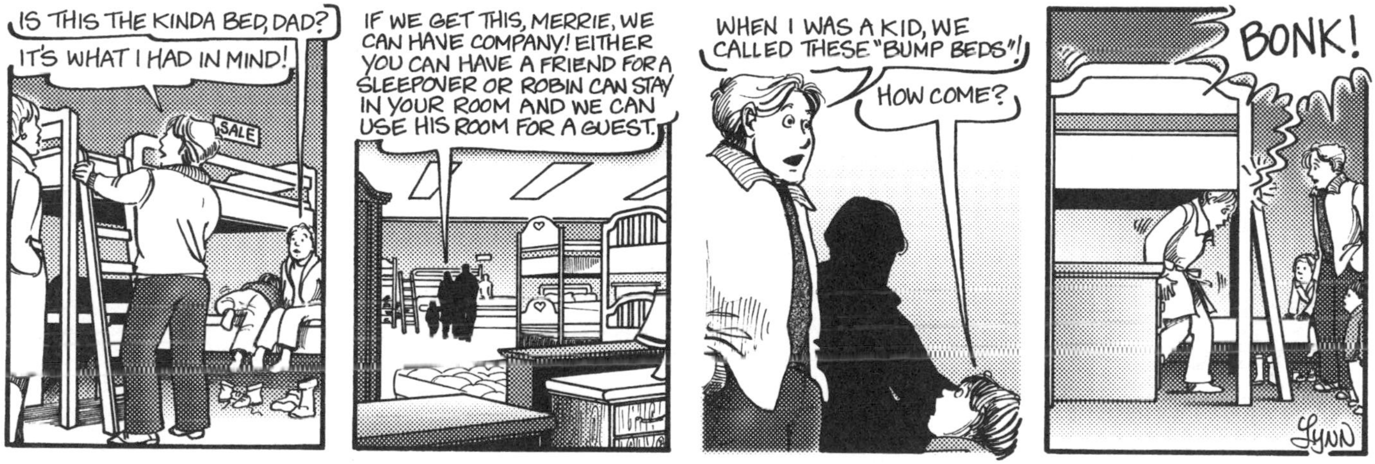
IS THIS THE KINDA BED, DAD?
IT'S WHAT I HAD IN MIND!
SALE
IF WE GET THIS, MERRIE, WE CAN HAVE COMPANY! EITHER YOU CAN HAVE A FRIEND FOR A SLEEPOVER OR ROBIN CAN STAY IN YOUR ROOM AND WE CAN USE HIS ROOM FOR A GUEST.
WHEN I WAS A KID, WE CALLED THESE "BUMP BEDS"!
HOW COME?
BONK!
LYNN

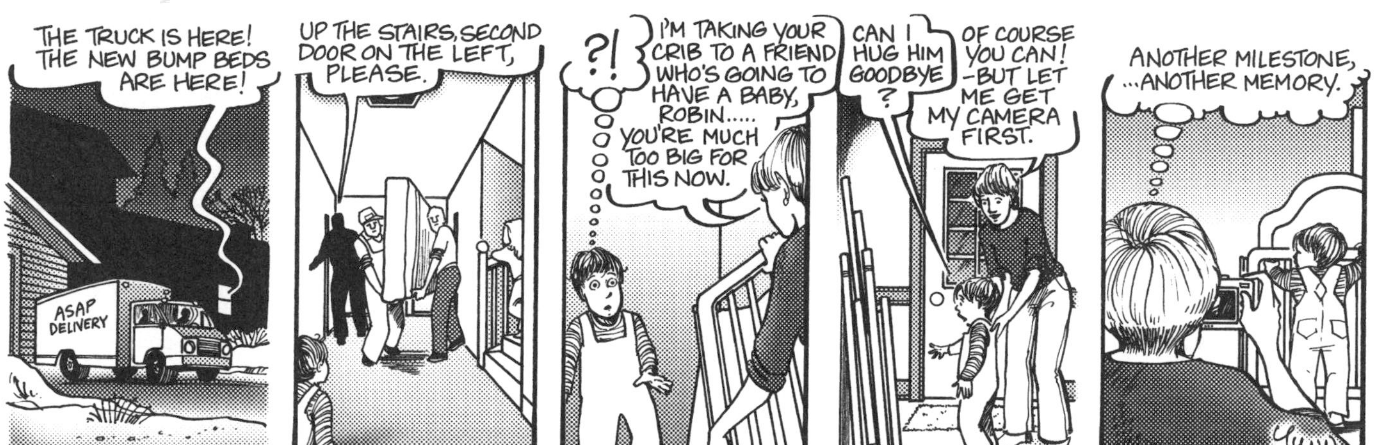
THE TRUCK IS HERE! THE NEW BUMP BEDS ARE HERE!
ASAP DELIVERY
UP THE STAIRS, SECOND DOOR ON THE LEFT, PLEASE.
?!
I'M TAKING YOUR CRIB TO A FRIEND WHO'S GOING TO HAVE A BABY, ROBIN..... YOU'RE MUCH TOO BIG FOR THIS NOW.
CAN I HUG HIM GOODBYE?
OF COURSE YOU CAN! -BUT LET ME GET MY CAMERA FIRST.
ANOTHER MILESTONE, ...ANOTHER MEMORY.
LYNN

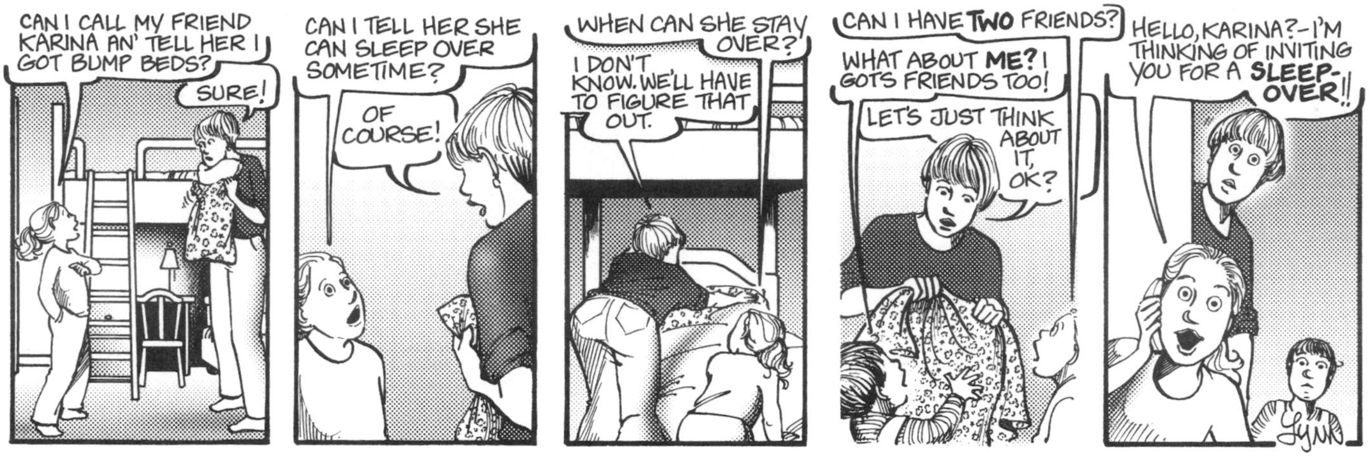
CAN I CALL MY FRIEND KARINA AN' TELL HER I GOT BUMP BEDS?
SURE!
CAN I TELL HER SHE CAN SLEEP OVER SOMETIME?
OF COURSE!
WHEN CAN SHE STAY OVER?
I DON'T KNOW. WE'LL HAVE TO FIGURE THAT OUT.
CAN I HAVE TWO FRIENDS?
WHAT ABOUT ME? I GOTS FRIENDS TOO!
LET'S JUST THINK ABOUT IT, OK?
HELLO, KARINA?– I'M THINKING OF INVITING YOU FOR A SLEEP-OVER!!
LYNN

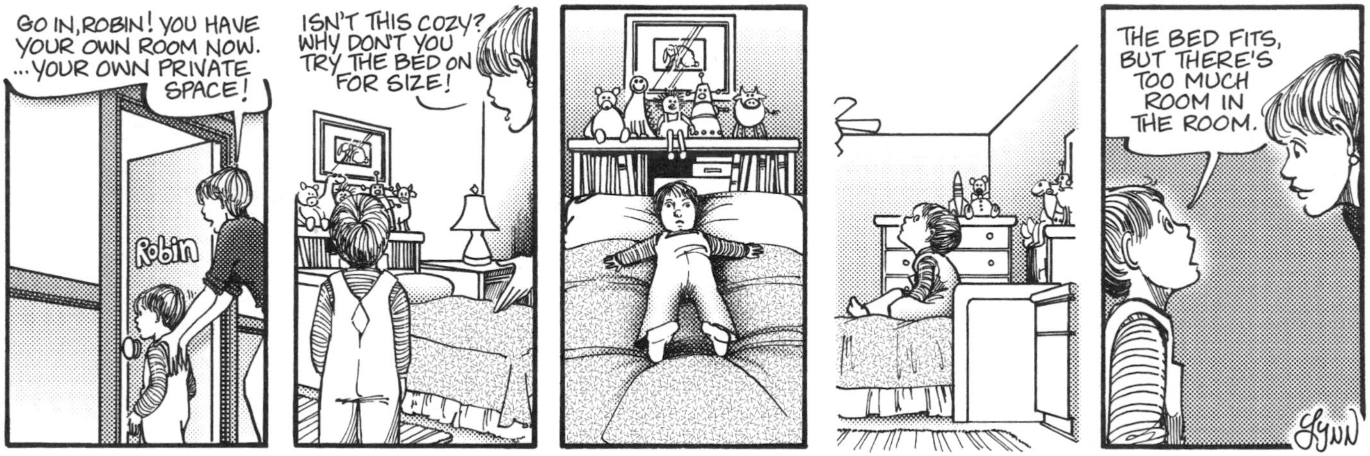
GO IN, ROBIN! YOU HAVE YOUR OWN ROOM NOW. ...YOUR OWN PRIVATE SPACE!
Robin
ISN'T THIS COZY? WHY DON'T YOU TRY THE BED ON FOR SIZE!
THE BED FITS, BUT THERE'S TOO MUCH ROOM IN THE ROOM.
LYNN

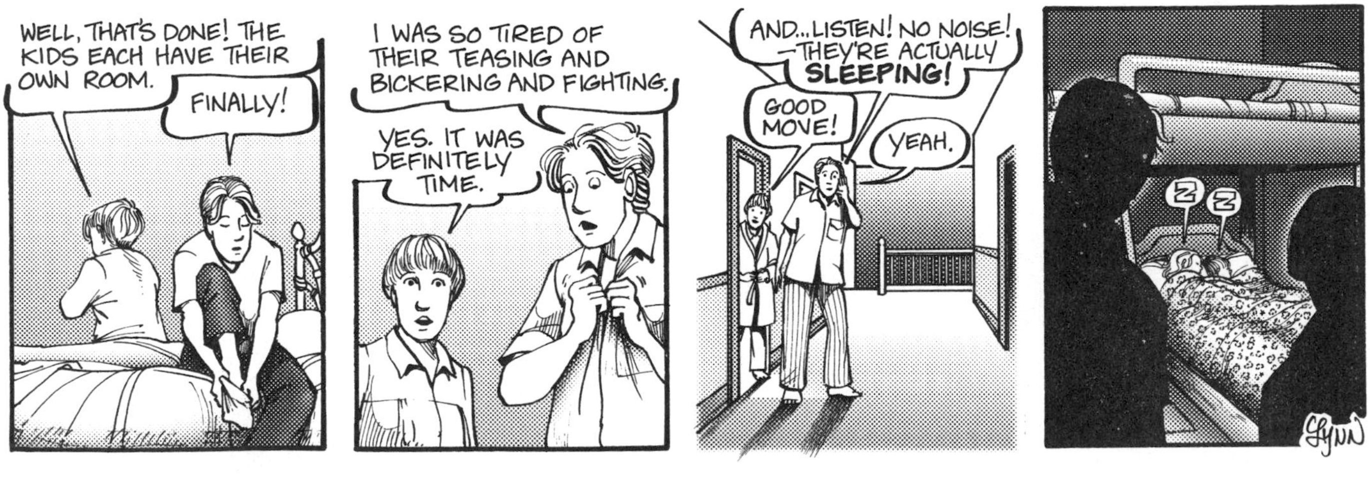
WELL, THAT'S DONE! THE KIDS EACH HAVE THEIR OWN ROOM.
FINALLY!
I WAS SO TIRED OF THEIR TEASING AND BICKERING AND FIGHTING.
YES. IT WAS DEFINITELY TIME.
AND...LISTEN! NO NOISE! –THEY'RE ACTUALLY SLEEPING!
GOOD MOVE!
YEAH.
Z Z
LYNN

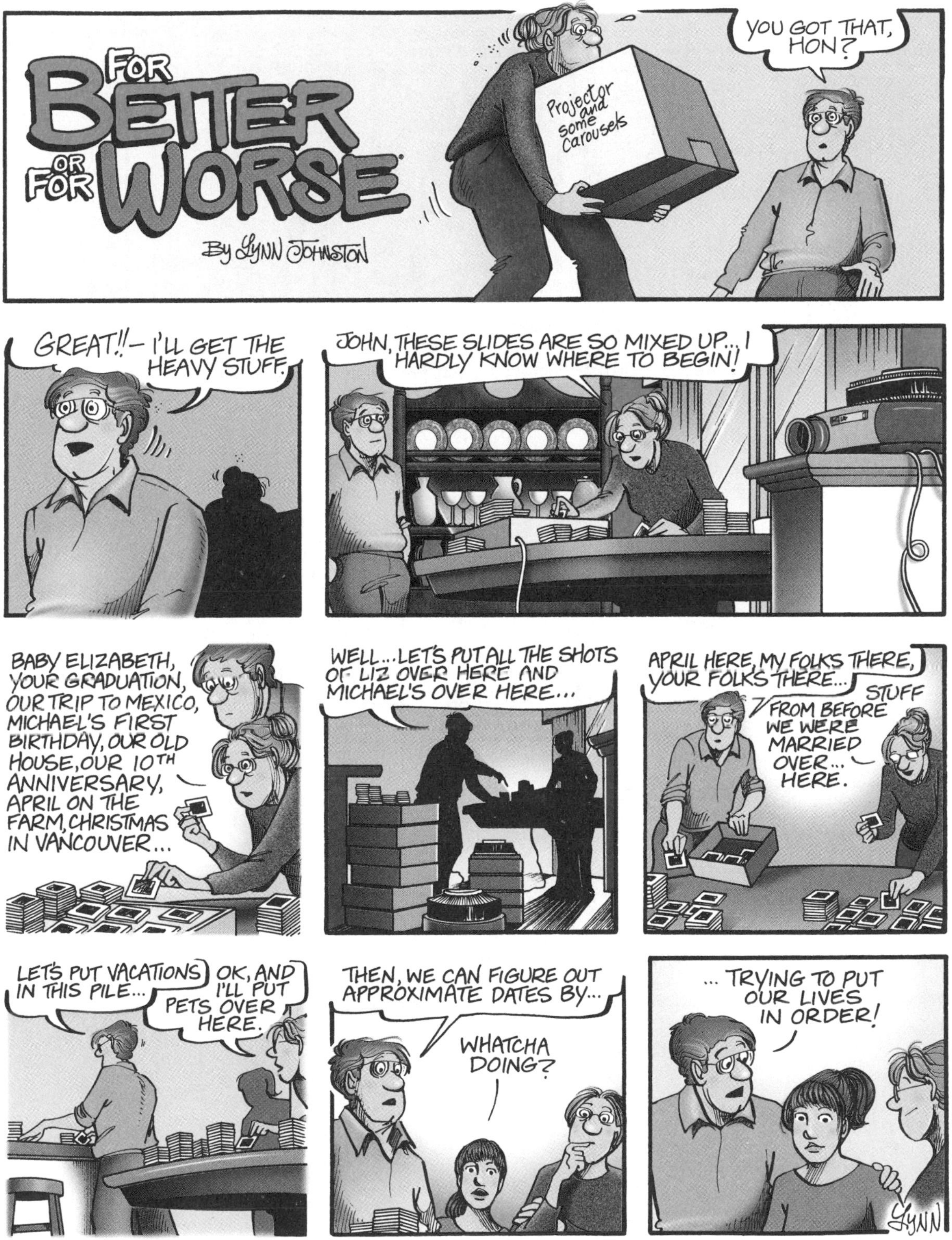

FOR BETTER OR FOR WORSE
BY LYNN JOHNSTON
Projector and some carousels
YOU GOT THAT, HON?
GREAT!!– I'LL GET THE HEAVY STUFF.
JOHN, THESE SLIDES ARE SO MIXED UP... I HARDLY KNOW WHERE TO BEGIN!
BABY ELIZABETH, YOUR GRADUATION, OUR TRIP TO MEXICO, MICHAEL'S FIRST BIRTHDAY, OUR OLD HOUSE, OUR 10TH ANNIVERSARY, APRIL ON THE FARM, CHRISTMAS IN VANCOUVER...
WELL... LET'S PUT ALL THE SHOTS OF LIZ OVER HERE AND MICHAEL'S OVER HERE...
APRIL HERE, MY FOLKS THERE, YOUR FOLKS THERE...
STUFF FROM BEFORE WE WERE MARRIED OVER... HERE.
LET'S PUT VACATIONS IN THIS PILE...
OK, AND I'LL PUT PETS OVER HERE.
THEN, WE CAN FIGURE OUT APPROXIMATE DATES BY...
WHATCHA DOING?
... TRYING TO PUT OUR LIVES IN ORDER!
LYNN

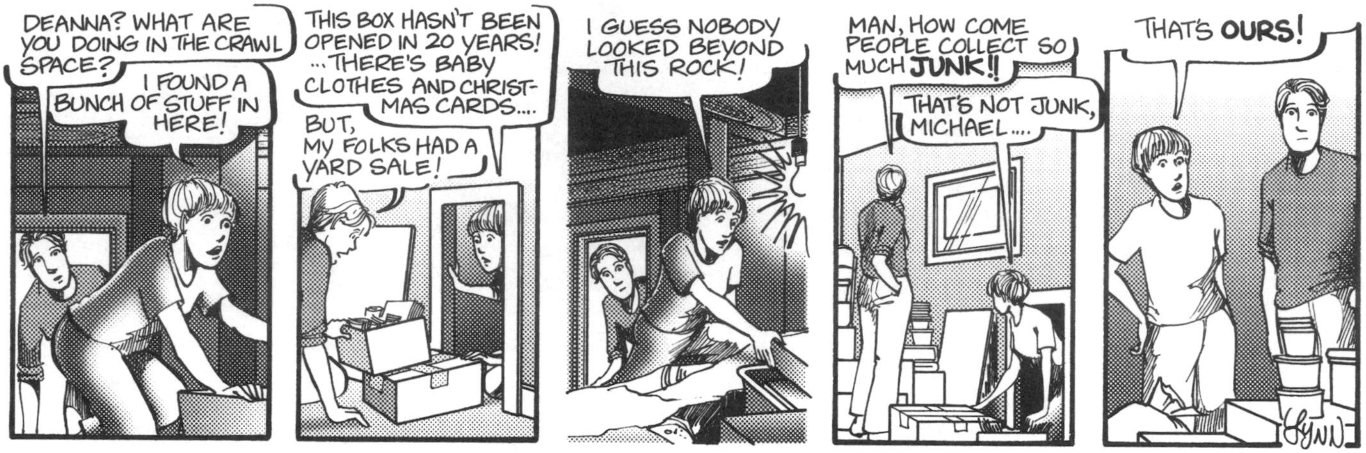
DEANNA? WHAT ARE YOU DOING IN THE CRAWL SPACE?
I FOUND A BUNCH OF STUFF IN HERE!
THIS BOX HASN'T BEEN OPENED IN 20 YEARS! ...THERE'S BABY CLOTHES AND CHRISTMAS CARDS....
BUT, MY FOLKS HAD A YARD SALE!
I GUESS NOBODY LOOKED BEYOND THIS ROCK!
MAN, HOW COME PEOPLE COLLECT SO MUCH **JUNK**!!
THAT'S NOT JUNK, MICHAEL....
THAT'S **OURS**!

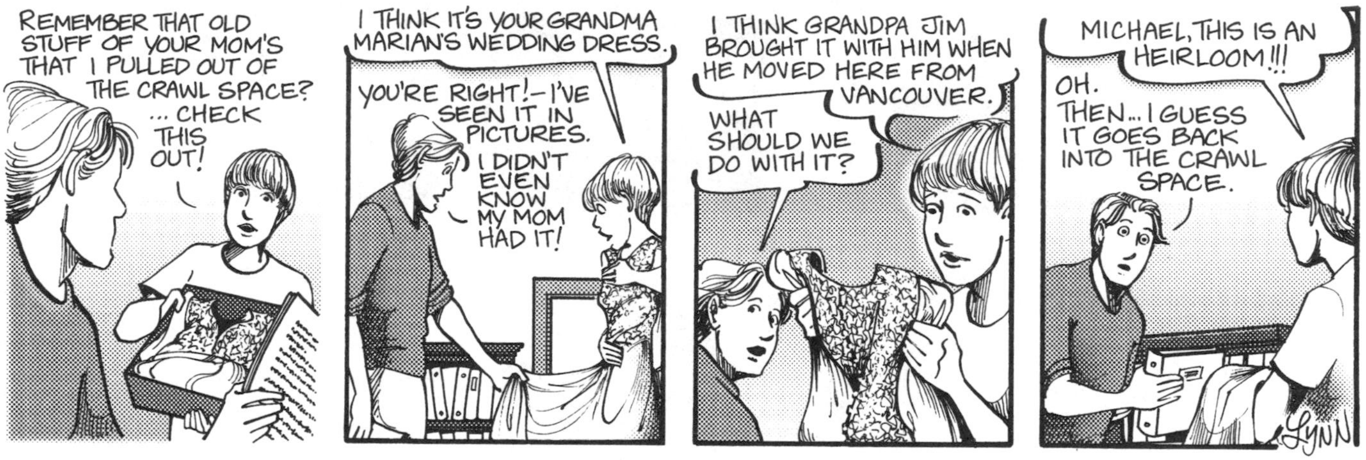
REMEMBER THAT OLD STUFF OF YOUR MOM'S THAT I PULLED OUT OF THE CRAWL SPACE? ... CHECK THIS OUT!
I THINK IT'S YOUR GRANDMA MARIAN'S WEDDING DRESS.
YOU'RE RIGHT! – I'VE SEEN IT IN PICTURES.
I DIDN'T EVEN KNOW MY MOM HAD IT!
I THINK GRANDPA JIM BROUGHT IT WITH HIM WHEN HE MOVED HERE FROM VANCOUVER.
WHAT SHOULD WE DO WITH IT?
MICHAEL, THIS IS AN HEIRLOOM!!!
OH. THEN... I GUESS IT GOES BACK INTO THE CRAWL SPACE.

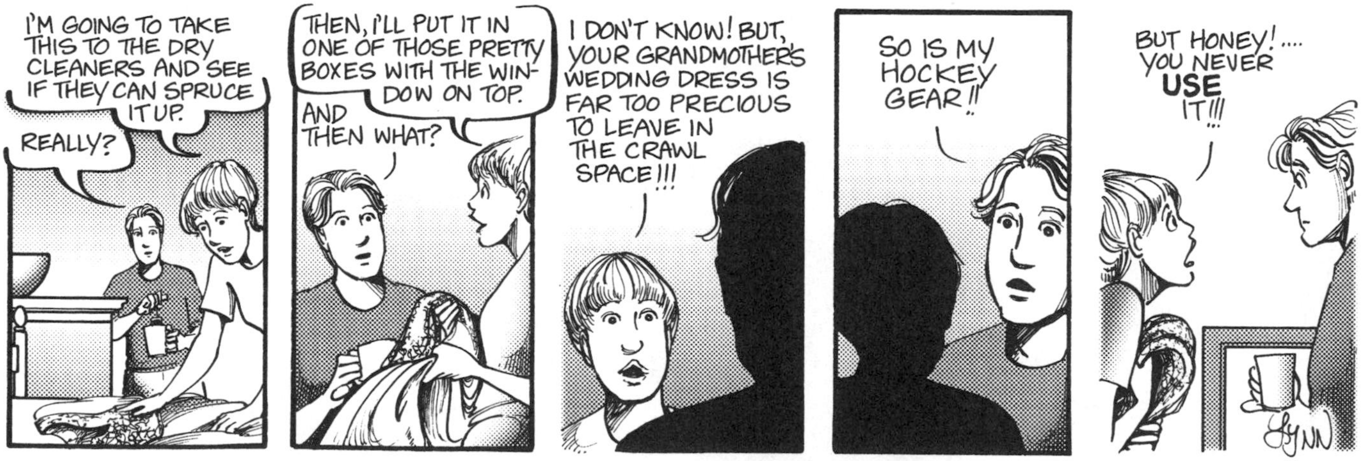
I'M GOING TO TAKE THIS TO THE DRY CLEANERS AND SEE IF THEY CAN SPRUCE IT UP.
REALLY?
THEN, I'LL PUT IT IN ONE OF THOSE PRETTY BOXES WITH THE WINDOW ON TOP.
AND THEN WHAT?
I DON'T KNOW! BUT, YOUR GRANDMOTHER'S WEDDING DRESS IS FAR TOO PRECIOUS TO LEAVE IN THE CRAWL SPACE!!!
SO IS MY HOCKEY GEAR!!
BUT HONEY!.... YOU NEVER **USE** IT!!!

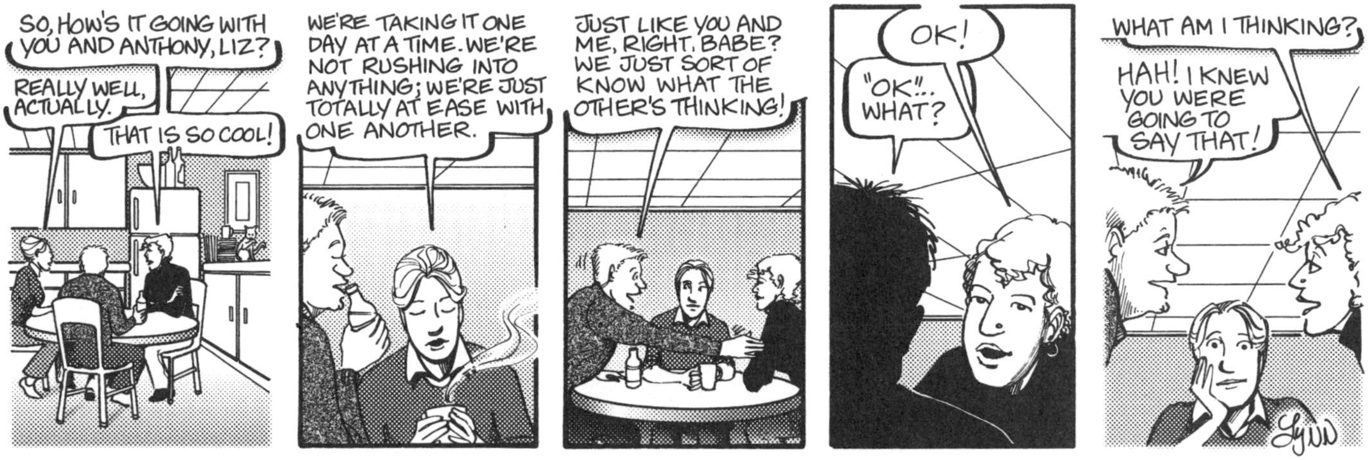
SO, HOW'S IT GOING WITH YOU AND ANTHONY, LIZ?
REALLY WELL, ACTUALLY.
THAT IS SO COOL!
WE'RE TAKING IT ONE DAY AT A TIME. WE'RE NOT RUSHING INTO ANYTHING; WE'RE JUST TOTALLY AT EASE WITH ONE ANOTHER.
JUST LIKE YOU AND ME, RIGHT, BABE? WE JUST SORT OF KNOW WHAT THE OTHER'S THINKING!
OK!
"OK!".. WHAT?
WHAT AM I THINKING?
HAH! I KNEW YOU WERE GOING TO SAY THAT!
Lynn

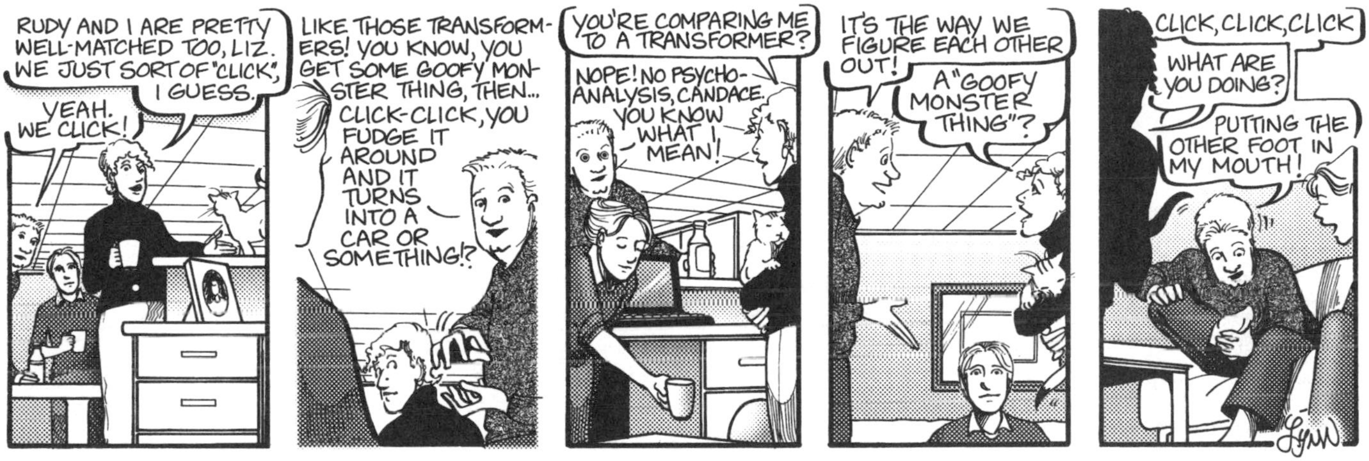
RUDY AND I ARE PRETTY WELL-MATCHED TOO, LIZ. WE JUST SORT OF "CLICK", I GUESS.
YEAH. WE CLICK!
LIKE THOSE TRANSFORMERS! YOU KNOW, YOU GET SOME GOOFY MONSTER THING, THEN... CLICK-CLICK, YOU FUDGE IT AROUND AND IT TURNS INTO A CAR OR SOMETHING!?
YOU'RE COMPARING ME TO A TRANSFORMER?
NOPE! NO PSYCHO-ANALYSIS, CANDACE. YOU KNOW WHAT I MEAN!
IT'S THE WAY WE FIGURE EACH OTHER OUT!
A "GOOFY MONSTER THING"?
CLICK, CLICK, CLICK
WHAT ARE YOU DOING?
PUTTING THE OTHER FOOT IN MY MOUTH!
Lynn

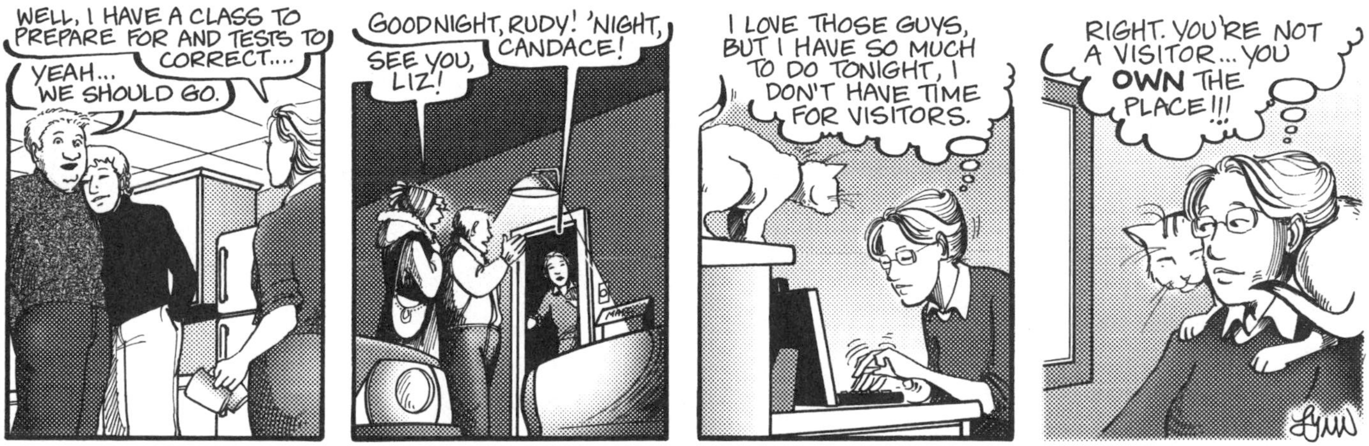
WELL, I HAVE A CLASS TO PREPARE FOR AND TESTS TO CORRECT....
YEAH... WE SHOULD GO.
GOODNIGHT, RUDY! 'NIGHT, CANDACE!
SEE YOU, LIZ!
I LOVE THOSE GUYS, BUT I HAVE SO MUCH TO DO TONIGHT, I DON'T HAVE TIME FOR VISITORS.
RIGHT. YOU'RE NOT A VISITOR... YOU **OWN** THE PLACE!!!
Lynn

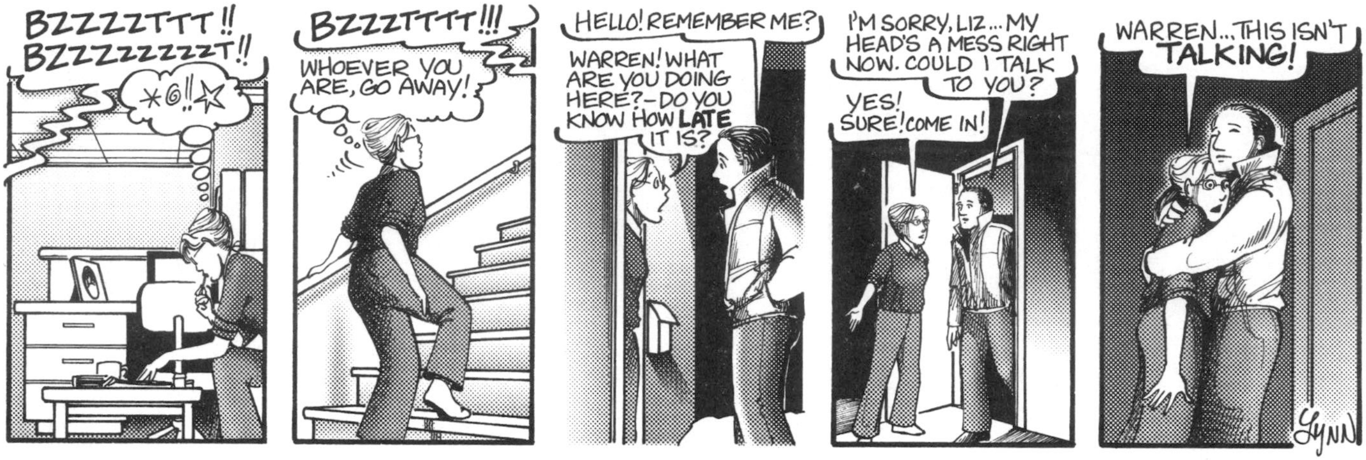
BZZZZTTT!! BZZZZZZZZT!!
*@!!☆
BZZZTTTT!!!
WHOEVER YOU ARE, GO AWAY!
HELLO! REMEMBER ME?
WARREN! WHAT ARE YOU DOING HERE?–DO YOU KNOW HOW **LATE** IT IS?
I'M SORRY, LIZ... MY HEAD'S A MESS RIGHT NOW. COULD I TALK TO YOU?
YES! SURE! COME IN!
WARREN... THIS ISN'T **TALKING!**
LYNN

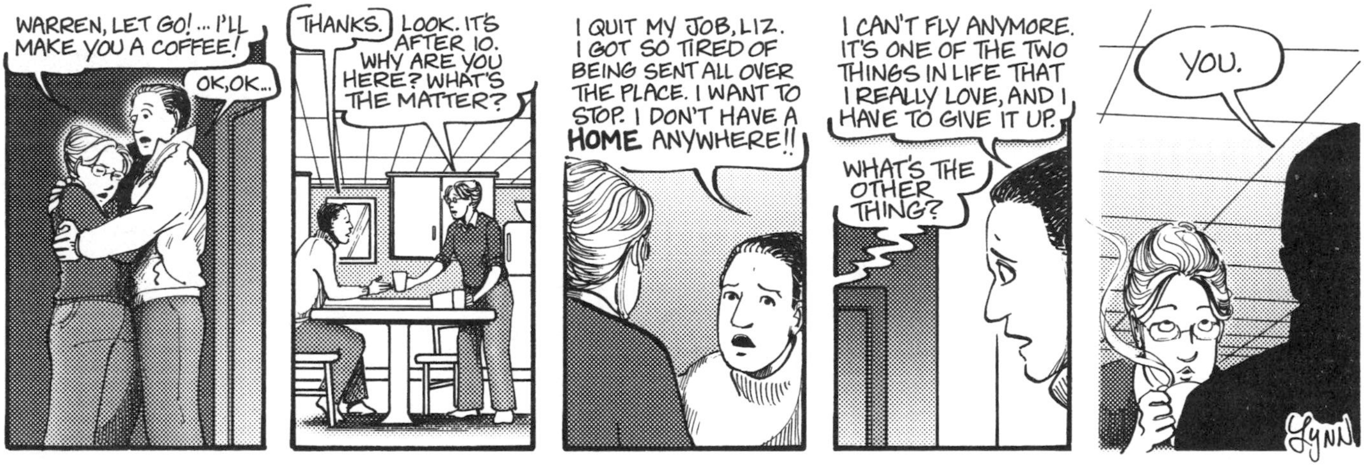
WARREN, LET GO! ... I'LL MAKE YOU A COFFEE!
OK, OK...
THANKS.
LOOK. IT'S AFTER 10. WHY ARE YOU HERE? WHAT'S THE MATTER?
I QUIT MY JOB, LIZ. I GOT SO TIRED OF BEING SENT ALL OVER THE PLACE. I WANT TO STOP. I DON'T HAVE A **HOME** ANYWHERE!!
I CAN'T FLY ANYMORE. IT'S ONE OF THE TWO THINGS IN LIFE THAT I REALLY LOVE, AND I HAVE TO GIVE IT UP.
WHAT'S THE OTHER THING?
YOU.
LYNN

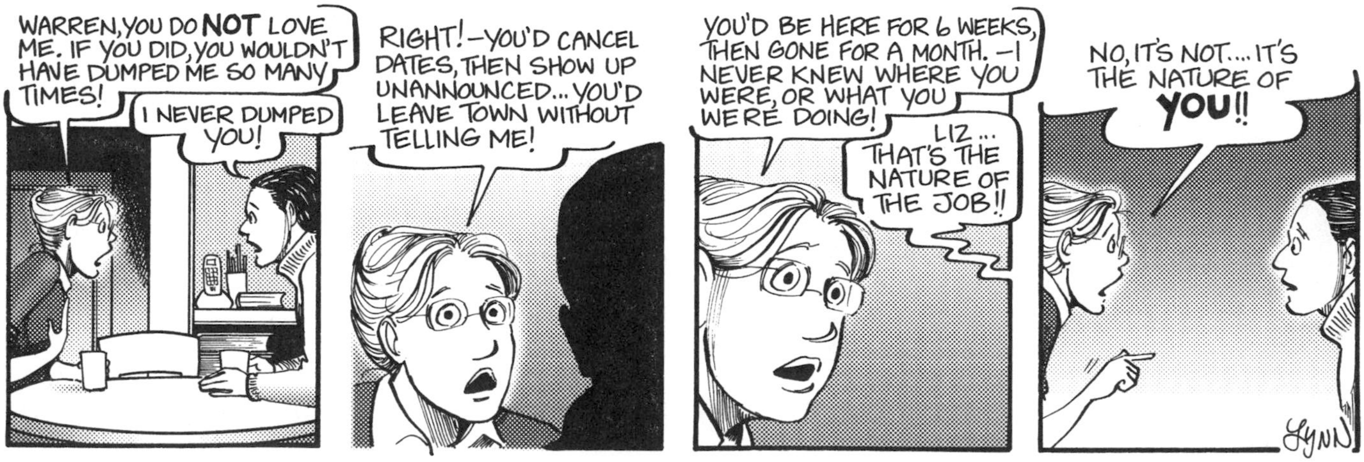
WARREN, YOU DO **NOT** LOVE ME. IF YOU DID, YOU WOULDN'T HAVE DUMPED ME SO MANY TIMES!
I NEVER DUMPED YOU!
RIGHT! –YOU'D CANCEL DATES, THEN SHOW UP UNANNOUNCED... YOU'D LEAVE TOWN WITHOUT TELLING ME!
YOU'D BE HERE FOR 6 WEEKS, THEN GONE FOR A MONTH. –I NEVER KNEW WHERE YOU WERE, OR WHAT YOU WERE DOING!
LIZ... THAT'S THE NATURE OF THE JOB!!
NO, IT'S NOT.... IT'S THE NATURE OF **YOU!!**
LYNN

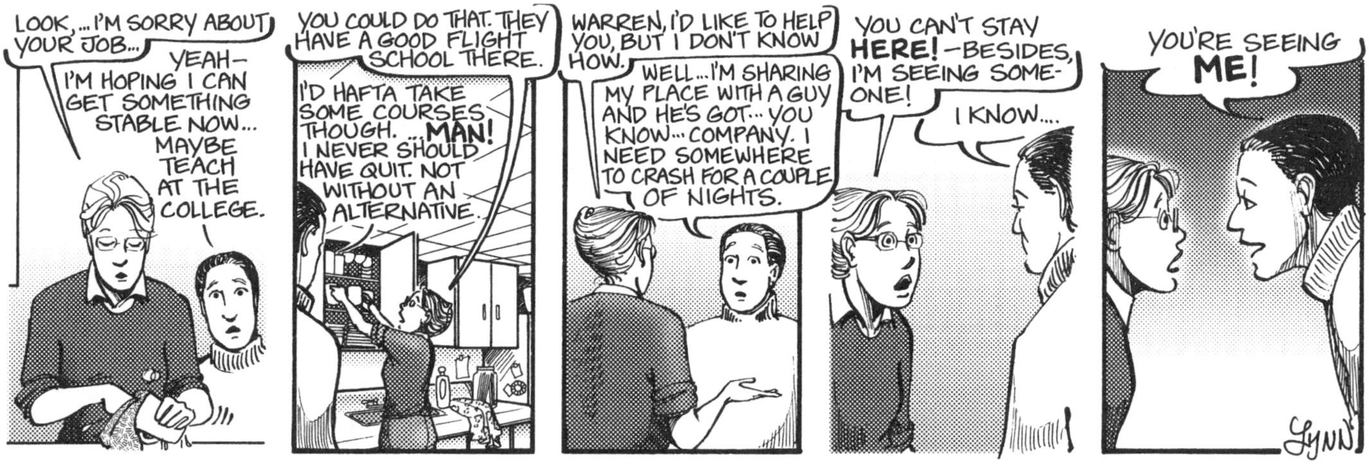
LOOK, ... I'M SORRY ABOUT YOUR JOB...
YEAH– I'M HOPING I CAN GET SOMETHING STABLE NOW... MAYBE TEACH AT THE COLLEGE.
YOU COULD DO THAT. THEY HAVE A GOOD FLIGHT SCHOOL THERE.
I'D HAFTA TAKE SOME COURSES THOUGH. ...**MAN!** I NEVER SHOULD HAVE QUIT. NOT WITHOUT AN ALTERNATIVE.
WARREN, I'D LIKE TO HELP YOU, BUT I DON'T KNOW HOW.
WELL... I'M SHARING MY PLACE WITH A GUY AND HE'S GOT... YOU KNOW... COMPANY. I NEED SOMEWHERE TO CRASH FOR A COUPLE OF NIGHTS.
YOU CAN'T STAY **HERE!** –BESIDES, I'M SEEING SOME-ONE!
I KNOW....
YOU'RE SEEING **ME!**
LYNN

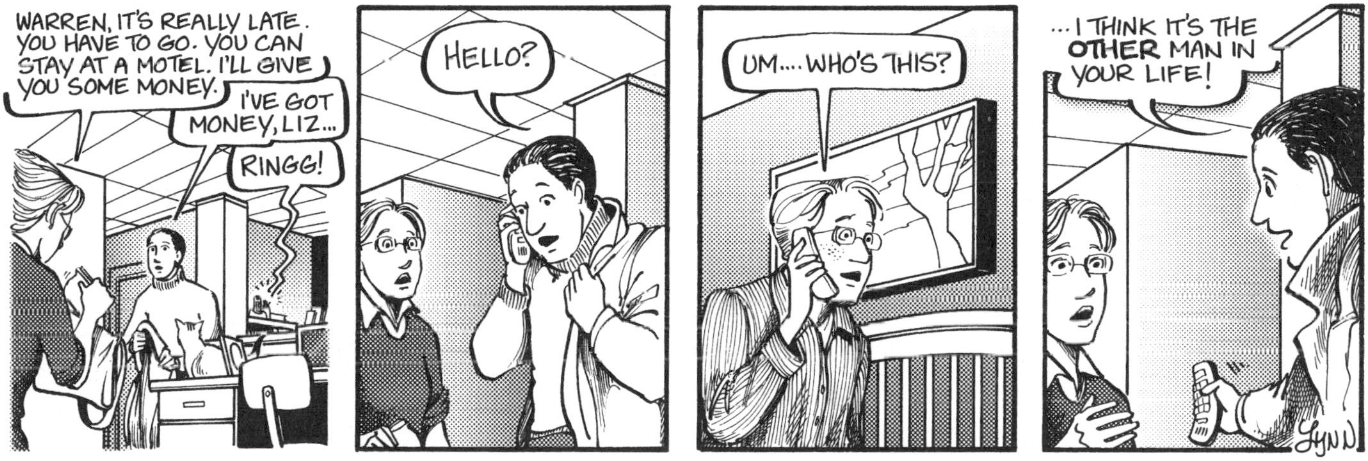
WARREN, IT'S REALLY LATE. YOU HAVE TO GO. YOU CAN STAY AT A MOTEL. I'LL GIVE YOU SOME MONEY.
I'VE GOT MONEY, LIZ...
RINGG!
HELLO?
UM.... WHO'S THIS?
... I THINK IT'S THE **OTHER** MAN IN YOUR LIFE!
LYNN

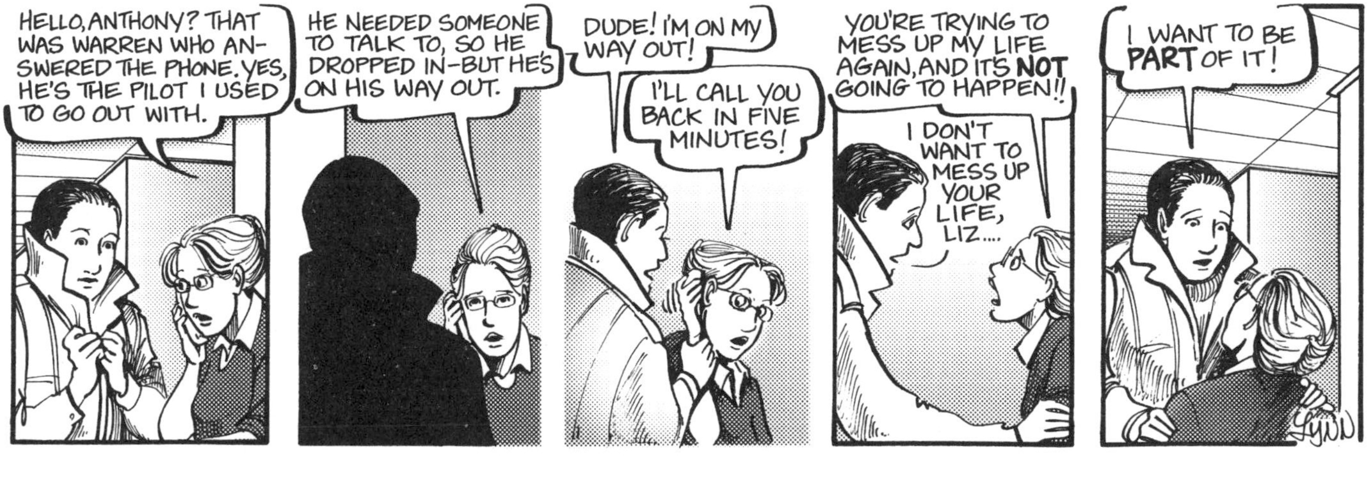
HELLO, ANTHONY? THAT WAS WARREN WHO AN-SWERED THE PHONE. YES, HE'S THE PILOT I USED TO GO OUT WITH.
HE NEEDED SOMEONE TO TALK TO, SO HE DROPPED IN–BUT HE'S ON HIS WAY OUT.
DUDE! I'M ON MY WAY OUT!
I'LL CALL YOU BACK IN FIVE MINUTES!
YOU'RE TRYING TO MESS UP MY LIFE AGAIN, AND IT'S **NOT** GOING TO HAPPEN!!
I DON'T WANT TO MESS UP YOUR LIFE, LIZ....
I WANT TO BE **PART** OF IT!
LYNN

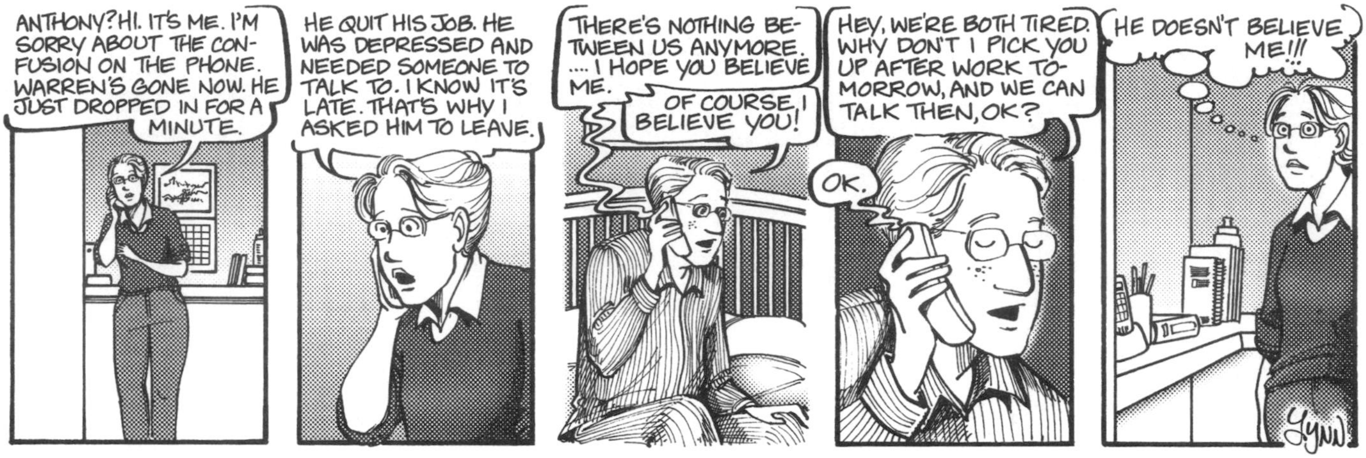
ANTHONY? HI. IT'S ME. I'M SORRY ABOUT THE CON-FUSION ON THE PHONE. WARREN'S GONE NOW. HE JUST DROPPED IN FOR A MINUTE.
HE QUIT HIS JOB. HE WAS DEPRESSED AND NEEDED SOMEONE TO TALK TO. I KNOW IT'S LATE. THAT'S WHY I ASKED HIM TO LEAVE.
THERE'S NOTHING BE-TWEEN US ANYMORE. .... I HOPE YOU BELIEVE ME.
OF COURSE, I BELIEVE YOU!
HEY, WE'RE BOTH TIRED. WHY DON'T I PICK YOU UP AFTER WORK TO-MORROW, AND WE CAN TALK THEN, OK?
OK.
HE DOESN'T BELIEVE ME!!!

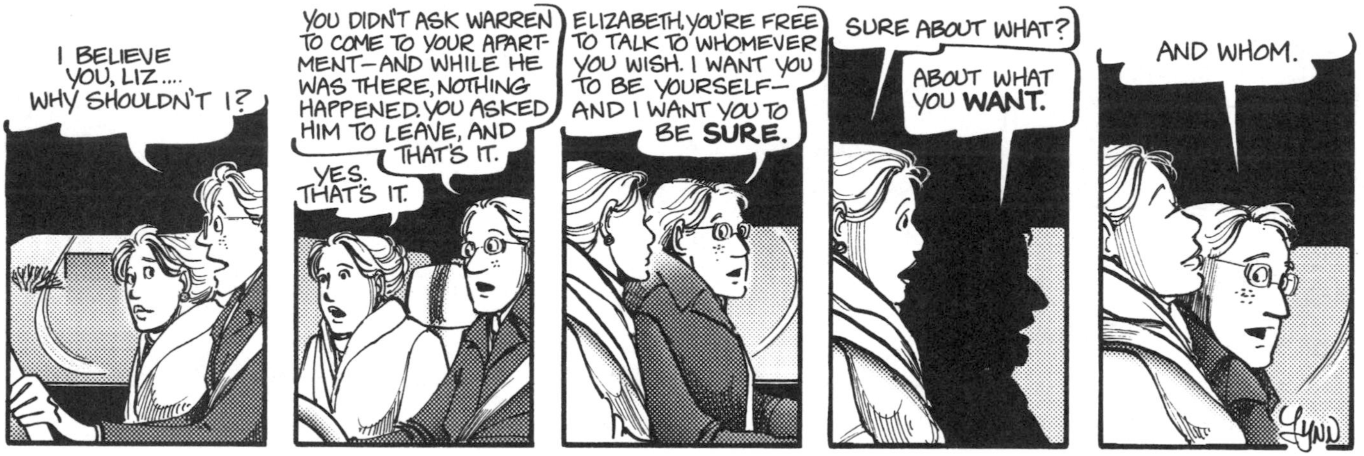
I BELIEVE YOU, LIZ.... WHY SHOULDN'T I?
YOU DIDN'T ASK WARREN TO COME TO YOUR APART-MENT—AND WHILE HE WAS THERE, NOTHING HAPPENED. YOU ASKED HIM TO LEAVE, AND THAT'S IT.
YES. THAT'S IT.
ELIZABETH, YOU'RE FREE TO TALK TO WHOMEVER YOU WISH. I WANT YOU TO BE YOURSELF— AND I WANT YOU TO BE **SURE.**
SURE ABOUT WHAT?
ABOUT WHAT YOU **WANT.**
AND WHOM.

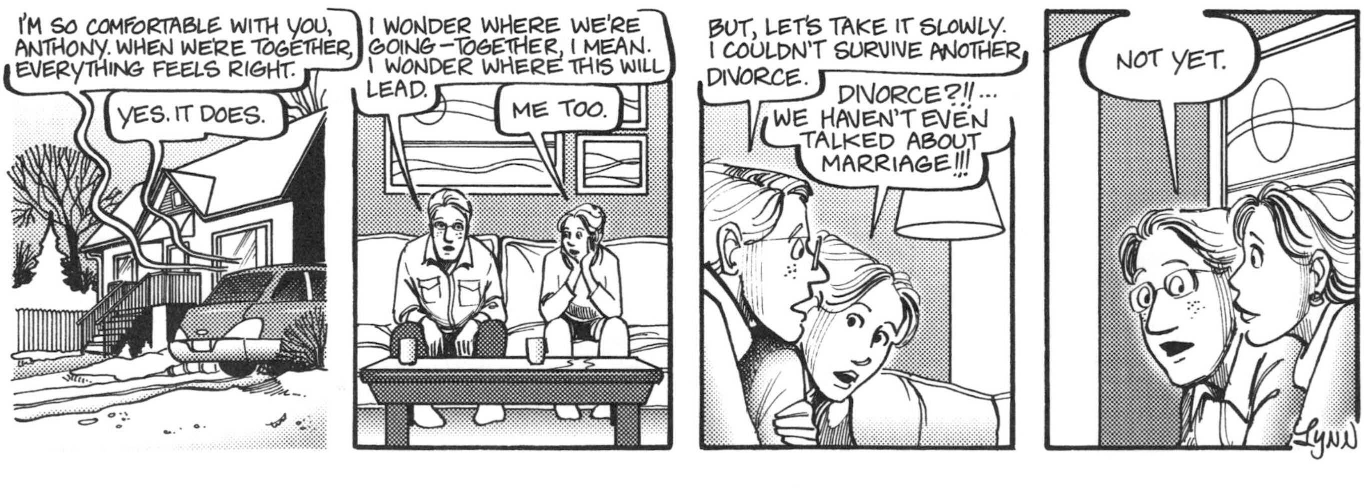
I'M SO COMFORTABLE WITH YOU, ANTHONY. WHEN WE'RE TOGETHER, EVERYTHING FEELS RIGHT.
YES. IT DOES.
I WONDER WHERE WE'RE GOING—TOGETHER, I MEAN. I WONDER WHERE THIS WILL LEAD.
ME TOO.
BUT, LET'S TAKE IT SLOWLY. I COULDN'T SURVIVE ANOTHER DIVORCE.
DIVORCE?!!... WE HAVEN'T EVEN TALKED ABOUT MARRIAGE!!!
NOT YET.

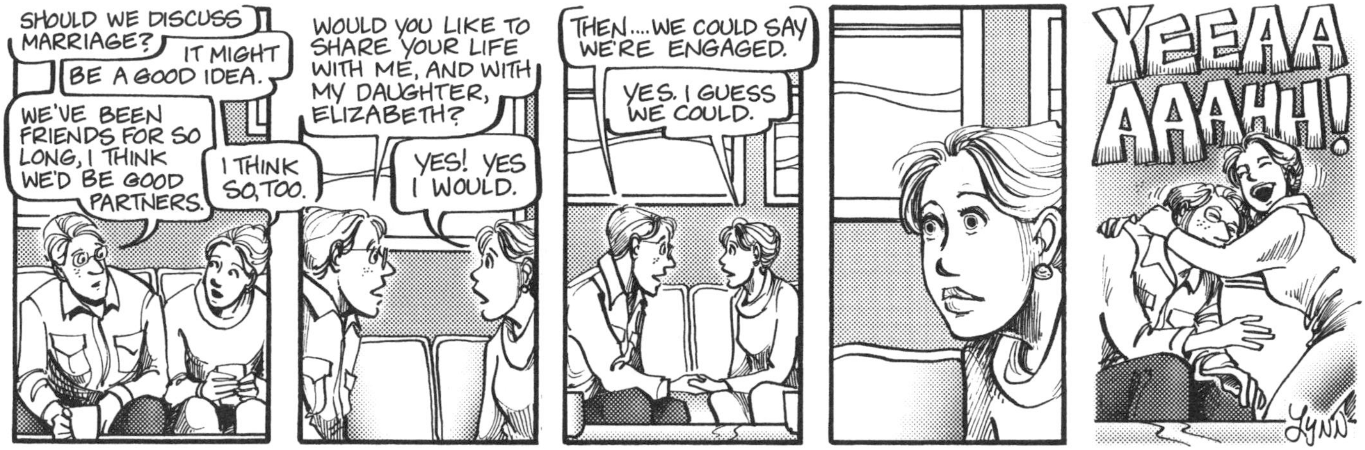
SHOULD WE DISCUSS MARRIAGE?
IT MIGHT BE A GOOD IDEA.
WE'VE BEEN FRIENDS FOR SO LONG, I THINK WE'D BE GOOD PARTNERS.
I THINK SO, TOO.
WOULD YOU LIKE TO SHARE YOUR LIFE WITH ME, AND WITH MY DAUGHTER, ELIZABETH?
YES! YES I WOULD.
THEN.... WE COULD SAY WE'RE ENGAGED.
YES. I GUESS WE COULD.
YEEAA AAAHH!
LYNN

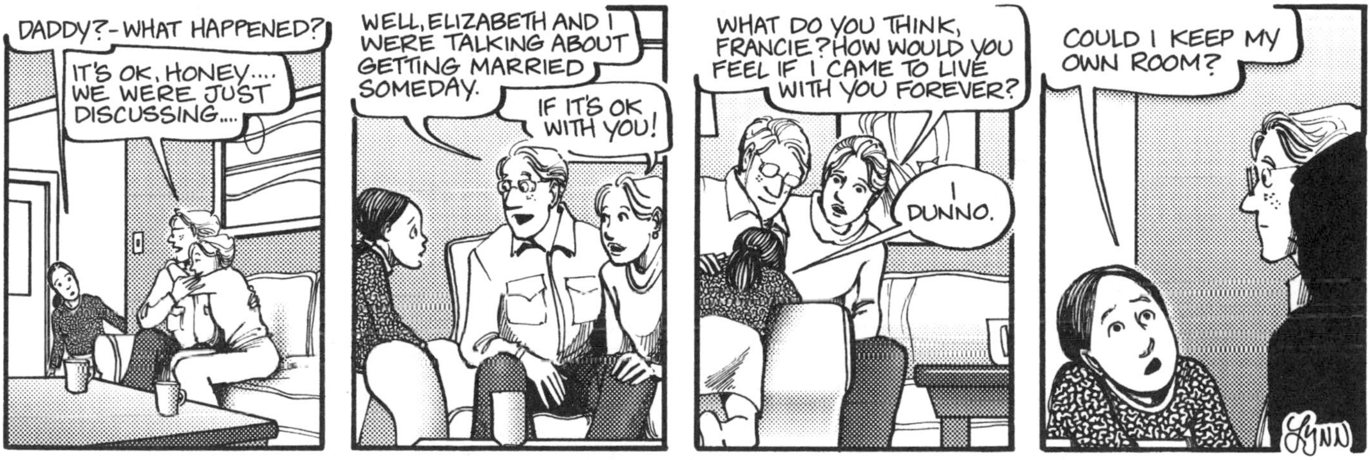
DADDY?- WHAT HAPPENED?
IT'S OK, HONEY.... WE WERE JUST DISCUSSING....
WELL, ELIZABETH AND I WERE TALKING ABOUT GETTING MARRIED SOMEDAY.
IF IT'S OK WITH YOU!
WHAT DO YOU THINK, FRANCIE? HOW WOULD YOU FEEL IF I CAME TO LIVE WITH YOU FOREVER?
I DUNNO.
COULD I KEEP MY OWN ROOM?
LYNN

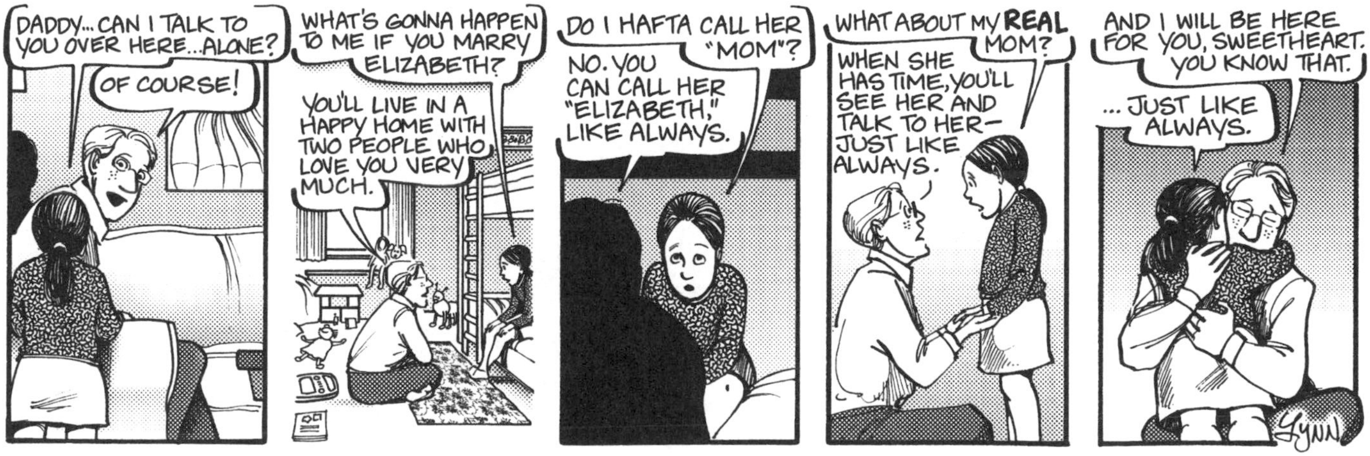
DADDY... CAN I TALK TO YOU OVER HERE... ALONE?
OF COURSE!
WHAT'S GONNA HAPPEN TO ME IF YOU MARRY ELIZABETH?
YOU'LL LIVE IN A HAPPY HOME WITH TWO PEOPLE WHO LOVE YOU VERY MUCH.
DO I HAFTA CALL HER "MOM"?
NO. YOU CAN CALL HER "ELIZABETH," LIKE ALWAYS.
WHAT ABOUT MY **REAL** MOM?
WHEN SHE HAS TIME, YOU'LL SEE HER AND TALK TO HER— JUST LIKE ALWAYS.
AND I WILL BE HERE FOR YOU, SWEETHEART. YOU KNOW THAT.
... JUST LIKE ALWAYS.
LYNN

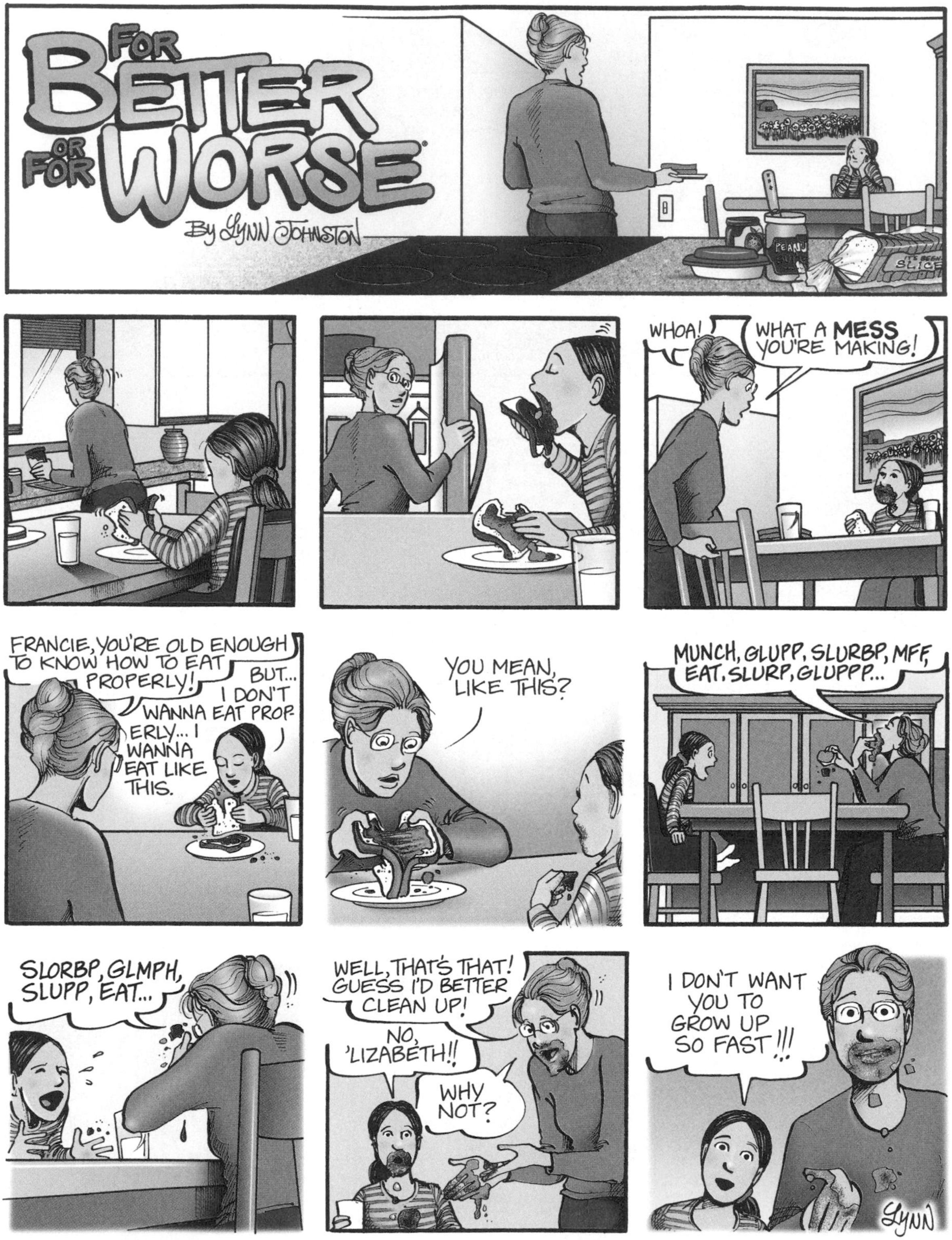
FOR BETTER OR FOR WORSE
By Lynn Johnston
WHOA!
WHAT A MESS YOU'RE MAKING!
FRANCIE, YOU'RE OLD ENOUGH TO KNOW HOW TO EAT PROPERLY!
BUT... I DON'T WANNA EAT PROPERLY... I WANNA EAT LIKE THIS.
YOU MEAN, LIKE THIS?
MUNCH, GLUPP, SLURBP, MFF, EAT, SLURP, GLUPPP...
SLORBP, GLMPH, SLUPP, EAT...
WELL, THAT'S THAT! GUESS I'D BETTER CLEAN UP!
NO, 'LIZABETH!!
WHY NOT?
I DON'T WANT YOU TO GROW UP SO FAST!!!
LYNN

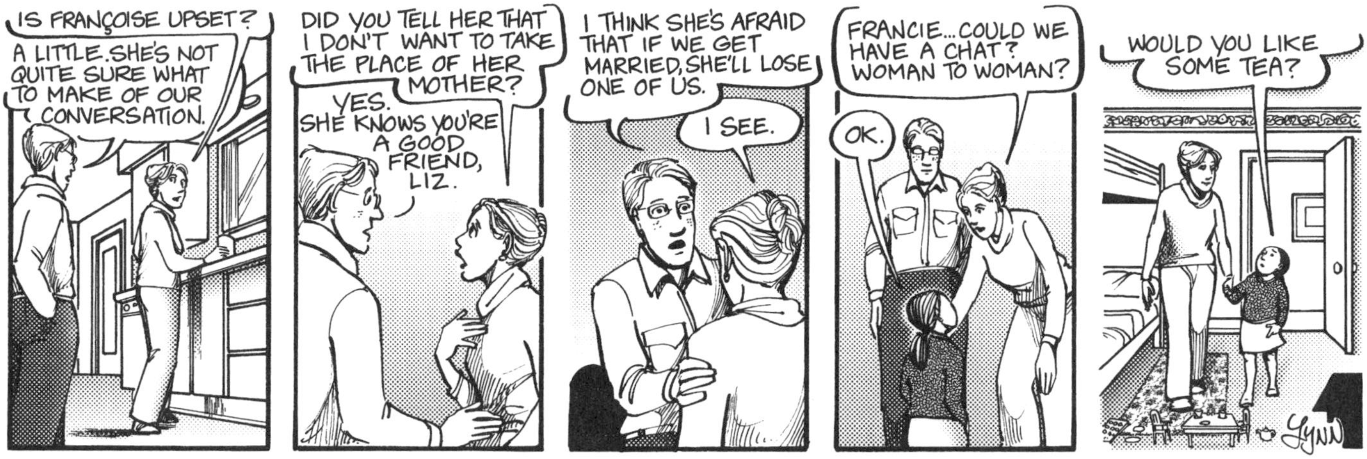
IS FRANÇOISE UPSET?
A LITTLE. SHE'S NOT QUITE SURE WHAT TO MAKE OF OUR CONVERSATION.
DID YOU TELL HER THAT I DON'T WANT TO TAKE THE PLACE OF HER MOTHER?
YES. SHE KNOWS YOU'RE A GOOD FRIEND, LIZ.
I THINK SHE'S AFRAID THAT IF WE GET MARRIED, SHE'LL LOSE ONE OF US.
I SEE.
FRANCIE... COULD WE HAVE A CHAT? WOMAN TO WOMAN?
OK.
WOULD YOU LIKE SOME TEA?
Lynn

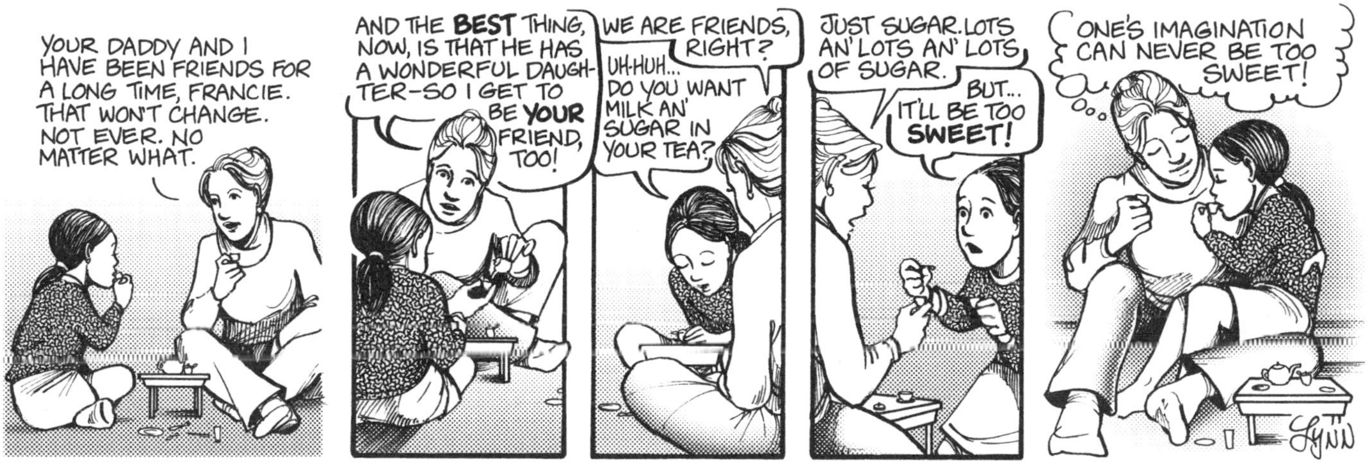
YOUR DADDY AND I HAVE BEEN FRIENDS FOR A LONG TIME, FRANCIE. THAT WON'T CHANGE. NOT EVER. NO MATTER WHAT.
AND THE BEST THING, NOW, IS THAT HE HAS A WONDERFUL DAUGHTER–SO I GET TO BE YOUR FRIEND, TOO!
WE ARE FRIENDS, RIGHT?
UH-HUH... DO YOU WANT MILK AN' SUGAR IN YOUR TEA?
JUST SUGAR. LOTS AN' LOTS AN' LOTS OF SUGAR.
BUT... IT'LL BE TOO SWEET!
ONE'S IMAGINATION CAN NEVER BE TOO SWEET!
Lynn

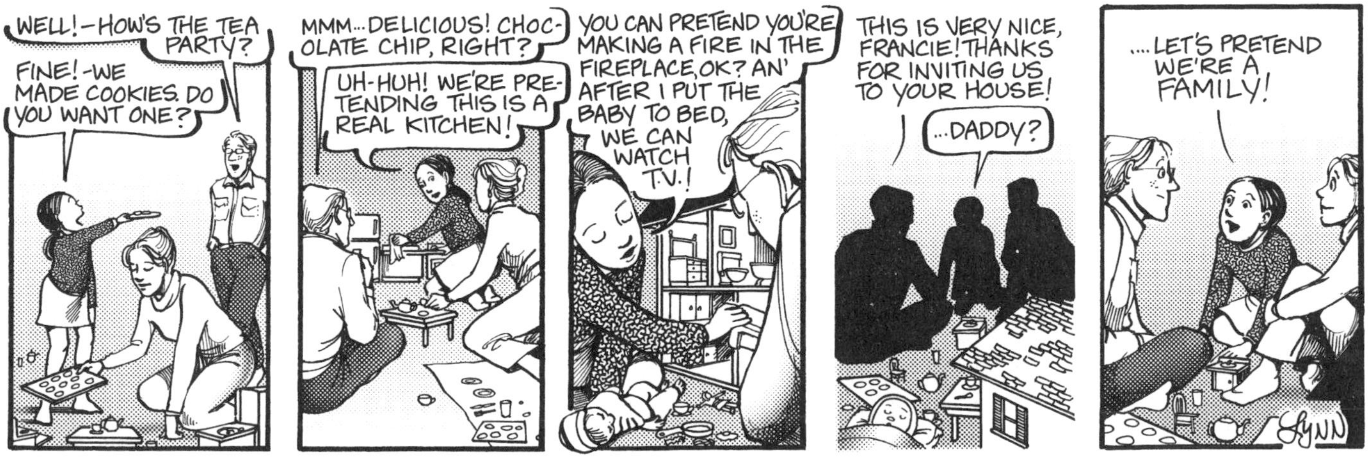
WELL! –HOW'S THE TEA PARTY?
FINE! –WE MADE COOKIES. DO YOU WANT ONE?
MMM... DELICIOUS! CHOCOLATE CHIP, RIGHT?
UH-HUH! WE'RE PRETENDING THIS IS A REAL KITCHEN!
YOU CAN PRETEND YOU'RE MAKING A FIRE IN THE FIREPLACE, OK? AN' AFTER I PUT THE BABY TO BED, WE CAN WATCH T.V.!
THIS IS VERY NICE, FRANCIE! THANKS FOR INVITING US TO YOUR HOUSE!
...DADDY?
....LET'S PRETEND WE'RE A FAMILY!
Lynn

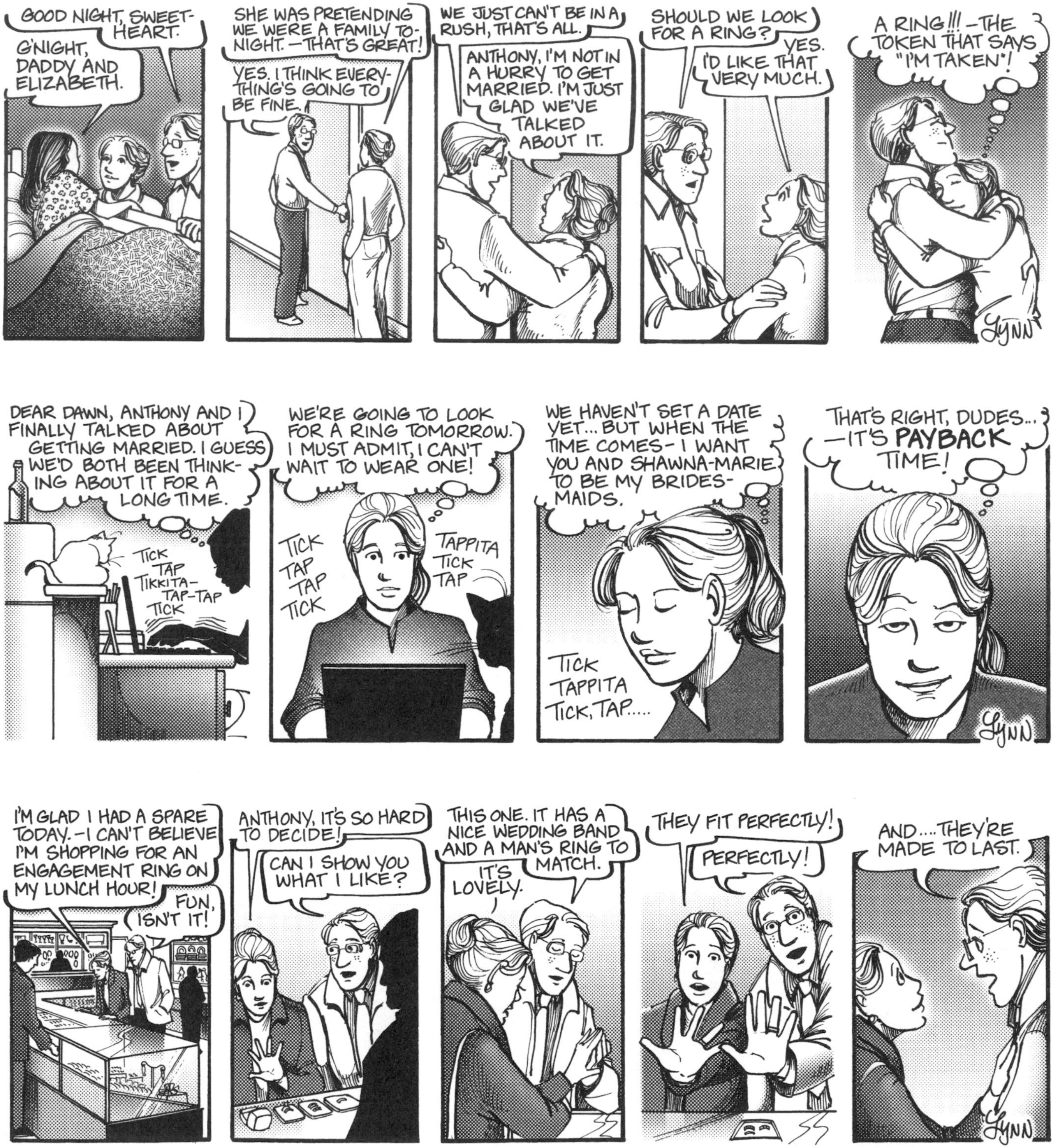
GOOD NIGHT, SWEET-HEART.
G'NIGHT, DADDY AND ELIZABETH.
SHE WAS PRETENDING WE WERE A FAMILY TO-NIGHT. —THAT'S GREAT!
YES. I THINK EVERY-THING'S GOING TO BE FINE.
WE JUST CAN'T BE IN A RUSH, THAT'S ALL.
ANTHONY, I'M NOT IN A HURRY TO GET MARRIED. I'M JUST GLAD WE'VE TALKED ABOUT IT.
SHOULD WE LOOK FOR A RING?
YES. I'D LIKE THAT VERY MUCH.
A RING!!! —THE TOKEN THAT SAYS "I'M TAKEN"!
LYNN
DEAR DAWN, ANTHONY AND I FINALLY TALKED ABOUT GETTING MARRIED. I GUESS WE'D BOTH BEEN THINK-ING ABOUT IT FOR A LONG TIME.
TICK TAP TIKKITA-TAP-TAP TICK
WE'RE GOING TO LOOK FOR A RING TOMORROW. I MUST ADMIT, I CAN'T WAIT TO WEAR ONE!
TICK TAP TAP TICK
TAPPITA TICK TAP
WE HAVEN'T SET A DATE YET... BUT WHEN THE TIME COMES- I WANT YOU AND SHAWNA-MARIE TO BE MY BRIDES-MAIDS.
TICK TAPPITA TICK, TAP.....
THAT'S RIGHT, DUDES... —IT'S PAYBACK TIME!
LYNN
I'M GLAD I HAD A SPARE TODAY. —I CAN'T BELIEVE I'M SHOPPING FOR AN ENGAGEMENT RING ON MY LUNCH HOUR!
FUN, ISN'T IT!
ANTHONY, IT'S SO HARD TO DECIDE!
CAN I SHOW YOU WHAT I LIKE?
THIS ONE. IT HAS A NICE WEDDING BAND AND A MAN'S RING TO MATCH.
IT'S LOVELY.
THEY FIT PERFECTLY!
PERFECTLY!
AND.... THEY'RE MADE TO LAST.
LYNN

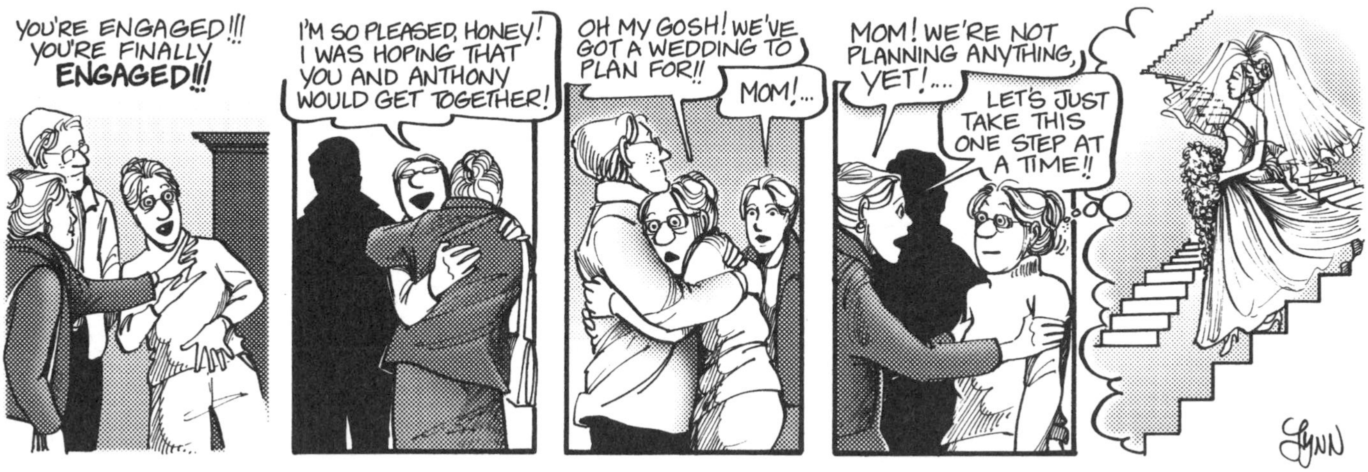
YOU'RE ENGAGED!!! YOU'RE FINALLY ENGAGED!!!
I'M SO PLEASED, HONEY! I WAS HOPING THAT YOU AND ANTHONY WOULD GET TOGETHER!
OH MY GOSH! WE'VE GOT A WEDDING TO PLAN FOR!!
MOM!...
MOM! WE'RE NOT PLANNING ANYTHING, YET!...
LET'S JUST TAKE THIS ONE STEP AT A TIME!!
LYNN

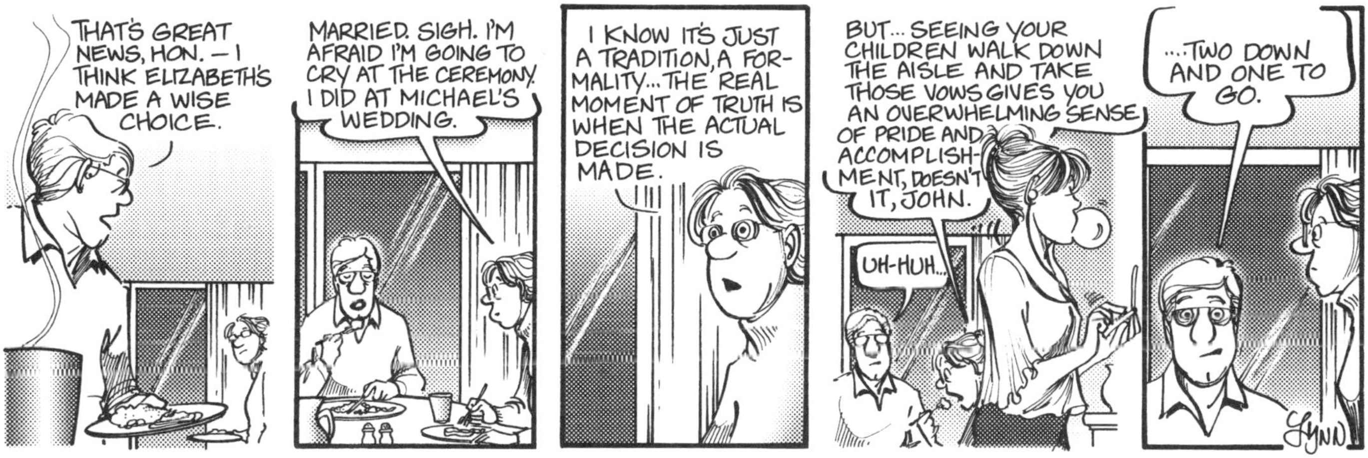
THAT'S GREAT NEWS, HON. – I THINK ELIZABETH'S MADE A WISE CHOICE.
MARRIED. SIGH. I'M AFRAID I'M GOING TO CRY AT THE CEREMONY. I DID AT MICHAEL'S WEDDING.
I KNOW IT'S JUST A TRADITION, A FORMALITY... THE REAL MOMENT OF TRUTH IS WHEN THE ACTUAL DECISION IS MADE.
BUT... SEEING YOUR CHILDREN WALK DOWN THE AISLE AND TAKE THOSE VOWS GIVES YOU AN OVERWHELMING SENSE OF PRIDE AND ACCOMPLISHMENT, DOESN'T IT, JOHN.
UH-HUH...
...TWO DOWN AND ONE TO GO.
LYNN

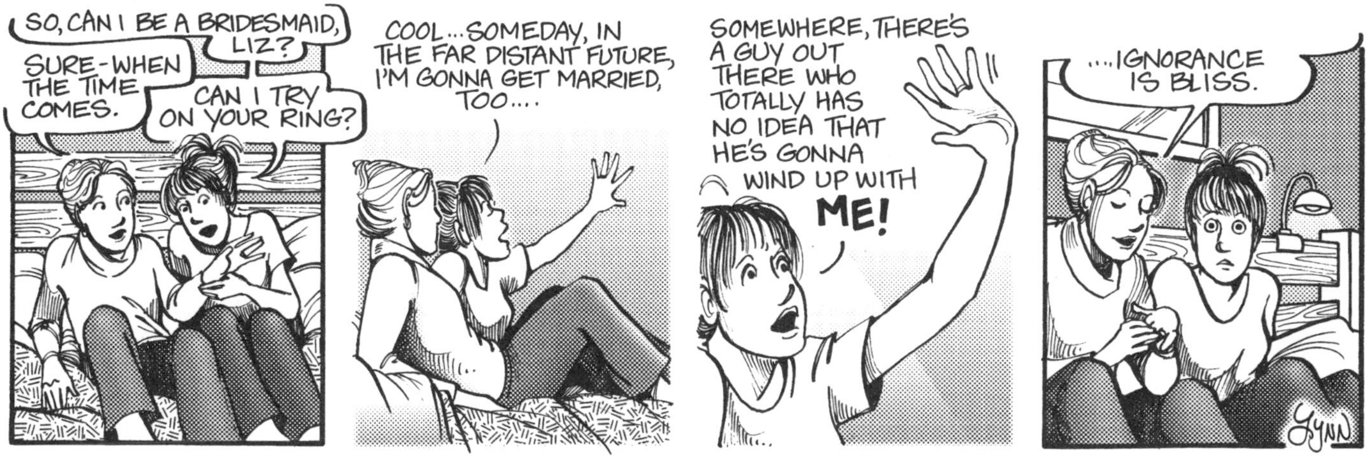
SO, CAN I BE A BRIDESMAID, LIZ?
SURE- WHEN THE TIME COMES.
CAN I TRY ON YOUR RING?
COOL... SOMEDAY, IN THE FAR DISTANT FUTURE, I'M GONNA GET MARRIED, TOO....
SOMEWHERE, THERE'S A GUY OUT THERE WHO TOTALLY HAS NO IDEA THAT HE'S GONNA WIND UP WITH ME!
....IGNORANCE IS BLISS.
LYNN

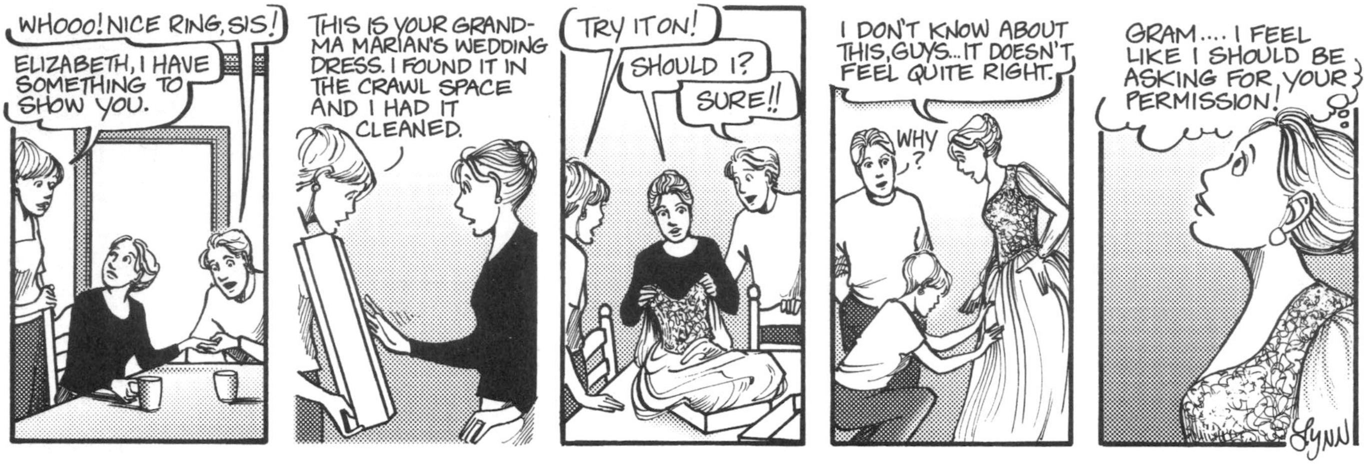
WHOOO! NICE RING, SIS!
ELIZABETH, I HAVE SOMETHING TO SHOW YOU.
THIS IS YOUR GRANDMA MARIAN'S WEDDING DRESS. I FOUND IT IN THE CRAWL SPACE AND I HAD IT CLEANED.
TRY IT ON!
SHOULD I?
SURE!!
I DON'T KNOW ABOUT THIS, GUYS... IT DOESN'T FEEL QUITE RIGHT.
WHY?
GRAM.... I FEEL LIKE I SHOULD BE ASKING FOR YOUR PERMISSION!
LYNN

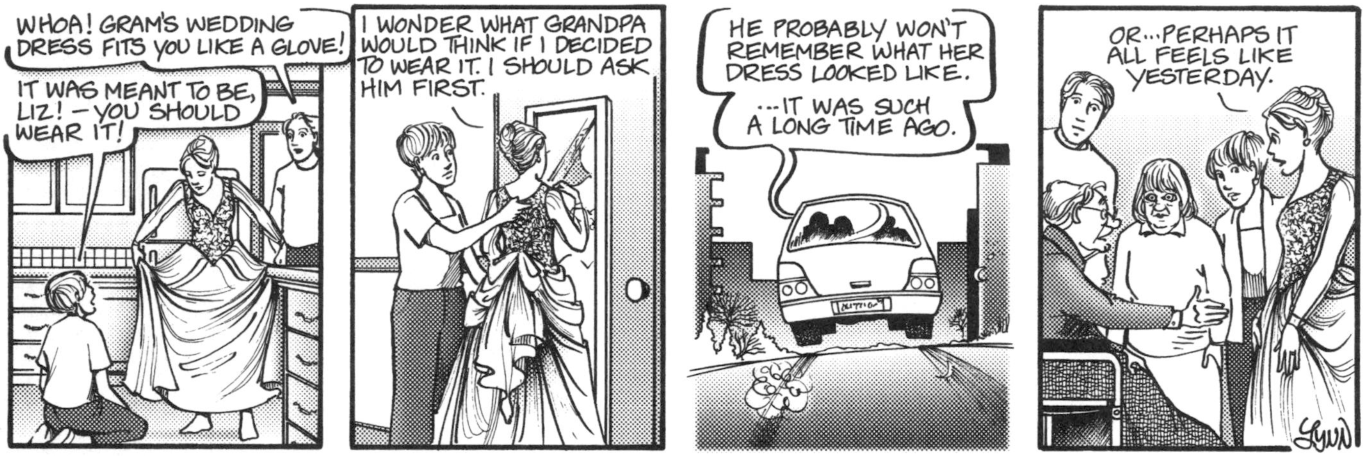
WHOA! GRAM'S WEDDING DRESS FITS YOU LIKE A GLOVE!
IT WAS MEANT TO BE, LIZ! – YOU SHOULD WEAR IT!
I WONDER WHAT GRANDPA WOULD THINK IF I DECIDED TO WEAR IT. I SHOULD ASK HIM FIRST.
HE PROBABLY WON'T REMEMBER WHAT HER DRESS LOOKED LIKE.
...IT WAS SUCH A LONG TIME AGO.
OR... PERHAPS IT ALL FEELS LIKE YESTERDAY.
LYNN

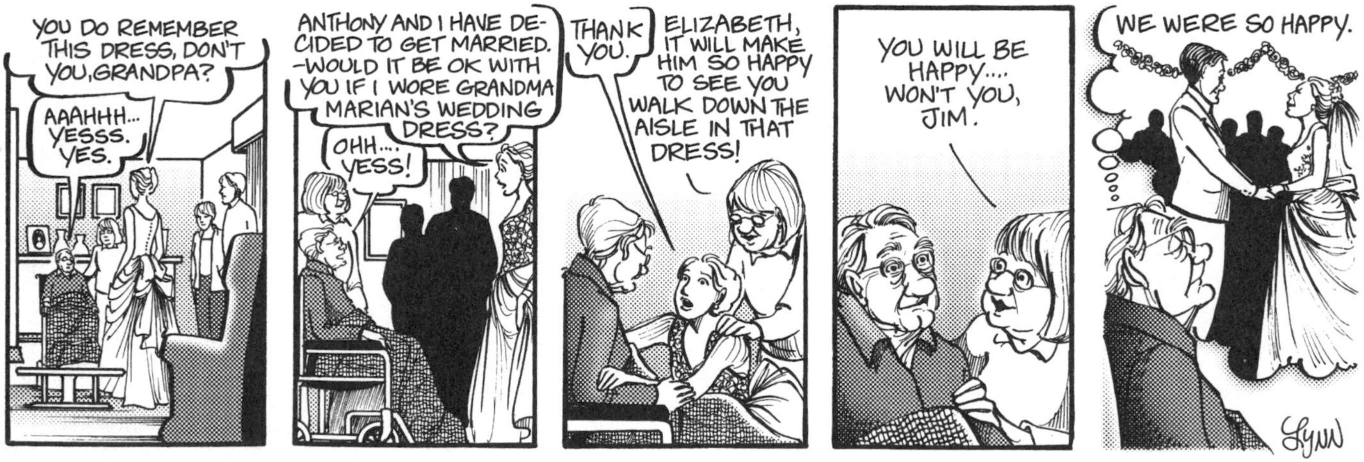
YOU DO REMEMBER THIS DRESS, DON'T YOU, GRANDPA?
AAAHHH... YESSS. YES.
ANTHONY AND I HAVE DECIDED TO GET MARRIED. -WOULD IT BE OK WITH YOU IF I WORE GRANDMA MARIAN'S WEDDING DRESS?
OHH.... YESS!
THANK YOU.
ELIZABETH, IT WILL MAKE HIM SO HAPPY TO SEE YOU WALK DOWN THE AISLE IN THAT DRESS!
YOU WILL BE HAPPY.... WON'T YOU, JIM.
WE WERE SO HAPPY.
LYNN

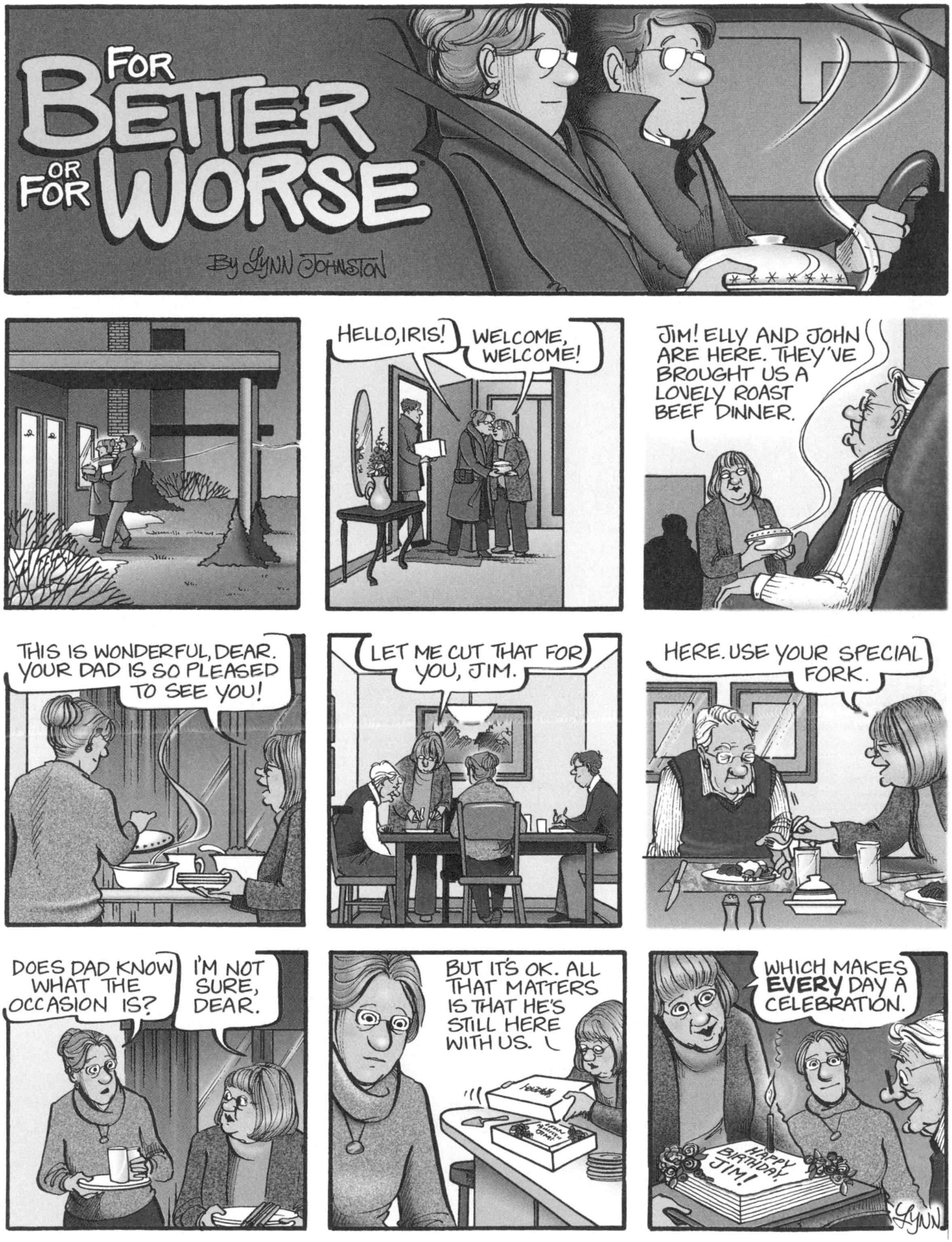
FOR BETTER OR FOR WORSE
BY LYNN JOHNSTON
HELLO, IRIS!
WELCOME, WELCOME!
JIM! ELLY AND JOHN ARE HERE. THEY'VE BROUGHT US A LOVELY ROAST BEEF DINNER.
THIS IS WONDERFUL, DEAR. YOUR DAD IS SO PLEASED TO SEE YOU!
LET ME CUT THAT FOR YOU, JIM.
HERE. USE YOUR SPECIAL FORK.
DOES DAD KNOW WHAT THE OCCASION IS?
I'M NOT SURE, DEAR.
BUT IT'S OK. ALL THAT MATTERS IS THAT HE'S STILL HERE WITH US.
WHICH MAKES **EVERY** DAY A CELEBRATION.
HAPPY BIRTHDAY, JIM!
LYNN

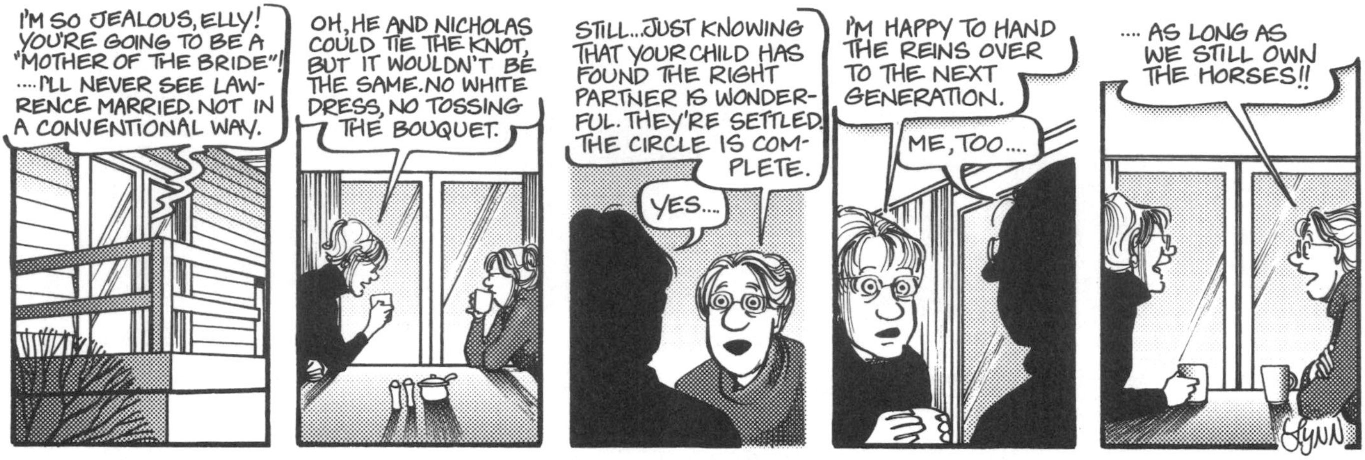
I'M SO JEALOUS, ELLY! YOU'RE GOING TO BE A "MOTHER OF THE BRIDE"! ....I'LL NEVER SEE LAWRENCE MARRIED. NOT IN A CONVENTIONAL WAY.
OH, HE AND NICHOLAS COULD TIE THE KNOT, BUT IT WOULDN'T BE THE SAME. NO WHITE DRESS, NO TOSSING THE BOUQUET.
STILL...JUST KNOWING THAT YOUR CHILD HAS FOUND THE RIGHT PARTNER IS WONDERFUL. THEY'RE SETTLED. THE CIRCLE IS COMPLETE.
YES....
I'M HAPPY TO HAND THE REINS OVER TO THE NEXT GENERATION.
ME, TOO....
.... AS LONG AS WE STILL OWN THE HORSES!!
LYNN

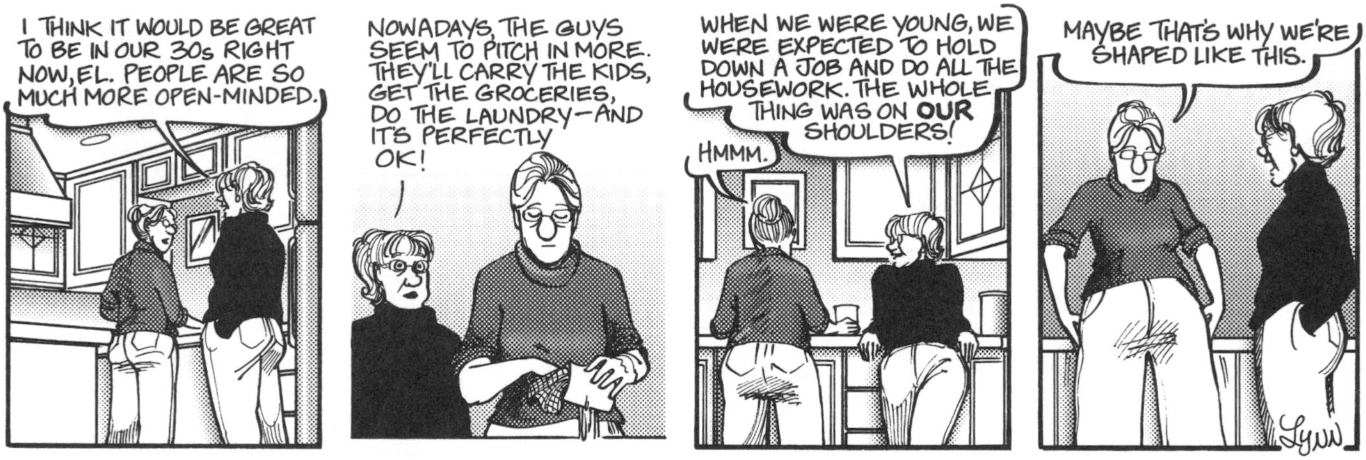
I THINK IT WOULD BE GREAT TO BE IN OUR 30s RIGHT NOW, EL. PEOPLE ARE SO MUCH MORE OPEN-MINDED.
NOWADAYS, THE GUYS SEEM TO PITCH IN MORE. THEY'LL CARRY THE KIDS, GET THE GROCERIES, DO THE LAUNDRY—AND IT'S PERFECTLY OK!
WHEN WE WERE YOUNG, WE WERE EXPECTED TO HOLD DOWN A JOB AND DO ALL THE HOUSEWORK. THE WHOLE THING WAS ON **OUR** SHOULDERS!
HMMM.
MAYBE THAT'S WHY WE'RE SHAPED LIKE THIS.
LYNN

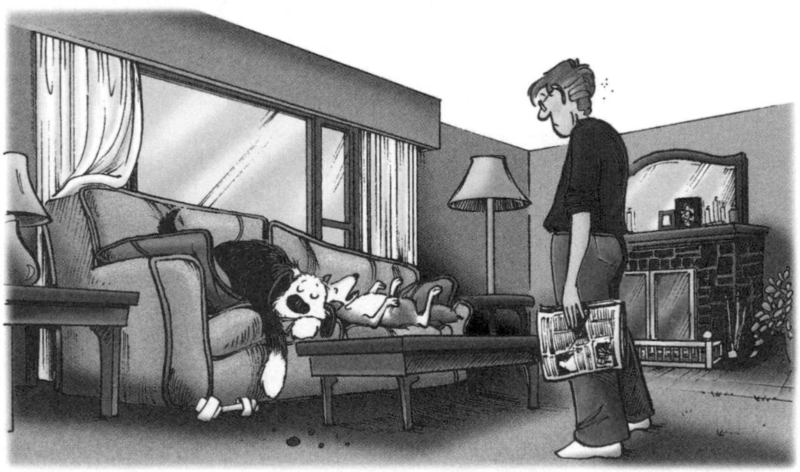

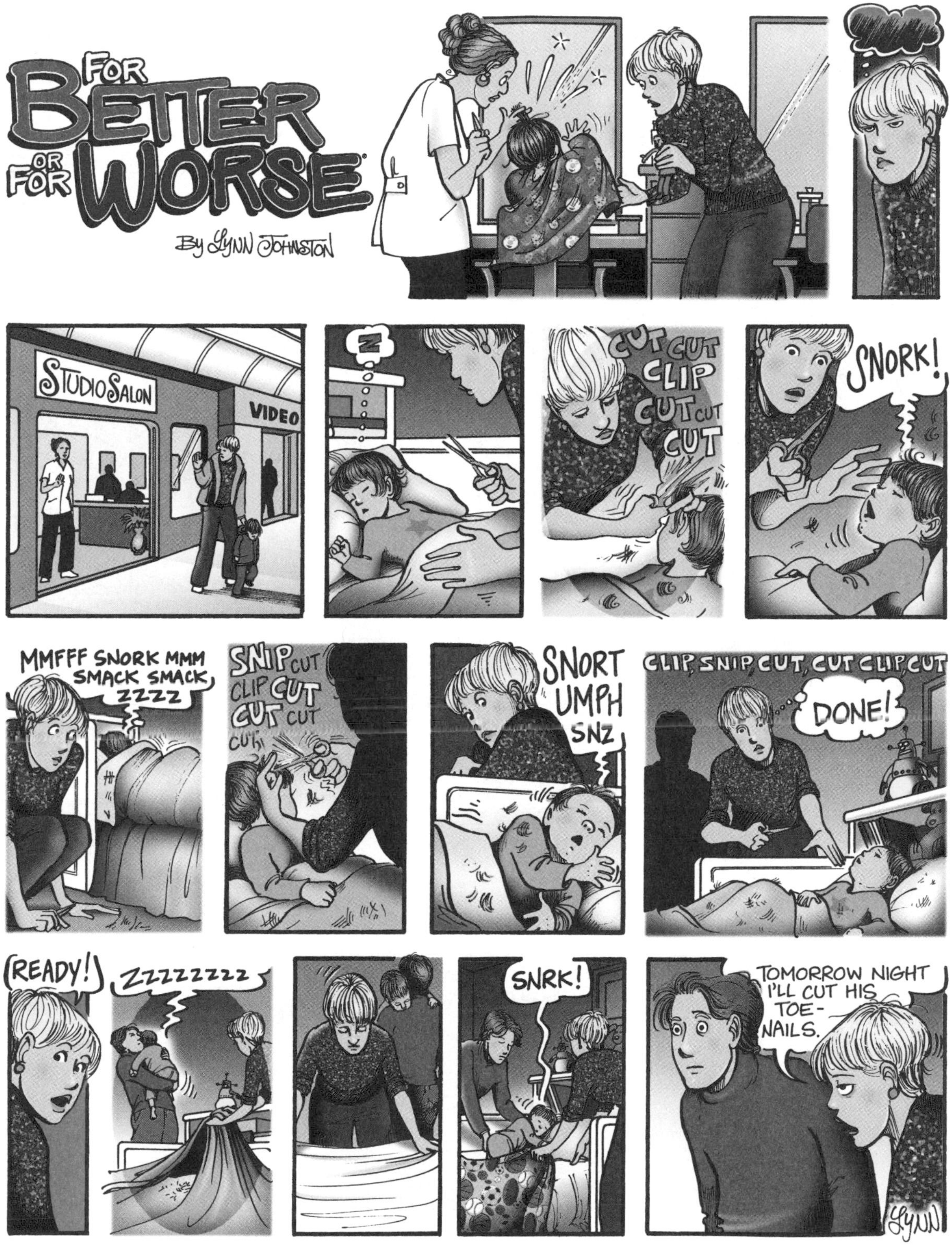
For Better or For Worse
By Lynn Johnston
STUDIO SALON
VIDEO
Z
CUT CUT
CLIP
CUT CUT
CUT
SNORK!
MMFFF SNORK MMM SMACK SMACK, ZZZZ
SNIP CUT
CLIP CUT
CUT CUT
CUT
SNORT UMPH SNZ
CLIP, SNIP, CUT, CUT CLIP, CUT
DONE!
READY!
ZZZZZZZZ
SNRK!
TOMORROW NIGHT I'LL CUT HIS TOE-NAILS.
LYNN

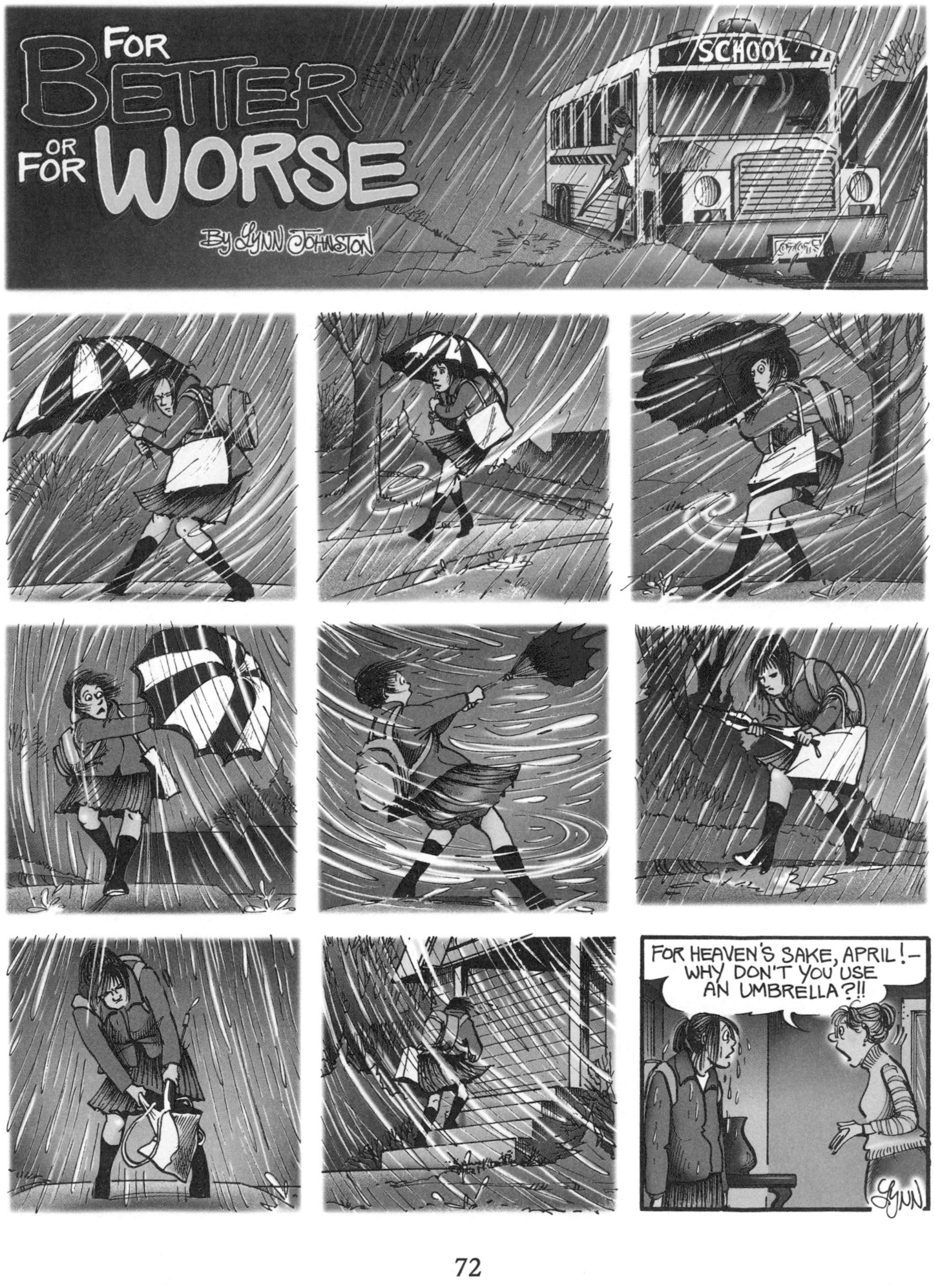
FOR BETTER OR FOR WORSE
By Lynn Johnston
SCHOOL
FOR HEAVEN'S SAKE, APRIL! – WHY DON'T YOU USE AN UMBRELLA?!!
LYNN

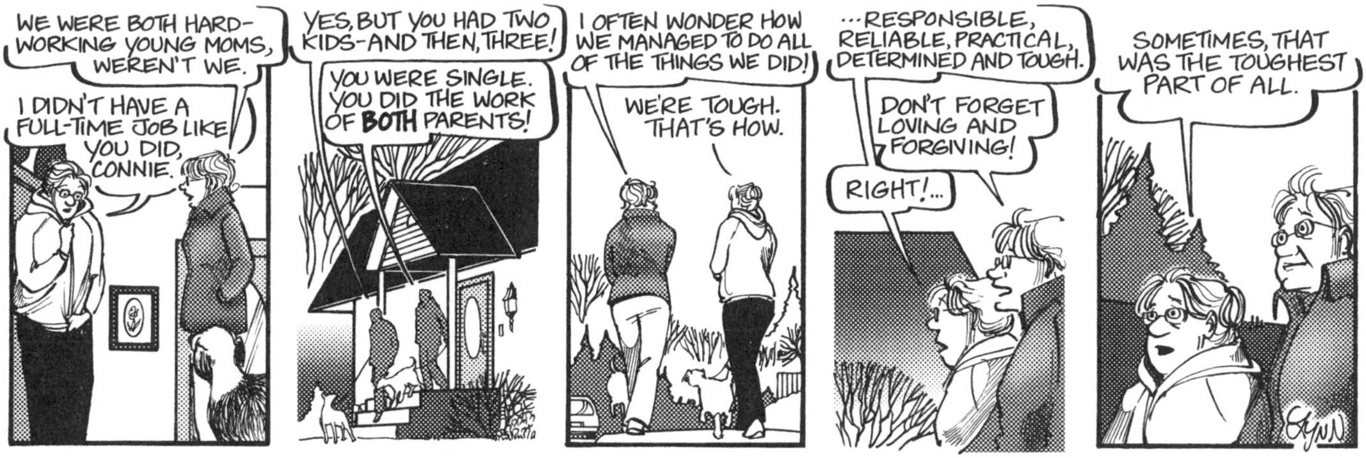
WE WERE BOTH HARD-WORKING YOUNG MOMS, WEREN'T WE.
I DIDN'T HAVE A FULL-TIME JOB LIKE YOU DID, CONNIE.
YES, BUT YOU HAD TWO KIDS-AND THEN, THREE!
YOU WERE SINGLE. YOU DID THE WORK OF BOTH PARENTS!
I OFTEN WONDER HOW WE MANAGED TO DO ALL OF THE THINGS WE DID!
WE'RE TOUGH. THAT'S HOW.
...RESPONSIBLE, RELIABLE, PRACTICAL, DETERMINED AND TOUGH.
RIGHT!...
DON'T FORGET LOVING AND FORGIVING!
SOMETIMES, THAT WAS THE TOUGHEST PART OF ALL.
LYNN

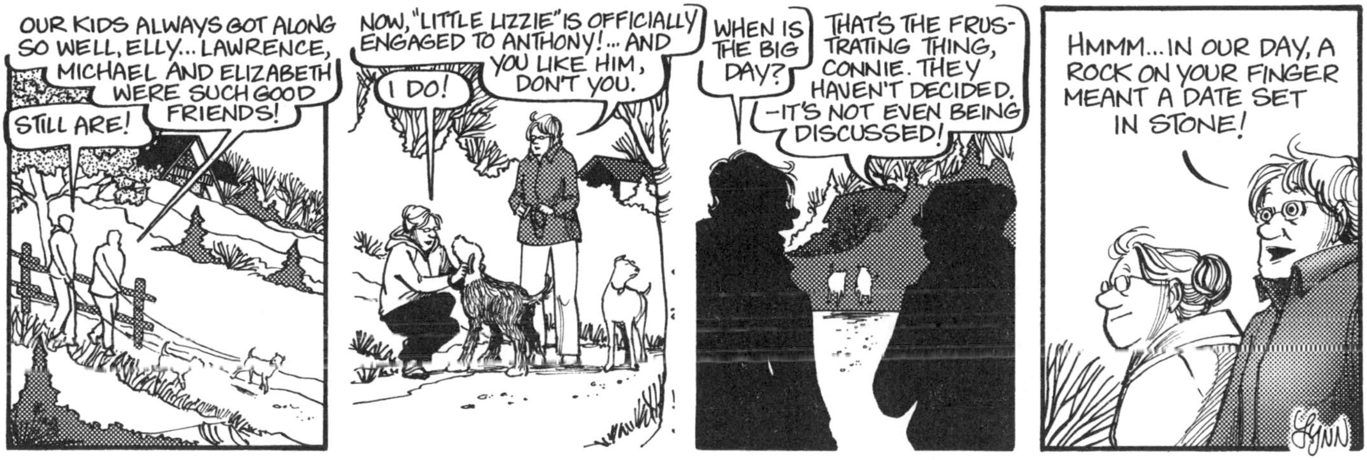
OUR KIDS ALWAYS GOT ALONG SO WELL, ELLY... LAWRENCE, MICHAEL AND ELIZABETH WERE SUCH GOOD FRIENDS!
STILL ARE!
NOW, "LITTLE LIZZIE" IS OFFICIALLY ENGAGED TO ANTHONY!... AND YOU LIKE HIM, DON'T YOU.
I DO!
WHEN IS THE BIG DAY?
THAT'S THE FRUS-TRATING THING, CONNIE. THEY HAVEN'T DECIDED. -IT'S NOT EVEN BEING DISCUSSED!
HMMM... IN OUR DAY, A ROCK ON YOUR FINGER MEANT A DATE SET IN STONE!
LYNN

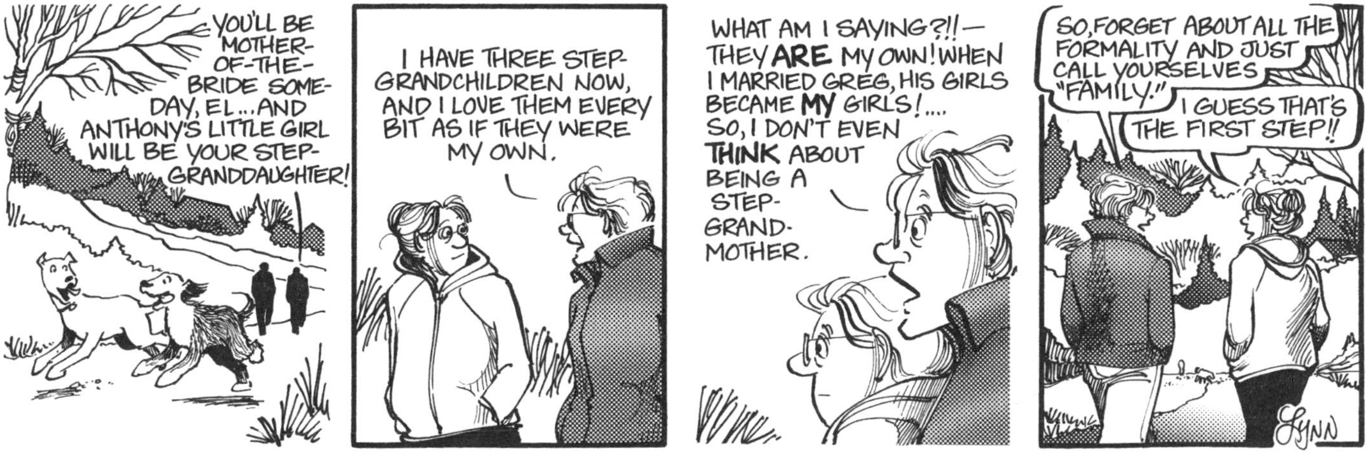
YOU'LL BE MOTHER-OF-THE-BRIDE SOME-DAY, EL... AND ANTHONY'S LITTLE GIRL WILL BE YOUR STEP-GRANDDAUGHTER!
I HAVE THREE STEP-GRANDCHILDREN NOW, AND I LOVE THEM EVERY BIT AS IF THEY WERE MY OWN.
WHAT AM I SAYING?!!— THEY ARE MY OWN! WHEN I MARRIED GREG, HIS GIRLS BECAME MY GIRLS!.... SO, I DON'T EVEN THINK ABOUT BEING A STEP-GRAND-MOTHER.
SO, FORGET ABOUT ALL THE FORMALITY AND JUST CALL YOURSELVES "FAMILY."
I GUESS THAT'S THE FIRST STEP!!
LYNN

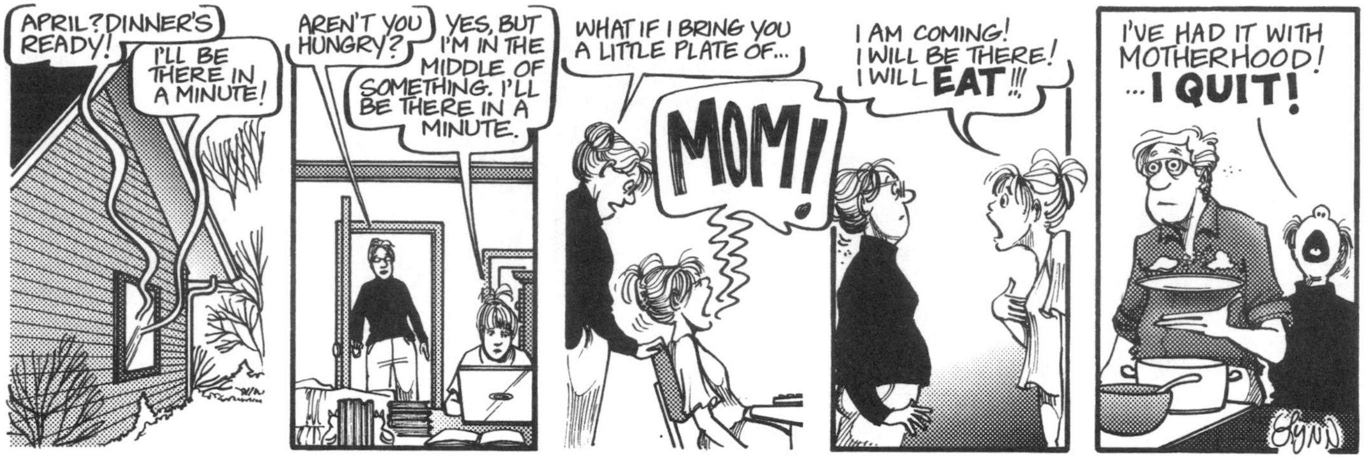
APRIL? DINNER'S READY!
I'LL BE THERE IN A MINUTE!
AREN'T YOU HUNGRY?
YES, BUT I'M IN THE MIDDLE OF SOMETHING. I'LL BE THERE IN A MINUTE.
WHAT IF I BRING YOU A LITTLE PLATE OF...
MOM!
I AM COMING! I WILL BE THERE! I WILL EAT!!!
I'VE HAD IT WITH MOTHERHOOD! ...I QUIT!

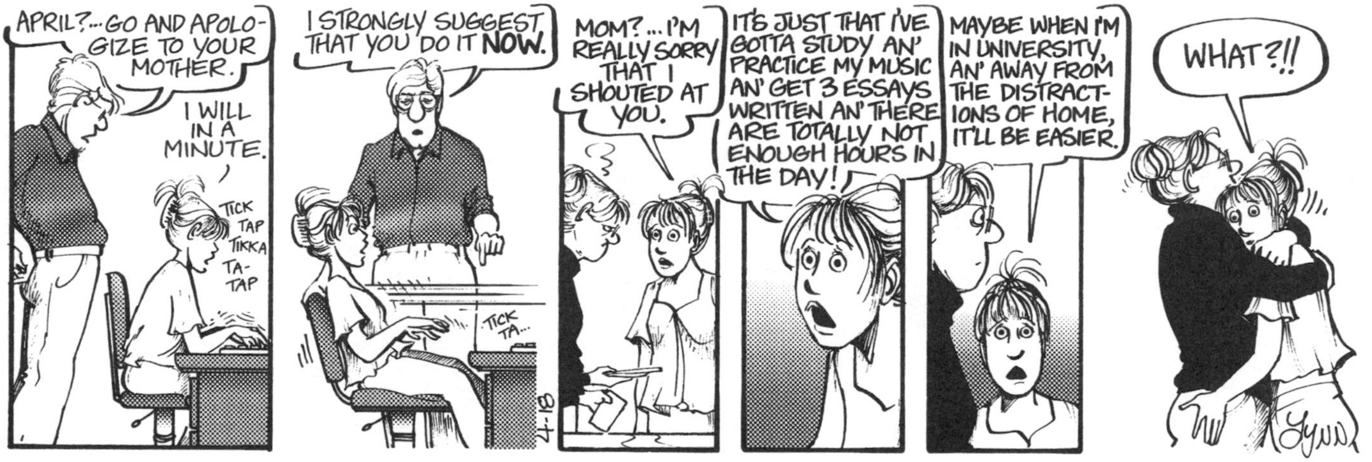
APRIL?...GO AND APOLOGIZE TO YOUR MOTHER.
I WILL IN A MINUTE.
TICK TAP TIKKA TA-TAP
I STRONGLY SUGGEST THAT YOU DO IT NOW.
TICK TA...
MOM?...I'M REALLY SORRY THAT I SHOUTED AT YOU.
IT'S JUST THAT I'VE GOTTA STUDY AN' PRACTICE MY MUSIC AN' GET 3 ESSAYS WRITTEN AN' THERE ARE TOTALLY NOT ENOUGH HOURS IN THE DAY!
MAYBE WHEN I'M IN UNIVERSITY, AN' AWAY FROM THE DISTRACTIONS OF HOME, IT'LL BE EASIER.
WHAT?!!

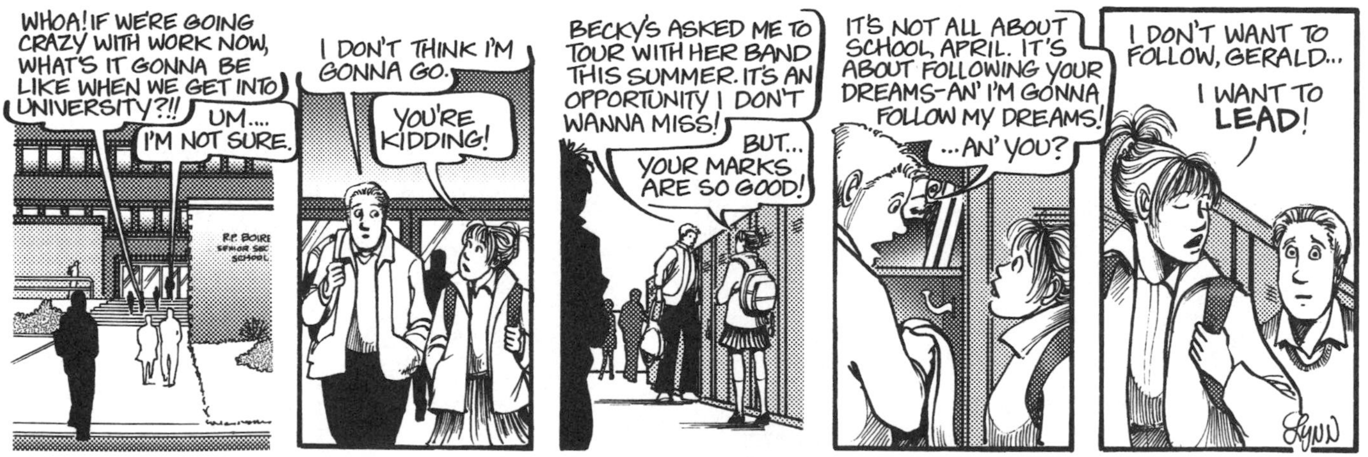
WHOA! IF WE'RE GOING CRAZY WITH WORK NOW, WHAT'S IT GONNA BE LIKE WHEN WE GET INTO UNIVERSITY?!!
UM.... I'M NOT SURE.
I DON'T THINK I'M GONNA GO.
YOU'RE KIDDING!
BECKY'S ASKED ME TO TOUR WITH HER BAND THIS SUMMER. IT'S AN OPPORTUNITY I DON'T WANNA MISS!
BUT... YOUR MARKS ARE SO GOOD!
IT'S NOT ALL ABOUT SCHOOL, APRIL. IT'S ABOUT FOLLOWING YOUR DREAMS-AN' I'M GONNA FOLLOW MY DREAMS!
...AN' YOU?
I DON'T WANT TO FOLLOW, GERALD...
I WANT TO LEAD!

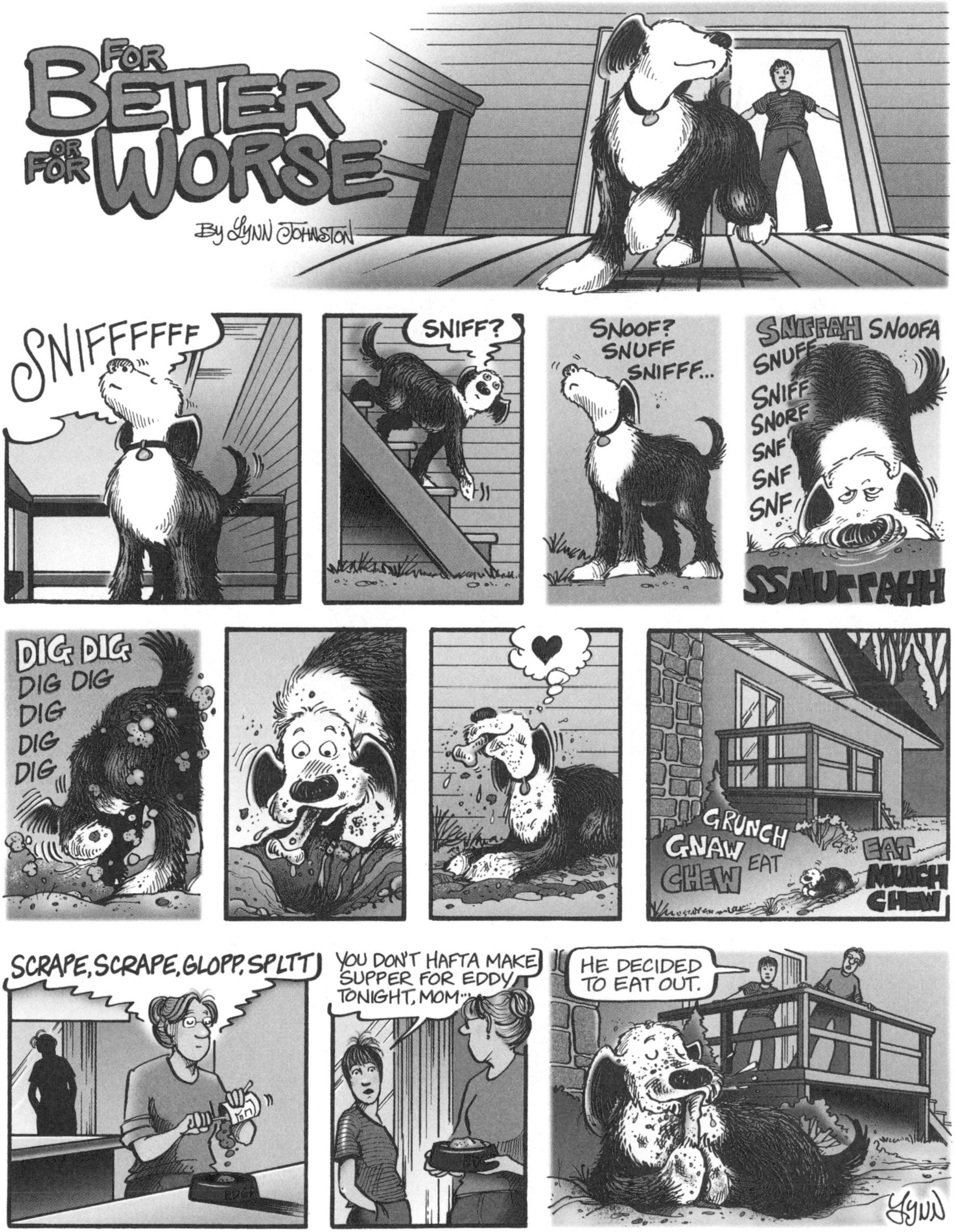
FOR BETTER OR FOR WORSE
BY LYNN JOHNSTON
SNIFFFFFF
SNIFF?
SNOOF? SNUFF SNIFFF...
SNIFFAH SNOOFA
SNUFF
SNIFF
SNORF
SNF
SNF
SNF
SSNUFFAHH
DIG DIG
DIG DIG
DIG
DIG
DIG
GRUNCH
GNAW
EAT
CHEW
EAT
MUNCH
CHEW
SCRAPE, SCRAPE, GLOPP, SPLTT
YOU DON'T HAFTA MAKE SUPPER FOR EDDY TONIGHT, MOM...
HE DECIDED TO EAT OUT.
LYNN

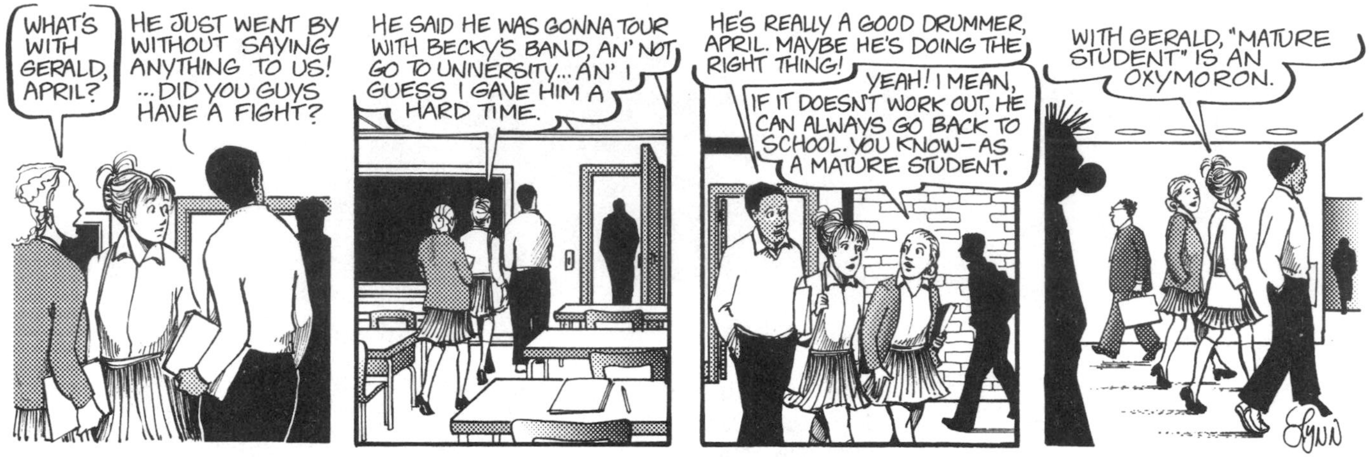
WHAT'S WITH GERALD, APRIL?
HE JUST WENT BY WITHOUT SAYING ANYTHING TO US! ...DID YOU GUYS HAVE A FIGHT?
HE SAID HE WAS GONNA TOUR WITH BECKY'S BAND, AN' NOT GO TO UNIVERSITY... AN' I GUESS I GAVE HIM A HARD TIME.
HE'S REALLY A GOOD DRUMMER, APRIL. MAYBE HE'S DOING THE RIGHT THING!
YEAH! I MEAN, IF IT DOESN'T WORK OUT, HE CAN ALWAYS GO BACK TO SCHOOL. YOU KNOW—AS A MATURE STUDENT.
WITH GERALD, "MATURE STUDENT" IS AN OXYMORON.
Lynn

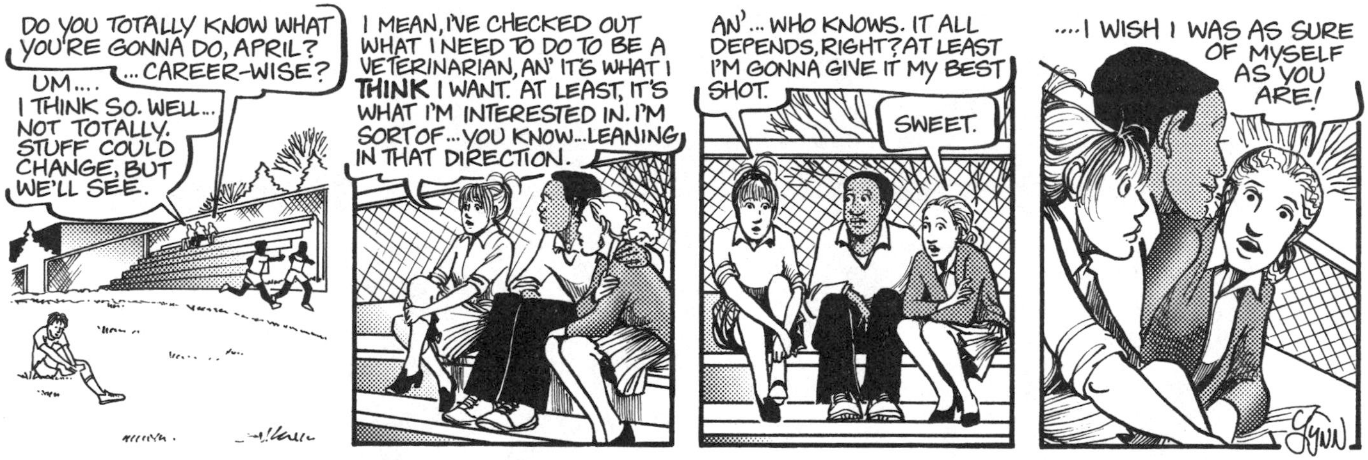
DO YOU TOTALLY KNOW WHAT YOU'RE GONNA DO, APRIL? ...CAREER-WISE?
UM.... I THINK SO. WELL... NOT TOTALLY. STUFF COULD CHANGE, BUT WE'LL SEE.
I MEAN, I'VE CHECKED OUT WHAT I NEED TO DO TO BE A VETERINARIAN, AN' IT'S WHAT I **THINK** I WANT. AT LEAST, IT'S WHAT I'M INTERESTED IN. I'M SORT OF... YOU KNOW... LEANING IN THAT DIRECTION.
AN'... WHO KNOWS. IT ALL DEPENDS, RIGHT? AT LEAST I'M GONNA GIVE IT MY BEST SHOT.
SWEET.
....I WISH I WAS AS SURE OF MYSELF AS YOU ARE!
Lynn

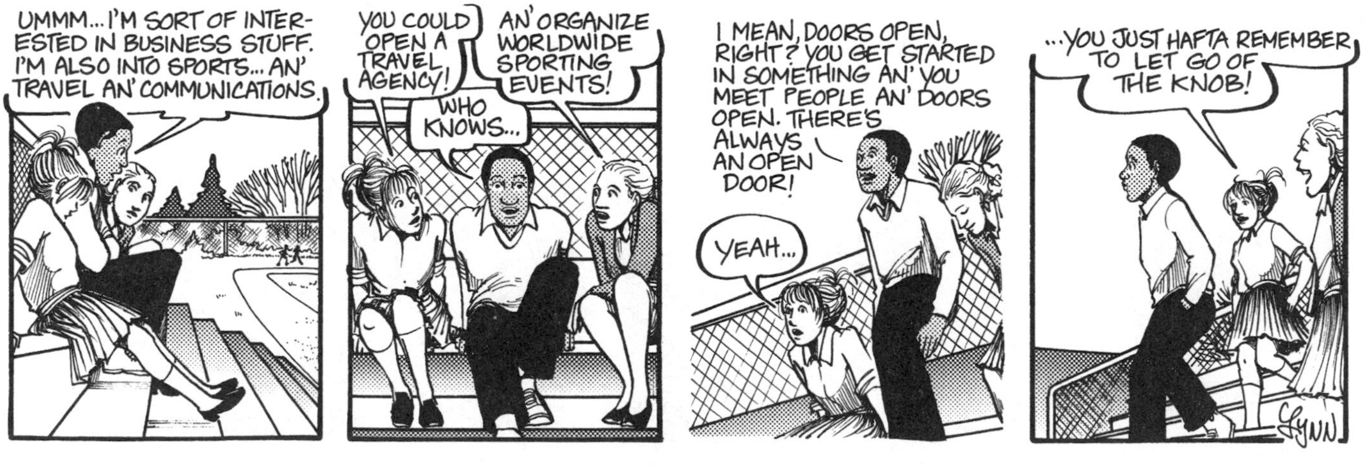
UMMM... I'M SORT OF INTERESTED IN BUSINESS STUFF. I'M ALSO INTO SPORTS... AN' TRAVEL AN' COMMUNICATIONS.
YOU COULD OPEN A TRAVEL AGENCY!
AN' ORGANIZE WORLDWIDE SPORTING EVENTS!
WHO KNOWS...
I MEAN, DOORS OPEN, RIGHT? YOU GET STARTED IN SOMETHING AN' YOU MEET PEOPLE AN' DOORS OPEN. THERE'S ALWAYS AN OPEN DOOR!
YEAH...
...YOU JUST HAFTA REMEMBER TO LET GO OF THE KNOB!
Lynn

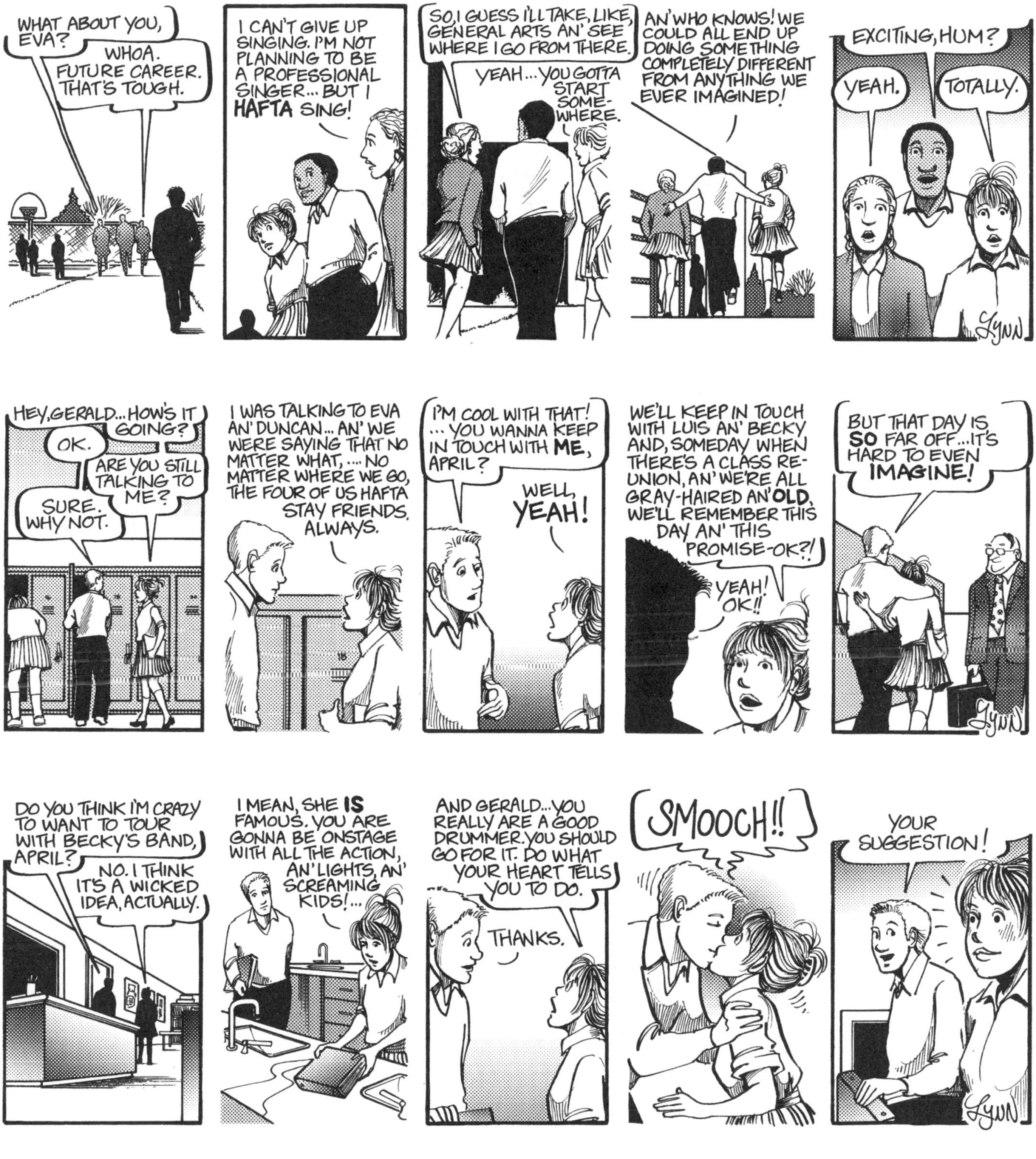
WHAT ABOUT YOU, EVA?
WHOA. FUTURE CAREER. THAT'S TOUGH.
I CAN'T GIVE UP SINGING. I'M NOT PLANNING TO BE A PROFESSIONAL SINGER... BUT I HAFTA SING!
SO, I GUESS I'LL TAKE, LIKE, GENERAL ARTS AN' SEE WHERE I GO FROM THERE.
YEAH... YOU GOTTA START SOME-WHERE.
AN' WHO KNOWS! WE COULD ALL END UP DOING SOMETHING COMPLETELY DIFFERENT FROM ANYTHING WE EVER IMAGINED!
EXCITING, HUM?
YEAH.
TOTALLY.
LYNN
HEY, GERALD... HOW'S IT GOING?
OK.
ARE YOU STILL TALKING TO ME?
SURE. WHY NOT.
I WAS TALKING TO EVA AN' DUNCAN... AN' WE WERE SAYING THAT NO MATTER WHAT, ... NO MATTER WHERE WE GO, THE FOUR OF US HAFTA STAY FRIENDS. ALWAYS.
I'M COOL WITH THAT! ... YOU WANNA KEEP IN TOUCH WITH ME, APRIL?
WELL, YEAH!
WE'LL KEEP IN TOUCH WITH LUIS AN' BECKY AND, SOMEDAY WHEN THERE'S A CLASS RE-UNION, AN' WE'RE ALL GRAY-HAIRED AN' OLD, WE'LL REMEMBER THIS DAY AN' THIS PROMISE-OK?!
YEAH! OK!!
BUT THAT DAY IS SO FAR OFF... IT'S HARD TO EVEN IMAGINE!
LYNN
DO YOU THINK I'M CRAZY TO WANT TO TOUR WITH BECKY'S BAND, APRIL?
NO. I THINK IT'S A WICKED IDEA, ACTUALLY.
I MEAN, SHE IS FAMOUS. YOU ARE GONNA BE ONSTAGE WITH ALL THE ACTION, AN' LIGHTS, AN' SCREAMING KIDS!...
AND GERALD... YOU REALLY ARE A GOOD DRUMMER. YOU SHOULD GO FOR IT. DO WHAT YOUR HEART TELLS YOU TO DO.
THANKS.
SMOOCH!!
YOUR SUGGESTION!
LYNN

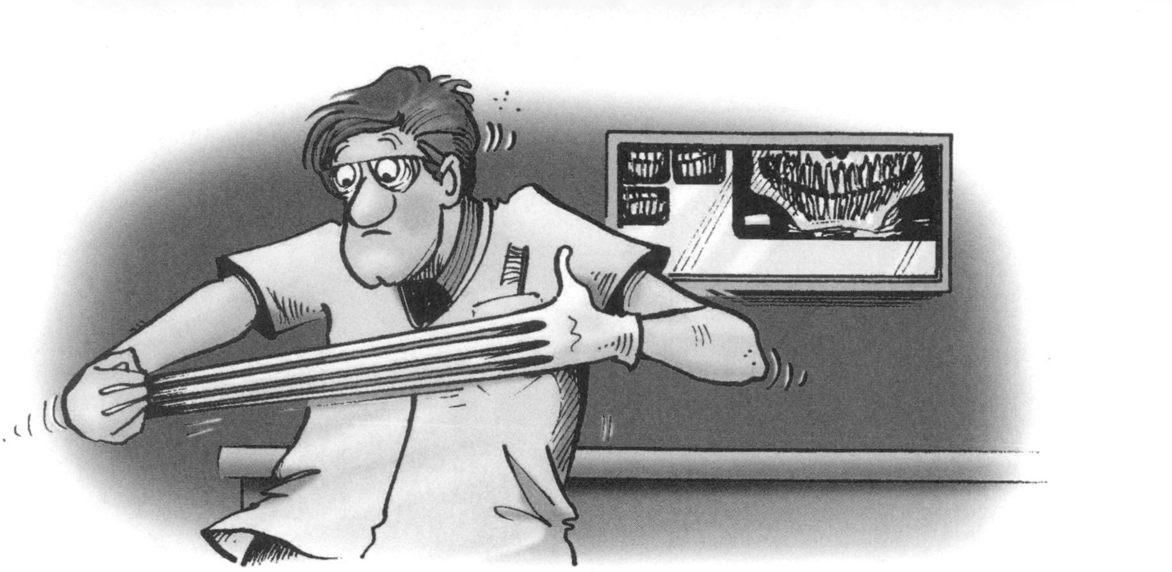

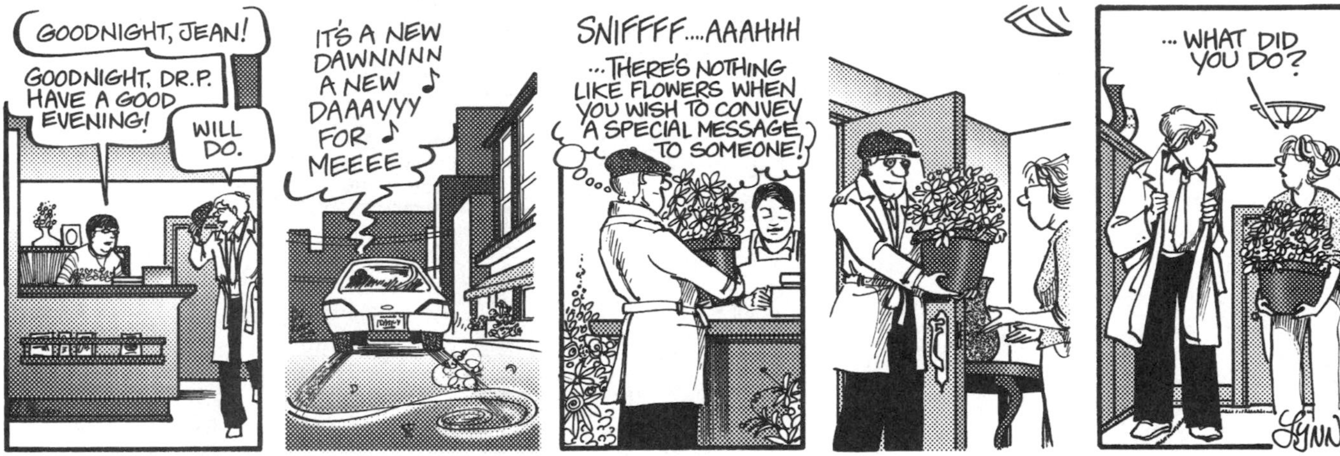

GOODNIGHT, JEAN!
GOODNIGHT, DR. P. HAVE A GOOD EVENING!
WILL DO.
IT'S A NEW DAWNNNN A NEW DAAAYYY FOR MEEEE
SNIFFFF....AAAHHH
...THERE'S NOTHING LIKE FLOWERS WHEN YOU WISH TO CONVEY A SPECIAL MESSAGE TO SOMEONE!
...WHAT DID YOU DO?
LYNN

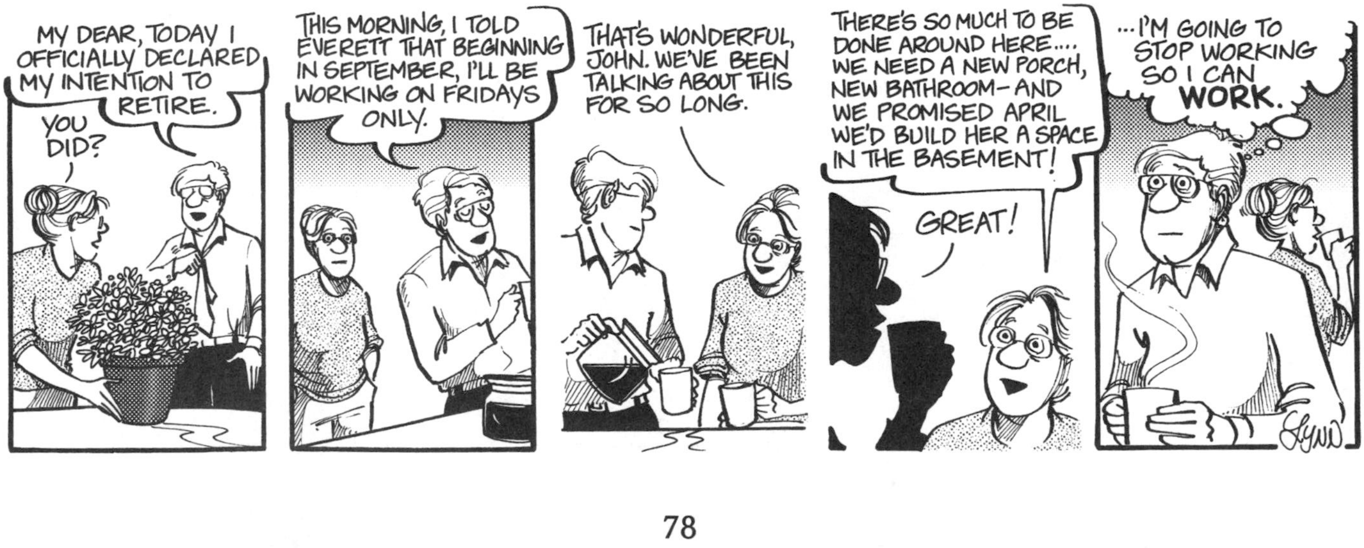

MY DEAR, TODAY I OFFICIALLY DECLARED MY INTENTION TO RETIRE.
YOU DID?
THIS MORNING, I TOLD EVERETT THAT BEGINNING IN SEPTEMBER, I'LL BE WORKING ON FRIDAYS ONLY.
THAT'S WONDERFUL, JOHN. WE'VE BEEN TALKING ABOUT THIS FOR SO LONG.
THERE'S SO MUCH TO BE DONE AROUND HERE.... WE NEED A NEW PORCH, NEW BATHROOM– AND WE PROMISED APRIL WE'D BUILD HER A SPACE IN THE BASEMENT!
GREAT!
...I'M GOING TO STOP WORKING SO I CAN **WORK**.
LYNN

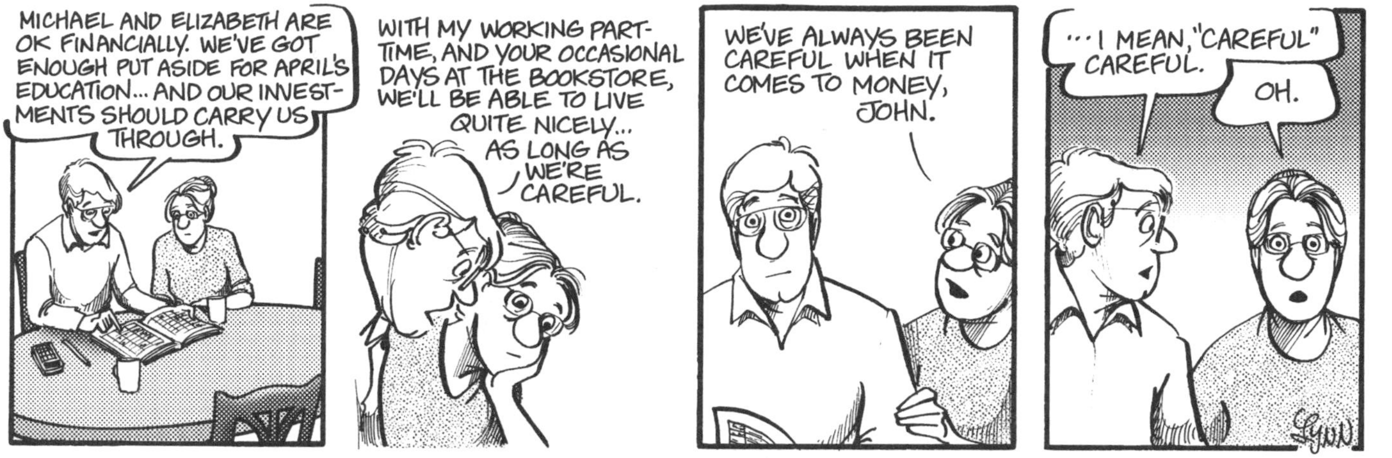
MICHAEL AND ELIZABETH ARE OK FINANCIALLY. WE'VE GOT ENOUGH PUT ASIDE FOR APRIL'S EDUCATION... AND OUR INVESTMENTS SHOULD CARRY US THROUGH.
WITH MY WORKING PART-TIME, AND YOUR OCCASIONAL DAYS AT THE BOOKSTORE, WE'LL BE ABLE TO LIVE QUITE NICELY...
AS LONG AS WE'RE CAREFUL.
WE'VE ALWAYS BEEN CAREFUL WHEN IT COMES TO MONEY, JOHN.
...I MEAN, "CAREFUL" CAREFUL.
OH.
LYNN

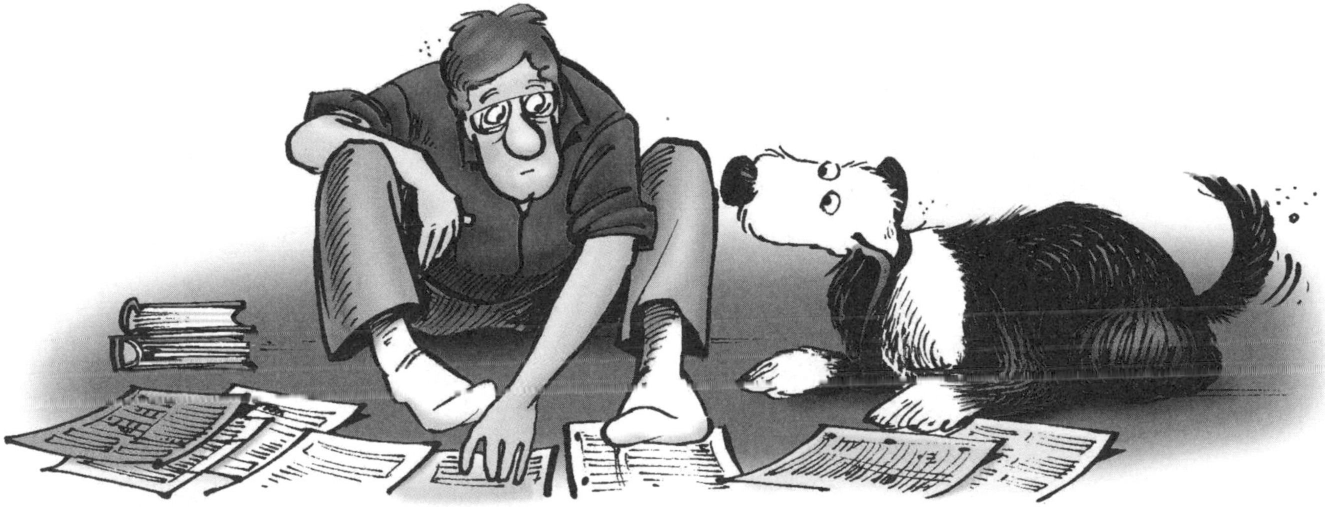

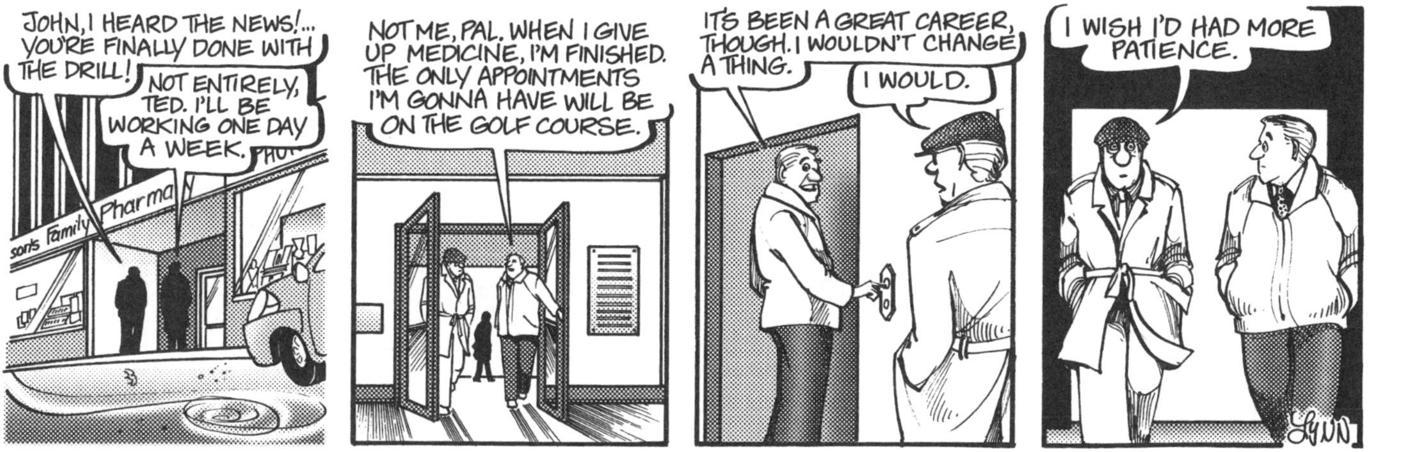
JOHN, I HEARD THE NEWS!... YOU'RE FINALLY DONE WITH THE DRILL!
NOT ENTIRELY, TED. I'LL BE WORKING ONE DAY A WEEK.
sons Family Pharma
NOT ME, PAL. WHEN I GIVE UP MEDICINE, I'M FINISHED. THE ONLY APPOINTMENTS I'M GONNA HAVE WILL BE ON THE GOLF COURSE.
IT'S BEEN A GREAT CAREER, THOUGH. I WOULDN'T CHANGE A THING.
I WOULD.
I WISH I'D HAD MORE PATIENCE.
LYNN

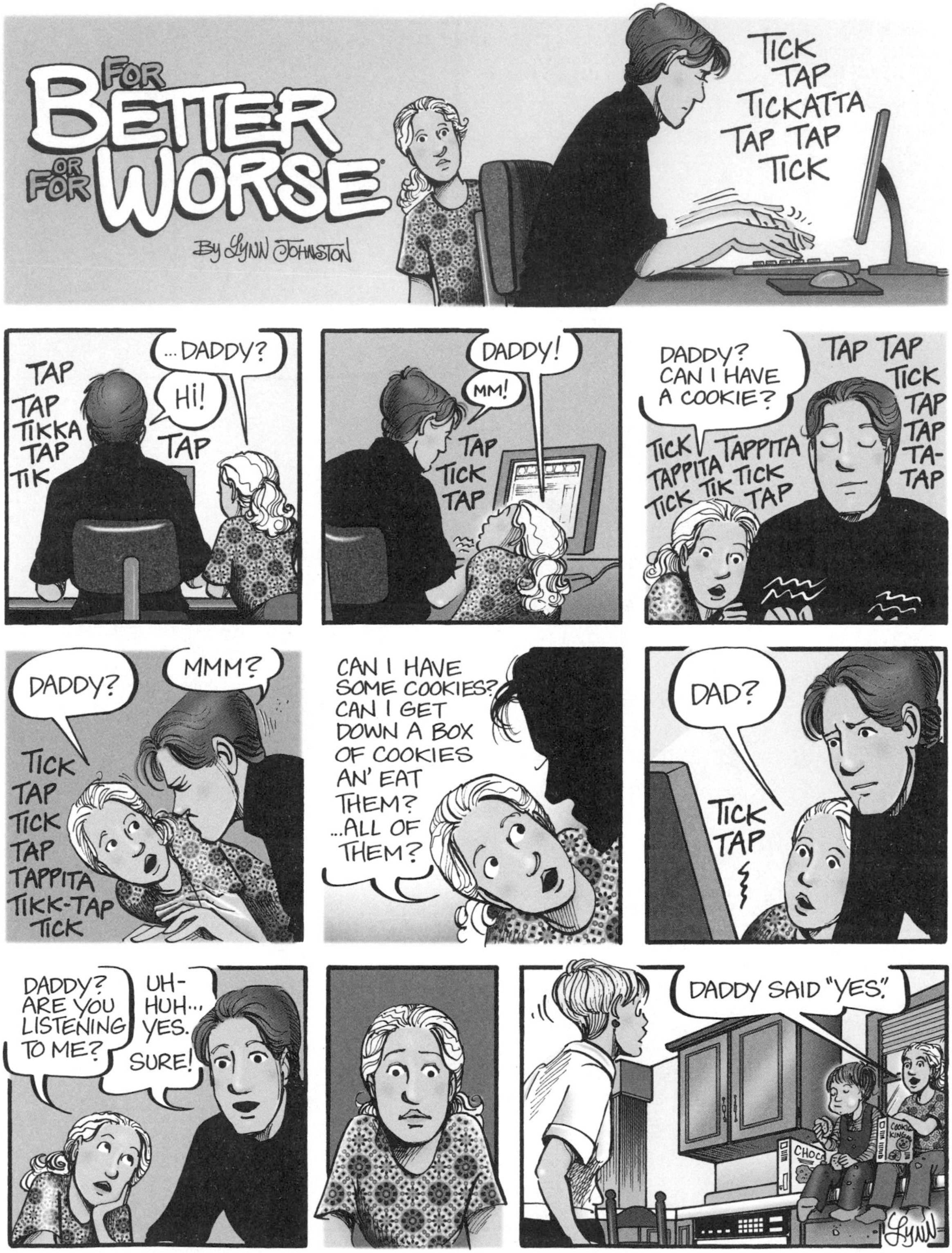
For Better or for Worse
By Lynn Johnston
TICK TAP TICKATTA TAP TAP TICK
TAP TAP TIKKA TAP TIK
...DADDY?
HI!
TAP
DADDY!
MM!
TAP TICK TAP
DADDY? CAN I HAVE A COOKIE?
TAP TAP TICK TAP TAP TA-TAP
TICK TAPPITA TICK TAPPITA TIK TICK TAP
DADDY?
MMM?
TICK TAP TICK TAP TAPPITA TIKK-TAP TICK
CAN I HAVE SOME COOKIES? CAN I GET DOWN A BOX OF COOKIES AN' EAT THEM? ...ALL OF THEM?
DAD?
TICK TAP
DADDY? ARE YOU LISTENING TO ME?
UH-HUH..., YES. SURE!
DADDY SAID "YES."
LYNN

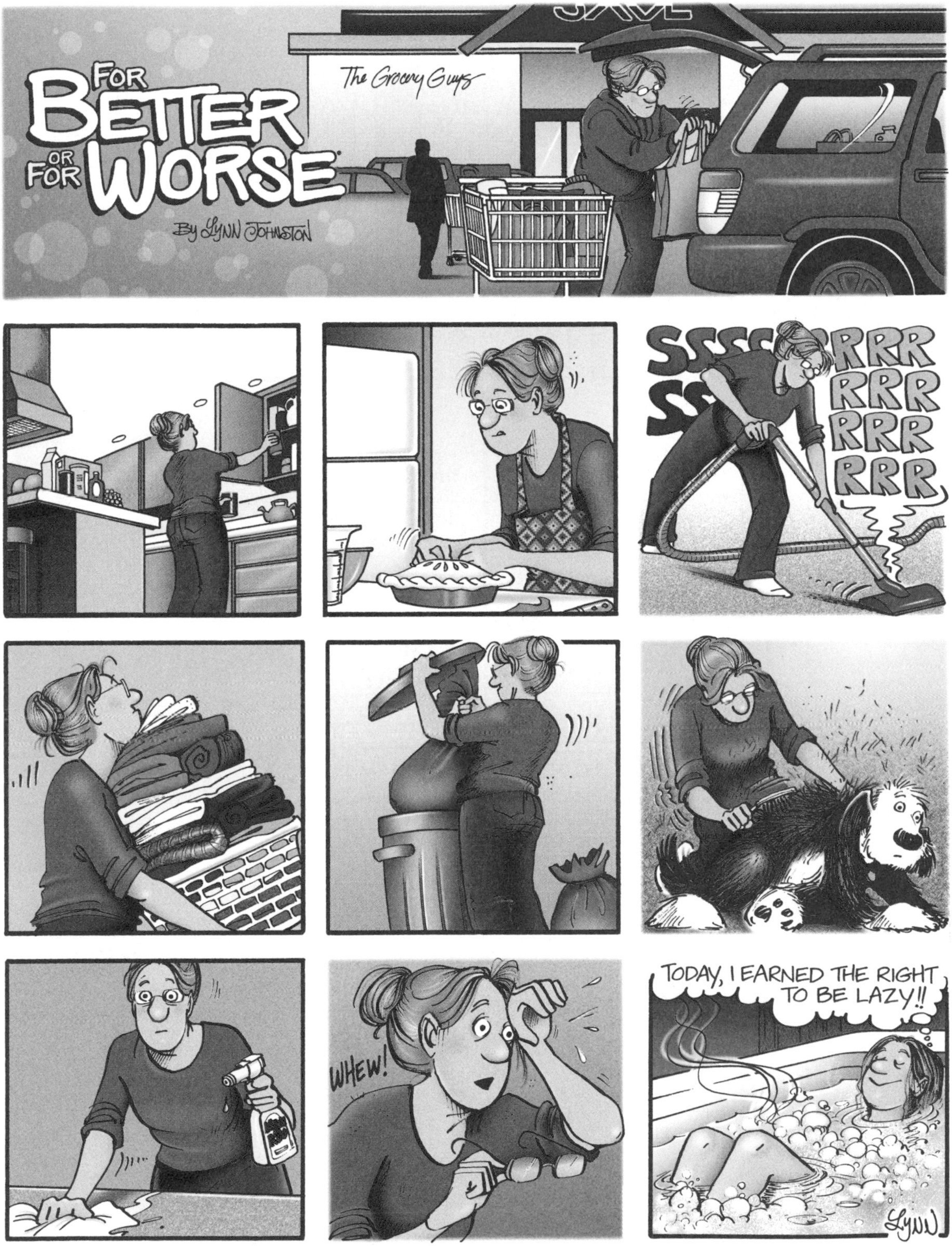
SAVE
The Grocery Guys
FOR BETTER OR FOR WORSE
By Lynn Johnston
SSSSS
SS
RRR
RRR
RRR
RRR
WHEW!
TODAY, I EARNED THE RIGHT TO BE LAZY!!
Lynn

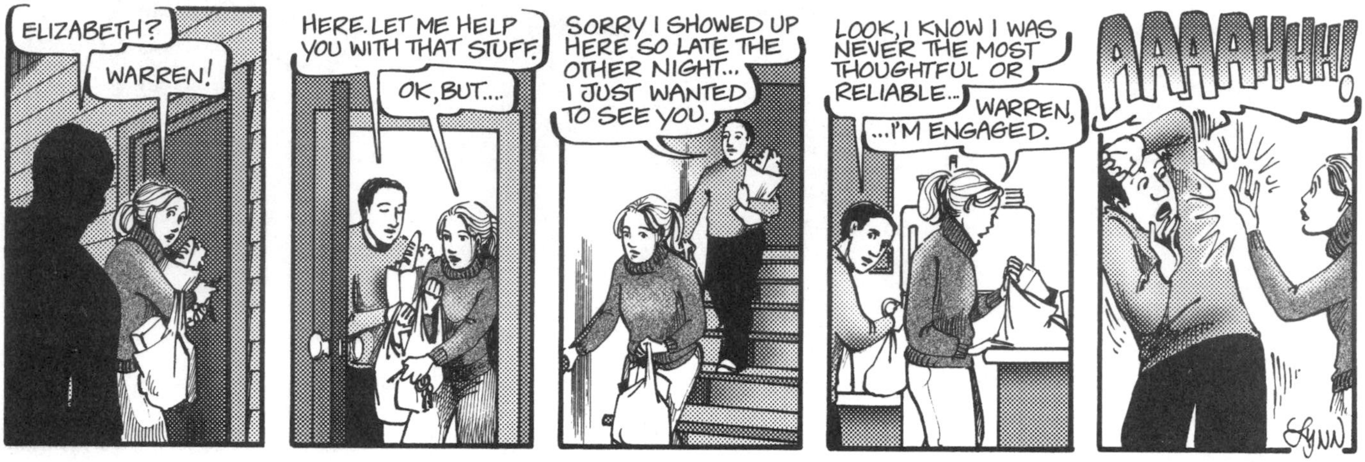
ELIZABETH?
WARREN!
HERE. LET ME HELP YOU WITH THAT STUFF.
OK, BUT....
SORRY I SHOWED UP HERE SO LATE THE OTHER NIGHT... I JUST WANTED TO SEE YOU.
LOOK, I KNOW I WAS NEVER THE MOST THOUGHTFUL OR RELIABLE...
WARREN, ...I'M ENGAGED.
AAAAHHH!
LYNN

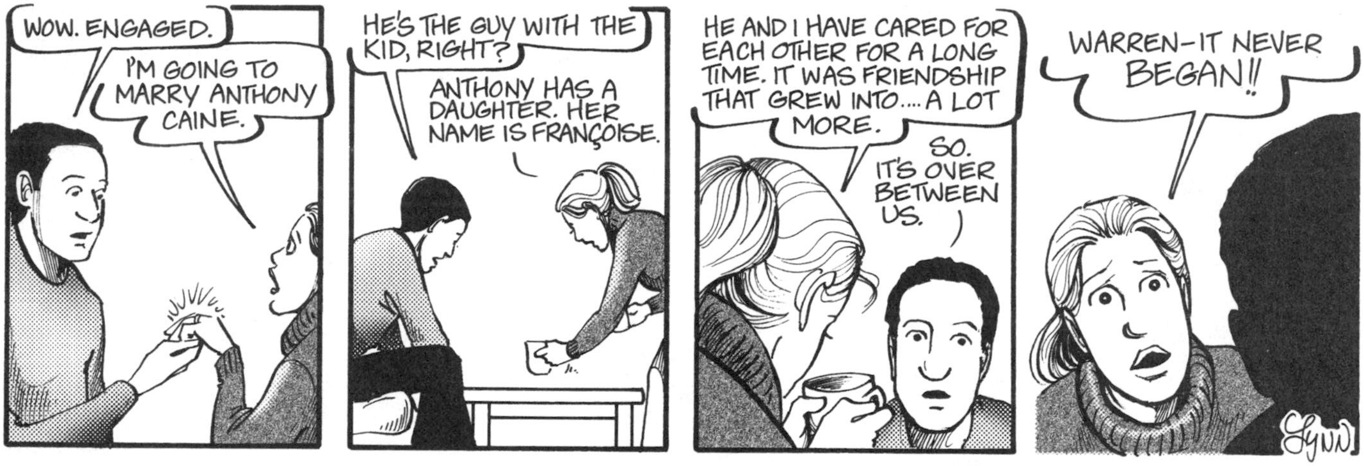
WOW. ENGAGED.
I'M GOING TO MARRY ANTHONY CAINE.
HE'S THE GUY WITH THE KID, RIGHT?
ANTHONY HAS A DAUGHTER. HER NAME IS FRANÇOISE.
HE AND I HAVE CARED FOR EACH OTHER FOR A LONG TIME. IT WAS FRIENDSHIP THAT GREW INTO.... A LOT MORE.
SO. IT'S OVER BETWEEN US.
WARREN– IT NEVER BEGAN!!
LYNN

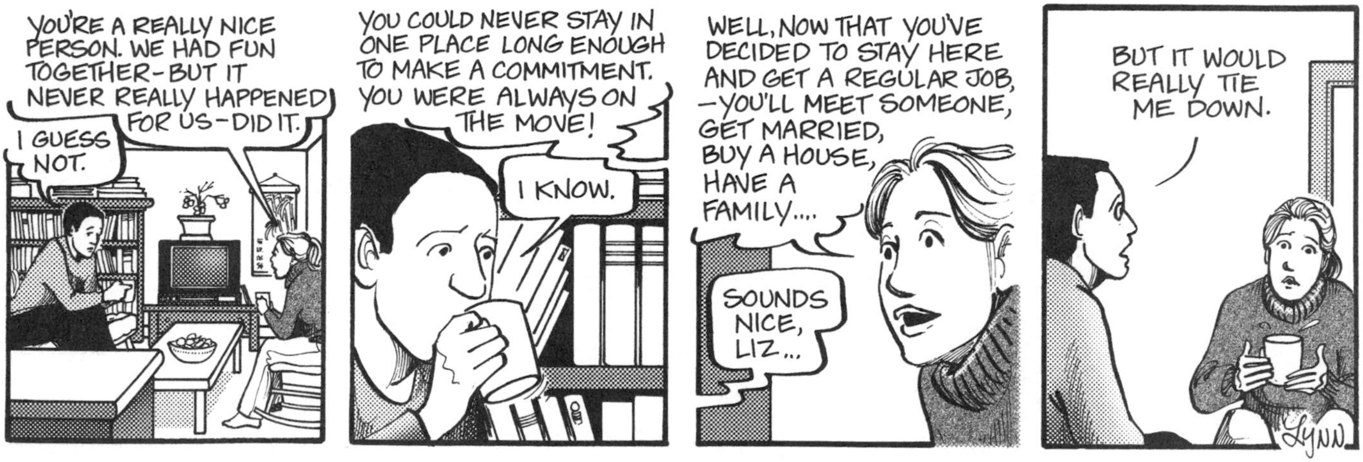
YOU'RE A REALLY NICE PERSON. WE HAD FUN TOGETHER– BUT IT NEVER REALLY HAPPENED FOR US– DID IT.
I GUESS NOT.
YOU COULD NEVER STAY IN ONE PLACE LONG ENOUGH TO MAKE A COMMITMENT. YOU WERE ALWAYS ON THE MOVE!
I KNOW.
WELL, NOW THAT YOU'VE DECIDED TO STAY HERE AND GET A REGULAR JOB, –YOU'LL MEET SOMEONE, GET MARRIED, BUY A HOUSE, HAVE A FAMILY....
SOUNDS NICE, LIZ...
BUT IT WOULD REALLY TIE ME DOWN.
LYNN

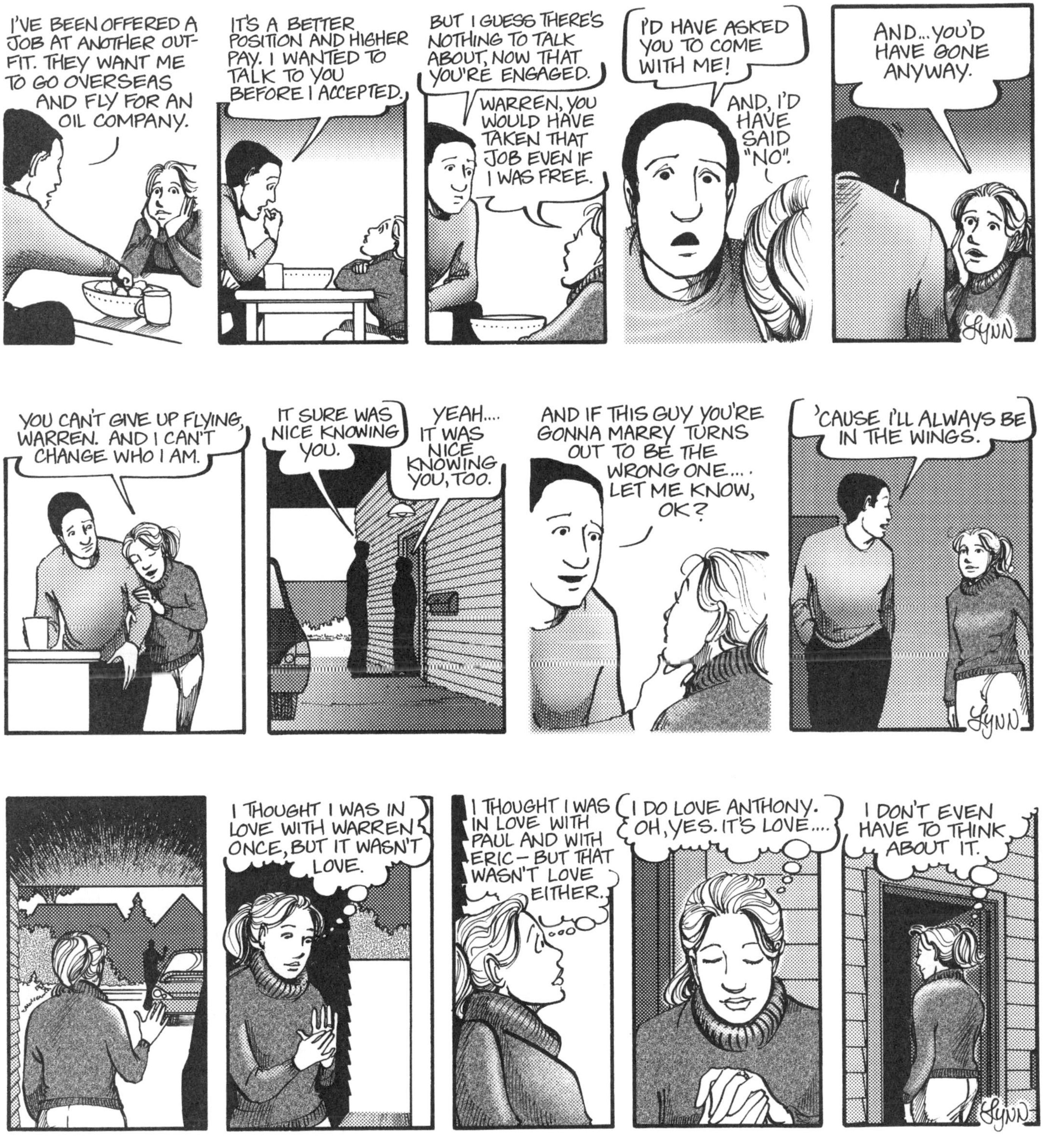
I'VE BEEN OFFERED A JOB AT ANOTHER OUT-FIT. THEY WANT ME TO GO OVERSEAS AND FLY FOR AN OIL COMPANY.
IT'S A BETTER POSITION AND HIGHER PAY. I WANTED TO TALK TO YOU BEFORE I ACCEPTED.
BUT I GUESS THERE'S NOTHING TO TALK ABOUT, NOW THAT YOU'RE ENGAGED.
WARREN, YOU WOULD HAVE TAKEN THAT JOB EVEN IF I WAS FREE.
I'D HAVE ASKED YOU TO COME WITH ME!
AND, I'D HAVE SAID "NO".
AND... YOU'D HAVE GONE ANYWAY.
LYNN
YOU CAN'T GIVE UP FLYING, WARREN. AND I CAN'T CHANGE WHO I AM.
IT SURE WAS NICE KNOWING YOU.
YEAH.... IT WAS NICE KNOWING YOU, TOO.
AND IF THIS GUY YOU'RE GONNA MARRY TURNS OUT TO BE THE WRONG ONE.... LET ME KNOW, OK?
'CAUSE I'LL ALWAYS BE IN THE WINGS.
LYNN
I THOUGHT I WAS IN LOVE WITH WARREN ONCE, BUT IT WASN'T LOVE.
I THOUGHT I WAS IN LOVE WITH PAUL AND WITH ERIC – BUT THAT WASN'T LOVE EITHER.
I DO LOVE ANTHONY. OH, YES. IT'S LOVE....
I DON'T EVEN HAVE TO THINK ABOUT IT.
LYNN

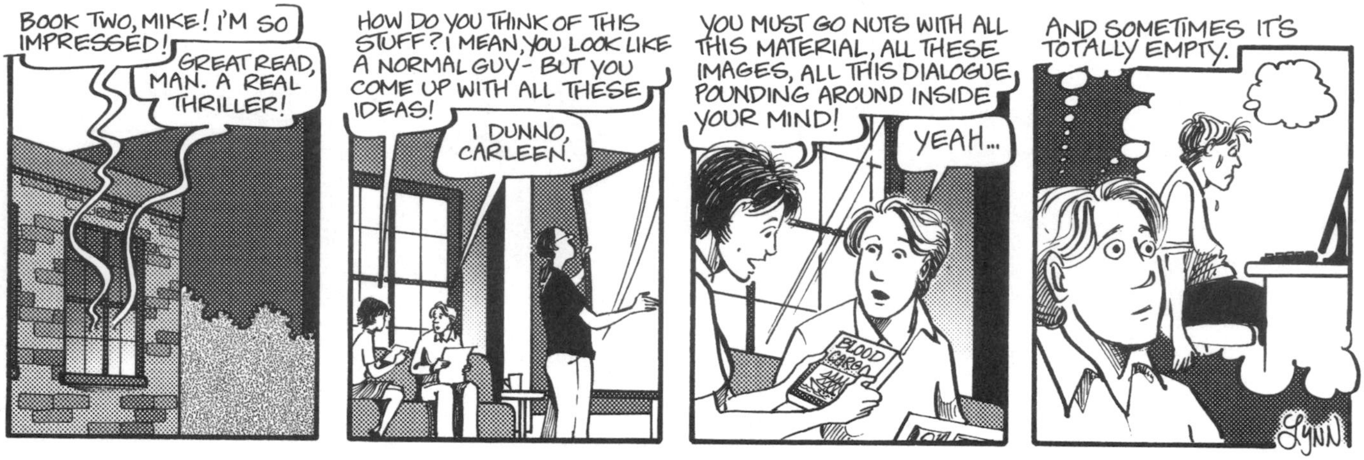
BOOK TWO, MIKE! I'M SO IMPRESSED!
GREAT READ, MAN. A REAL THRILLER!
HOW DO YOU THINK OF THIS STUFF? I MEAN, YOU LOOK LIKE A NORMAL GUY - BUT YOU COME UP WITH ALL THESE IDEAS!
I DUNNO, CARLEEN.
YOU MUST GO NUTS WITH ALL THIS MATERIAL, ALL THESE IMAGES, ALL THIS DIALOGUE POUNDING AROUND INSIDE YOUR MIND!
YEAH...
BLOOD CARGO
AND SOMETIMES IT'S TOTALLY EMPTY.
LYNN

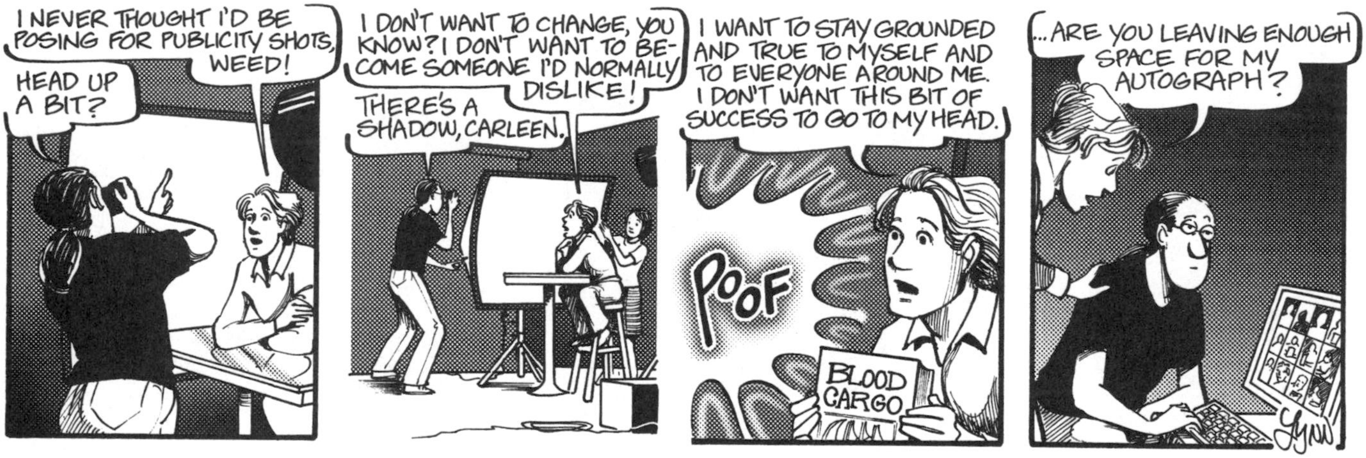
I NEVER THOUGHT I'D BE POSING FOR PUBLICITY SHOTS, WEED!
HEAD UP A BIT?
I DON'T WANT TO CHANGE, YOU KNOW? I DON'T WANT TO BECOME SOMEONE I'D NORMALLY DISLIKE!
THERE'S A SHADOW, CARLEEN.
I WANT TO STAY GROUNDED AND TRUE TO MYSELF AND TO EVERYONE AROUND ME. I DON'T WANT THIS BIT OF SUCCESS TO GO TO MY HEAD.
POOF
BLOOD CARGO
...ARE YOU LEAVING ENOUGH SPACE FOR MY AUTOGRAPH?
LYNN

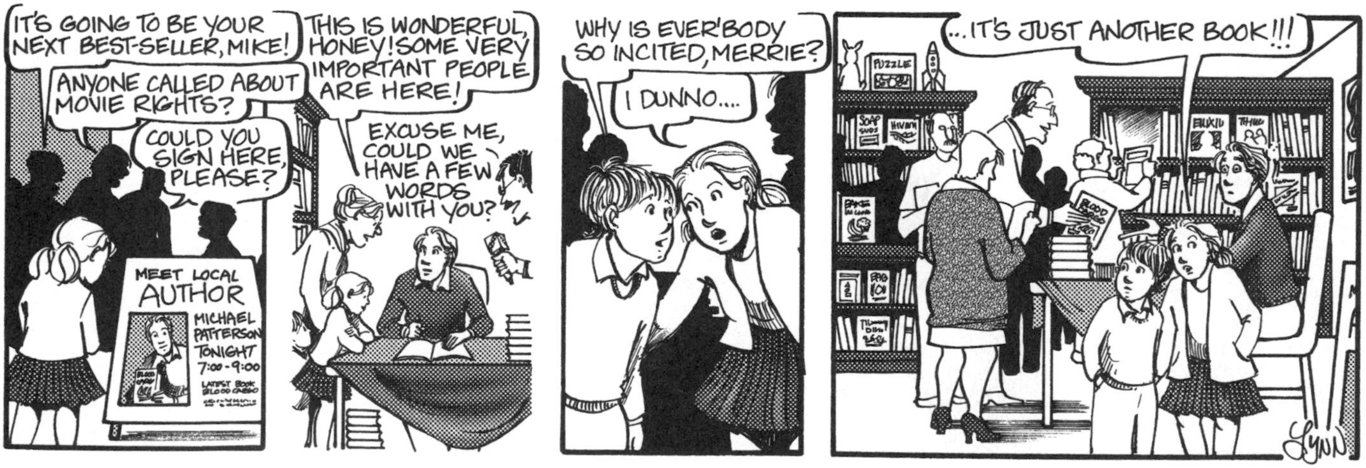
IT'S GOING TO BE YOUR NEXT BEST-SELLER, MIKE!
ANYONE CALLED ABOUT MOVIE RIGHTS?
COULD YOU SIGN HERE, PLEASE?
MEET LOCAL AUTHOR
MICHAEL PATTERSON
TONIGHT
7:00 - 9:00
THIS IS WONDERFUL, HONEY! SOME VERY IMPORTANT PEOPLE ARE HERE!
EXCUSE ME, COULD WE HAVE A FEW WORDS WITH YOU?
WHY IS EVER'BODY SO INCITED, MERRIE?
I DUNNO....
...IT'S JUST ANOTHER BOOK!!!
PUZZLE
LYNN

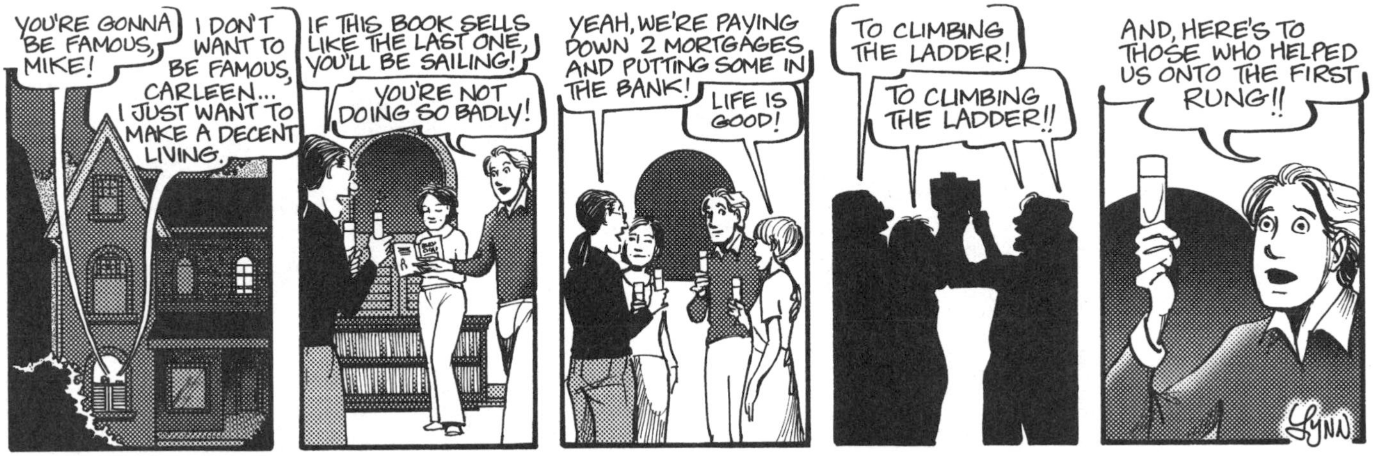
YOU'RE GONNA BE FAMOUS, MIKE!
I DON'T WANT TO BE FAMOUS, CARLEEN... I JUST WANT TO MAKE A DECENT LIVING.
IF THIS BOOK SELLS LIKE THE LAST ONE, YOU'LL BE SAILING!
YOU'RE NOT DOING SO BADLY!
YEAH, WE'RE PAYING DOWN 2 MORTGAGES AND PUTTING SOME IN THE BANK!
LIFE IS GOOD!
TO CLIMBING THE LADDER!
TO CLIMBING THE LADDER!!
AND, HERE'S TO THOSE WHO HELPED US ONTO THE FIRST RUNG!!
LYNN

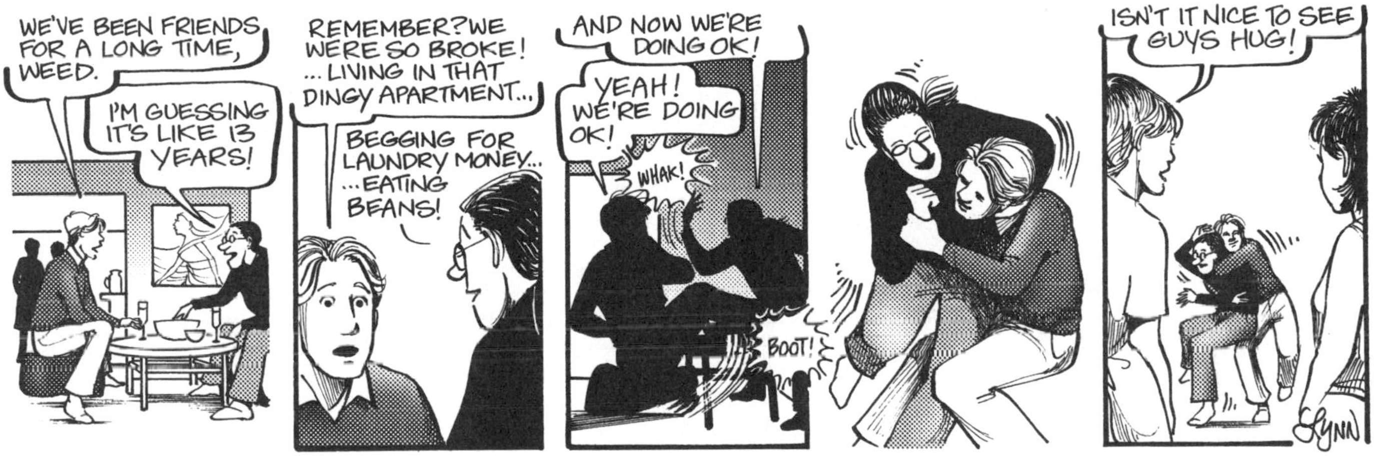
WE'VE BEEN FRIENDS FOR A LONG TIME, WEED.
I'M GUESSING IT'S LIKE 13 YEARS!
REMEMBER? WE WERE SO BROKE! ...LIVING IN THAT DINGY APARTMENT...
BEGGING FOR LAUNDRY MONEY... ...EATING BEANS!
AND NOW WE'RE DOING OK!
YEAH! WE'RE DOING OK!
WHAK!
BOOT!
ISN'T IT NICE TO SEE GUYS HUG!
LYNN

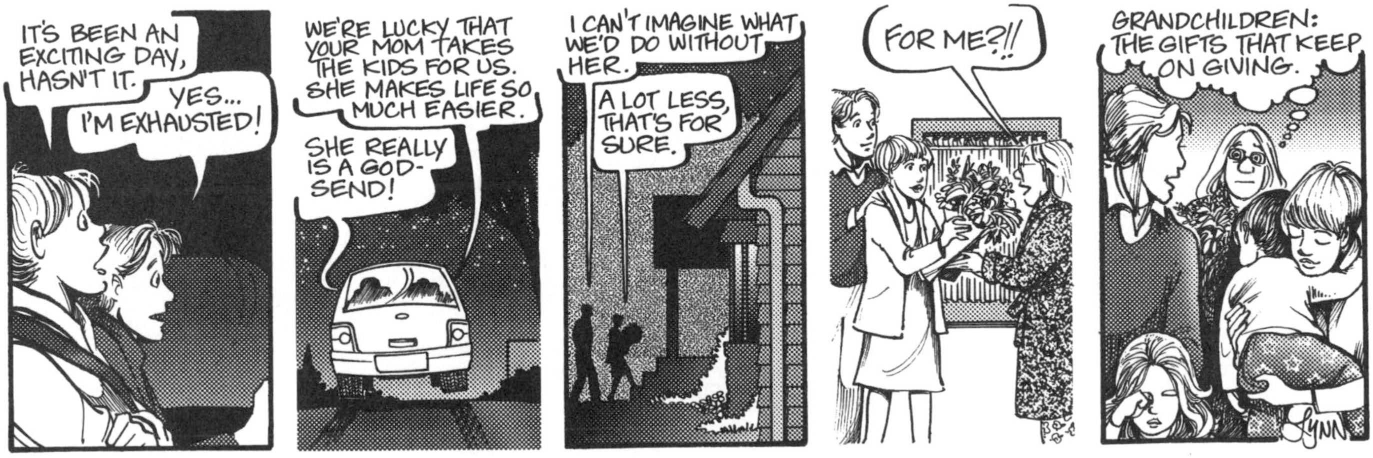
IT'S BEEN AN EXCITING DAY, HASN'T IT.
YES... I'M EXHAUSTED!
WE'RE LUCKY THAT YOUR MOM TAKES THE KIDS FOR US. SHE MAKES LIFE SO MUCH EASIER.
SHE REALLY IS A GOD-SEND!
I CAN'T IMAGINE WHAT WE'D DO WITHOUT HER.
A LOT LESS, THAT'S FOR SURE.
FOR ME?!!
GRANDCHILDREN: THE GIFTS THAT KEEP ON GIVING.
LYNN

ARE YOU GIRLS COMFORTABLE BACK THERE?

UH-HUH.

IT'S TAKING A LONG TIME TO GET DOWNTOWN. THERE'S SO MUCH TRAFFIC.

YOU TWO ARE AWFULLY QUIET! DON'T YOU HAVE ANYTHING TO SAY TO EACH OTHER?

YEAH! SURE!

BUT NOT ALOUD.

TICKA TICK TEXT TICK TICK

Lynn

THE WHOLE TIME WE WERE DRIVING THEM TO THE MALL, APRIL AND EVA WERE TEXT-MESSAGING EACH OTHER!

KIDS!

CBI*386

APRIL AND HER FRIENDS ARE CONSTANTLY SENDING LITTLE NOTES TO EACH OTHER. ≀TSK≀ ... THEY CAN'T JUST SAVE IT ALL UP AND HAVE A CONVERSATION!

AND, THEY USE SOME KIND OF CODE! KIDS! THEIR LANGUAGE IS ERODING AND NOBODY CARES. THEY DON'T EVEN KNOW HOW TO WRITE ANYMORE! WRITING'S BECOME A LOST ART!!

DID THEY SAY WHERE THEY WANTED TO BE PICKED UP?

NO!

...I'LL SEND THEM A MESSAGE.

TICK-A TAPPA TIK TAP

Lynn

I'M GLAD YOU FELT LIKE GOING OUT TONIGHT, CONNIE. JOHN'S AWAY AND I DIDN'T FEEL LIKE SPENDING THE EVENING ALONE.

HEY, ANY TIME!

HE'S STILL GOING TO DENTAL CONVENTIONS? —I THOUGHT HE WAS SEMI-RETIRED!

HE IS. BUT HE LIKES TO KEEP UP.

I REMEMBER WHEN HE FIRST STARTED HIS PRACTICE AND YOU WORKED AS HIS ASSISTANT!

HE DIDN'T HAVE THE MONEY TO HIRE ONE!

MOCHAFRAPPALATTE... TRI CHAI TEA... COL... ILLA RE... OFFEE... DR... OAST...

...WE WERE LIVING HAND-TO-MOUTH.

Lynn

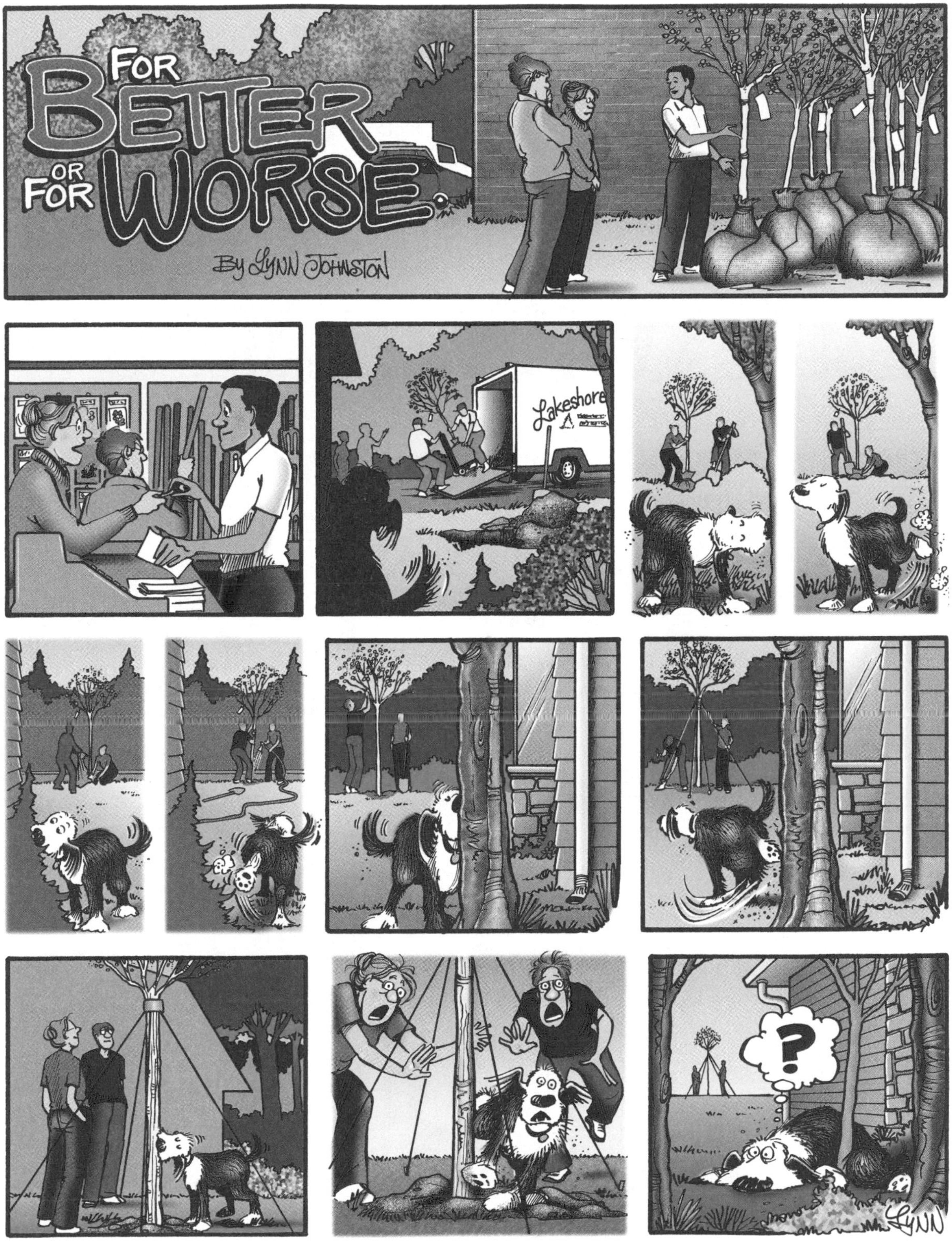
FOR BETTER OR FOR WORSE
BY LYNN JOHNSTON
Lakeshore
?
LYNN

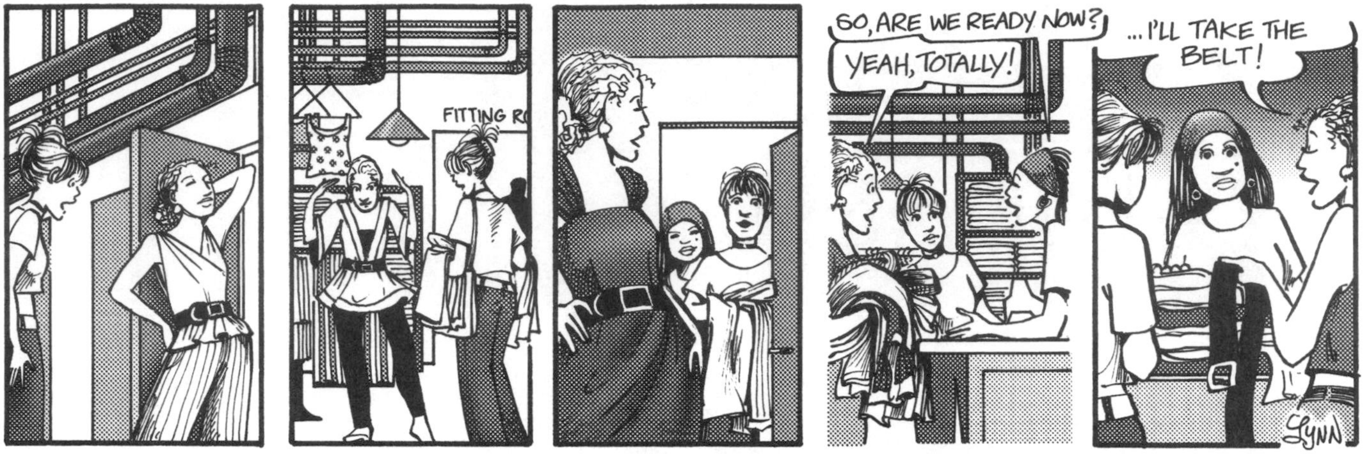
SO, ARE WE READY NOW?
YEAH, TOTALLY!
...I'LL TAKE THE BELT!
LYNN

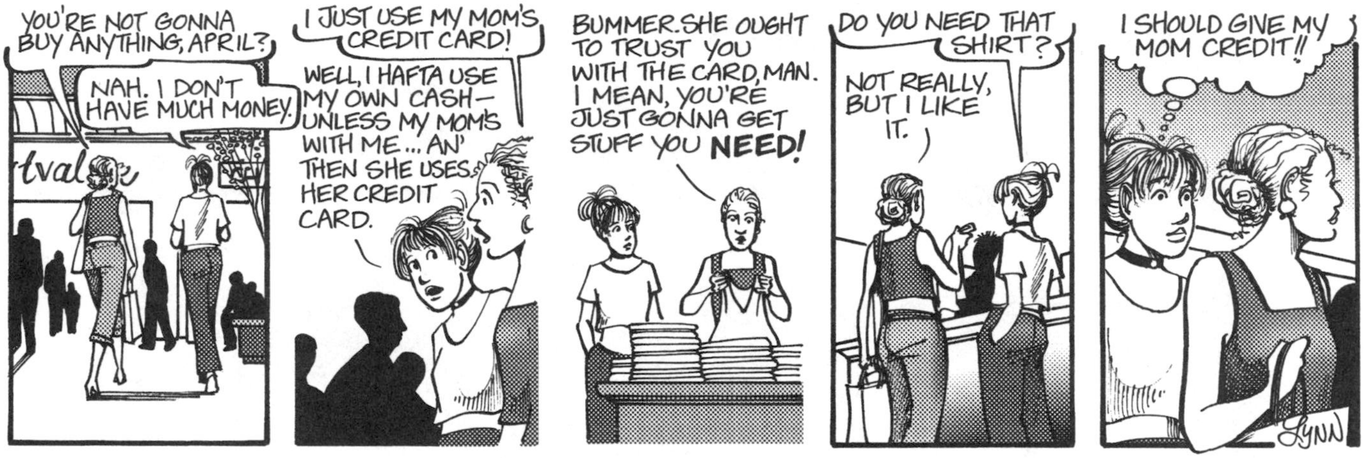
YOU'RE NOT GONNA BUY ANYTHING, APRIL?
NAH. I DON'T HAVE MUCH MONEY.
I JUST USE MY MOM'S CREDIT CARD!
WELL, I HAFTA USE MY OWN CASH— UNLESS MY MOM'S WITH ME... AN' THEN SHE USES HER CREDIT CARD.
BUMMER. SHE OUGHT TO TRUST YOU WITH THE CARD, MAN. I MEAN, YOU'RE JUST GONNA GET STUFF YOU **NEED!**
DO YOU NEED THAT SHIRT?
NOT REALLY, BUT I LIKE IT.
I SHOULD GIVE MY MOM CREDIT!!
LYNN

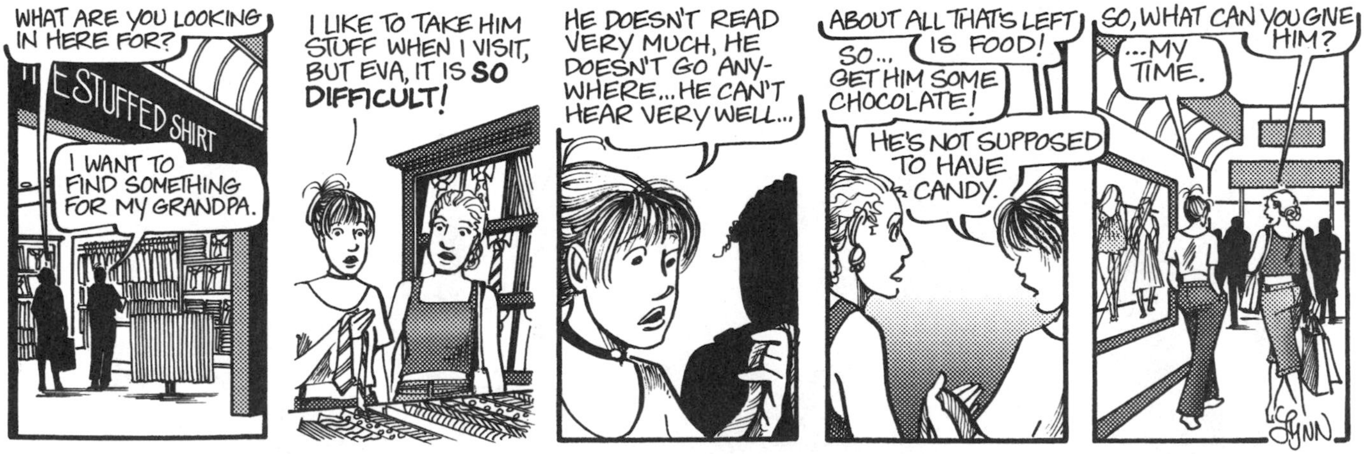
WHAT ARE YOU LOOKING IN HERE FOR?
I WANT TO FIND SOMETHING FOR MY GRANDPA.
I LIKE TO TAKE HIM STUFF WHEN I VISIT, BUT EVA, IT IS **SO DIFFICULT!**
HE DOESN'T READ VERY MUCH, HE DOESN'T GO ANY-WHERE... HE CAN'T HEAR VERY WELL...
ABOUT ALL THAT'S LEFT IS FOOD!
SO... GET HIM SOME CHOCOLATE!
HE'S NOT SUPPOSED TO HAVE CANDY.
SO, WHAT CAN YOU GIVE HIM?
...MY TIME.
LYNN

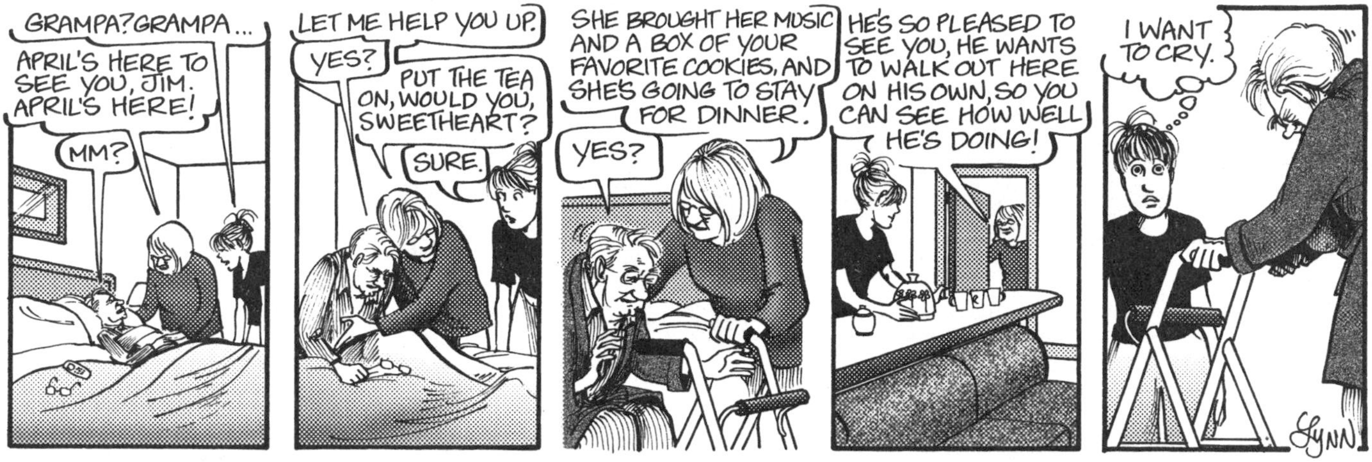
GRAMPA? GRAMPA...
APRIL'S HERE TO SEE YOU, JIM. APRIL'S HERE!
MM?
LET ME HELP YOU UP.
YES?
PUT THE TEA ON, WOULD YOU, SWEETHEART?
SURE.
SHE BROUGHT HER MUSIC AND A BOX OF YOUR FAVORITE COOKIES, AND SHE'S GOING TO STAY FOR DINNER.
YES?
HE'S SO PLEASED TO SEE YOU, HE WANTS TO WALK OUT HERE ON HIS OWN, SO YOU CAN SEE HOW WELL HE'S DOING!
I WANT TO CRY.
LYNN

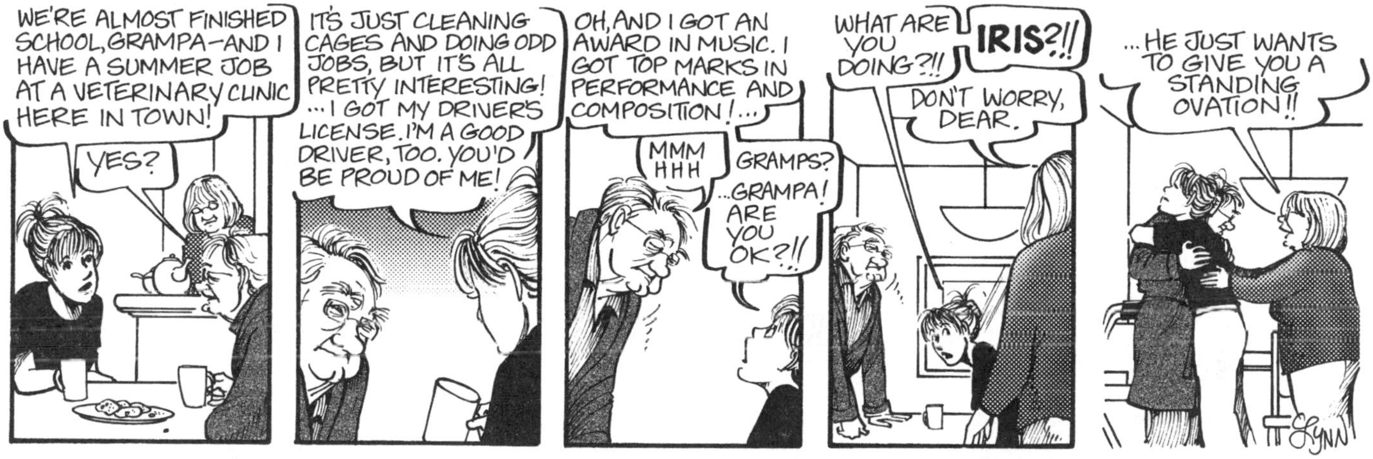
WE'RE ALMOST FINISHED SCHOOL, GRAMPA—AND I HAVE A SUMMER JOB AT A VETERINARY CLINIC HERE IN TOWN!
YES?
IT'S JUST CLEANING CAGES AND DOING ODD JOBS, BUT IT'S ALL PRETTY INTERESTING! ...I GOT MY DRIVER'S LICENSE. I'M A GOOD DRIVER, TOO. YOU'D BE PROUD OF ME!
OH, AND I GOT AN AWARD IN MUSIC. I GOT TOP MARKS IN PERFORMANCE AND COMPOSITION!...
MMM HHH
GRAMPS?
...GRAMPA! ARE YOU OK?!!
WHAT ARE YOU DOING?!!
IRIS?!!
DON'T WORRY, DEAR.
...HE JUST WANTS TO GIVE YOU A STANDING OVATION!!
LYNN

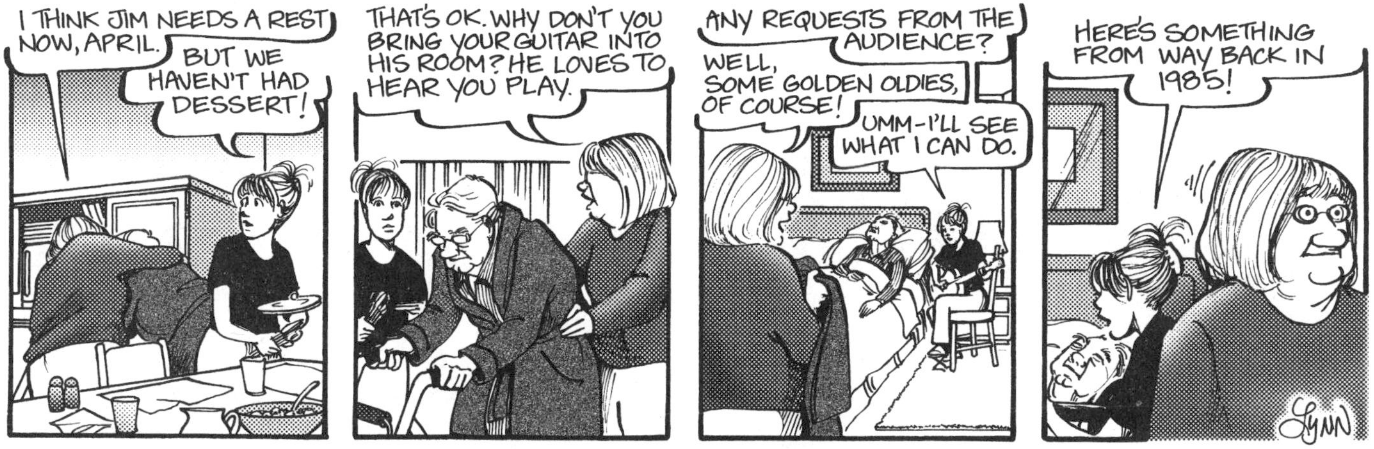
I THINK JIM NEEDS A REST NOW, APRIL.
BUT WE HAVEN'T HAD DESSERT!
THAT'S OK. WHY DON'T YOU BRING YOUR GUITAR INTO HIS ROOM? HE LOVES TO HEAR YOU PLAY.
ANY REQUESTS FROM THE AUDIENCE?
WELL, SOME GOLDEN OLDIES, OF COURSE!
UMM-I'LL SEE WHAT I CAN DO.
HERE'S SOMETHING FROM WAY BACK IN 1985!
LYNN

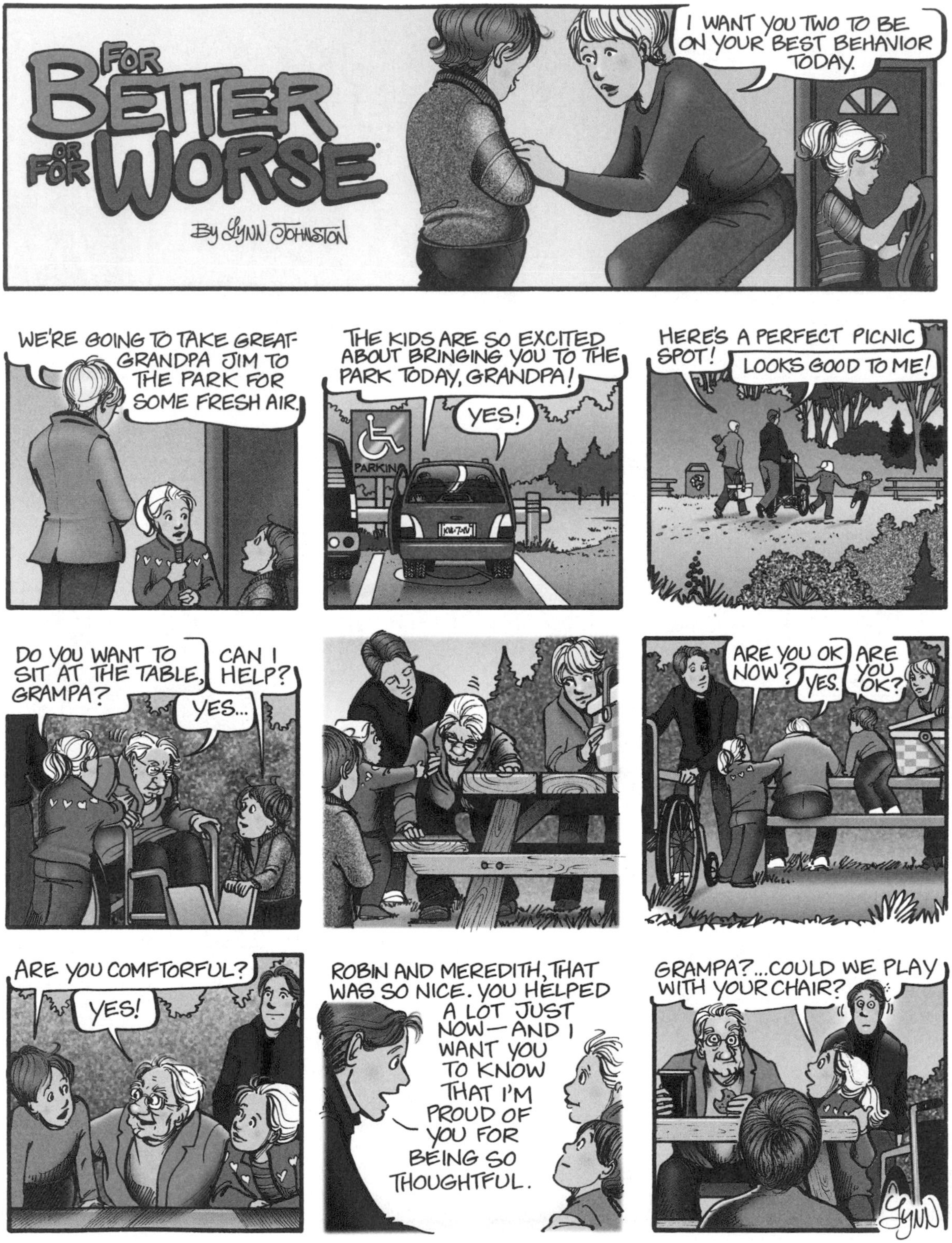
FOR BETTER OR FOR WORSE
BY LYNN JOHNSTON
I WANT YOU TWO TO BE ON YOUR BEST BEHAVIOR TODAY.
WE'RE GOING TO TAKE GREAT-GRANDPA JIM TO THE PARK FOR SOME FRESH AIR.
THE KIDS ARE SO EXCITED ABOUT BRINGING YOU TO THE PARK TODAY, GRANDPA!
YES!
PARKING
HERE'S A PERFECT PICNIC SPOT!
LOOKS GOOD TO ME!
DO YOU WANT TO SIT AT THE TABLE, GRAMPA?
CAN I HELP?
YES...
ARE YOU OK NOW?
YES.
ARE YOU OK?
ARE YOU COMFTORFUL?
YES!
ROBIN AND MEREDITH, THAT WAS SO NICE. YOU HELPED A LOT JUST NOW—AND I WANT YOU TO KNOW THAT I'M PROUD OF YOU FOR BEING SO THOUGHTFUL.
GRAMPA?...COULD WE PLAY WITH YOUR CHAIR?
LYNN

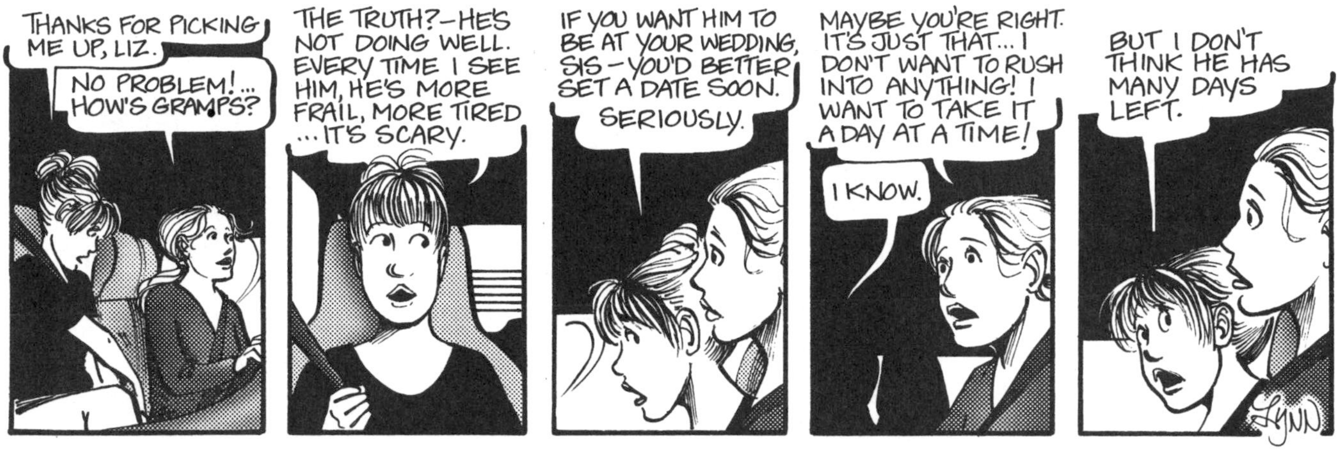
THANKS FOR PICKING ME UP, LIZ.
NO PROBLEM!... HOW'S GRAMPS?
THE TRUTH?—HE'S NOT DOING WELL. EVERY TIME I SEE HIM, HE'S MORE FRAIL, MORE TIRED ...IT'S SCARY.
IF YOU WANT HIM TO BE AT YOUR WEDDING, SIS—YOU'D BETTER SET A DATE SOON.
SERIOUSLY.
MAYBE YOU'RE RIGHT. IT'S JUST THAT... I DON'T WANT TO RUSH INTO ANYTHING! I WANT TO TAKE IT A DAY AT A TIME!
I KNOW.
BUT I DON'T THINK HE HAS MANY DAYS LEFT.
LYNN

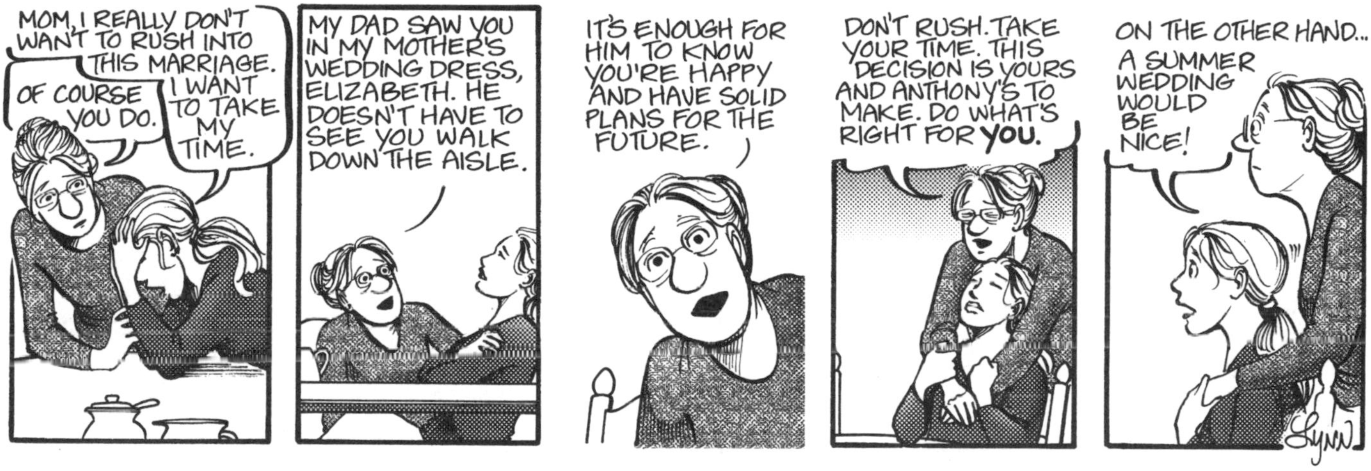
MOM, I REALLY DON'T WANT TO RUSH INTO THIS MARRIAGE.
OF COURSE YOU DO.
I WANT TO TAKE MY TIME.
MY DAD SAW YOU IN MY MOTHER'S WEDDING DRESS, ELIZABETH. HE DOESN'T HAVE TO SEE YOU WALK DOWN THE AISLE.
IT'S ENOUGH FOR HIM TO KNOW YOU'RE HAPPY AND HAVE SOLID PLANS FOR THE FUTURE.
DON'T RUSH. TAKE YOUR TIME. THIS DECISION IS YOURS AND ANTHONY'S TO MAKE. DO WHAT'S RIGHT FOR YOU.
ON THE OTHER HAND...
A SUMMER WEDDING WOULD BE NICE!
LYNN

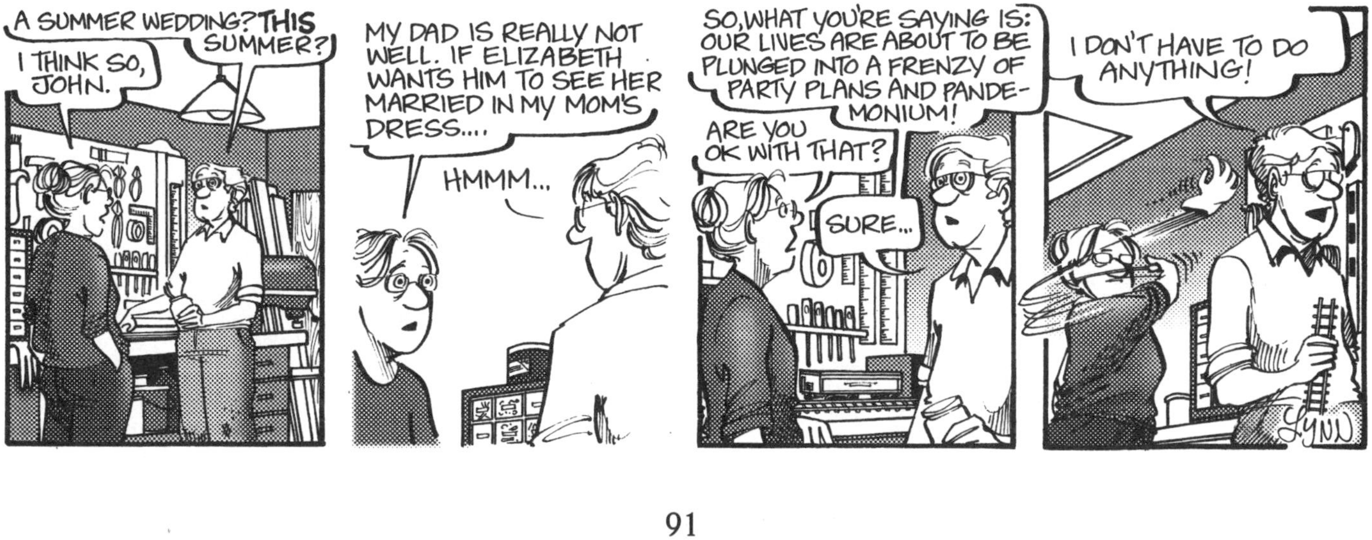
A SUMMER WEDDING? THIS SUMMER?
I THINK SO, JOHN.
MY DAD IS REALLY NOT WELL. IF ELIZABETH WANTS HIM TO SEE HER MARRIED IN MY MOM'S DRESS....
HMMM...
SO, WHAT YOU'RE SAYING IS: OUR LIVES ARE ABOUT TO BE PLUNGED INTO A FRENZY OF PARTY PLANS AND PANDEMONIUM!
ARE YOU OK WITH THAT?
SURE...
I DON'T HAVE TO DO ANYTHING!
LYNN

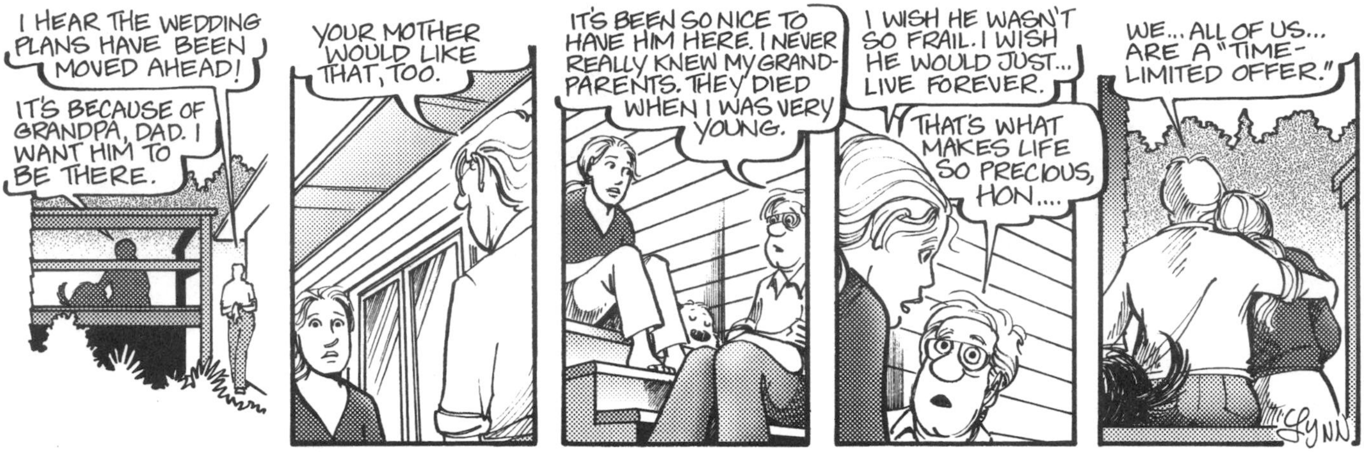
I HEAR THE WEDDING PLANS HAVE BEEN MOVED AHEAD!
IT'S BECAUSE OF GRANDPA, DAD. I WANT HIM TO BE THERE.
YOUR MOTHER WOULD LIKE THAT, TOO.
IT'S BEEN SO NICE TO HAVE HIM HERE. I NEVER REALLY KNEW MY GRAND-PARENTS. THEY DIED WHEN I WAS VERY YOUNG.
I WISH HE WASN'T SO FRAIL. I WISH HE WOULD JUST... LIVE FOREVER.
THAT'S WHAT MAKES LIFE SO PRECIOUS, HON....
WE... ALL OF US... ARE A "TIME-LIMITED OFFER."
LYNN

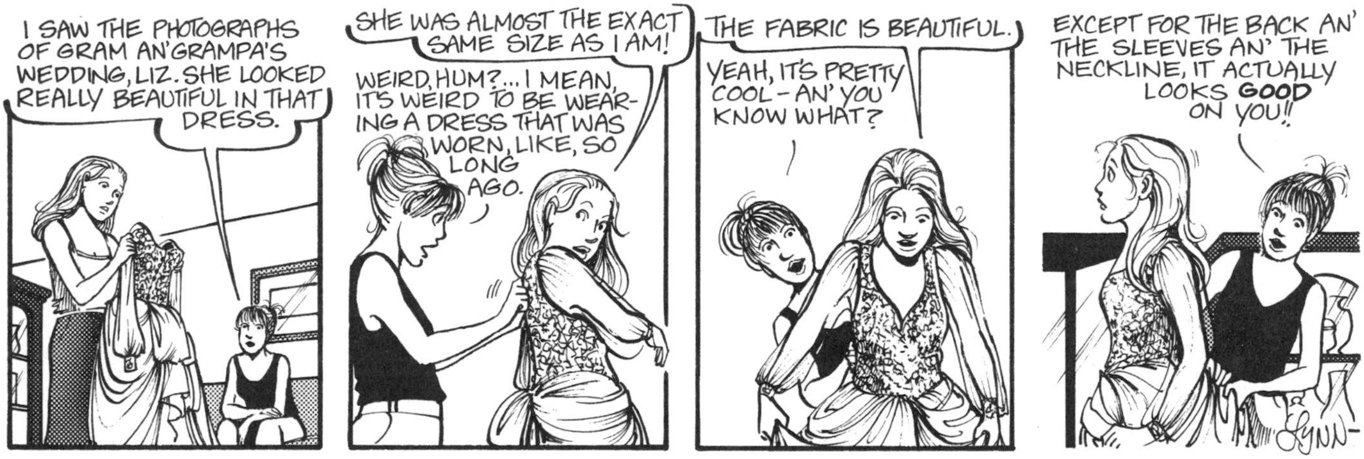
I SAW THE PHOTOGRAPHS OF GRAM AN' GRAMPA'S WEDDING, LIZ. SHE LOOKED REALLY BEAUTIFUL IN THAT DRESS.
SHE WAS ALMOST THE EXACT SAME SIZE AS I AM!
WEIRD, HUM?... I MEAN, IT'S WEIRD TO BE WEAR-ING A DRESS THAT WAS WORN, LIKE, SO LONG AGO.
THE FABRIC IS BEAUTIFUL.
YEAH, IT'S PRETTY COOL – AN' YOU KNOW WHAT?
EXCEPT FOR THE BACK AN' THE SLEEVES AN' THE NECKLINE, IT ACTUALLY LOOKS **GOOD** ON YOU!!
LYNN

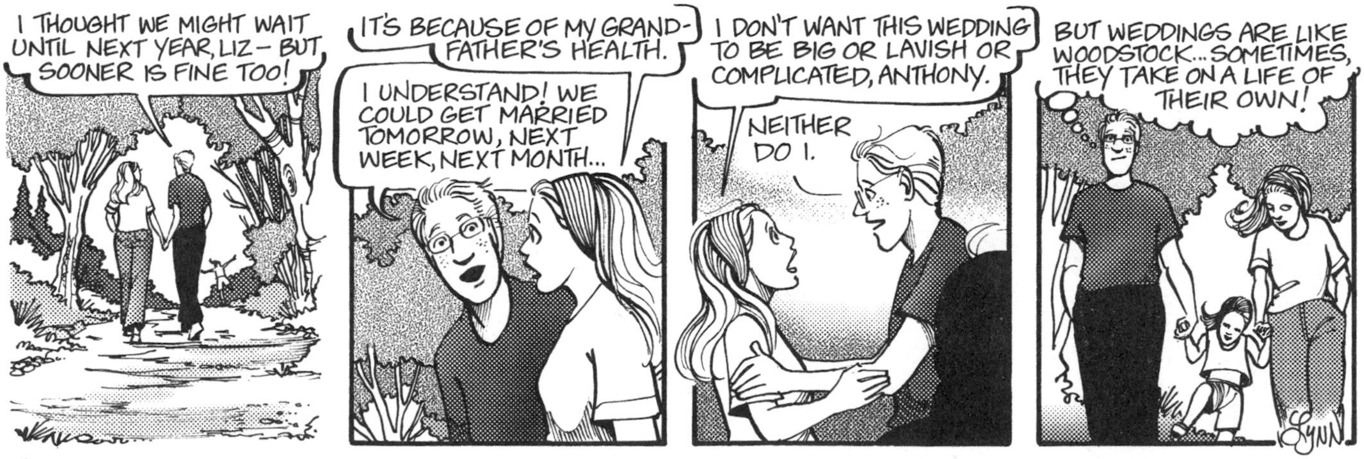
I THOUGHT WE MIGHT WAIT UNTIL NEXT YEAR, LIZ – BUT, SOONER IS FINE TOO!
IT'S BECAUSE OF MY GRAND-FATHER'S HEALTH.
I UNDERSTAND! WE COULD GET MARRIED TOMORROW, NEXT WEEK, NEXT MONTH...
I DON'T WANT THIS WEDDING TO BE BIG OR LAVISH OR COMPLICATED, ANTHONY.
NEITHER DO I.
BUT WEDDINGS ARE LIKE WOODSTOCK... SOMETIMES, THEY TAKE ON A LIFE OF THEIR OWN!
LYNN

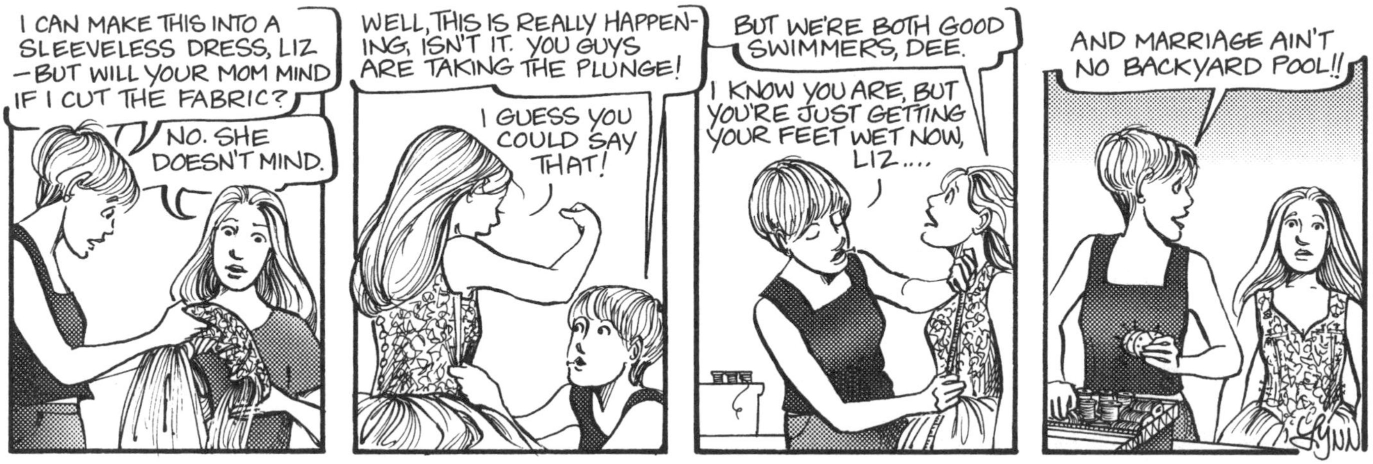
I CAN MAKE THIS INTO A SLEEVELESS DRESS, LIZ —BUT WILL YOUR MOM MIND IF I CUT THE FABRIC?
NO. SHE DOESN'T MIND.
WELL, THIS IS REALLY HAPPEN-ING, ISN'T IT. YOU GUYS ARE TAKING THE PLUNGE!
I GUESS YOU COULD SAY THAT!
BUT WE'RE BOTH GOOD SWIMMERS, DEE.
I KNOW YOU ARE, BUT YOU'RE JUST GETTING YOUR FEET WET NOW, LIZ....
AND MARRIAGE AIN'T NO BACKYARD POOL!!
LYNN

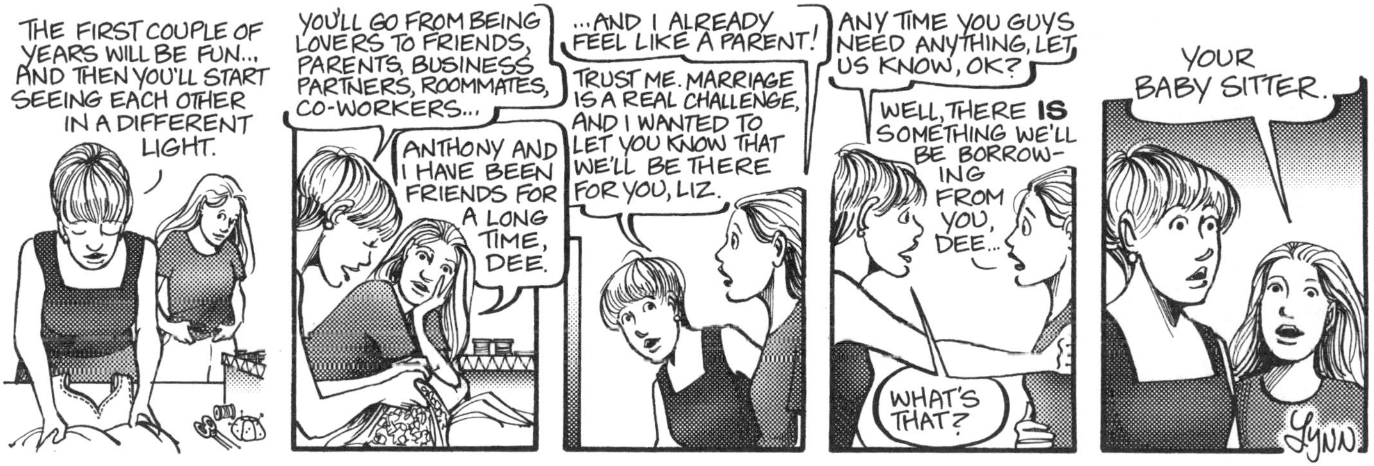
THE FIRST COUPLE OF YEARS WILL BE FUN..., AND THEN YOU'LL START SEEING EACH OTHER IN A DIFFERENT LIGHT.
YOU'LL GO FROM BEING LOVERS TO FRIENDS, PARENTS, BUSINESS PARTNERS, ROOMMATES, CO-WORKERS...
ANTHONY AND I HAVE BEEN FRIENDS FOR A LONG TIME, DEE.
...AND I ALREADY FEEL LIKE A PARENT!
TRUST ME. MARRIAGE IS A REAL CHALLENGE, AND I WANTED TO LET YOU KNOW THAT WE'LL BE THERE FOR YOU, LIZ.
ANY TIME YOU GUYS NEED ANYTHING, LET US KNOW, OK?
WELL, THERE IS SOMETHING WE'LL BE BORROW-ING FROM YOU, DEE...
WHAT'S THAT?
YOUR BABY SITTER.
LYNN

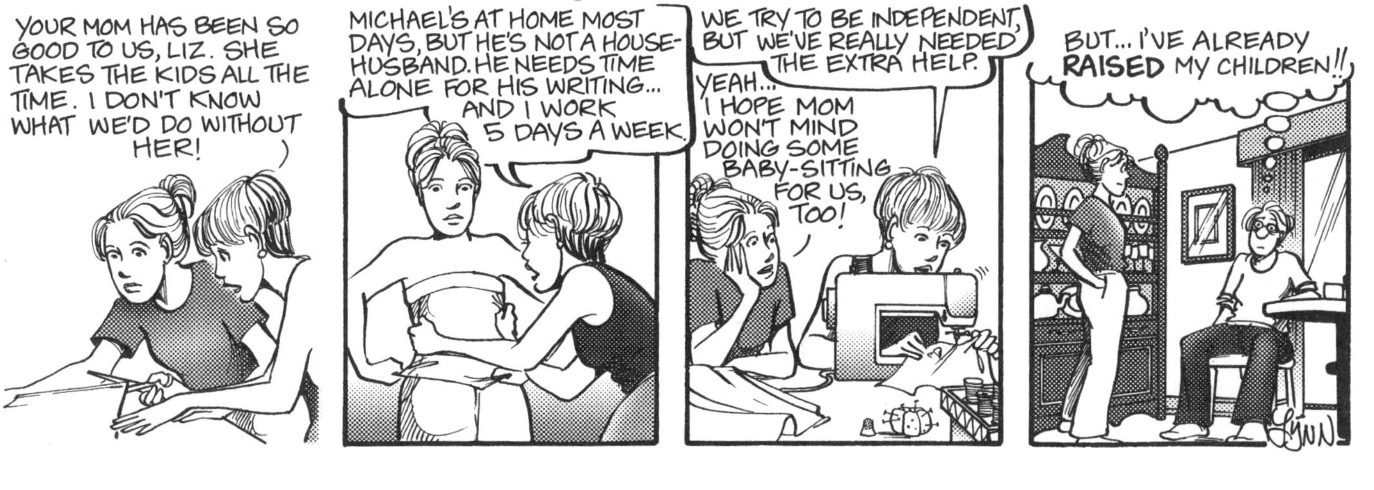
YOUR MOM HAS BEEN SO GOOD TO US, LIZ. SHE TAKES THE KIDS ALL THE TIME. I DON'T KNOW WHAT WE'D DO WITHOUT HER!
MICHAEL'S AT HOME MOST DAYS, BUT HE'S NOT A HOUSE-HUSBAND. HE NEEDS TIME ALONE FOR HIS WRITING... AND I WORK 5 DAYS A WEEK.
WE TRY TO BE INDEPENDENT, BUT WE'VE REALLY NEEDED THE EXTRA HELP.
YEAH... I HOPE MOM WON'T MIND DOING SOME BABY-SITTING FOR US, TOO!
BUT... I'VE ALREADY RAISED MY CHILDREN!!
LYNN

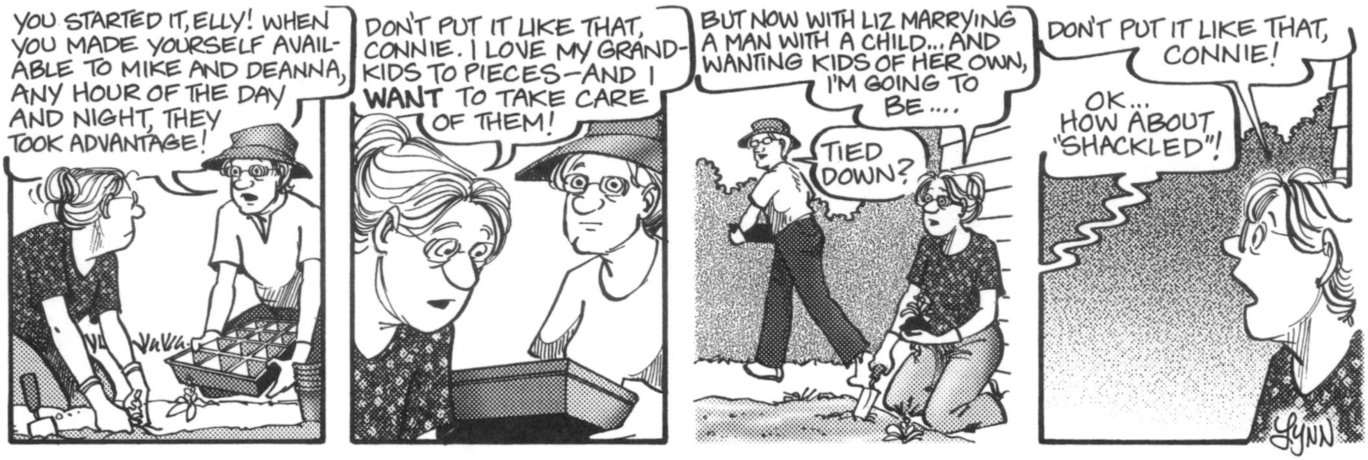
YOU STARTED IT, ELLY! WHEN YOU MADE YOURSELF AVAILABLE TO MIKE AND DEANNA, ANY HOUR OF THE DAY AND NIGHT, THEY TOOK ADVANTAGE!
DON'T PUT IT LIKE THAT, CONNIE. I LOVE MY GRANDKIDS TO PIECES—AND I WANT TO TAKE CARE OF THEM!
BUT NOW WITH LIZ MARRYING A MAN WITH A CHILD... AND WANTING KIDS OF HER OWN, I'M GOING TO BE....
TIED DOWN?
DON'T PUT IT LIKE THAT, CONNIE!
OK... HOW ABOUT "SHACKLED"?!
LYNN

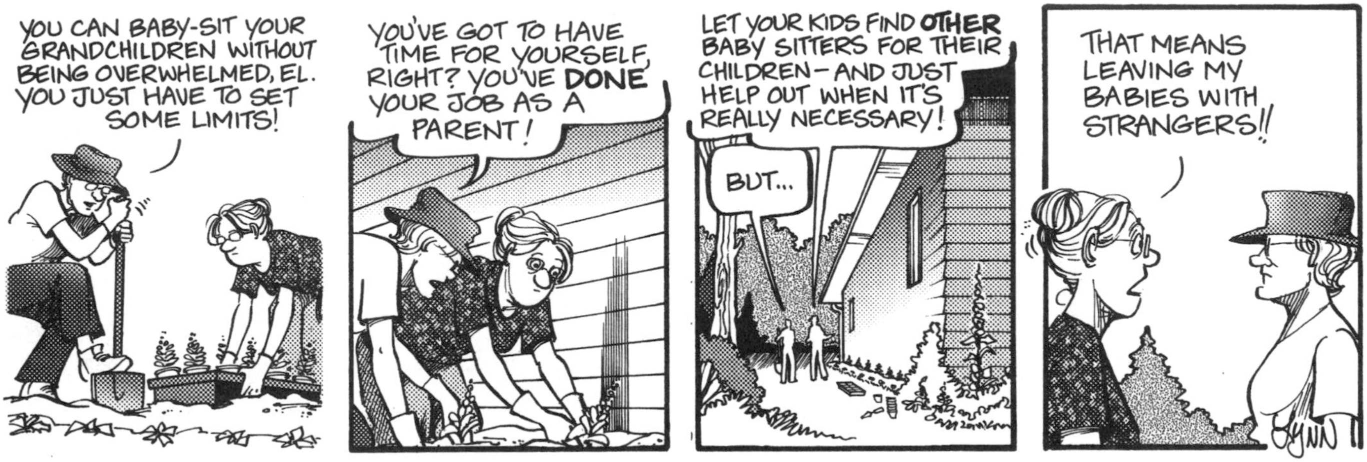
YOU CAN BABY-SIT YOUR GRANDCHILDREN WITHOUT BEING OVERWHELMED, EL. YOU JUST HAVE TO SET SOME LIMITS!
YOU'VE GOT TO HAVE TIME FOR YOURSELF, RIGHT? YOU'VE DONE YOUR JOB AS A PARENT!
LET YOUR KIDS FIND OTHER BABY SITTERS FOR THEIR CHILDREN—AND JUST HELP OUT WHEN IT'S REALLY NECESSARY!
BUT...
THAT MEANS LEAVING MY BABIES WITH STRANGERS!!
LYNN

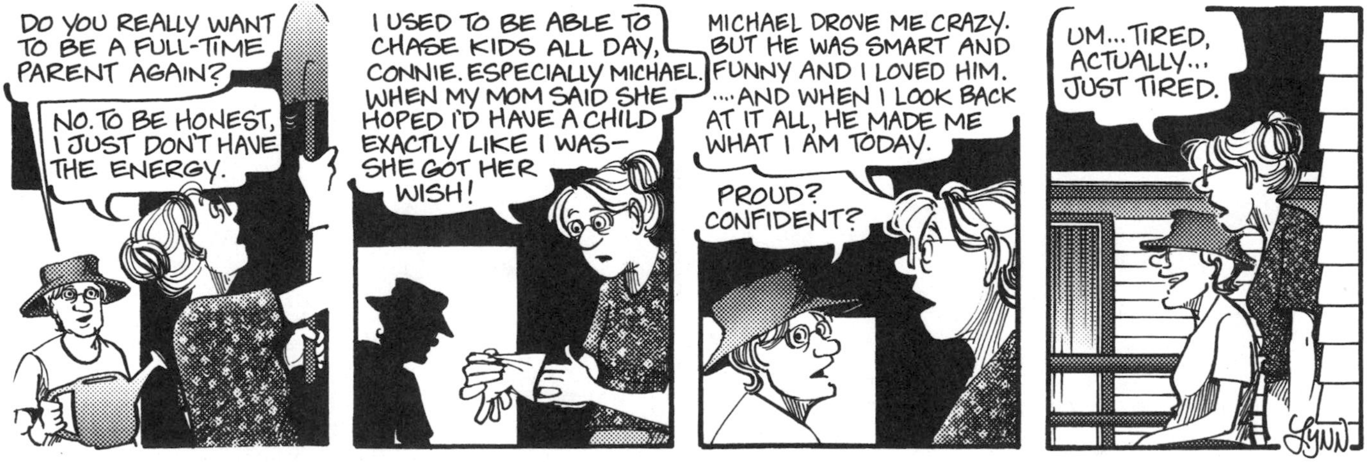
DO YOU REALLY WANT TO BE A FULL-TIME PARENT AGAIN?
NO. TO BE HONEST, I JUST DON'T HAVE THE ENERGY.
I USED TO BE ABLE TO CHASE KIDS ALL DAY, CONNIE. ESPECIALLY MICHAEL. WHEN MY MOM SAID SHE HOPED I'D HAVE A CHILD EXACTLY LIKE I WAS—SHE GOT HER WISH!
MICHAEL DROVE ME CRAZY. BUT HE WAS SMART AND FUNNY AND I LOVED HIM. ....AND WHEN I LOOK BACK AT IT ALL, HE MADE ME WHAT I AM TODAY.
PROUD? CONFIDENT?
UM... TIRED, ACTUALLY... JUST TIRED.
LYNN

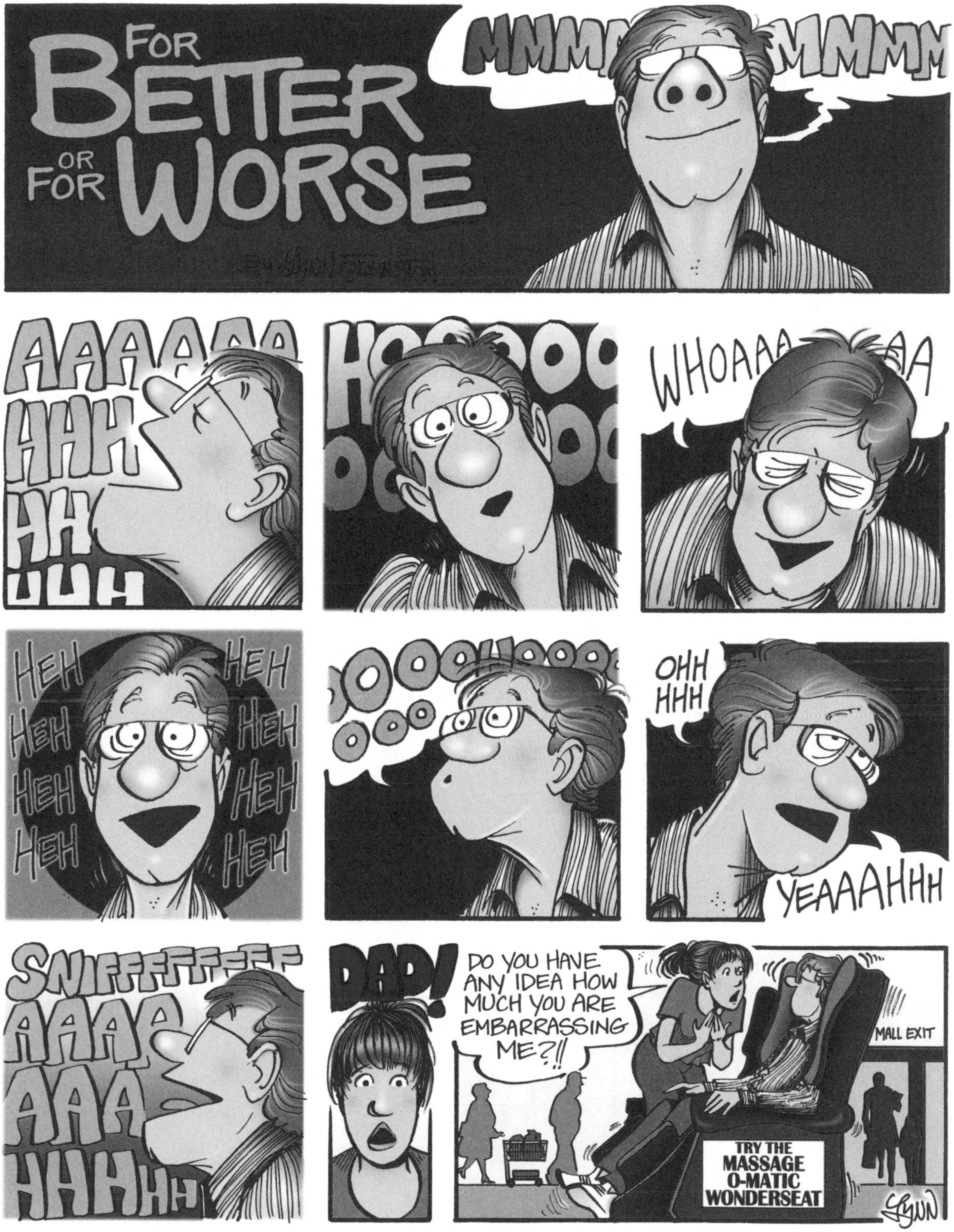
FOR BETTER OR FOR WORSE
BY LYNN JOHNSTON
MMMMMMMMM
AAAAAAHHHHHUUH
HOOOOOOOOO
WHOAAAAA
HEH HEH HEH HEH HEH HEH HEH HEH
OOOOHOOOOOOO
OHHHHH
YEAAAHHH
SNIFFFFFFFFF
AAAAAAAHHHHHH
DAD!
DO YOU HAVE ANY IDEA HOW MUCH YOU ARE EMBARRASSING ME?!!
MALL EXIT
TRY THE MASSAGE O-MATIC WONDERSEAT
LYNN

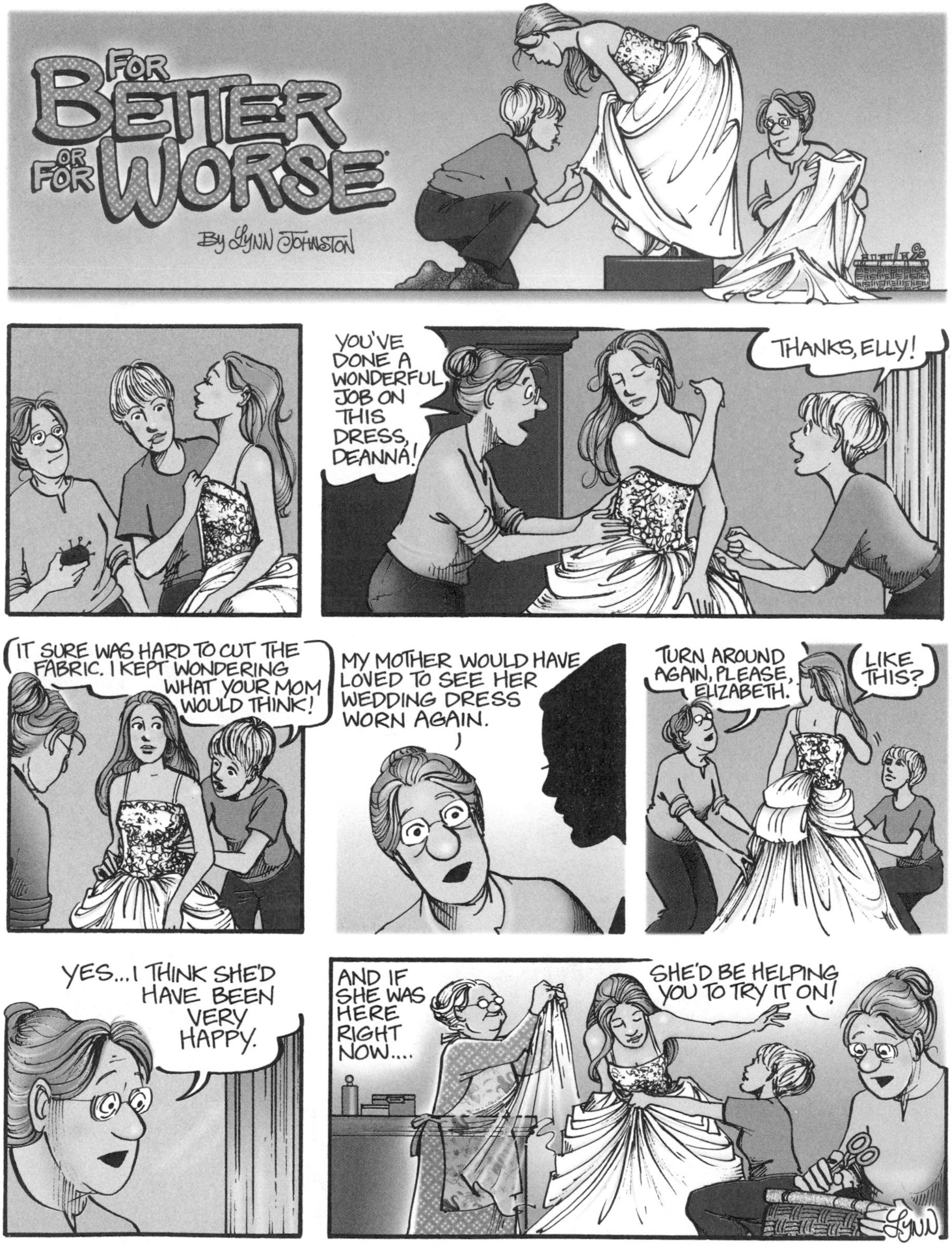
FOR BETTER OR FOR WORSE
By Lynn Johnston
YOU'VE DONE A WONDERFUL JOB ON THIS DRESS, DEANNA!
THANKS, ELLY!
IT SURE WAS HARD TO CUT THE FABRIC. I KEPT WONDERING WHAT YOUR MOM WOULD THINK!
MY MOTHER WOULD HAVE LOVED TO SEE HER WEDDING DRESS WORN AGAIN.
TURN AROUND AGAIN, PLEASE, ELIZABETH.
LIKE THIS?
YES...I THINK SHE'D HAVE BEEN VERY HAPPY.
AND IF SHE WAS HERE RIGHT NOW....
SHE'D BE HELPING YOU TO TRY IT ON!
LYNN

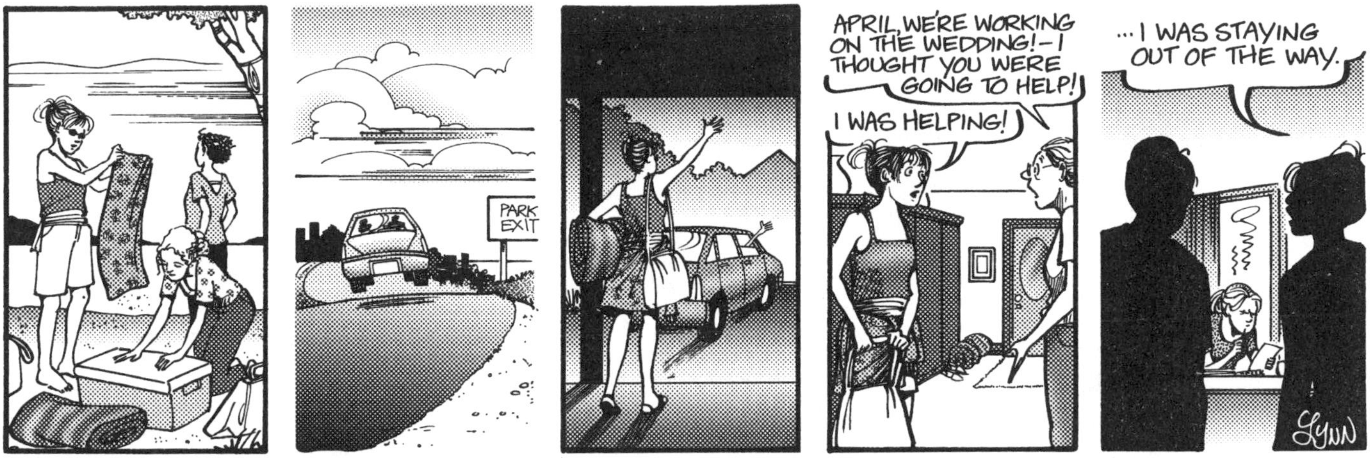
PARK EXIT
APRIL, WE'RE WORKING ON THE WEDDING! - I THOUGHT YOU WERE GOING TO HELP!
I WAS HELPING!
... I WAS STAYING OUT OF THE WAY.
LYNN

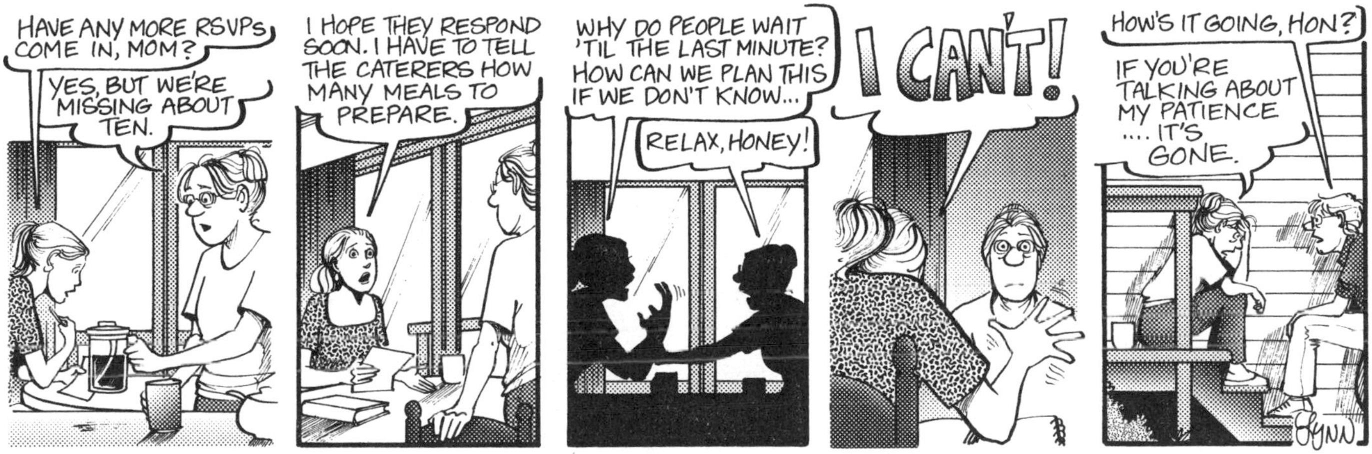
HAVE ANY MORE RSVPs COME IN, MOM?
YES, BUT WE'RE MISSING ABOUT TEN.
I HOPE THEY RESPOND SOON. I HAVE TO TELL THE CATERERS HOW MANY MEALS TO PREPARE.
WHY DO PEOPLE WAIT 'TIL THE LAST MINUTE? HOW CAN WE PLAN THIS IF WE DON'T KNOW...
RELAX, HONEY!
I CAN'T!
HOW'S IT GOING, HON?
IF YOU'RE TALKING ABOUT MY PATIENCE .... IT'S GONE.
LYNN

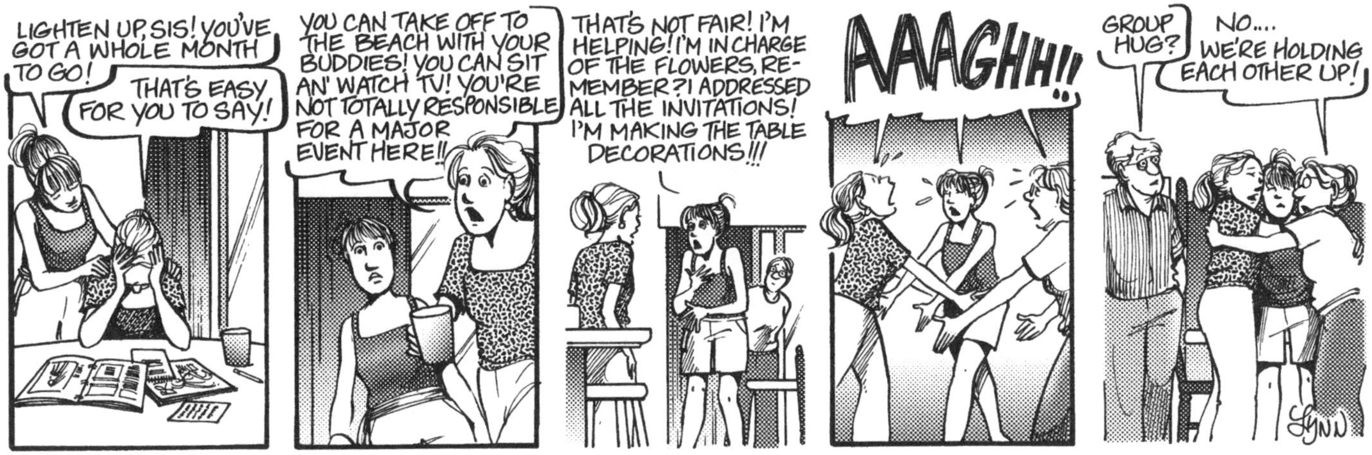
LIGHTEN UP, SIS! YOU'VE GOT A WHOLE MONTH TO GO!
THAT'S EASY FOR YOU TO SAY!
YOU CAN TAKE OFF TO THE BEACH WITH YOUR BUDDIES! YOU CAN SIT AN' WATCH TV! YOU'RE NOT TOTALLY RESPONSIBLE FOR A MAJOR EVENT HERE!!
THAT'S NOT FAIR! I'M HELPING! I'M IN CHARGE OF THE FLOWERS, RE-MEMBER?! I ADDRESSED ALL THE INVITATIONS! I'M MAKING THE TABLE DECORATIONS!!!
AAAGHH!!
GROUP HUG?
NO.... WE'RE HOLDING EACH OTHER UP!
LYNN

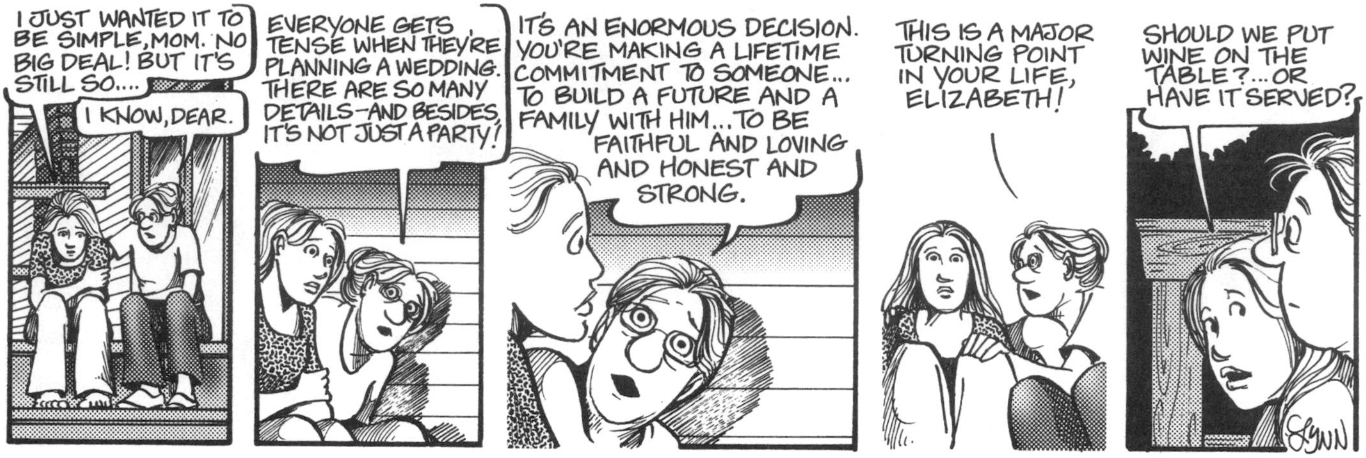
I JUST WANTED IT TO BE SIMPLE, MOM. NO BIG DEAL! BUT IT'S STILL SO....
I KNOW, DEAR.
EVERYONE GETS TENSE WHEN THEY'RE PLANNING A WEDDING. THERE ARE SO MANY DETAILS–AND BESIDES, IT'S NOT JUST A PARTY!
IT'S AN ENORMOUS DECISION. YOU'RE MAKING A LIFETIME COMMITMENT TO SOMEONE... TO BUILD A FUTURE AND A FAMILY WITH HIM... TO BE FAITHFUL AND LOVING AND HONEST AND STRONG.
THIS IS A MAJOR TURNING POINT IN YOUR LIFE, ELIZABETH!
SHOULD WE PUT WINE ON THE TABLE?...OR HAVE IT SERVED?
LYNN

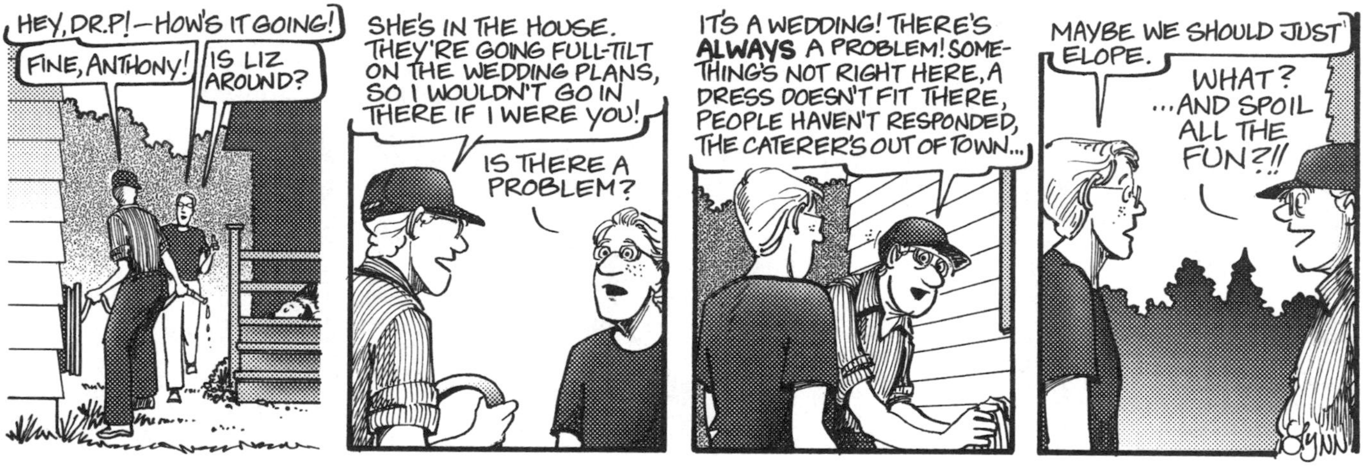
HEY, DR.P!–HOW'S IT GOING!
FINE, ANTHONY!
IS LIZ AROUND?
SHE'S IN THE HOUSE. THEY'RE GOING FULL-TILT ON THE WEDDING PLANS, SO I WOULDN'T GO IN THERE IF I WERE YOU!
IS THERE A PROBLEM?
IT'S A WEDDING! THERE'S ALWAYS A PROBLEM! SOMETHING'S NOT RIGHT HERE, A DRESS DOESN'T FIT THERE, PEOPLE HAVEN'T RESPONDED, THE CATERER'S OUT OF TOWN...
MAYBE WE SHOULD JUST ELOPE.
WHAT? ...AND SPOIL ALL THE FUN?!!
LYNN

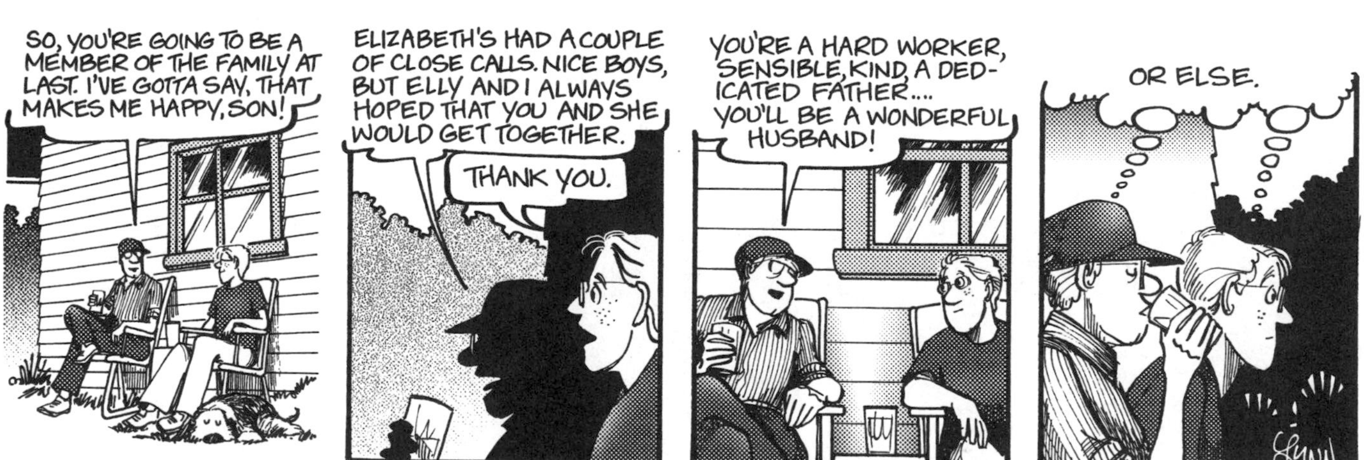
SO, YOU'RE GOING TO BE A MEMBER OF THE FAMILY AT LAST. I'VE GOTTA SAY, THAT MAKES ME HAPPY, SON!
ELIZABETH'S HAD A COUPLE OF CLOSE CALLS. NICE BOYS, BUT ELLY AND I ALWAYS HOPED THAT YOU AND SHE WOULD GET TOGETHER.
THANK YOU.
YOU'RE A HARD WORKER, SENSIBLE, KIND, A DEDICATED FATHER.... YOU'LL BE A WONDERFUL HUSBAND!
OR ELSE.
LYNN

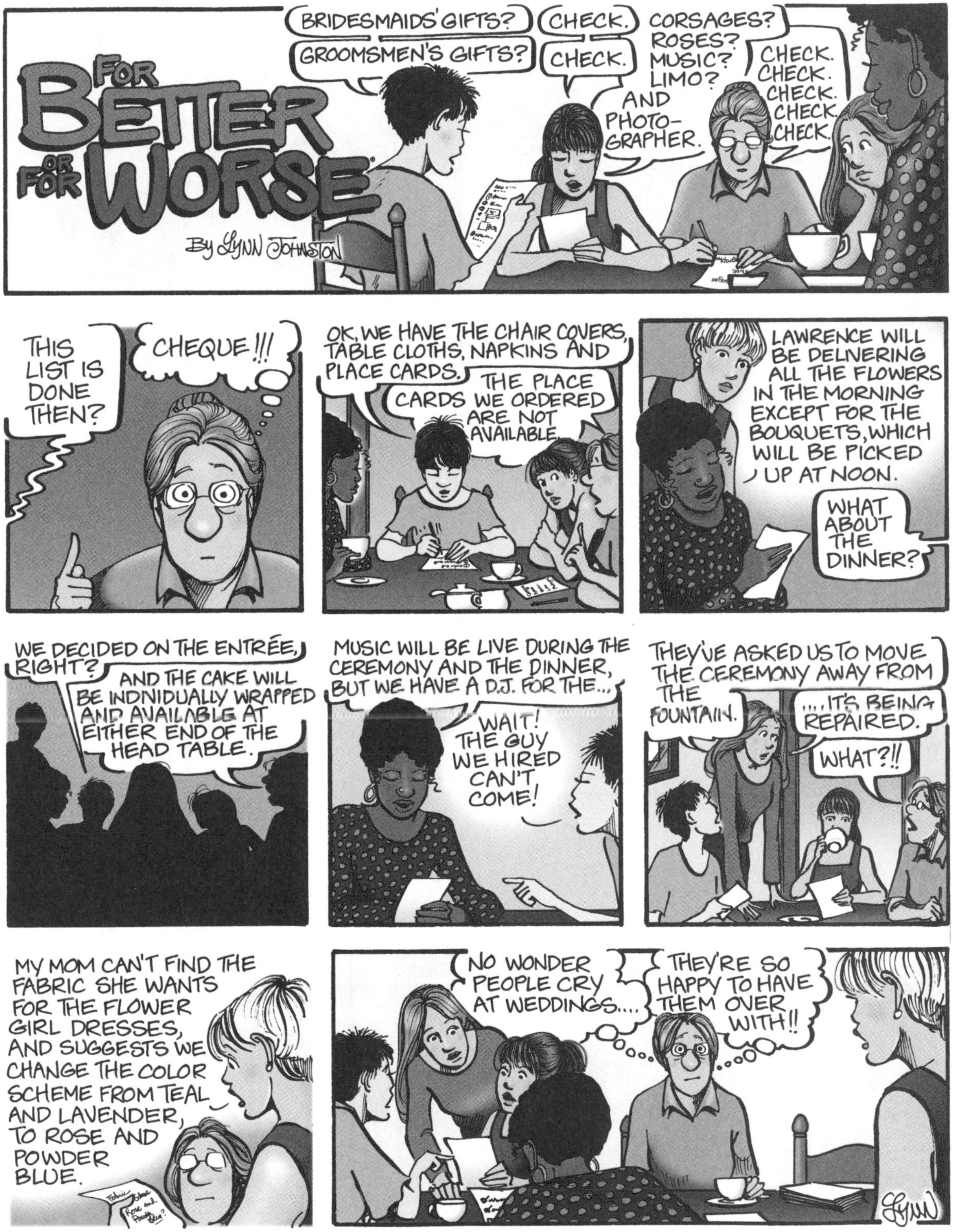

FOR BETTER OR FOR WORSE
By Lynn Johnston
BRIDESMAIDS' GIFTS?
CHECK.
GROOMSMEN'S GIFTS?
CHECK.
CORSAGES? ROSES? MUSIC? LIMO?
AND PHOTOGRAPHER.
CHECK. CHECK. CHECK. CHECK. CHECK.
THIS LIST IS DONE THEN?
CHEQUE!!!
OK, WE HAVE THE CHAIR COVERS, TABLE CLOTHS, NAPKINS AND PLACE CARDS.
THE PLACE CARDS WE ORDERED ARE NOT AVAILABLE.
LAWRENCE WILL BE DELIVERING ALL THE FLOWERS IN THE MORNING EXCEPT FOR THE BOUQUETS, WHICH WILL BE PICKED UP AT NOON.
WHAT ABOUT THE DINNER?
WE DECIDED ON THE ENTRÉE, RIGHT?
AND THE CAKE WILL BE INDIVIDUALLY WRAPPED AND AVAILABLE AT EITHER END OF THE HEAD TABLE.
MUSIC WILL BE LIVE DURING THE CEREMONY AND THE DINNER, BUT WE HAVE A D.J. FOR THE...
WAIT! THE GUY WE HIRED CAN'T COME!
THEY'VE ASKED US TO MOVE THE CEREMONY AWAY FROM THE FOUNTAIN.
...IT'S BEING REPAIRED.
WHAT?!!
MY MOM CAN'T FIND THE FABRIC SHE WANTS FOR THE FLOWER GIRL DRESSES, AND SUGGESTS WE CHANGE THE COLOR SCHEME FROM TEAL AND LAVENDER, TO ROSE AND POWDER BLUE.
NO WONDER PEOPLE CRY AT WEDDINGS....
THEY'RE SO HAPPY TO HAVE THEM OVER WITH!!
LYNN

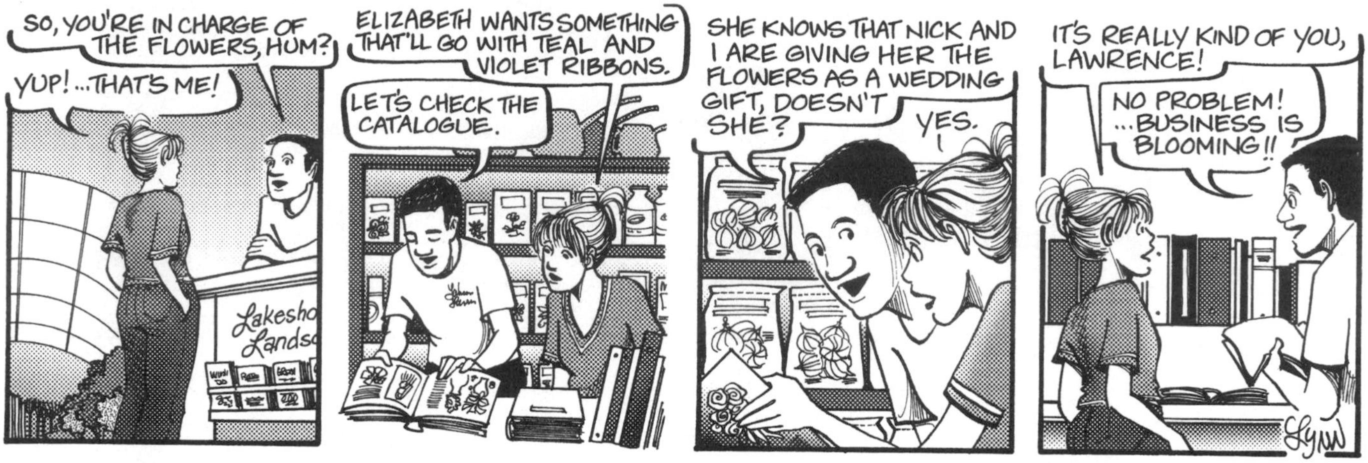
SO, YOU'RE IN CHARGE OF THE FLOWERS, HUM?
YUP! ...THAT'S ME!
ELIZABETH WANTS SOMETHING THAT'LL GO WITH TEAL AND VIOLET RIBBONS.
LET'S CHECK THE CATALOGUE.
SHE KNOWS THAT NICK AND I ARE GIVING HER THE FLOWERS AS A WEDDING GIFT, DOESN'T SHE?
YES.
IT'S REALLY KIND OF YOU, LAWRENCE!
NO PROBLEM! ...BUSINESS IS BLOOMING!!

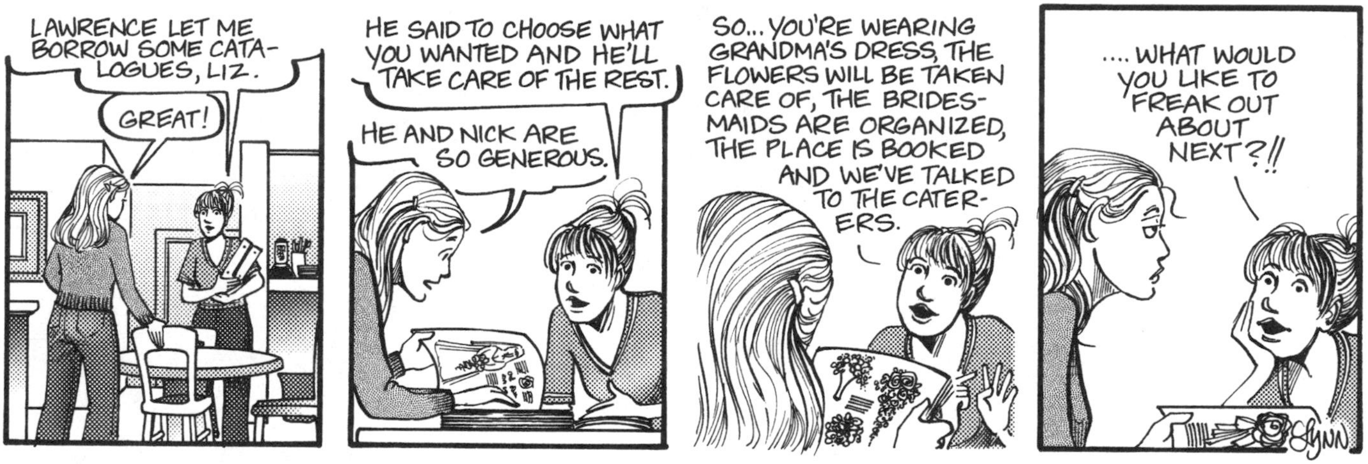
LAWRENCE LET ME BORROW SOME CATA-LOGUES, LIZ.
GREAT!
HE SAID TO CHOOSE WHAT YOU WANTED AND HE'LL TAKE CARE OF THE REST.
HE AND NICK ARE SO GENEROUS.
SO... YOU'RE WEARING GRANDMA'S DRESS, THE FLOWERS WILL BE TAKEN CARE OF, THE BRIDES-MAIDS ARE ORGANIZED, THE PLACE IS BOOKED AND WE'VE TALKED TO THE CATER-ERS.
.... WHAT WOULD YOU LIKE TO FREAK OUT ABOUT NEXT?!!

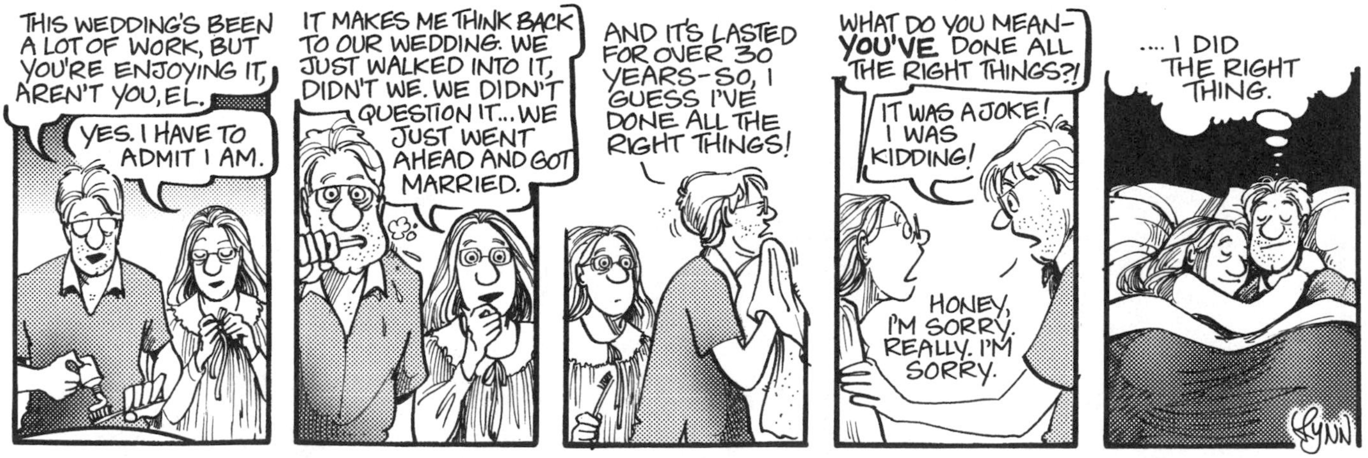
THIS WEDDING'S BEEN A LOT OF WORK, BUT YOU'RE ENJOYING IT, AREN'T YOU, EL.
YES. I HAVE TO ADMIT I AM.
IT MAKES ME THINK BACK TO OUR WEDDING. WE JUST WALKED INTO IT, DIDN'T WE. WE DIDN'T QUESTION IT... WE JUST WENT AHEAD AND GOT MARRIED.
AND IT'S LASTED FOR OVER 30 YEARS–SO, I GUESS I'VE DONE ALL THE RIGHT THINGS!
WHAT DO YOU MEAN–**YOU'VE** DONE ALL THE RIGHT THINGS?!
IT WAS A JOKE! I WAS KIDDING!
HONEY, I'M SORRY. REALLY. I'M SORRY.
.... I DID THE RIGHT THING.

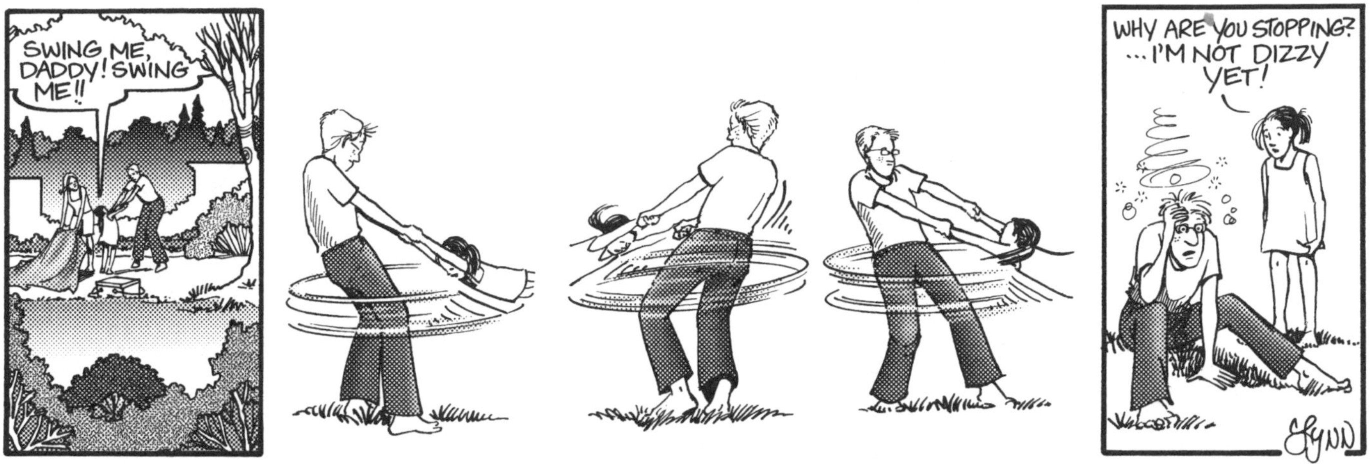
SWING ME, DADDY! SWING ME!!
WHY ARE YOU STOPPING? ...I'M NOT DIZZY YET!
LYNN

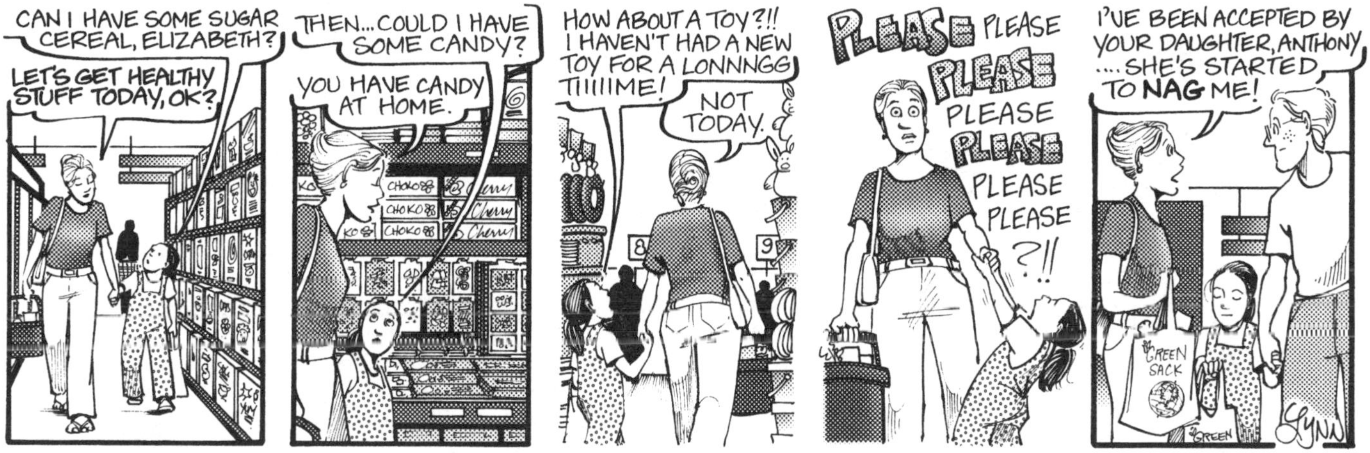
CAN I HAVE SOME SUGAR CEREAL, ELIZABETH?
LET'S GET HEALTHY STUFF TODAY, OK?
THEN...COULD I HAVE SOME CANDY?
YOU HAVE CANDY AT HOME.
HOW ABOUT A TOY?!! I HAVEN'T HAD A NEW TOY FOR A LONNNGG TIIIIIME!
NOT TODAY.
PLEASE PLEASE PLEASE PLEASE PLEASE PLEASE PLEASE ?!!
I'VE BEEN ACCEPTED BY YOUR DAUGHTER, ANTHONY ....SHE'S STARTED TO NAG ME!
GREEN SACK
LYNN

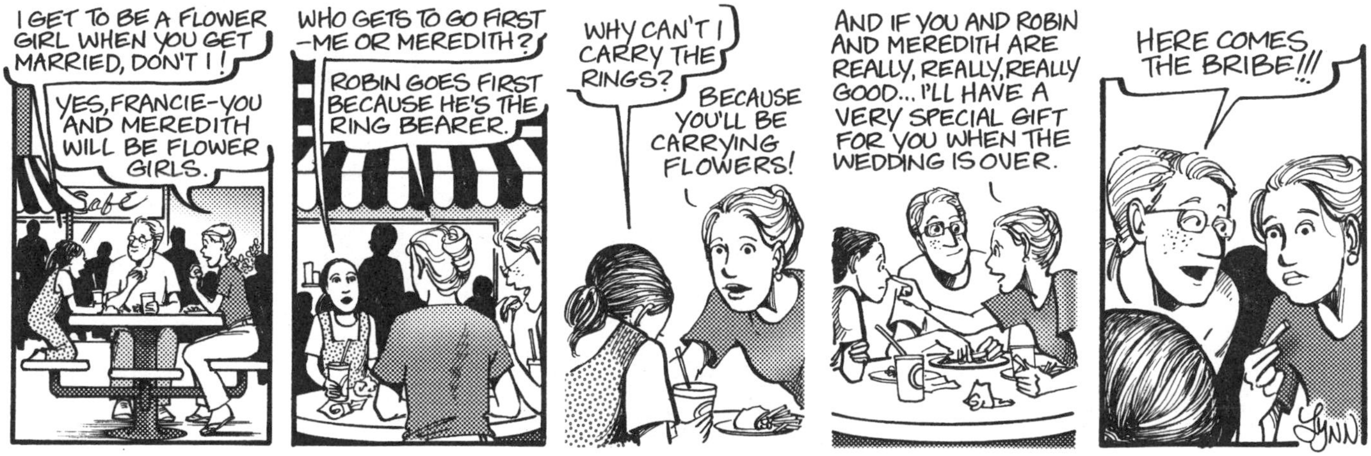
I GET TO BE A FLOWER GIRL WHEN YOU GET MARRIED, DON'T I!
YES, FRANCIE-YOU AND MEREDITH WILL BE FLOWER GIRLS.
WHO GETS TO GO FIRST -ME OR MEREDITH?
ROBIN GOES FIRST BECAUSE HE'S THE RING BEARER.
WHY CAN'T I CARRY THE RINGS?
BECAUSE YOU'LL BE CARRYING FLOWERS!
AND IF YOU AND ROBIN AND MEREDITH ARE REALLY, REALLY, REALLY GOOD... I'LL HAVE A VERY SPECIAL GIFT FOR YOU WHEN THE WEDDING IS OVER.
HERE COMES THE BRIBE!!!
LYNN

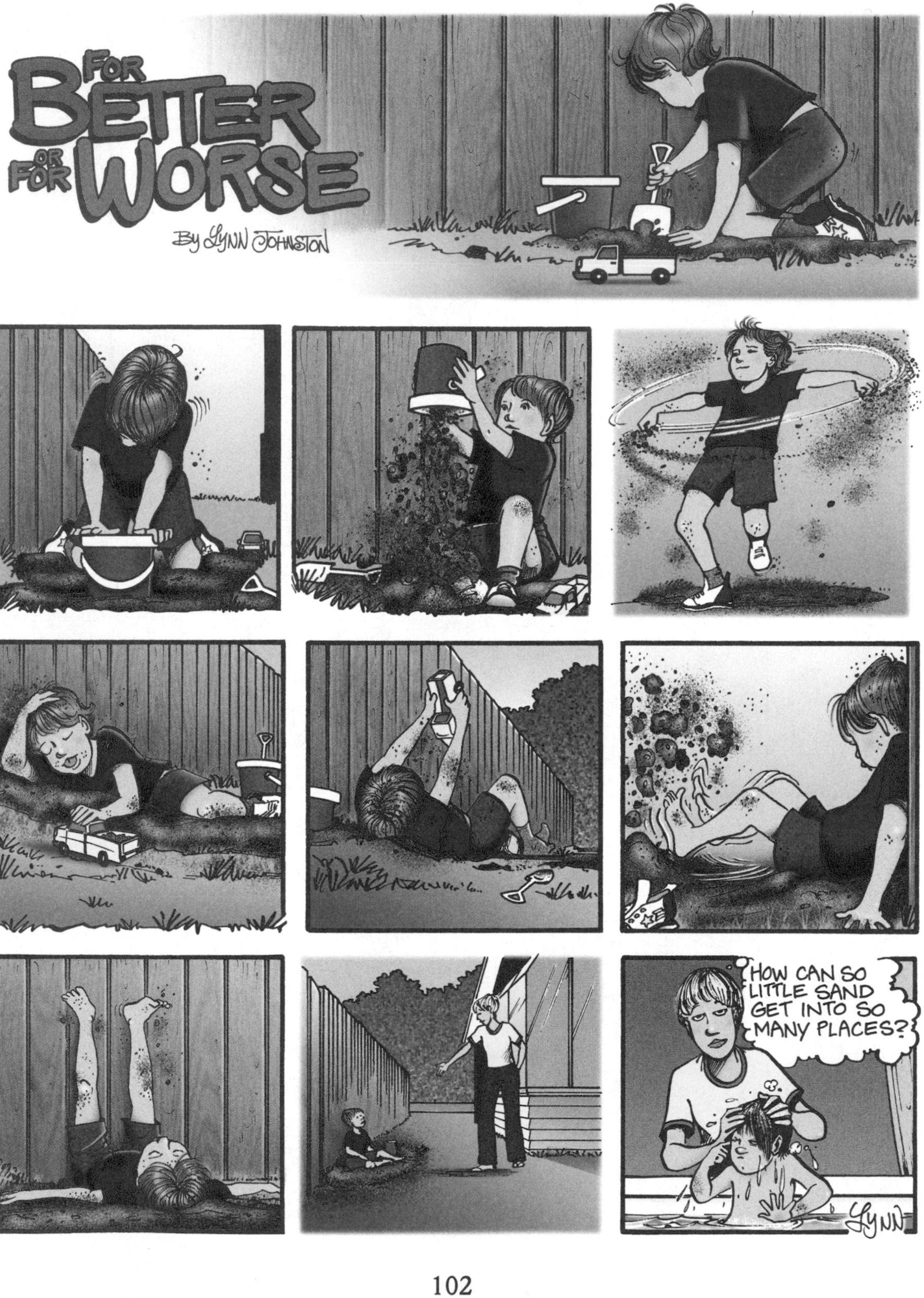
FOR BETTER OR FOR WORSE
BY LYNN JOHNSTON
HOW CAN SO LITTLE SAND GET INTO SO MANY PLACES?
LYNN

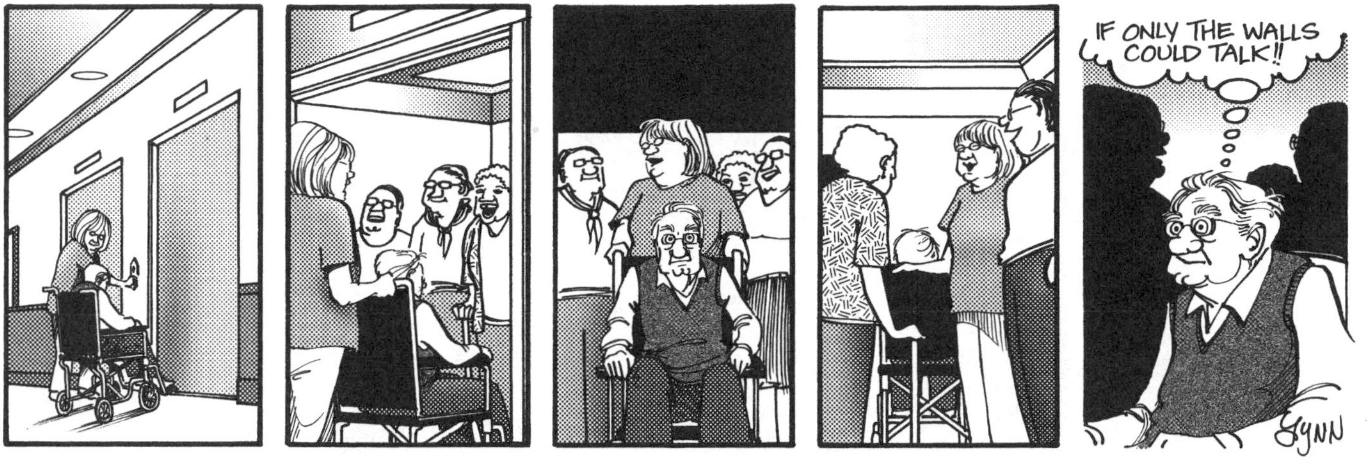
IF ONLY THE WALLS COULD TALK!!
LYNN

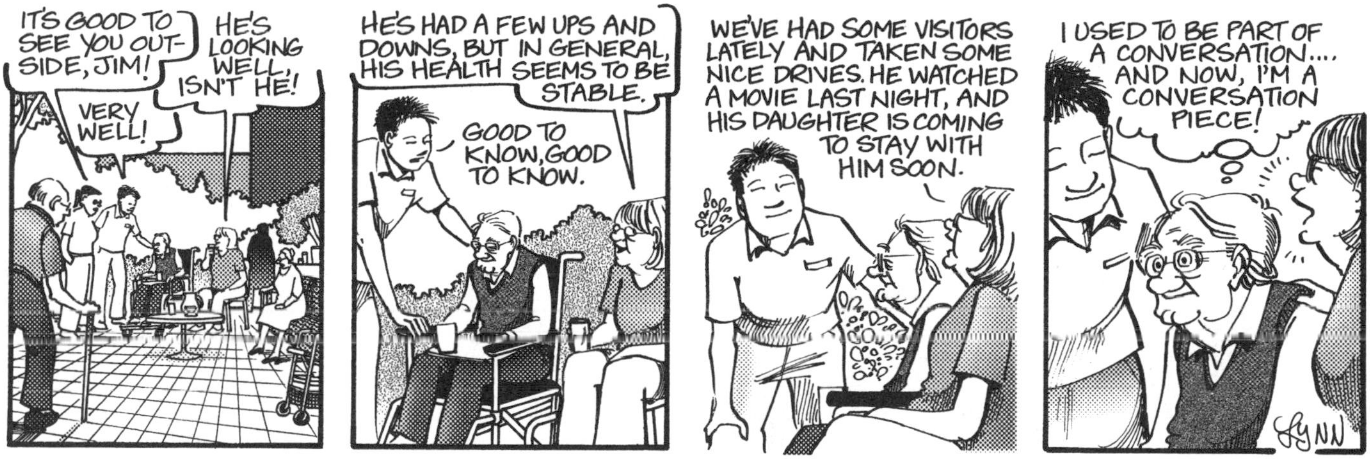
IT'S GOOD TO SEE YOU OUTSIDE, JIM!
HE'S LOOKING WELL, ISN'T HE!
VERY WELL!
HE'S HAD A FEW UPS AND DOWNS, BUT IN GENERAL, HIS HEALTH SEEMS TO BE STABLE.
GOOD TO KNOW, GOOD TO KNOW.
WE'VE HAD SOME VISITORS LATELY AND TAKEN SOME NICE DRIVES. HE WATCHED A MOVIE LAST NIGHT, AND HIS DAUGHTER IS COMING TO STAY WITH HIM SOON.
I USED TO BE PART OF A CONVERSATION.... AND NOW, I'M A CONVERSATION PIECE!
LYNN

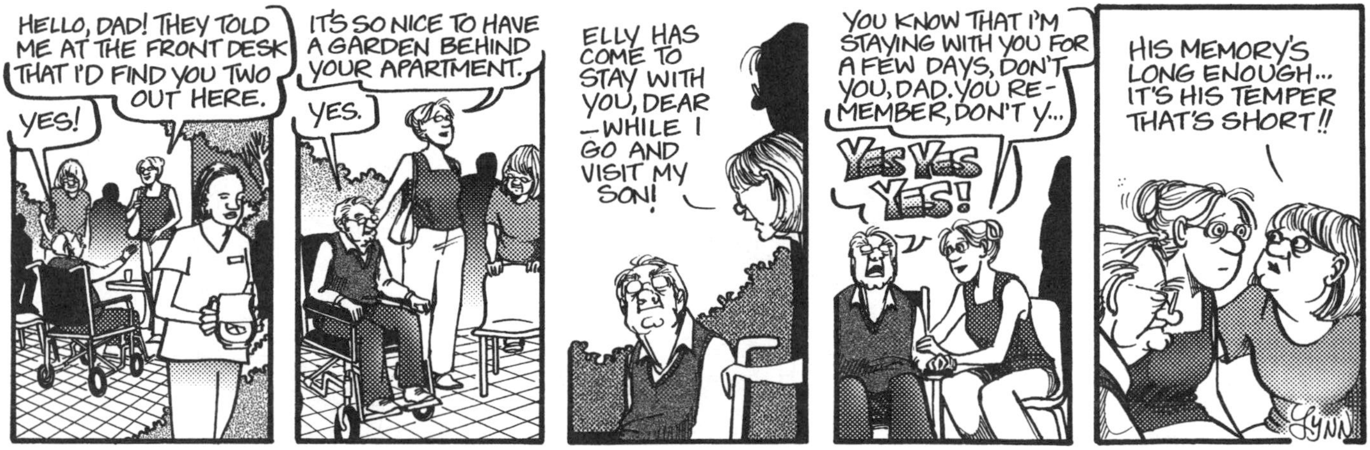
HELLO, DAD! THEY TOLD ME AT THE FRONT DESK THAT I'D FIND YOU TWO OUT HERE.
YES!
IT'S SO NICE TO HAVE A GARDEN BEHIND YOUR APARTMENT.
YES.
ELLY HAS COME TO STAY WITH YOU, DEAR —WHILE I GO AND VISIT MY SON!
YOU KNOW THAT I'M STAYING WITH YOU FOR A FEW DAYS, DON'T YOU, DAD. YOU REMEMBER, DON'T Y...
YES YES YES!
HIS MEMORY'S LONG ENOUGH... IT'S HIS TEMPER THAT'S SHORT!!
LYNN

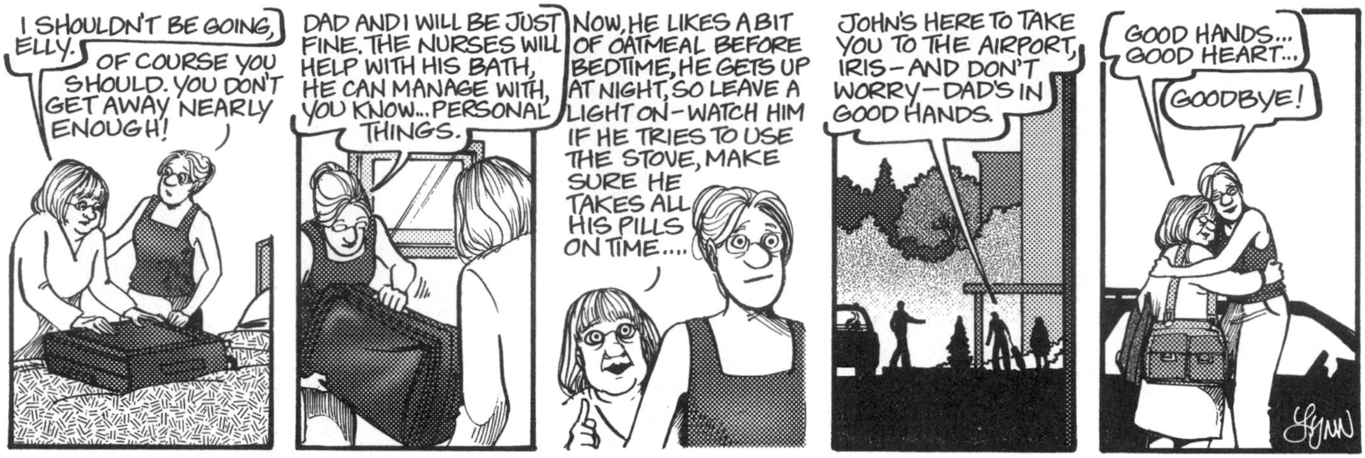
I SHOULDN'T BE GOING, ELLY.
OF COURSE YOU SHOULD. YOU DON'T GET AWAY NEARLY ENOUGH!
DAD AND I WILL BE JUST FINE. THE NURSES WILL HELP WITH HIS BATH, HE CAN MANAGE WITH, YOU KNOW... PERSONAL THINGS.
NOW, HE LIKES A BIT OF OATMEAL BEFORE BEDTIME, HE GETS UP AT NIGHT, SO LEAVE A LIGHT ON - WATCH HIM IF HE TRIES TO USE THE STOVE, MAKE SURE HE TAKES ALL HIS PILLS ON TIME....
JOHN'S HERE TO TAKE YOU TO THE AIRPORT, IRIS - AND DON'T WORRY - DAD'S IN GOOD HANDS.
GOOD HANDS... GOOD HEART...
GOODBYE!
LYNN

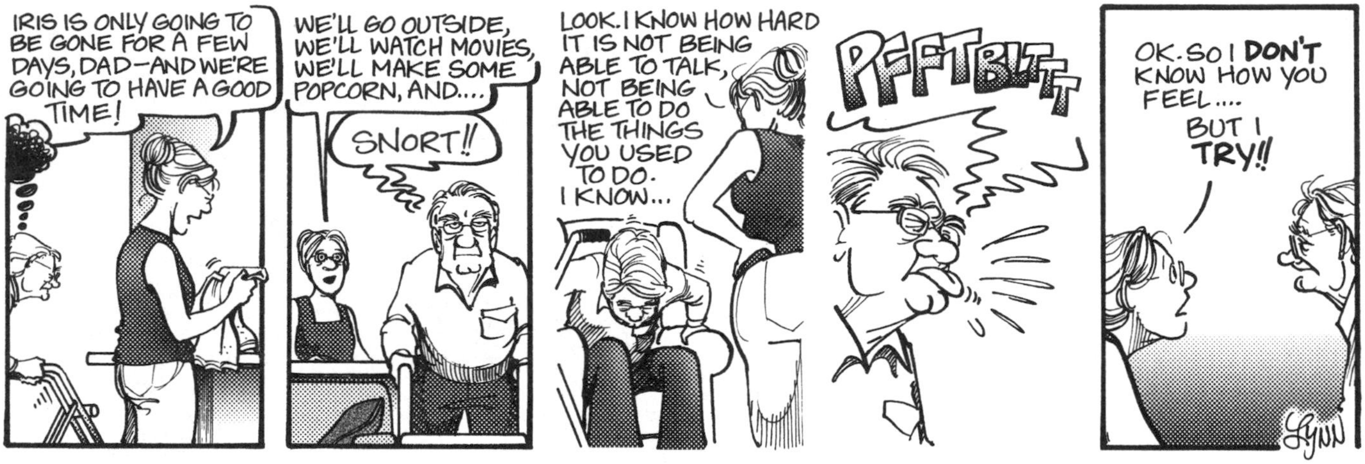
IRIS IS ONLY GOING TO BE GONE FOR A FEW DAYS, DAD - AND WE'RE GOING TO HAVE A GOOD TIME!
WE'LL GO OUTSIDE, WE'LL WATCH MOVIES, WE'LL MAKE SOME POPCORN, AND....
SNORT!!
LOOK. I KNOW HOW HARD IT IS NOT BEING ABLE TO TALK, NOT BEING ABLE TO DO THE THINGS YOU USED TO DO. I KNOW...
PFFTBLTTT
OK. SO I **DON'T** KNOW HOW YOU FEEL.... BUT I **TRY**!!
LYNN

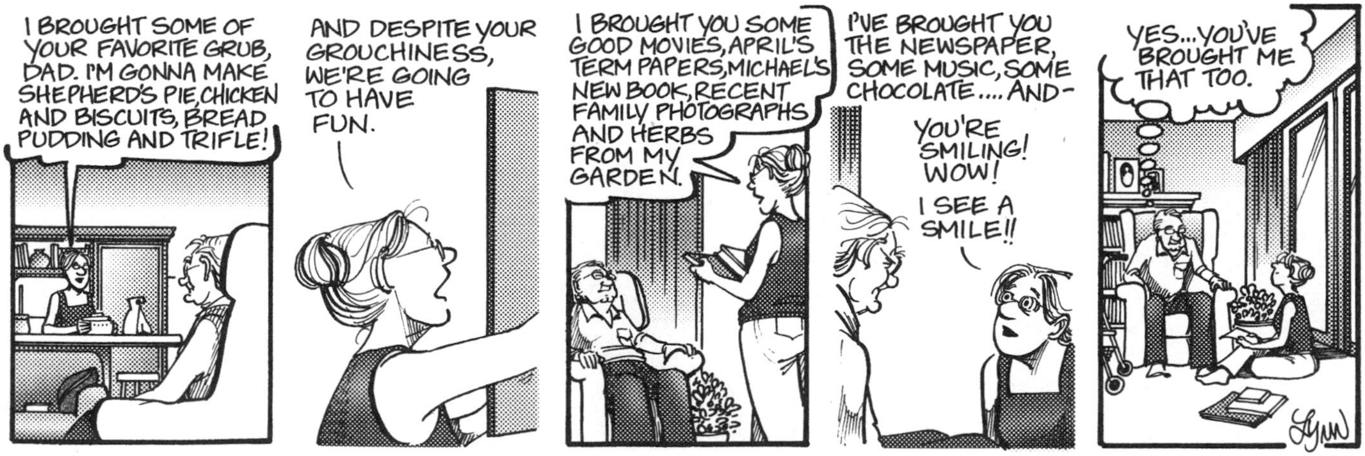
I BROUGHT SOME OF YOUR FAVORITE GRUB, DAD. I'M GONNA MAKE SHEPHERD'S PIE, CHICKEN AND BISCUITS, BREAD PUDDING AND TRIFLE!
AND DESPITE YOUR GROUCHINESS, WE'RE GOING TO HAVE FUN.
I BROUGHT YOU SOME GOOD MOVIES, APRIL'S TERM PAPERS, MICHAEL'S NEW BOOK, RECENT FAMILY PHOTOGRAPHS AND HERBS FROM MY GARDEN.
I'VE BROUGHT YOU THE NEWSPAPER, SOME MUSIC, SOME CHOCOLATE.... AND-
YOU'RE SMILING! WOW!
I SEE A SMILE!!
YES... YOU'VE BROUGHT ME THAT TOO.
LYNN

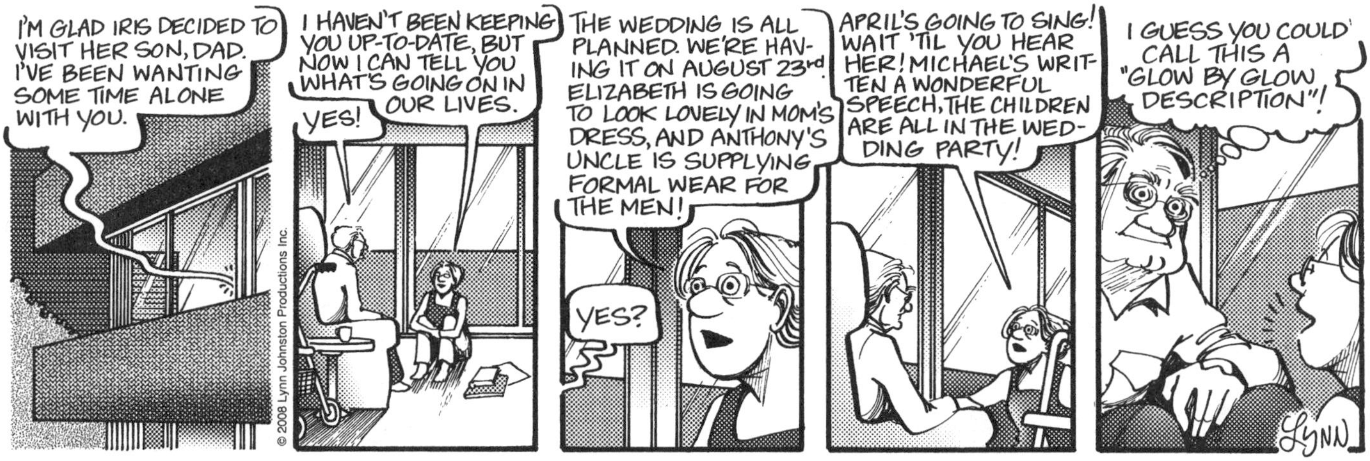
I'M GLAD IRIS DECIDED TO VISIT HER SON, DAD. I'VE BEEN WANTING SOME TIME ALONE WITH YOU.
I HAVEN'T BEEN KEEPING YOU UP-TO-DATE, BUT NOW I CAN TELL YOU WHAT'S GOING ON IN OUR LIVES.
YES!
THE WEDDING IS ALL PLANNED. WE'RE HAVING IT ON AUGUST 23rd. ELIZABETH IS GOING TO LOOK LOVELY IN MOM'S DRESS, AND ANTHONY'S UNCLE IS SUPPLYING FORMAL WEAR FOR THE MEN!
YES?
APRIL'S GOING TO SING! WAIT 'TIL YOU HEAR HER! MICHAEL'S WRITTEN A WONDERFUL SPEECH, THE CHILDREN ARE ALL IN THE WEDDING PARTY!
I GUESS YOU COULD CALL THIS A "GLOW BY GLOW DESCRIPTION"!
LYNN

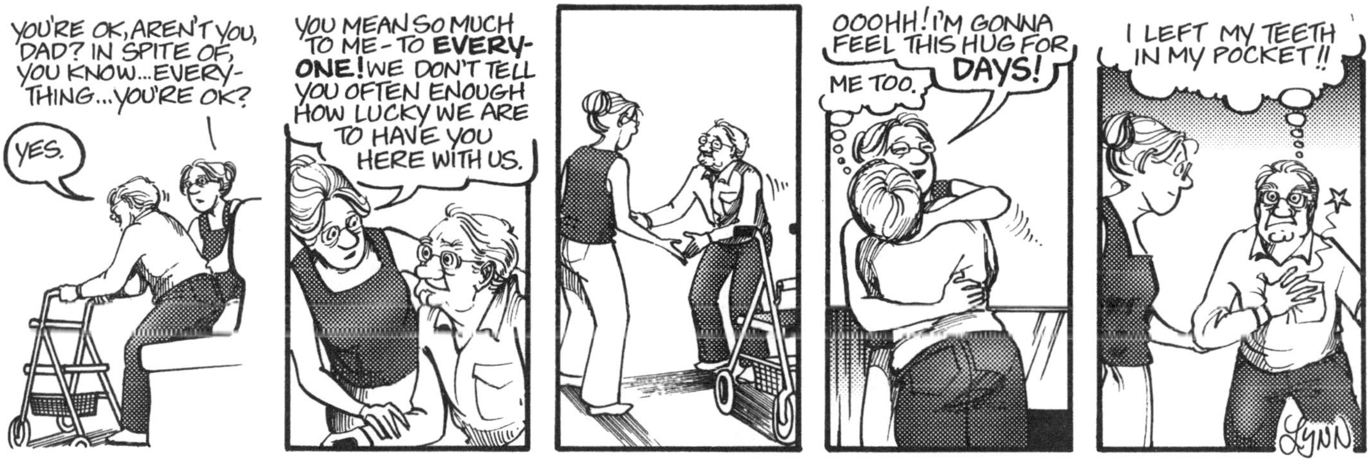
YOU'RE OK, AREN'T YOU, DAD? IN SPITE OF, YOU KNOW...EVERYTHING...YOU'RE OK?
YES.
YOU MEAN SO MUCH TO ME - TO **EVERYONE!** WE DON'T TELL YOU OFTEN ENOUGH HOW LUCKY WE ARE TO HAVE YOU HERE WITH US.
OOOHH! I'M GONNA FEEL THIS HUG FOR **DAYS!**
ME TOO.
I LEFT MY TEETH IN MY POCKET!!
LYNN

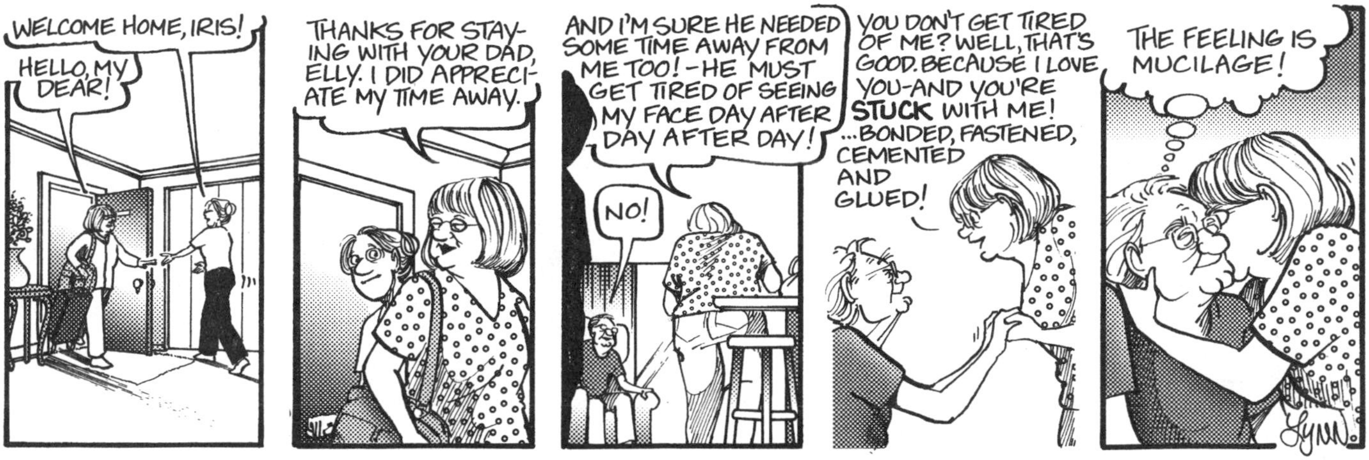
WELCOME HOME, IRIS!
HELLO, MY DEAR!
THANKS FOR STAYING WITH YOUR DAD, ELLY. I DID APPRECIATE MY TIME AWAY.
AND I'M SURE HE NEEDED SOME TIME AWAY FROM ME TOO! - HE MUST GET TIRED OF SEEING MY FACE DAY AFTER DAY AFTER DAY!
NO!
YOU DON'T GET TIRED OF ME? WELL, THAT'S GOOD. BECAUSE I LOVE YOU - AND YOU'RE **STUCK** WITH ME! ...BONDED, FASTENED, CEMENTED AND GLUED!
THE FEELING IS MUCILAGE!
LYNN

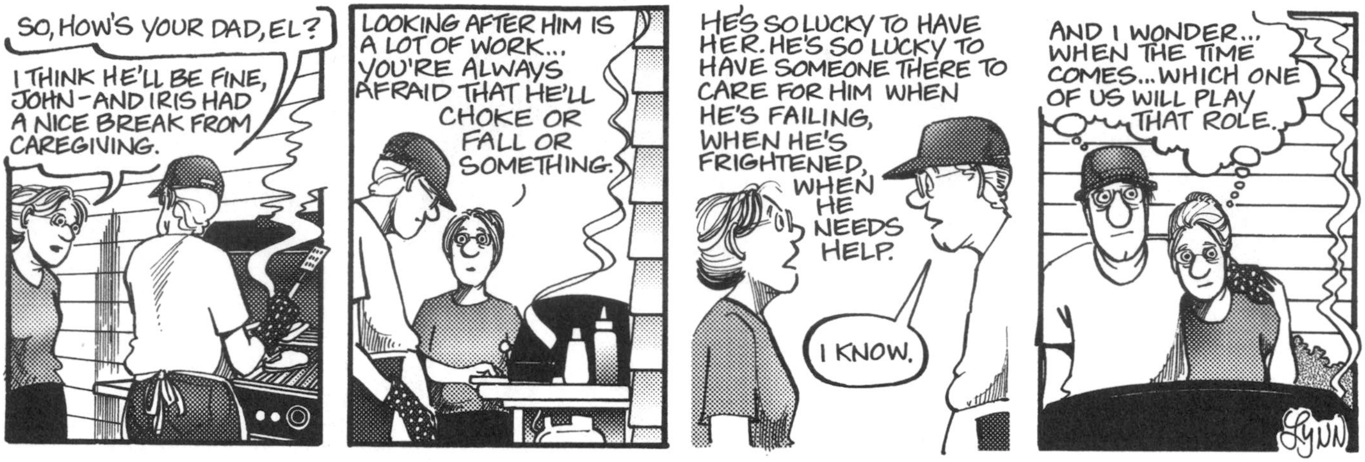
SO, HOW'S YOUR DAD, EL?
I THINK HE'LL BE FINE, JOHN - AND IRIS HAD A NICE BREAK FROM CAREGIVING.
LOOKING AFTER HIM IS A LOT OF WORK... YOU'RE ALWAYS AFRAID THAT HE'LL CHOKE OR FALL OR SOMETHING.
HE'S SO LUCKY TO HAVE HER. HE'S SO LUCKY TO HAVE SOMEONE THERE TO CARE FOR HIM WHEN HE'S FAILING, WHEN HE'S FRIGHTENED, WHEN HE NEEDS HELP.
I KNOW.
AND I WONDER... WHEN THE TIME COMES... WHICH ONE OF US WILL PLAY THAT ROLE.
LYNN

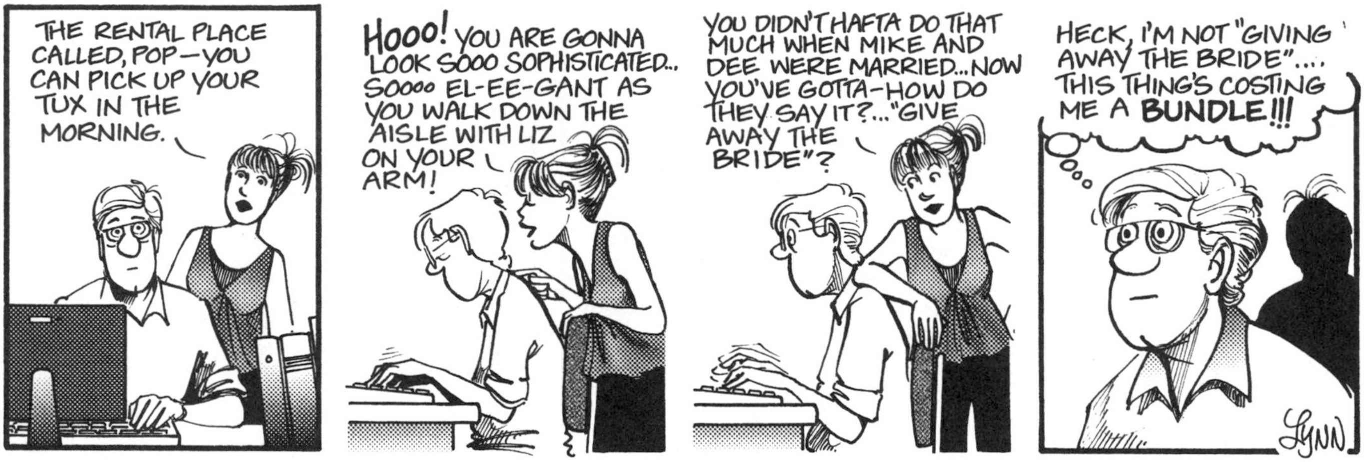
THE RENTAL PLACE CALLED, POP - YOU CAN PICK UP YOUR TUX IN THE MORNING.
HOOO! YOU ARE GONNA LOOK SOOO SOPHISTICATED.. SOOOO EL-EE-GANT AS YOU WALK DOWN THE AISLE WITH LIZ ON YOUR ARM!
YOU DIDN'T HAFTA DO THAT MUCH WHEN MIKE AND DEE WERE MARRIED...NOW YOU'VE GOTTA - HOW DO THEY SAY IT?..."GIVE AWAY THE BRIDE"?
HECK, I'M NOT "GIVING AWAY THE BRIDE".... THIS THING'S COSTING ME A BUNDLE!!!
LYNN

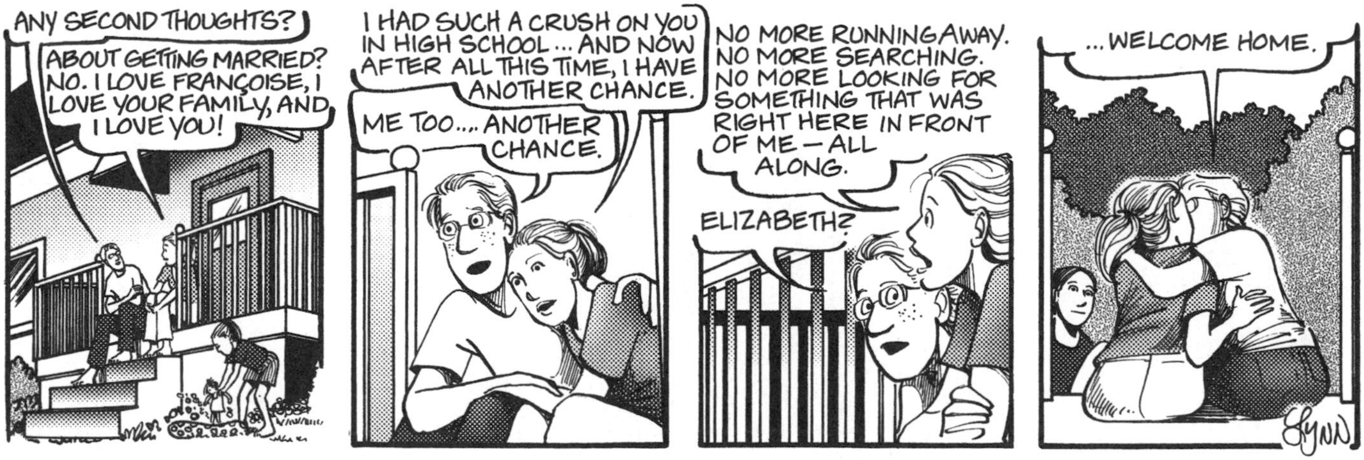
ANY SECOND THOUGHTS?
ABOUT GETTING MARRIED? NO. I LOVE FRANÇOISE, I LOVE YOUR FAMILY, AND I LOVE YOU!
I HAD SUCH A CRUSH ON YOU IN HIGH SCHOOL... AND NOW AFTER ALL THIS TIME, I HAVE ANOTHER CHANCE.
ME TOO.... ANOTHER CHANCE.
NO MORE RUNNING AWAY. NO MORE SEARCHING. NO MORE LOOKING FOR SOMETHING THAT WAS RIGHT HERE IN FRONT OF ME - ALL ALONG.
ELIZABETH?
... WELCOME HOME.
LYNN

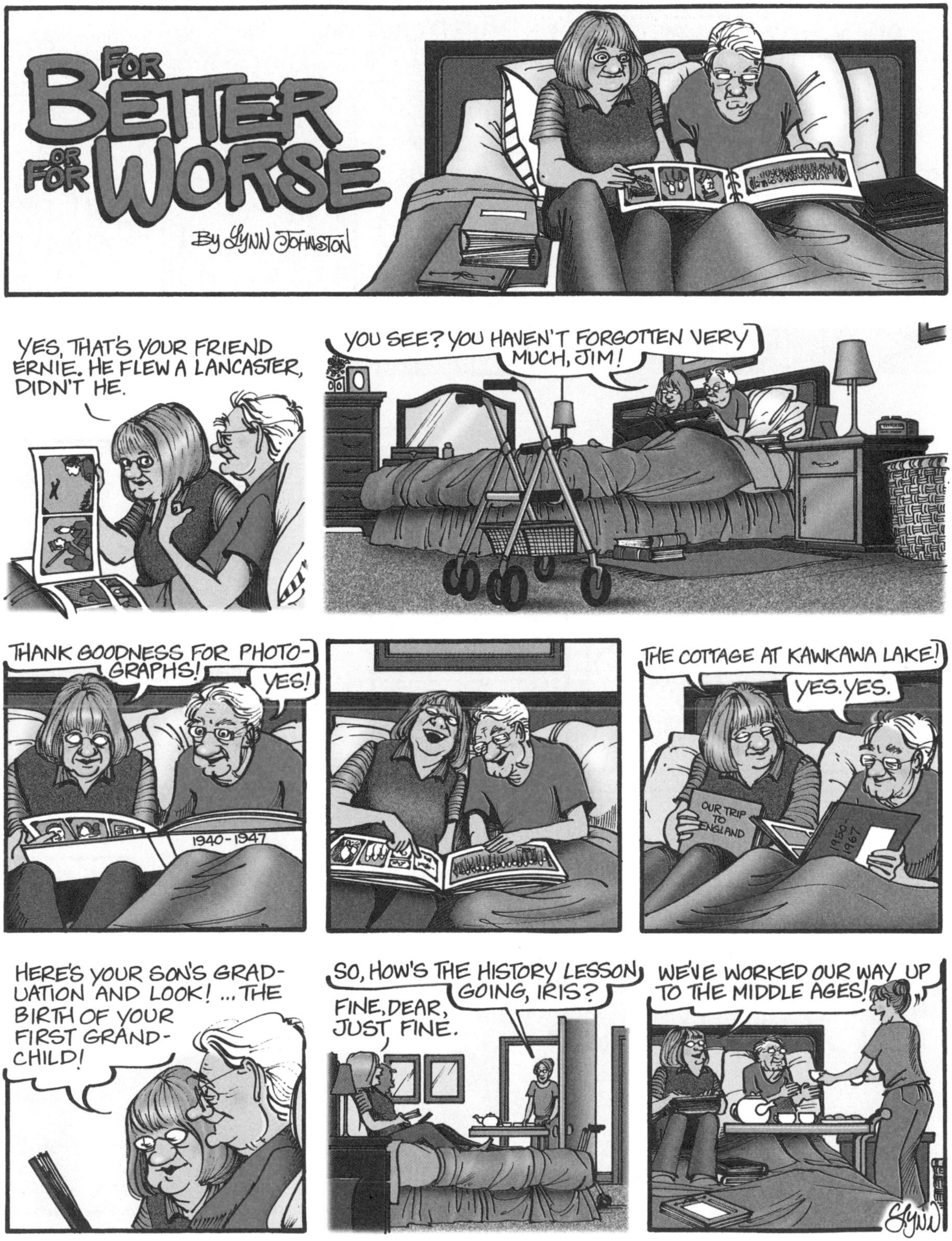
FOR BETTER OR FOR WORSE
BY LYNN JOHNSTON
YES, THAT'S YOUR FRIEND ERNIE. HE FLEW A LANCASTER, DIDN'T HE.
YOU SEE? YOU HAVEN'T FORGOTTEN VERY MUCH, JIM!
THANK GOODNESS FOR PHOTOGRAPHS!
YES!
1940-1947
THE COTTAGE AT KAWKAWA LAKE!
YES. YES.
OUR TRIP TO ENGLAND
1950-1967
HERE'S YOUR SON'S GRADUATION AND LOOK! ... THE BIRTH OF YOUR FIRST GRANDCHILD!
SO, HOW'S THE HISTORY LESSON GOING, IRIS?
FINE, DEAR, JUST FINE.
WE'VE WORKED OUR WAY UP TO THE MIDDLE AGES!
LYNN

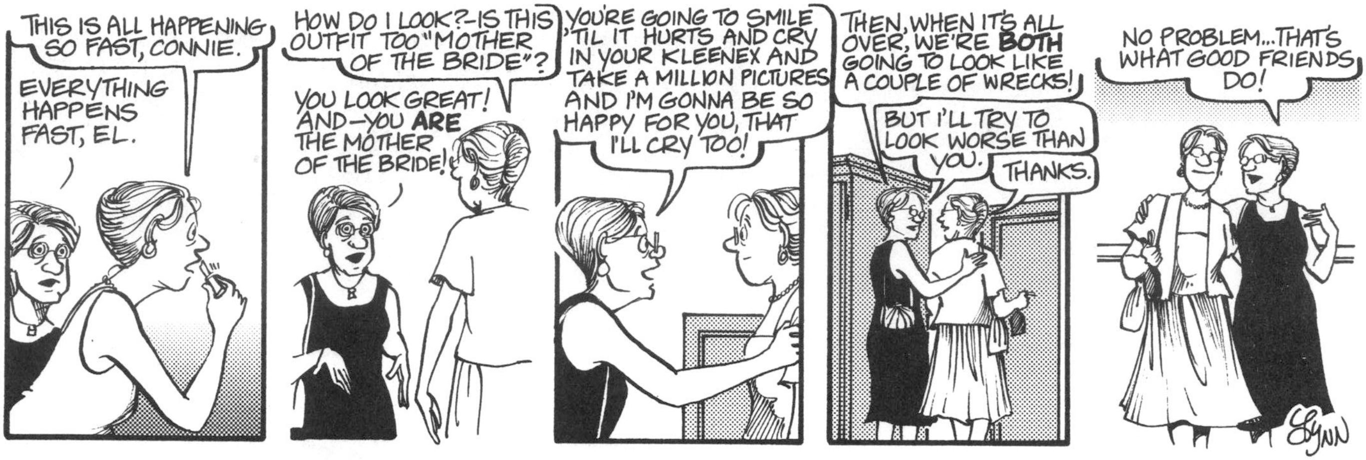
THIS IS ALL HAPPENING SO FAST, CONNIE.
EVERYTHING HAPPENS FAST, EL.
HOW DO I LOOK?–IS THIS OUTFIT TOO "MOTHER OF THE BRIDE"?
YOU LOOK GREAT! AND–YOU **ARE** THE MOTHER OF THE BRIDE!
YOU'RE GOING TO SMILE 'TIL IT HURTS AND CRY IN YOUR KLEENEX AND TAKE A MILLION PICTURES AND I'M GONNA BE SO HAPPY FOR YOU, THAT I'LL CRY TOO!
THEN, WHEN IT'S ALL OVER, WE'RE **BOTH** GOING TO LOOK LIKE A COUPLE OF WRECKS!
BUT I'LL TRY TO LOOK WORSE THAN YOU.
THANKS.
NO PROBLEM...THAT'S WHAT GOOD FRIENDS DO!
LYNN

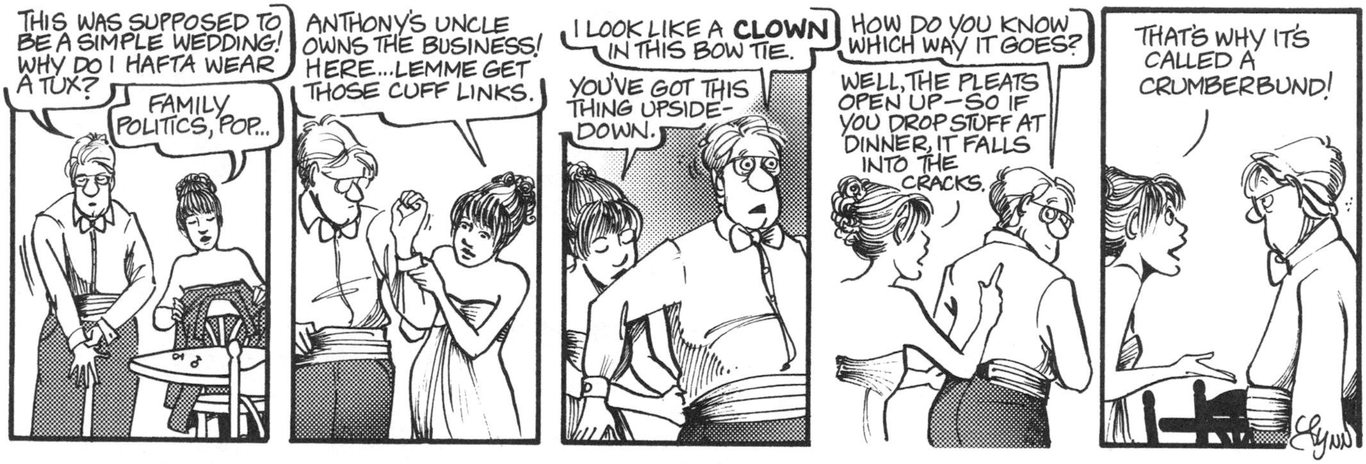
THIS WAS SUPPOSED TO BE A SIMPLE WEDDING! WHY DO I HAFTA WEAR A TUX?
FAMILY POLITICS, POP...
ANTHONY'S UNCLE OWNS THE BUSINESS! HERE...LEMME GET THOSE CUFF LINKS.
I LOOK LIKE A **CLOWN** IN THIS BOW TIE.
YOU'VE GOT THIS THING UPSIDE-DOWN.
HOW DO YOU KNOW WHICH WAY IT GOES?
WELL, THE PLEATS OPEN UP–SO IF YOU DROP STUFF AT DINNER, IT FALLS INTO THE CRACKS.
THAT'S WHY IT'S CALLED A CRUMBERBUND!
LYNN

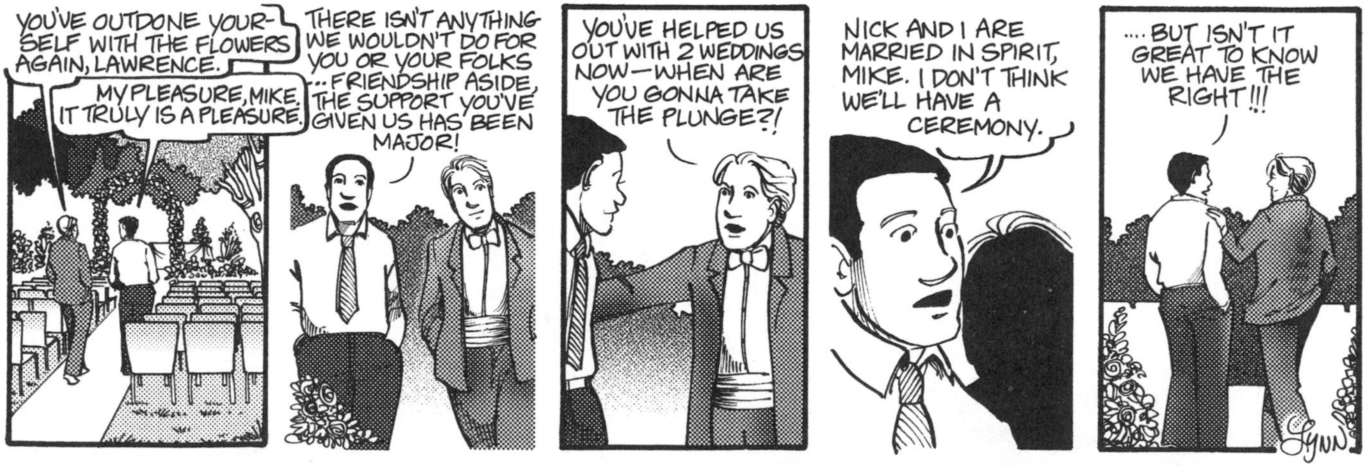
YOU'VE OUTDONE YOURSELF WITH THE FLOWERS AGAIN, LAWRENCE.
MY PLEASURE, MIKE. IT TRULY IS A PLEASURE.
THERE ISN'T ANYTHING WE WOULDN'T DO FOR YOU OR YOUR FOLKS ...FRIENDSHIP ASIDE, THE SUPPORT YOU'VE GIVEN US HAS BEEN MAJOR!
YOU'VE HELPED US OUT WITH 2 WEDDINGS NOW–WHEN ARE YOU GONNA TAKE THE PLUNGE?!
NICK AND I ARE MARRIED IN SPIRIT, MIKE. I DON'T THINK WE'LL HAVE A CEREMONY.
....BUT ISN'T IT GREAT TO KNOW WE HAVE THE RIGHT!!!
LYNN

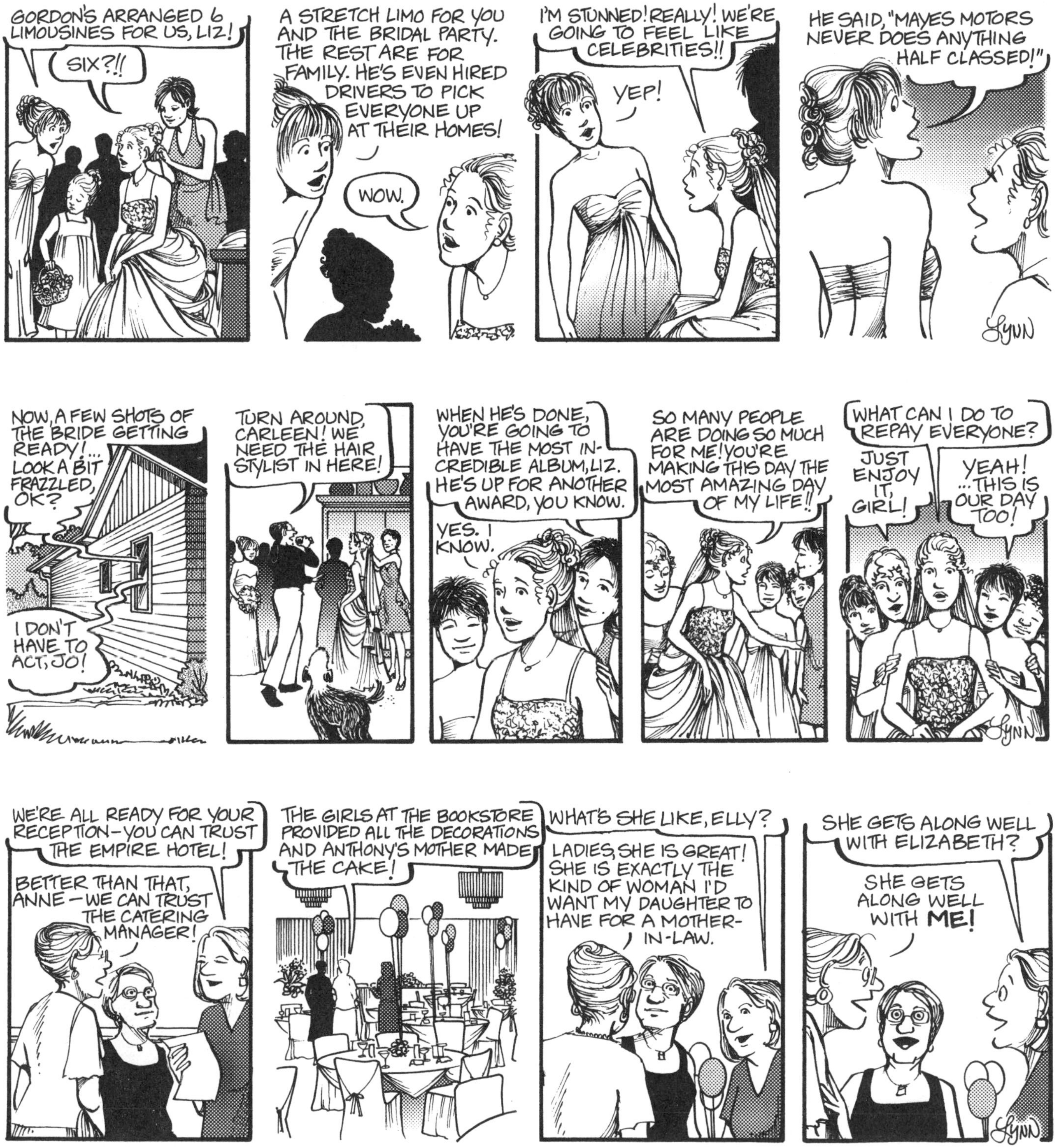
GORDON'S ARRANGED 6 LIMOUSINES FOR US, LIZ!
SIX?!!
A STRETCH LIMO FOR YOU AND THE BRIDAL PARTY. THE REST ARE FOR FAMILY. HE'S EVEN HIRED DRIVERS TO PICK EVERYONE UP AT THEIR HOMES!
WOW.
I'M STUNNED! REALLY! WE'RE GOING TO FEEL LIKE CELEBRITIES!!
YEP!
HE SAID, "MAYES MOTORS NEVER DOES ANYTHING HALF CLASSED!"
LYNN
NOW, A FEW SHOTS OF THE BRIDE GETTING READY!... LOOK A BIT FRAZZLED, OK?
I DON'T HAVE TO ACT, JO!
TURN AROUND, CARLEEN! WE NEED THE HAIR STYLIST IN HERE!
WHEN HE'S DONE, YOU'RE GOING TO HAVE THE MOST INCREDIBLE ALBUM, LIZ. HE'S UP FOR ANOTHER AWARD, YOU KNOW.
YES. I KNOW.
SO MANY PEOPLE ARE DOING SO MUCH FOR ME! YOU'RE MAKING THIS DAY THE MOST AMAZING DAY OF MY LIFE!!
WHAT CAN I DO TO REPAY EVERYONE?
JUST ENJOY IT, GIRL!
YEAH! ...THIS IS OUR DAY TOO!
LYNN
WE'RE ALL READY FOR YOUR RECEPTION—YOU CAN TRUST THE EMPIRE HOTEL!
BETTER THAN THAT, ANNE—WE CAN TRUST THE CATERING MANAGER!
THE GIRLS AT THE BOOKSTORE PROVIDED ALL THE DECORATIONS AND ANTHONY'S MOTHER MADE THE CAKE!
WHAT'S SHE LIKE, ELLY?
LADIES, SHE IS GREAT! SHE IS EXACTLY THE KIND OF WOMAN I'D WANT MY DAUGHTER TO HAVE FOR A MOTHER-IN-LAW.
SHE GETS ALONG WELL WITH ELIZABETH?
SHE GETS ALONG WELL WITH **ME!**
LYNN

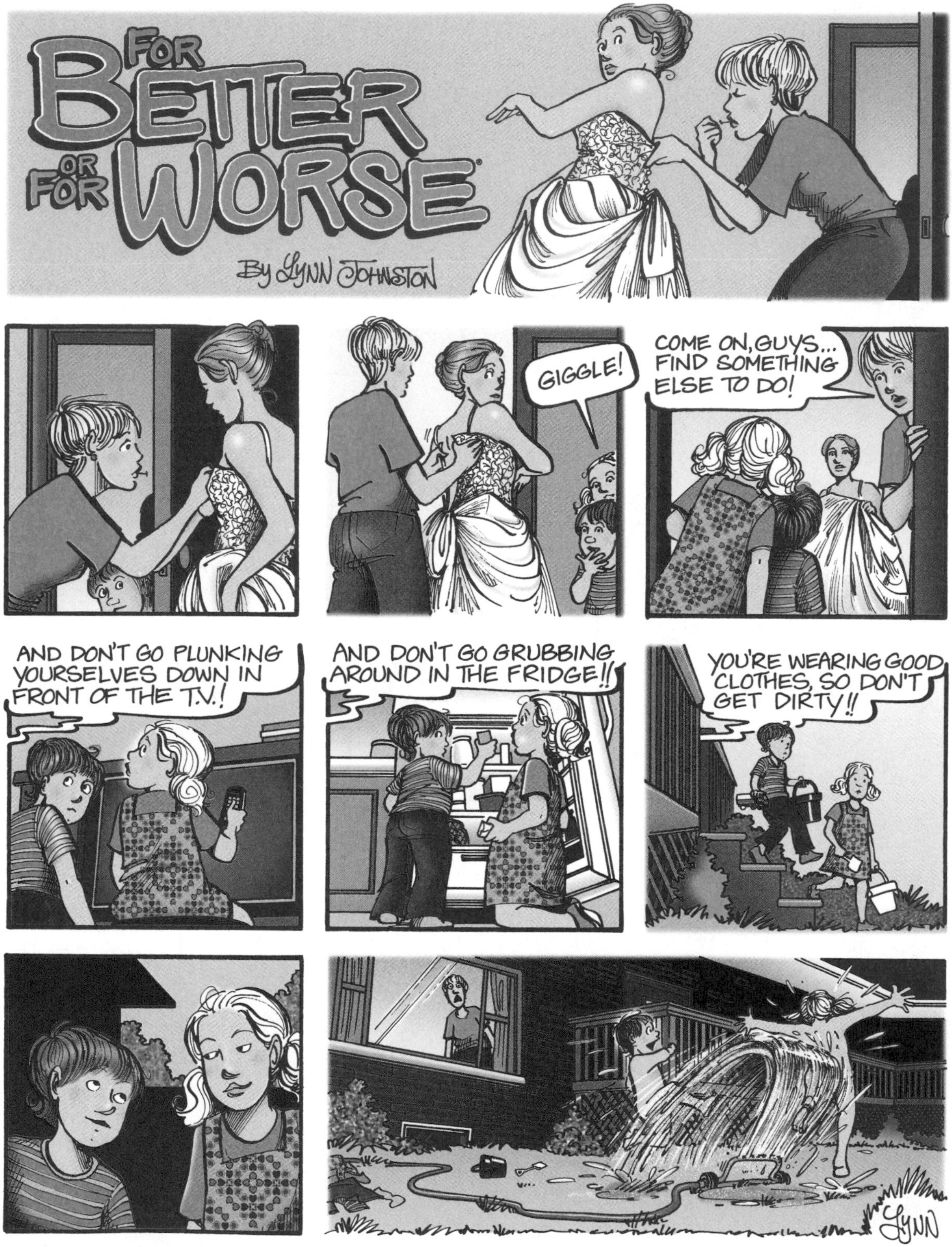
FOR BETTER OR FOR WORSE
BY LYNN JOHNSTON
GIGGLE!
COME ON, GUYS... FIND SOMETHING ELSE TO DO!
AND DON'T GO PLUNKING YOURSELVES DOWN IN FRONT OF THE T.V.!
AND DON'T GO GRUBBING AROUND IN THE FRIDGE!!
YOU'RE WEARING GOOD CLOTHES, SO DON'T GET DIRTY!!
LYNN

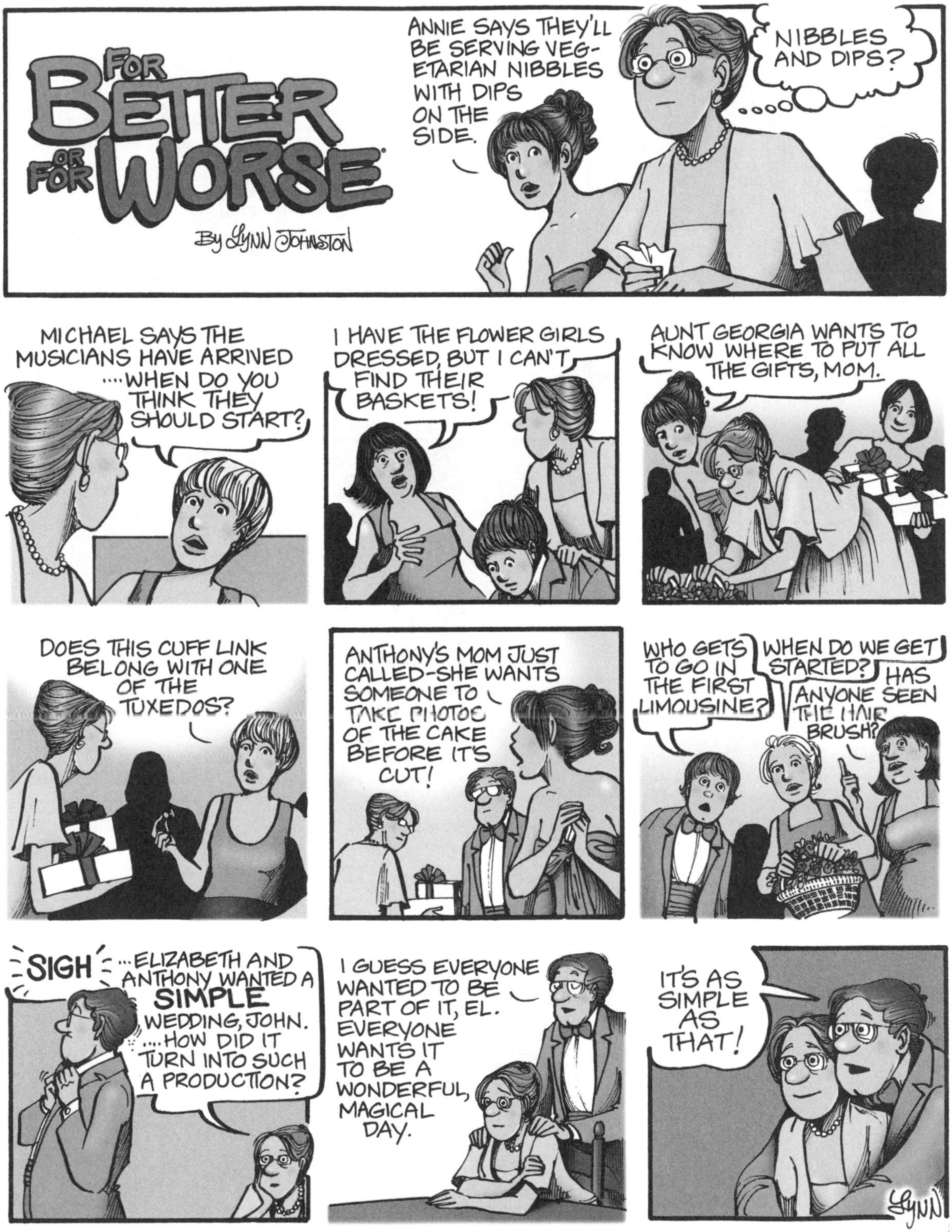

FOR BETTER OR FOR WORSE
BY LYNN JOHNSTON
ANNIE SAYS THEY'LL BE SERVING VEG-ETARIAN NIBBLES WITH DIPS ON THE SIDE.
NIBBLES AND DIPS?
MICHAEL SAYS THE MUSICIANS HAVE ARRIVED ....WHEN DO YOU THINK THEY SHOULD START?
I HAVE THE FLOWER GIRLS DRESSED, BUT I CAN'T FIND THEIR BASKETS!
AUNT GEORGIA WANTS TO KNOW WHERE TO PUT ALL THE GIFTS, MOM.
DOES THIS CUFF LINK BELONG WITH ONE OF THE TUXEDOS?
ANTHONY'S MOM JUST CALLED-SHE WANTS SOMEONE TO TAKE PHOTOS OF THE CAKE BEFORE IT'S CUT!
WHO GETS TO GO IN THE FIRST LIMOUSINE?
WHEN DO WE GET STARTED?
HAS ANYONE SEEN THE HAIR BRUSH?
SIGH
...ELIZABETH AND ANTHONY WANTED A SIMPLE WEDDING, JOHN. ....HOW DID IT TURN INTO SUCH A PRODUCTION?
I GUESS EVERYONE WANTED TO BE PART OF IT, EL. EVERYONE WANTS IT TO BE A WONDERFUL, MAGICAL DAY.
IT'S AS SIMPLE AS THAT!
LYNN

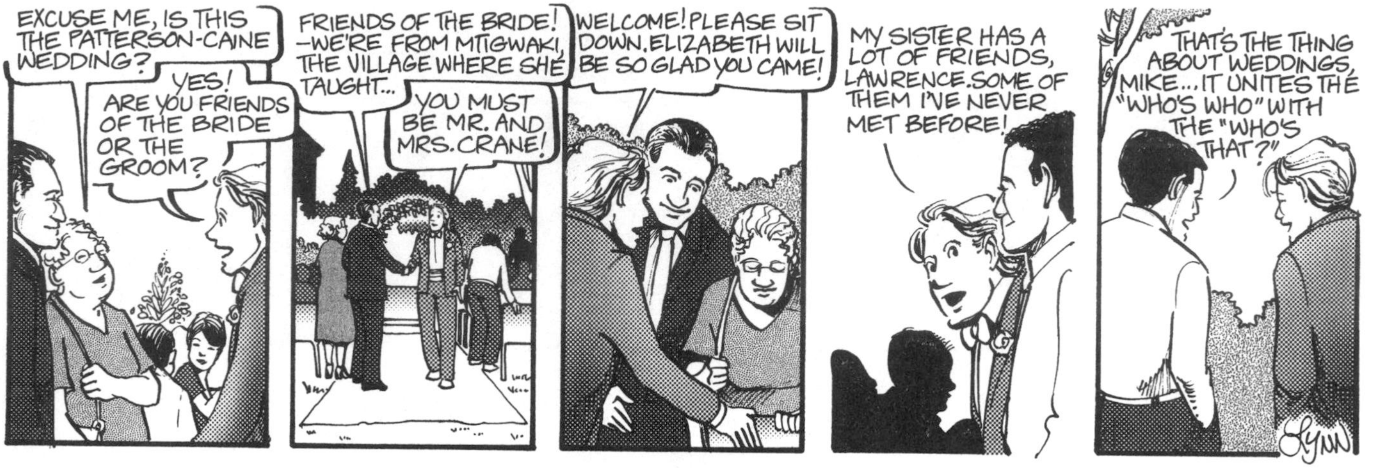
EXCUSE ME, IS THIS THE PATTERSON-CAINE WEDDING?
YES! ARE YOU FRIENDS OF THE BRIDE OR THE GROOM?
FRIENDS OF THE BRIDE! –WE'RE FROM MTIGWAKI, THE VILLAGE WHERE SHE TAUGHT...
YOU MUST BE MR. AND MRS. CRANE!
WELCOME! PLEASE SIT DOWN. ELIZABETH WILL BE SO GLAD YOU CAME!
MY SISTER HAS A LOT OF FRIENDS, LAWRENCE. SOME OF THEM I'VE NEVER MET BEFORE!
THAT'S THE THING ABOUT WEDDINGS, MIKE... IT UNITES THE "WHO'S WHO" WITH THE "WHO'S THAT?"
LYNN

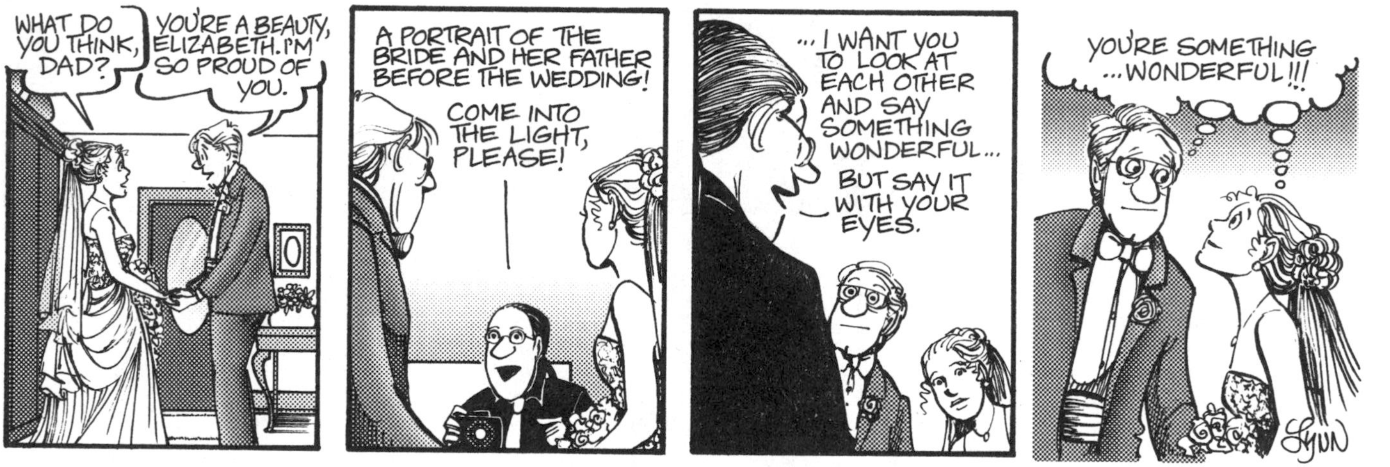
WHAT DO YOU THINK, DAD?
YOU'RE A BEAUTY, ELIZABETH. I'M SO PROUD OF YOU.
A PORTRAIT OF THE BRIDE AND HER FATHER BEFORE THE WEDDING!
COME INTO THE LIGHT, PLEASE!
...I WANT YOU TO LOOK AT EACH OTHER AND SAY SOMETHING WONDERFUL...
BUT SAY IT WITH YOUR EYES.
YOU'RE SOMETHING ...WONDERFUL!!!
LYNN

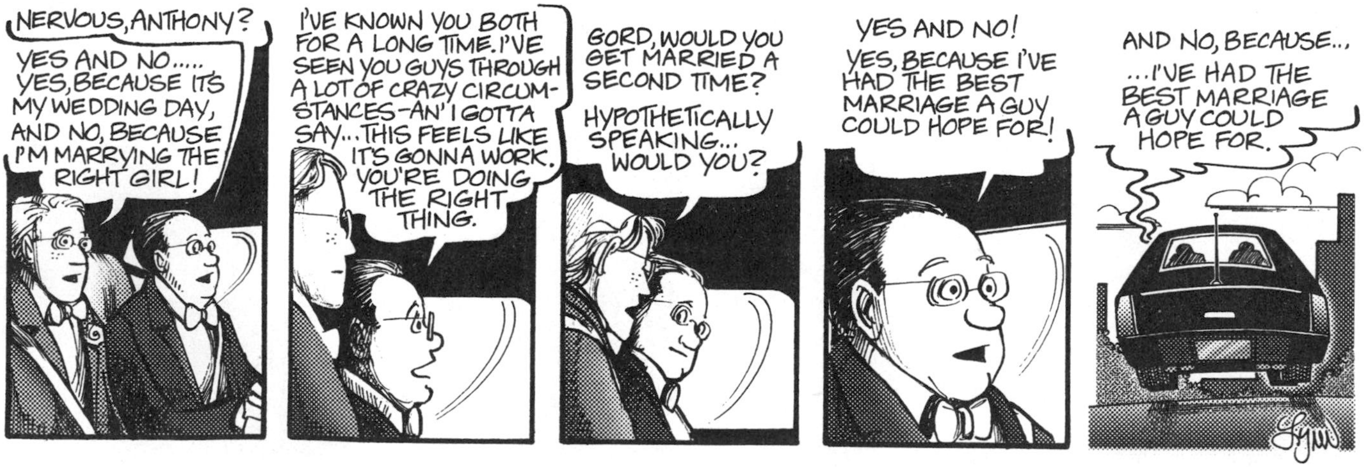
NERVOUS, ANTHONY?
YES AND NO..... YES, BECAUSE IT'S MY WEDDING DAY, AND NO, BECAUSE I'M MARRYING THE RIGHT GIRL!
I'VE KNOWN YOU BOTH FOR A LONG TIME. I'VE SEEN YOU GUYS THROUGH A LOT OF CRAZY CIRCUMSTANCES–AN' I GOTTA SAY... THIS FEELS LIKE IT'S GONNA WORK. YOU'RE DOING THE RIGHT THING.
GORD, WOULD YOU GET MARRIED A SECOND TIME?
HYPOTHETICALLY SPEAKING... WOULD YOU?
YES AND NO!
YES, BECAUSE I'VE HAD THE BEST MARRIAGE A GUY COULD HOPE FOR!
AND NO, BECAUSE...
...I'VE HAD THE BEST MARRIAGE A GUY COULD HOPE FOR.
LYNN

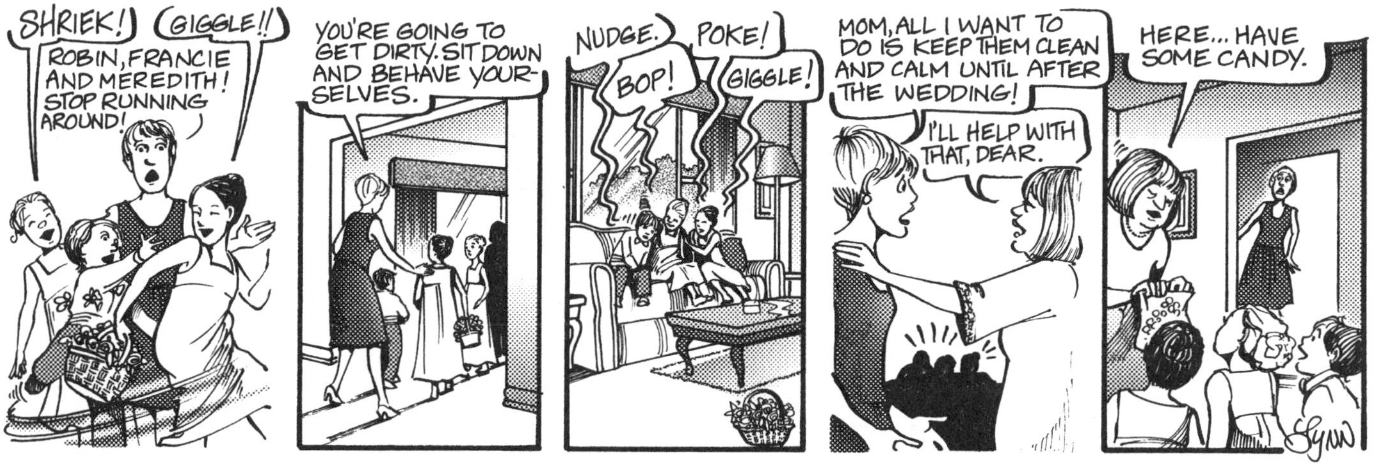
SHRIEK!
GIGGLE!!
ROBIN, FRANCIE AND MEREDITH! STOP RUNNING AROUND!
YOU'RE GOING TO GET DIRTY. SIT DOWN AND BEHAVE YOURSELVES.
NUDGE.
POKE!
BOP!
GIGGLE!
MOM, ALL I WANT TO DO IS KEEP THEM CLEAN AND CALM UNTIL AFTER THE WEDDING!
I'LL HELP WITH THAT, DEAR.
HERE... HAVE SOME CANDY.
LYNN

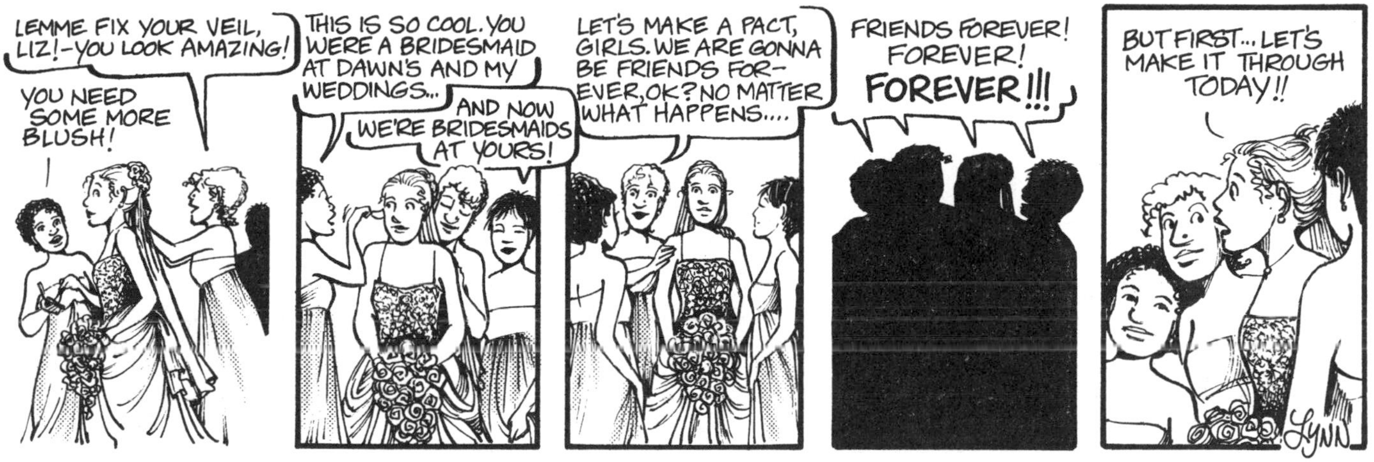
LEMME FIX YOUR VEIL, LIZ! - YOU LOOK AMAZING!
YOU NEED SOME MORE BLUSH!
THIS IS SO COOL. YOU WERE A BRIDESMAID AT DAWN'S AND MY WEDDINGS...
AND NOW WE'RE BRIDESMAIDS AT YOURS!
LET'S MAKE A PACT, GIRLS. WE ARE GONNA BE FRIENDS FOREVER, OK? NO MATTER WHAT HAPPENS....
FRIENDS FOREVER!
FOREVER!
FOREVER!!!
BUT FIRST... LET'S MAKE IT THROUGH TODAY!!
LYNN

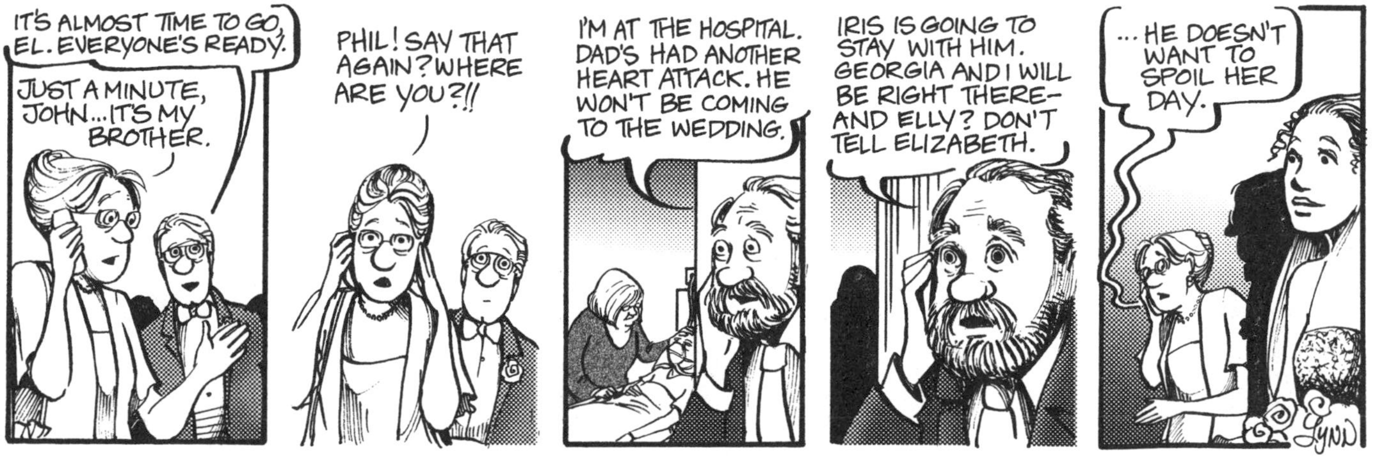
IT'S ALMOST TIME TO GO, EL. EVERYONE'S READY.
JUST A MINUTE, JOHN... IT'S MY BROTHER.
PHIL! SAY THAT AGAIN? WHERE ARE YOU?!!
I'M AT THE HOSPITAL. DAD'S HAD ANOTHER HEART ATTACK. HE WON'T BE COMING TO THE WEDDING.
IRIS IS GOING TO STAY WITH HIM. GEORGIA AND I WILL BE RIGHT THERE - AND ELLY? DON'T TELL ELIZABETH.
... HE DOESN'T WANT TO SPOIL HER DAY.
LYNN

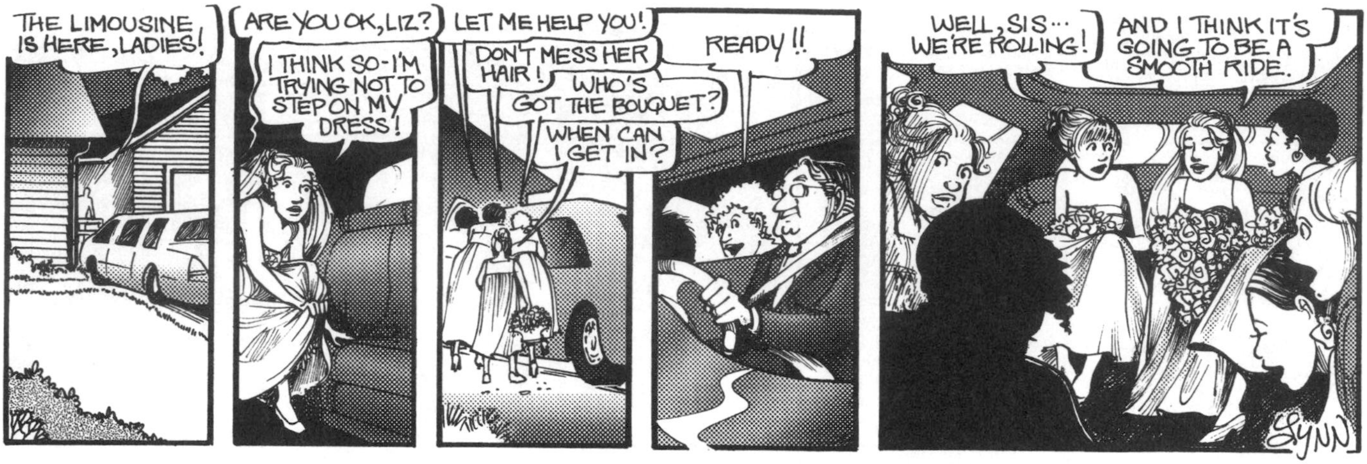
THE LIMOUSINE IS HERE, LADIES!
ARE YOU OK, LIZ?
I THINK SO-I'M TRYING NOT TO STEP ON MY DRESS!
LET ME HELP YOU!
DON'T MESS HER HAIR!
WHO'S GOT THE BOUQUET?
WHEN CAN I GET IN?
READY!!
WELL, SIS... WE'RE ROLLING!
AND I THINK IT'S GOING TO BE A SMOOTH RIDE.
LYNN

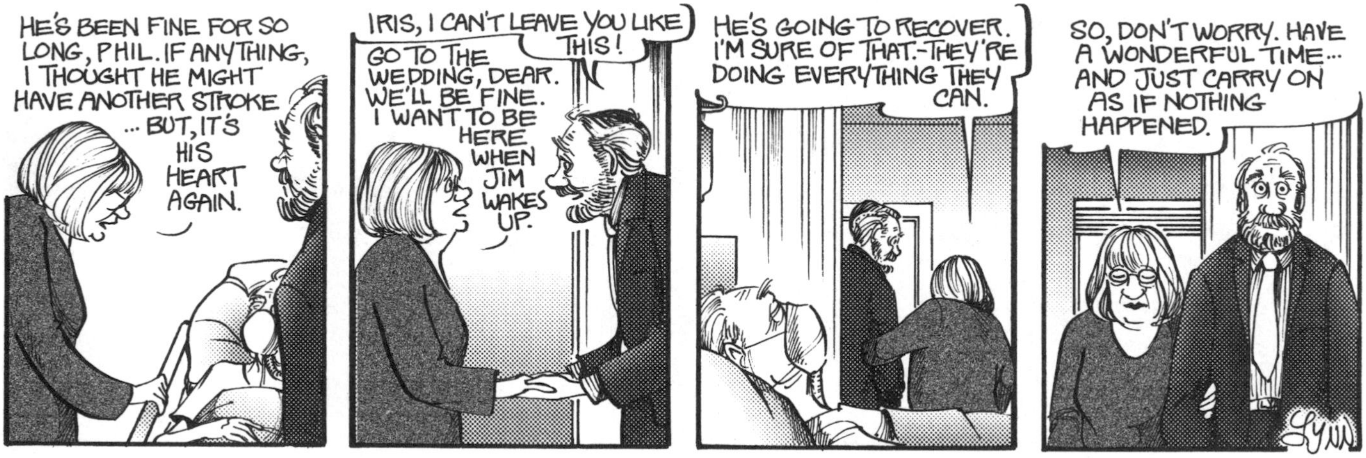
HE'S BEEN FINE FOR SO LONG, PHIL. IF ANYTHING, I THOUGHT HE MIGHT HAVE ANOTHER STROKE ... BUT, IT'S HIS HEART AGAIN.
IRIS, I CAN'T LEAVE YOU LIKE THIS!
GO TO THE WEDDING, DEAR. WE'LL BE FINE. I WANT TO BE HERE WHEN JIM WAKES UP.
HE'S GOING TO RECOVER. I'M SURE OF THAT.-THEY'RE DOING EVERYTHING THEY CAN.
SO, DON'T WORRY. HAVE A WONDERFUL TIME... AND JUST CARRY ON AS IF NOTHING HAPPENED.
LYNN

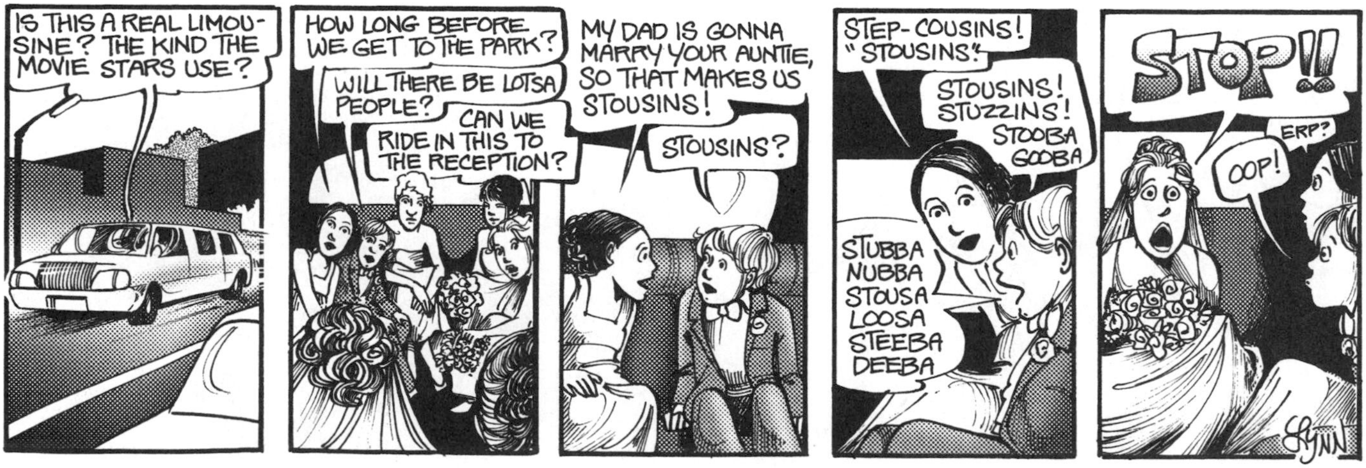
IS THIS A REAL LIMOUSINE? THE KIND THE MOVIE STARS USE?
HOW LONG BEFORE WE GET TO THE PARK?
WILL THERE BE LOTSA PEOPLE?
CAN WE RIDE IN THIS TO THE RECEPTION?
MY DAD IS GONNA MARRY YOUR AUNTIE, SO THAT MAKES US STOUSINS!
STOUSINS?
STEP-COUSINS! "STOUSINS"!
STOUSINS! STUZZINS! STOOBA GOOBA
STUBBA NUBBA STOUSA LOOSA STEEBA DEEBA
STOP!!
ERP?
OOP!
LYNN

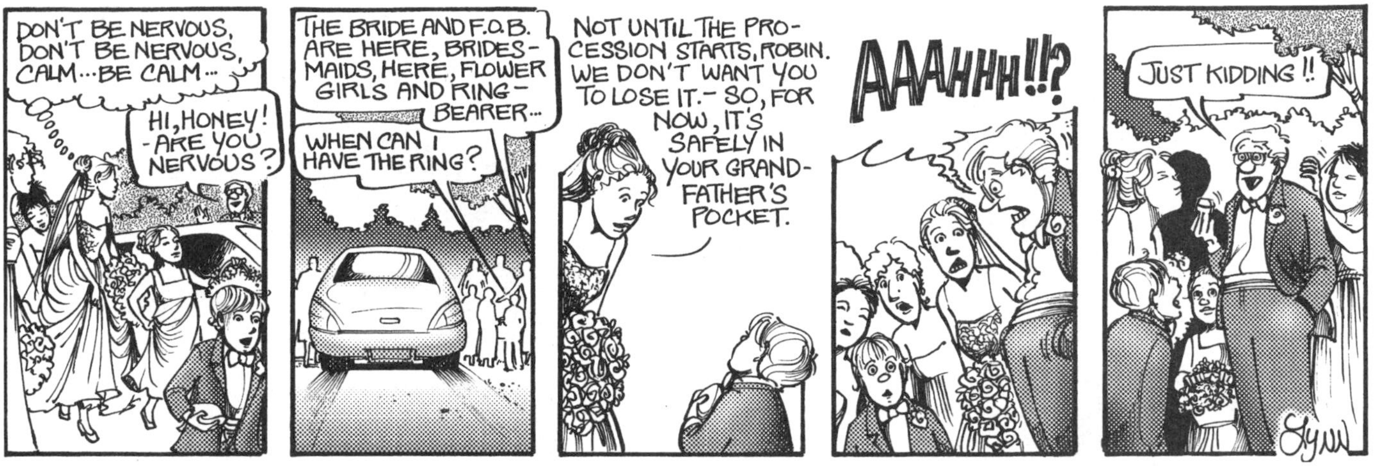
DON'T BE NERVOUS, DON'T BE NERVOUS, CALM... BE CALM...
HI, HONEY! - ARE YOU NERVOUS?
THE BRIDE AND F.O.B. ARE HERE, BRIDES-MAIDS, HERE, FLOWER GIRLS AND RING-BEARER...
WHEN CAN I HAVE THE RING?
NOT UNTIL THE PRO-CESSION STARTS, ROBIN. WE DON'T WANT YOU TO LOSE IT.- SO, FOR NOW, IT'S SAFELY IN YOUR GRAND-FATHER'S POCKET.
AAAHHH!!?
JUST KIDDING!!
LYNN

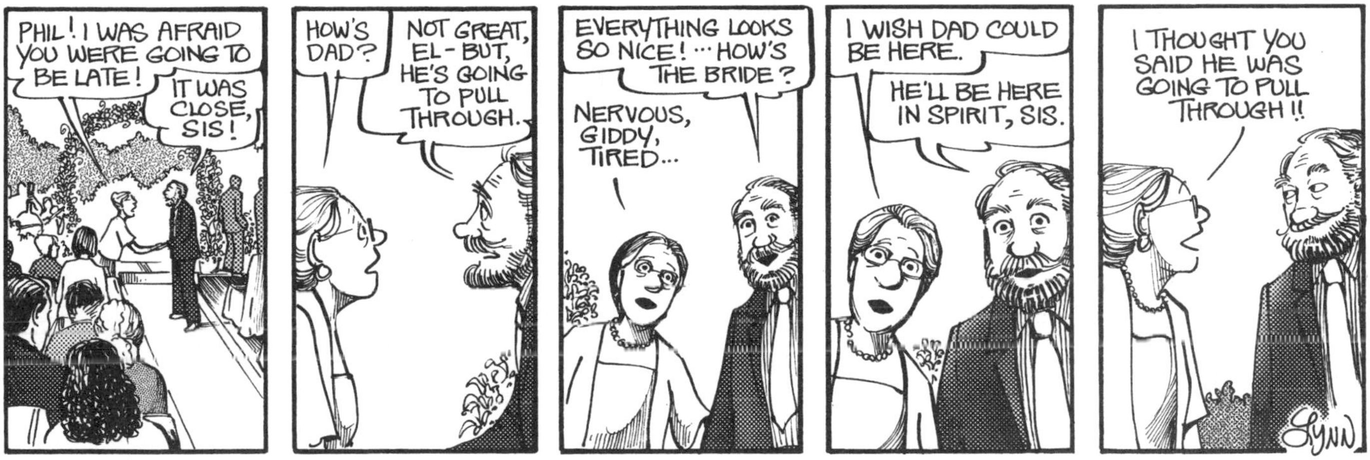
PHIL! I WAS AFRAID YOU WERE GOING TO BE LATE!
IT WAS CLOSE, SIS!
HOW'S DAD?
NOT GREAT, EL- BUT, HE'S GOING TO PULL THROUGH.
EVERYTHING LOOKS SO NICE! ...HOW'S THE BRIDE?
NERVOUS, GIDDY, TIRED...
I WISH DAD COULD BE HERE.
HE'LL BE HERE IN SPIRIT, SIS.
I THOUGHT YOU SAID HE WAS GOING TO PULL THROUGH!!
LYNN

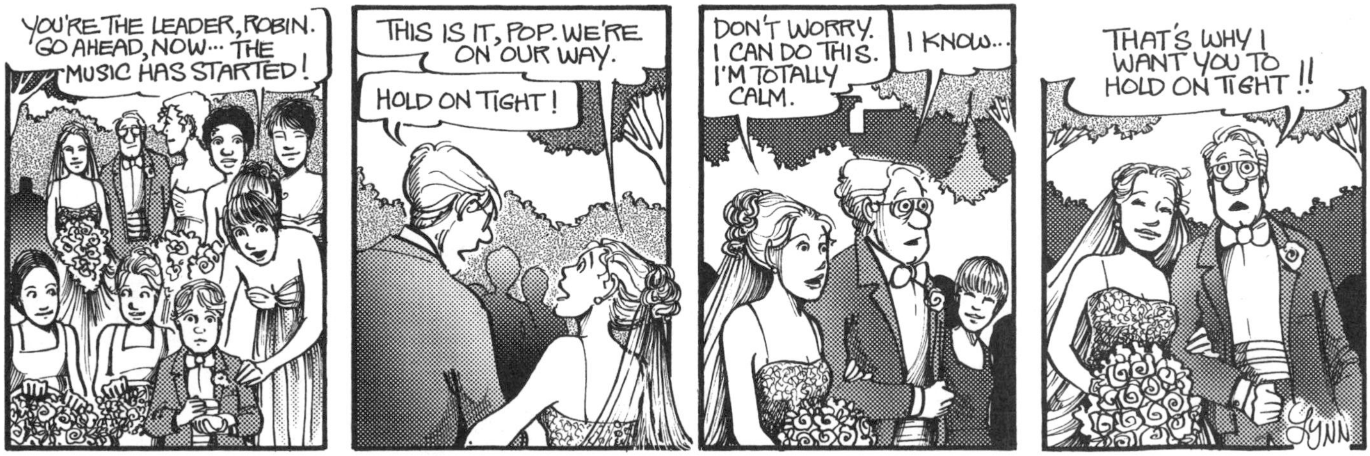
YOU'RE THE LEADER, ROBIN. GO AHEAD, NOW... THE MUSIC HAS STARTED!
THIS IS IT, POP. WE'RE ON OUR WAY.
HOLD ON TIGHT!
DON'T WORRY. I CAN DO THIS. I'M TOTALLY CALM.
I KNOW...
THAT'S WHY I WANT YOU TO HOLD ON TIGHT!!
LYNN

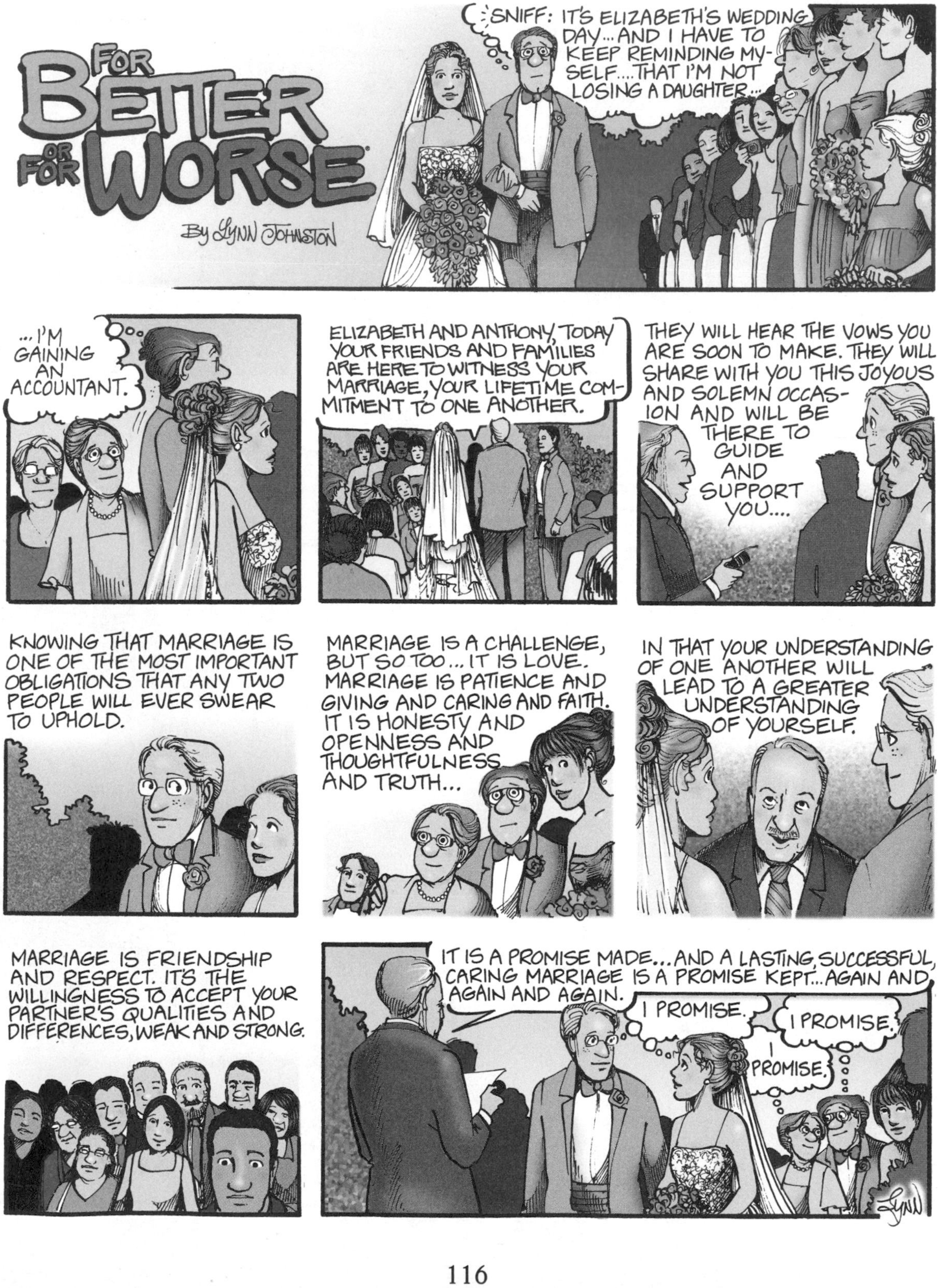
FOR BETTER OR FOR WORSE
BY LYNN JOHNSTON
SNIFF: IT'S ELIZABETH'S WEDDING DAY... AND I HAVE TO KEEP REMINDING MYSELF.... THAT I'M NOT LOSING A DAUGHTER...
...I'M GAINING AN ACCOUNTANT.
ELIZABETH AND ANTHONY, TODAY YOUR FRIENDS AND FAMILIES ARE HERE TO WITNESS YOUR MARRIAGE, YOUR LIFETIME COMMITMENT TO ONE ANOTHER.
THEY WILL HEAR THE VOWS YOU ARE SOON TO MAKE. THEY WILL SHARE WITH YOU THIS JOYOUS AND SOLEMN OCCASION AND WILL BE THERE TO GUIDE AND SUPPORT YOU....
KNOWING THAT MARRIAGE IS ONE OF THE MOST IMPORTANT OBLIGATIONS THAT ANY TWO PEOPLE WILL EVER SWEAR TO UPHOLD.
MARRIAGE IS A CHALLENGE, BUT SO TOO... IT IS LOVE. MARRIAGE IS PATIENCE AND GIVING AND CARING AND FAITH. IT IS HONESTY AND OPENNESS AND THOUGHTFULNESS AND TRUTH...
IN THAT YOUR UNDERSTANDING OF ONE ANOTHER WILL LEAD TO A GREATER UNDERSTANDING OF YOURSELF.
MARRIAGE IS FRIENDSHIP AND RESPECT. IT'S THE WILLINGNESS TO ACCEPT YOUR PARTNER'S QUALITIES AND DIFFERENCES, WEAK AND STRONG.
IT IS A PROMISE MADE... AND A LASTING, SUCCESSFUL, CARING MARRIAGE IS A PROMISE KEPT... AGAIN AND AGAIN AND AGAIN.
I PROMISE.
I PROMISE.
I PROMISE.
LYNN

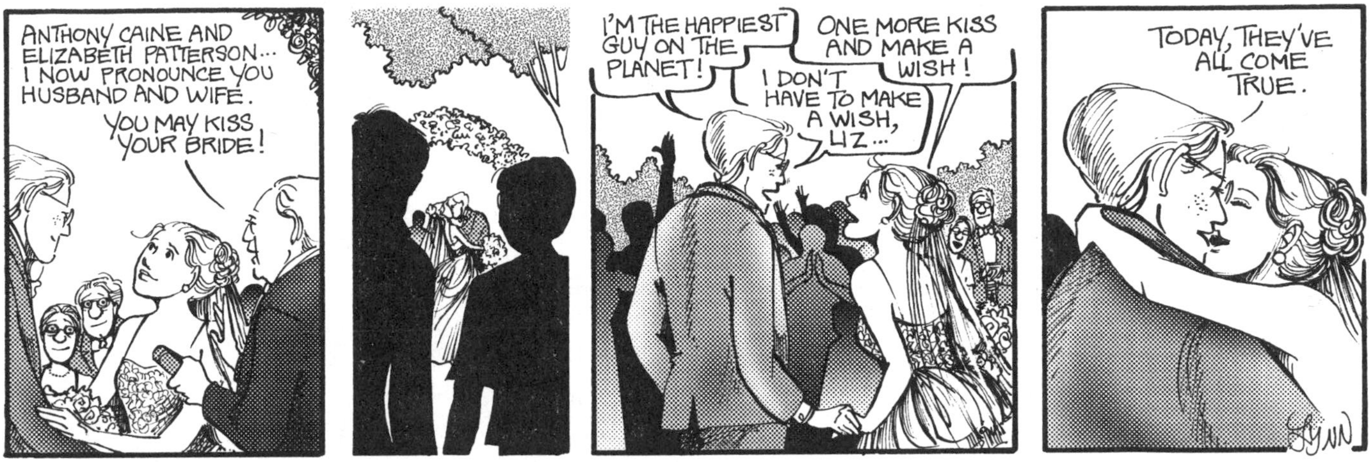
ANTHONY CAINE AND ELIZABETH PATTERSON... I NOW PRONOUNCE YOU HUSBAND AND WIFE.
YOU MAY KISS YOUR BRIDE!
I'M THE HAPPIEST GUY ON THE PLANET!
ONE MORE KISS AND MAKE A WISH!
I DON'T HAVE TO MAKE A WISH, LIZ...
TODAY, THEY'VE ALL COME TRUE.
LYNN

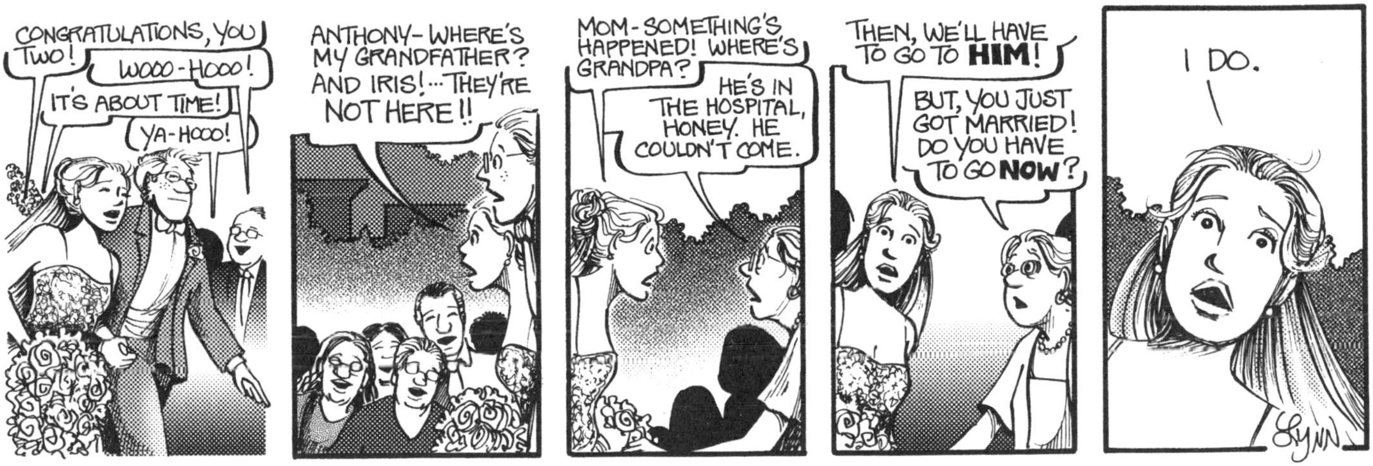
CONGRATULATIONS, YOU TWO!
WOOO-HOOO!
IT'S ABOUT TIME!
YA-HOOO!
ANTHONY- WHERE'S MY GRANDFATHER? AND IRIS!... THEY'RE NOT HERE!!
MOM- SOMETHING'S HAPPENED! WHERE'S GRANDPA?
HE'S IN THE HOSPITAL, HONEY. HE COULDN'T COME.
THEN, WE'LL HAVE TO GO TO HIM!
BUT, YOU JUST GOT MARRIED! DO YOU HAVE TO GO NOW?
I DO.
LYNN

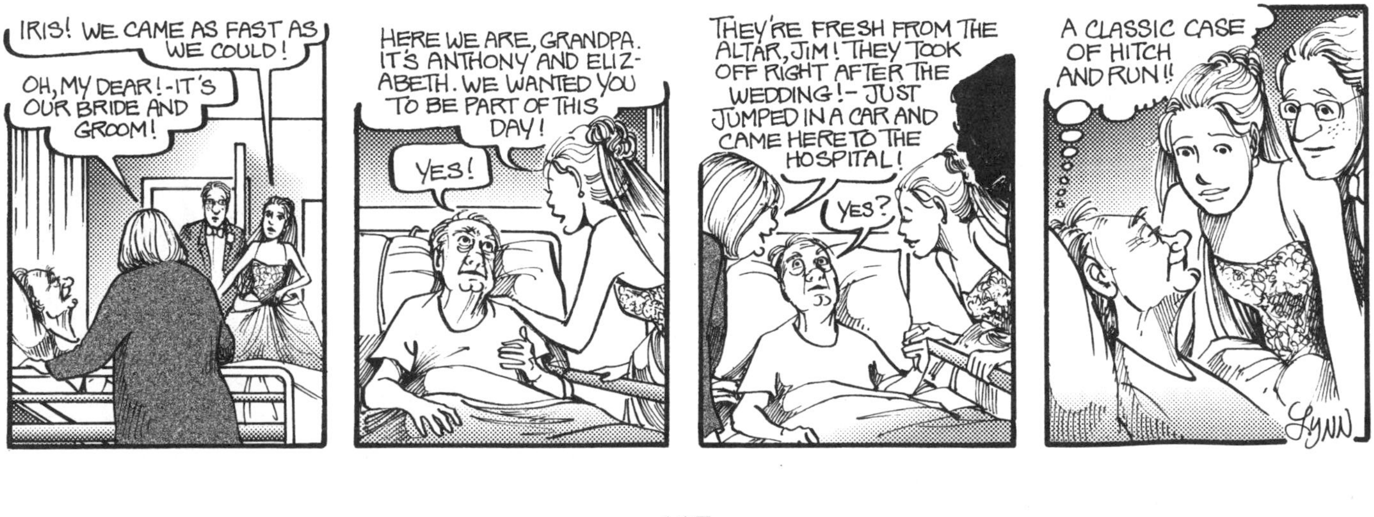
IRIS! WE CAME AS FAST AS WE COULD!
OH, MY DEAR! -IT'S OUR BRIDE AND GROOM!
HERE WE ARE, GRANDPA. IT'S ANTHONY AND ELIZABETH. WE WANTED YOU TO BE PART OF THIS DAY!
YES!
THEY'RE FRESH FROM THE ALTAR, JIM! THEY TOOK OFF RIGHT AFTER THE WEDDING! - JUST JUMPED IN A CAR AND CAME HERE TO THE HOSPITAL!
YES?
A CLASSIC CASE OF HITCH AND RUN!!
LYNN

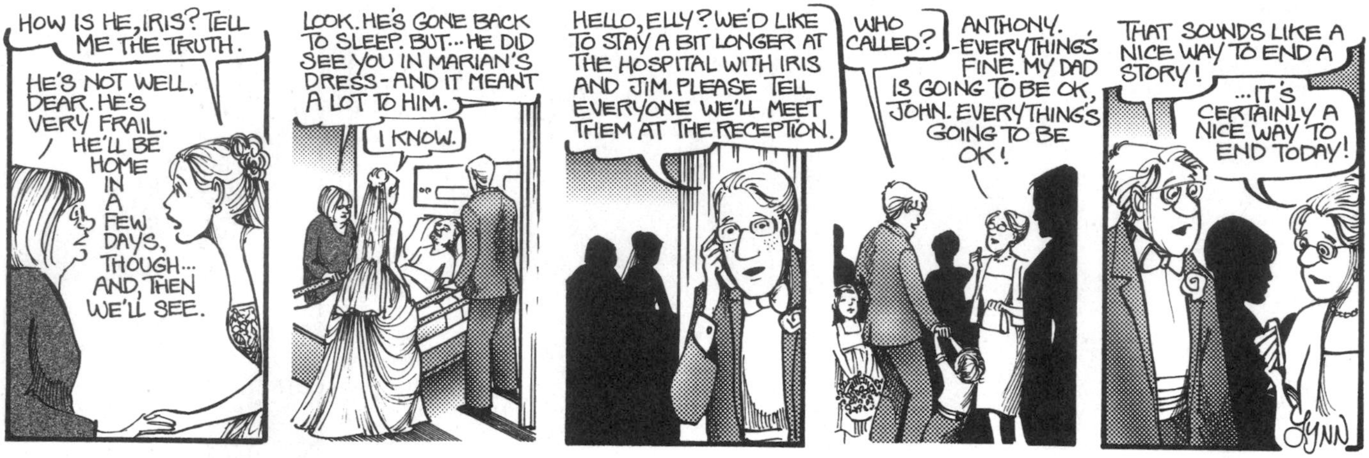
HOW IS HE, IRIS? TELL ME THE TRUTH.
HE'S NOT WELL, DEAR. HE'S VERY FRAIL.
HE'LL BE HOME IN A FEW DAYS, THOUGH... AND, THEN WE'LL SEE.
LOOK. HE'S GONE BACK TO SLEEP. BUT... HE DID SEE YOU IN MARIAN'S DRESS - AND IT MEANT A LOT TO HIM.
I KNOW.
HELLO, ELLY? WE'D LIKE TO STAY A BIT LONGER AT THE HOSPITAL WITH IRIS AND JIM. PLEASE TELL EVERYONE WE'LL MEET THEM AT THE RECEPTION.
WHO CALLED?
ANTHONY. - EVERYTHING'S FINE. MY DAD IS GOING TO BE OK, JOHN. EVERYTHING'S GOING TO BE OK!
THAT SOUNDS LIKE A NICE WAY TO END A STORY!
...IT'S CERTAINLY A NICE WAY TO END TODAY!
LYNN

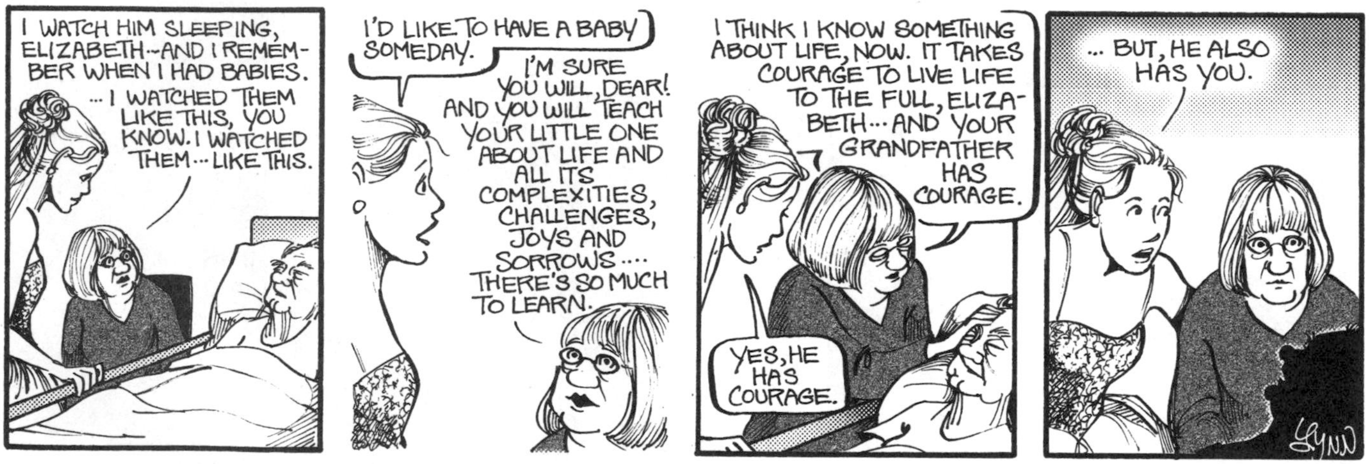
I WATCH HIM SLEEPING, ELIZABETH -- AND I REMEMBER WHEN I HAD BABIES.
... I WATCHED THEM LIKE THIS, YOU KNOW. I WATCHED THEM ... LIKE THIS.
I'D LIKE TO HAVE A BABY SOMEDAY.
I'M SURE YOU WILL, DEAR! AND YOU WILL TEACH YOUR LITTLE ONE ABOUT LIFE AND ALL ITS COMPLEXITIES, CHALLENGES, JOYS AND SORROWS .... THERE'S SO MUCH TO LEARN.
I THINK I KNOW SOMETHING ABOUT LIFE, NOW. IT TAKES COURAGE TO LIVE LIFE TO THE FULL, ELIZABETH... AND YOUR GRANDFATHER HAS COURAGE.
YES, HE HAS COURAGE.
... BUT, HE ALSO HAS YOU.
LYNN

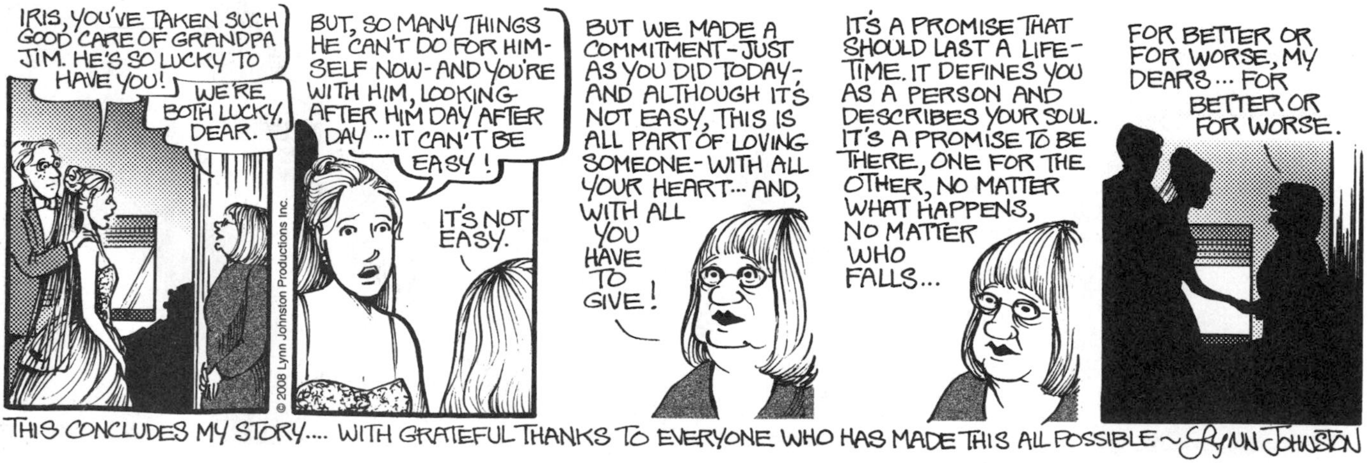
IRIS, YOU'VE TAKEN SUCH GOOD CARE OF GRANDPA JIM. HE'S SO LUCKY TO HAVE YOU!
WE'RE BOTH LUCKY, DEAR.
© 2008 Lynn Johnston Productions Inc.
BUT, SO MANY THINGS HE CAN'T DO FOR HIMSELF NOW - AND YOU'RE WITH HIM, LOOKING AFTER HIM DAY AFTER DAY ... IT CAN'T BE EASY!
IT'S NOT EASY.
BUT WE MADE A COMMITMENT - JUST AS YOU DID TODAY - AND ALTHOUGH IT'S NOT EASY, THIS IS ALL PART OF LOVING SOMEONE - WITH ALL YOUR HEART... AND, WITH ALL YOU HAVE TO GIVE!
IT'S A PROMISE THAT SHOULD LAST A LIFETIME. IT DEFINES YOU AS A PERSON AND DESCRIBES YOUR SOUL. IT'S A PROMISE TO BE THERE, ONE FOR THE OTHER, NO MATTER WHAT HAPPENS, NO MATTER WHO FALLS...
FOR BETTER OR FOR WORSE, MY DEARS... FOR BETTER OR FOR WORSE.

THIS CONCLUDES MY STORY.... WITH GRATEFUL THANKS TO EVERYONE WHO HAS MADE THIS ALL POSSIBLE ~ LYNN JOHNSTON

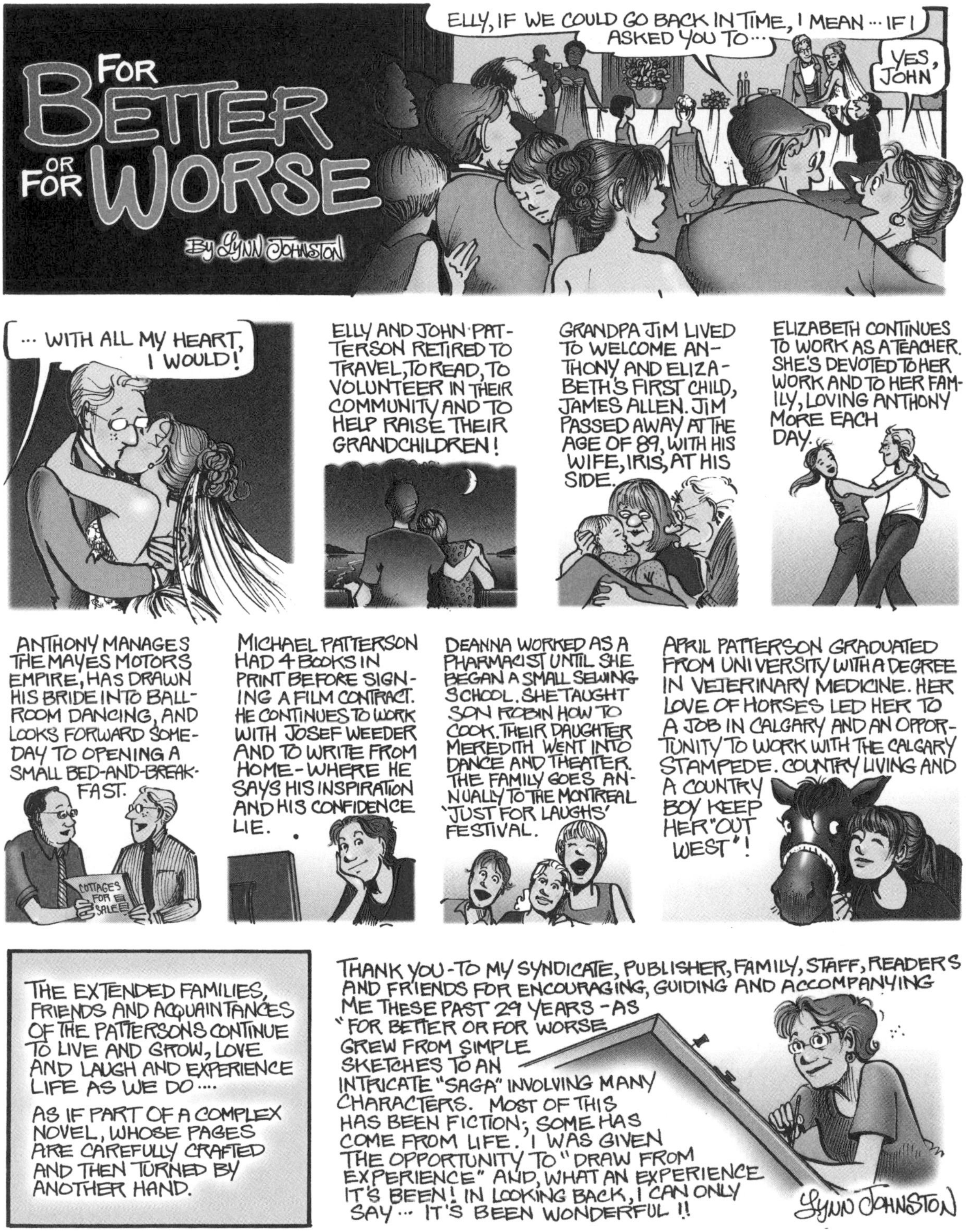
FOR BETTER OR FOR WORSE
BY LYNN JOHNSTON
ELLY, IF WE COULD GO BACK IN TIME, I MEAN ... IF I ASKED YOU TO...
YES, JOHN.
... WITH ALL MY HEART, I WOULD!
ELLY AND JOHN PATTERSON RETIRED TO TRAVEL, TO READ, TO VOLUNTEER IN THEIR COMMUNITY AND TO HELP RAISE THEIR GRANDCHILDREN!
GRANDPA JIM LIVED TO WELCOME ANTHONY AND ELIZABETH'S FIRST CHILD, JAMES ALLEN. JIM PASSED AWAY AT THE AGE OF 89, WITH HIS WIFE, IRIS, AT HIS SIDE.
ELIZABETH CONTINUES TO WORK AS A TEACHER. SHE'S DEVOTED TO HER WORK AND TO HER FAMILY, LOVING ANTHONY MORE EACH DAY.
ANTHONY MANAGES THE MAYES MOTORS EMPIRE, HAS DRAWN HIS BRIDE INTO BALLROOM DANCING, AND LOOKS FORWARD SOMEDAY TO OPENING A SMALL BED-AND-BREAKFAST.
COTTAGES FOR SALE
MICHAEL PATTERSON HAD 4 BOOKS IN PRINT BEFORE SIGNING A FILM CONTRACT. HE CONTINUES TO WORK WITH JOSEF WEEDER AND TO WRITE FROM HOME - WHERE HE SAYS HIS INSPIRATION AND HIS CONFIDENCE LIE.
DEANNA WORKED AS A PHARMACIST UNTIL SHE BEGAN A SMALL SEWING SCHOOL. SHE TAUGHT SON ROBIN HOW TO COOK. THEIR DAUGHTER MEREDITH WENT INTO DANCE AND THEATER. THE FAMILY GOES ANNUALLY TO THE MONTREAL 'JUST FOR LAUGHS' FESTIVAL.
APRIL PATTERSON GRADUATED FROM UNIVERSITY WITH A DEGREE IN VETERINARY MEDICINE. HER LOVE OF HORSES LED HER TO A JOB IN CALGARY AND AN OPPORTUNITY TO WORK WITH THE CALGARY STAMPEDE. COUNTRY LIVING AND A COUNTRY BOY KEEP HER "OUT WEST"!
THE EXTENDED FAMILIES, FRIENDS AND ACQUAINTANCES OF THE PATTERSONS CONTINUE TO LIVE AND GROW, LOVE AND LAUGH AND EXPERIENCE LIFE AS WE DO....
AS IF PART OF A COMPLEX NOVEL, WHOSE PAGES ARE CAREFULLY CRAFTED AND THEN TURNED BY ANOTHER HAND.
THANK YOU - TO MY SYNDICATE, PUBLISHER, FAMILY, STAFF, READERS AND FRIENDS FOR ENCOURAGING, GUIDING AND ACCOMPANYING ME THESE PAST 29 YEARS - AS "FOR BETTER OR FOR WORSE" GREW FROM SIMPLE SKETCHES TO AN INTRICATE "SAGA" INVOLVING MANY CHARACTERS. MOST OF THIS HAS BEEN FICTION; SOME HAS COME FROM LIFE. I WAS GIVEN THE OPPORTUNITY TO "DRAW FROM EXPERIENCE" AND, WHAT AN EXPERIENCE IT'S BEEN! IN LOOKING BACK, I CAN ONLY SAY... IT'S BEEN WONDERFUL!!
Lynn Johnston